DUBLIN'S
Fighting Story
1916 — 21

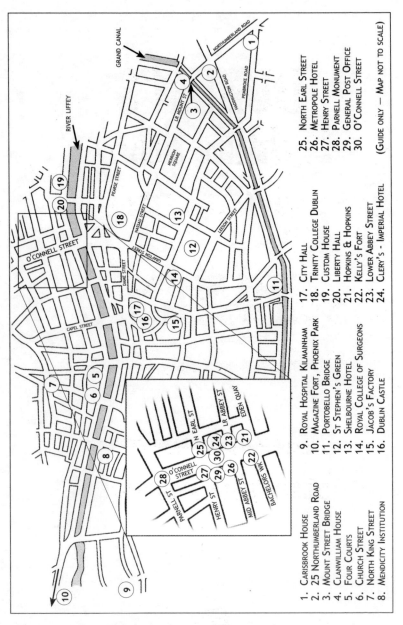

DUBLIN CITY CENTRE 1916

Map reproduced from A Walk Through Rebel Dublin 1916, *by kind permission of Mick O'Farrell.*

1. CARISBROOK HOUSE
2. 25 NORTHUMBERLAND ROAD
3. MOUNT STREET BRIDGE
4. CLANWILLIAM HOUSE
5. FOUR COURTS
6. CHURCH STREET
7. NORTH KING STREET
8. MENDICITY INSTITUTION
9. ROYAL HOSPITAL KILMAINHAM
10. MAGAZINE FORT, PHOENIX PARK
11. PORTOBELLO BRIDGE
12. ST STEPHEN'S GREEN
13. SHELBOURNE HOTEL
14. ROYAL COLLEGE OF SURGEONS
15. JACOB'S FACTORY
16. DUBLIN CASTLE
17. CITY HALL
18. TRINITY COLLEGE DUBLIN
19. CUSTOM HOUSE
20. LIBERTY HALL
21. HOPKINS & HOPKINS
22. KELLY'S FORT
23. LOWER ABBEY STREET
24. CLERY'S - IMPERIAL HOTEL
25. NORTH EARL STREET
26. METROPOLE HOTEL
27. HENRY STREET
28. PARNELL MONUMENT
29. GENERAL POST OFFICE
30. O'CONNELL STREET

(GUIDE ONLY — MAP NOT TO SCALE)

DUBLIN'S
Fighting Story
1916 — 21

Told By The
Men Who Made It

With a Unique Pictorial Record of the Period

INTRODUCTION BY DIARMAID FERRITER

SERIES EDITOR: BRIAN Ó CONCHUBHAIR

MERCIER PRESS
IRISH PUBLISHER – IRISH STORY

MERCIER PRESS

Cork

www.mercierpress.ie

Trade enquiries to CMD BookSource,
55a Spruce Avenue, Stillorgan Industrial Park,
Blackrock, County Dublin

Originally published by *The Kerryman*, 1948

This edition published by Mercier Press, 2009

© Preface: Brian Ó Conchubhair, 2009

© Introduction: Diarmaid Ferriter, 2009

© Text: Mercier Press, 2009

© Frontispiece Map: Mick O'Farrell, 1999

ISBN: 978 1 85635 643 5

10 9 8 7 6 5 4 3 2 1

A CIP record for this title is available from the British Library

Printed and bound in the EU.

CONTENTS

PREFACE (2009) BY BRIAN Ó CONCHUBHAIR   7

ACKNOWLEDGEMENTS   12

INTRODUCTION (2009) BY DIARMAID FERRITER   13

FOREWORD   21

HOW THE FIGHT BEGAN!   23

THE GREAT DUBLIN STRIKE AND LOCKOUT, 1913   35

THE IRISH CITIZEN ARMY   52

THE 1916 RISING   60
    The Magazine Fort raid   60
    The South Dublin Union   61
    Jacob's Factory   77
    Boland's Mills   83
    The North King Street area   98
    Citizen Army posts   107
    The Battle of Ashbourne   117
    The GPO   130
    The Surrender   146

THE EXECUTED LEADERS   156
    Pádraig Pearse   157
    James Connolly   162
    Tom Clarke   170
    Seán MacDiarmada   176
    Thomas MacDonagh   181
    Éamonn Ceannt   186
    Joseph Mary Plunkett   190
    Major John MacBride   197
    Michael O'Hanrahan   200
    Michael Mallin   202
    Ned Daly   204
    Con Colbert   208
    Seán Heuston   209
    William Pearse   211

FRONGOCH UNIVERSITY – AND AFTER 1916–1919   213

SAVING OF THE BATTALION DUMP   236

COLLINSTOWN AERODROME RAID   241

ATTACK ON LORD FRENCH   246

RAID ON THE KING'S INNS   253

FIGHT AT FERNSIDE   257

DEATH OF SEÁN TREACY   270

TORTURE AND EXECUTION OF KEVIN BARRY   278

BLOODY SUNDAY   283

ESCAPE FROM KILMAINHAM JAIL   295

INCHICORE RAILWAY WORKSHOP OCCUPIED BY IRA   301

BATTLE OF BRUNSWICK STREET   305

ATTACK ON RAF UNITS AT RED COW INN   309

THE BURNING OF THE CUSTOM HOUSE   313

BRITISH FORCES IN SCENE OF CONFUSION   322

ATTEMPTED RESCUE OF SEÁN MACEOIN FROM MOUNTJOY JAIL   327

    Leonard's story – Outside   329
    MacEoin's story – Inside   333
    Conclusion   335

ESCAPE FROM MOUNTJOY   337

WITH THE SIXTH BATTALION   346

THE FIGHT IN THE BRAY AREA   350

IN BRITISH JAILS   365

HOW IT WAS DONE – IRA INTELLIGENCE   376

FIANNA ÉIREANN – WITH THE DUBLIN BRIGADE   384

HOW THE WOMEN HELPED   395

MICHAEL COLLINS   406

ÉAMON DE VALERA   413

ARTHUR GRIFFITH   426

INDEX   435

PREFACE (2009)

As we approach the centenary of the 1916 Easter Rising and the Irish War of Independence/Anglo-Irish War (1919–1921), interest among scholars and the general public in these historic events gathers unrelenting pace. Recent years have witnessed a slew of books, articles, documentaries and films, emerge at home and abroad all dealing with the events and controversies involved in the struggle for political independence in the period 1916–1922. While many of these projects have re-evaluated and challenged the standard nationalist narrative that dominated for so long, and indeed have contributed to a more nuanced and complex appreciation of the events in question, the absence of the famous *Fighting Story* series – initially published by *The Kerryman* newspaper and subsequently republished by Anvil Books – is a notable and regrettable absence. First published in Christmas and special editions of *The Kerryman* newspaper in the years before the Second World War, the articles subsequently appeared in four independent collections entitled *Rebel Cork's Fighting Story, Kerry's Fighting Story, Limerick's Fighting Story* and *Dublin's Fighting Story* between 1947–49. The choice of counties reflects the geographical intensity of the campaign as Dr Peter Hart explains in his new introduction to *Rebel Cork's Fighting Story*: 'The Munster IRA ... was much more active than anywhere else except Longford, Roscommon and Dublin city.' Marketed as authentic accounts and as 'gripping episodes' by 'the men who made it', the series was dramatically described as 'more graphic than anything written of late war zones', with 'astonishing pictures' and sold 'at the very moderate price of two shillings'. Benefiting from *The Kerryman*'s wide distribution network and a competitive price, the books proved immediately popular at home and abroad, so much so that many, if not most, of the books were purchased by, and for, the

Irish Diaspora. This competitive price resulted in part from the fact that 'the producers were content to reduce their own profit and to produce the booklet at little above the mere cost of production'. Consequently, however, the volumes quickly disappeared from general circulation. Dr Ruán O'Donnell explains in the new introduction to *Limerick's Fighting Story*, 'The shelf life … was reduced by the poor production values they shared. This was a by-product of the stringent economies of their day when pricing, paper quality, binding and distribution costs had to be considered [which] rendered copies vulnerable to deterioration and unsuited to library utilisation.'

The books targeted not only the younger generation who knew about those times by hearsay only, but also the older generation who 'will recall vividly a memorable era and the men who made it'. Professor Diarmaid Ferriter notes in the new introduction to *Dublin's Fighting Story* that these volumes answered the perceived need for Volunteers to record their stories in their own words, in addition to ensuring the proper education and appreciation of a new generation for their predecessors' sacrifices. The narrative, he writes 'captures the excitement and the immediacy of the Irish War of Independence and the belief that the leaders of the revolution did not urge people to take dangerous courses they were not themselves prepared to take'. These four books deserve reprinting, therefore, not only for the important factual information they contain, and the resource they offer scholars of various disciplines, but also because of the valuable window they open on the mentality of the period. As Professor J.J. Lee observes in the introduction to *Kerry's Fighting Story*, for anyone 'trying to reconstruct in very different times the historical reality of what it felt like at the time, there is no substitute for contemporary accounts, however many questions these accounts may raise. We know what was to come. Contemporaries did not.' The insight these books offer on IRA organisation at local level suggest to Dr Peter Hart 'why IRA units were so resilient under pressure, and how untrained, inexperienced men could be such formidable soldiers … Irish guerrillas fought alongside their brothers, cousins, school and teammates, and childhood friends – often in the very lanes, fields and streets where they had spent their lives together'. In addition these texts reveal the vital roles, both active and passive, women played in the struggle of Irish independence.

The establishment of Anvil Books in 1962 saw a reissuing of certain volumes, Cork and Limerick in particular. The link between *The Kerryman* and Anvil Books was Dan Nolan (1910–1989). Son of Thomas Nolan, and nephew of Daniel Nolan and Maurice Griffin, he was related to all three founders of *The Kerryman* newspaper that commenced publishing in 1904. His obituary in that newspaper describes how he 'was only a nipper when he looked down the barrels of British guns as His Majesty's soldiers tried to arrest the proprietors of *The Kerryman* for refusing to publish recruitment advertisements. And he saw the paper and its employees being harassed by the Black and Tans.' On graduating from Castleknock College, he joined the paper's staff in 1928 replacing his recently deceased uncle, Maurice Griffin. His father's death in 1939 saw Dan Nolan become the paper's managing director and his tenure would, in due course, see a marked improvement in its commercial performance: circulation increased and ultimately exceeded 40,000 copies per week, and advertisement revenue also increased significantly. Under his stewardship *The Kerryman*, according to Séamus McConville in an obituary in the paper, 'became solidly established as the unchallenged leader in sales and stature among provincial newspapers'. Recognising his talent, the Provincial Newspaper Association elected him president in 1951. Among his projects were the Rose of Tralee Festival, Tralee Racecourse and Anvil Books. Founded in 1962 with Nolan and Rena Dardis as co-directors, Anvil Books established itself as the pre-eminent publishers of memoirs and accounts dealing with the Irish War of Independence. Indeed the first book published by Anvil Books was a 1962 reprint of *Rebel Cork's Fighting Story* in a print run of 10,000 copies.

Conscious, no doubt, of the potential for controversy, the original preface was careful not to present the *Fighting Stories* as 'a detailed or chronological history of the fight for independence', and acknowledged 'that in the collection of data about such a period errors and omissions can easily occur and so they will welcome the help of readers who may be able to throw more light upon the various episodes related in the series. Such additional information will be incorporated into the second edition of the booklets which the present rate of orders would seem to indicate will be called for in the very near future.' Subsequent editions of *Rebel Cork's Fighting Story* and *Limerick's Fighting Story* did appear in print with additional material as O'Donnell discusses in his enlightening introduction to *Limerick's Fighting Story*, but the proposed *Tipperary's Fighting Story*, as advertised in the Limerick volume with a suggested publication date of 1948 and a plea for relevant information or pictures, never materialised. This 2009 edition adheres to the original texts as first published by *The Kerryman* rather than the later editions by Anvil Books. A new preface, introduction and index frame the original texts that remain as first presented other than the silent correction of obvious typographical errors.

The preface to the final book, *Dublin's Fighting Story*, concluded by noting that the publishers 'would be satisfied if the series serves to preserve in the hearts of the younger generation that love of country and devotion to its interests which distinguished the men whose doings are related therein'. The overall story narrated in these four books is neither provincial nor insular, nor indeed limited to Ireland, but as Lee remarks in *Kerry's Fighting Story*, it is rather 'like that of kindred spirits elsewhere, at home and abroad, an example of the refusal of the human spirit to submit to arbitrary power'. The hasty and almost premature endings of several chapters may be attributed to the legacy of the Irish Civil War whose shadow constantly hovers at the edges, threatening to break into the narrative, and in fact does intrude in a few instances. Lee opines that writers avoided the Civil War as it 'was still too divisive, still too harrowing, a nightmare to be recalled into public memory. Hence the somewhat abrupt ending of several chapters at a moment when hopes were still high and the horrors to come yet unimagined.'

Ireland at the start of the twenty-first century is a very different place than it was when these books were first published. Irish historiography has undergone no less a transformation and to bridge the gap four eminent historians have written new introductions that set the four *Fighting Stories* in the context of recent research and shifts in Irish historiography. Yet Lee's assessment in reference to Kerry holds true for each of the four volumes: 'Whatever would happen subsequently, and however perspectives would inevitably be affected by hindsight, for better and for worse, *Kerry's Fighting Story* lays the foundation for all subsequent studies of these foundation years of an independent Irish state.' As we move toward the centenary of 1916, the War of Independence, the Anglo-Irish Treaty and the Civil War, it is appropriate and fitting that these key texts be once again part of the public debate of those events and it is sincerely hoped that as Ruán O'Donnell states: 'This new life of a classic of its genre will facilitate a fresh evaluation of its unique perspectives on the genesis of the modern Irish state.'

Dr Brian Ó Conchubhair

Series Editor

University of Notre Dame

Easter 2009

ACKNOWLEDGEMENTS

I AM GRATEFUL not only to the scholars who penned the new introductions for their time and expertise but also to the following who assisted in numerous ways: Beth Bland, Angela Carothers, Aedín Ní Bhroithe-Clements (Hesburgh Library), Professor Mike Cronin, Rena Dardis, Ken Garcia, Alan Hayes, Dr Diarmaid Ferriter, Mick O'Farrell, Dyann Mawhorr, Don and Patrica Nolan, Tara MacLeod, Seán Seosamh Ó Conchubhair, Interlibrary Loans at the Hesburgh Library, University of Notre Dame, and Eoin Purcell, Wendy Logue and the staff at Mercier Press. *Táim an-bhuíoch do gach éinne atá luaite thuas, m'athair ach go háirithe as a chuid foighne agus as a chuid saineolais a roinnt liom go fial agus do Thara uair amháin eile a d'fhulaing go foighneach agus an obair seo ar bun agam.*

DR BRIAN Ó CONCHUBHAIR

INTRODUCTION (2009)

In 1913, CONSTANCE Markievicz, a member of an Anglo-Irish aristocratic family, the Gore Booths of Lissadell in County Sligo, identified three 'great movements' in Ireland: the nationalist, women's and labour movements. She was just one example of an individual, whose background would suggest little sympathy for Irish separatism, caught up in the intense political awakening and excitement of the early twentieth century. Markievicz identified three strands of the newly politicised Ireland, but there were others, including the intense Ulster unionist resistance movement to Home Rule, the secret revolutionary Irish Republican Brotherhood (IRB) and the proponents of a distinctly Irish culture, history and education system. Nonetheless, it did not seem that a pre-revolutionary situation existed in Ireland in the few years before the 1916 Rising. Ireland had one hundred and three constituency seats at Westminster, seventy-five of which were held by the moderate Irish Parliamentary Party (IPP), led by John Redmond. The early twentieth century had witnessed this political party recovering from the fall-out of the political demise and death of Charles Stewart Parnell in 1891. Re-unified in 1900, it was dedicated to achieving Home Rule for Ireland through constitutional means, a commitment it succeeded in extracting from the British government in 1912. When the First World War broke out, the implementation of Home Rule was postponed until the conflict was over, and the nationalists were biding their time and hoping unionist opposition would be overruled.

Irish people generally enjoyed the right to free speech, free assembly, free organisation, and a varied and (mostly) uncensored media. Many initiatives had been taken by the British government to satisfy different sections of the population; old age pensions gave a weekly payment to

13

those aged over seventy, and the National University of Ireland Act of 1908 seemed to reflect an increasingly confident Catholic Church that had succeeded in achieving its demands in the area of education. Most Irish farmers owned their own land, some eleven million acres having been purchased as a result of the Land Acts of the late nineteenth and early twentieth centuries. After the First World War commenced, Irish agriculturalists benefited from the extra demand in Britain for Irish foodstuffs. Conscription to the armed forces was not imposed in Ireland, but many Irish men volunteered for service in the British army, with over 200,000 serving during the First World War. The Royal Irish Constabulary (RIC), mostly Catholic, and a respected force, was policing an island relatively free of serious crime.

On the surface therefore, the years before the Rising seemed some of the more peaceful and prosperous in Ireland's history. In many respects, it is necessary to go below the surface in order to locate what has sometimes been referred to as 'the legion of the excluded' that declared war on the British Empire in April 1916. Whatever about its stability, and the determination of most to take advantage of the opportunities provided by their citizenship of the United Kingdom, early twentieth-century Ireland also had its full share of petty resentments, snobberies, hypocrisies and frustrated expectations. Many felt excluded from the prevailing political establishment. John Redmond had many noble traits, but he also represented a generation of Irish nationalists who were arrogant and removed from the concerns of those who felt aggrieved. The Irish Parliamentary Party (IPP) tended to rely on pliant henchmen and it rarely had to contest hard-fought elections, many MPs being returned unopposed for decades.

The many small organisations and agitators, including the disgruntled working-class victims of the 1913 Lockout who formed the Irish Citizens Army (ICA), the women demanding the vote and a role in Irish nationalism, and those in the IRB intent on reviving the tradition of Irish defiance of British rule, were working hard to undermine what they identified as a prevailing smugness within the status quo. The extraordinarily prolific journalist, Arthur Griffith, was struggling to make his small Sinn Féin party relevant or attractive to the electorate; but it seemed to be in permanent decline by 1914. Like Patrick Pearse and Thomas MacDonagh – both teachers, language enthusiasts and poets – many were involved in the cultural revival, notably through membership of the Gaelic League and the Gaelic Athletic Association (GAA), but some wanted to move beyond that, and came to believe in the necessity of a military as well as a cultural struggle. Eoin MacNeill was an academic and chief-of-staff of the Irish Volunteers, an organisation dedicated to ensuring the implementation of Home Rule, which had been established in the aftermath of the formation of the Ulster Volunteer Force (UVF) in 1913, a group dedicated to resisting Home Rule. After the outbreak of the First World War the Irish Volunteers split as a result of John Redmond's decision to back the British war effort, with 150,000 remaining loyal to Redmond (now calling themselves the National Volunteers) and in the region of 2,500 opposing Redmond, retaining the organisation's original title.

The reason for MacNeill and his followers' decision not to back Redmond can be found in a book MacNeill published in 1915 in which he expressed a hatred for the way 'Ireland's representatives wheedled, fawned, begged, bargained and truckled for a provincial legislature'. Many wanted far more independence than was being provided for in the Home Rule Bill. Those who organised the Rising worked in MacNeill's shadow and found the Irish Volunteers a useful cover organisation. The IRB, originally established in 1858 and dedicated to achieving its aims through rebellion, had been revitalised in the early twentieth century by a new generation, with the help of the older Tom Clarke, determined since 1907 to see a rebellion launched in his lifetime. Denis McCullough, a future president of the IRB Supreme Council, put it bluntly: 'I cleared out most of the older men (including my father) most of whom I considered of no further use to us.' The eager youth were tired of the veteran Fenians' tendency to sit around drinking and reminiscing about past glorious failures. They were also pleased that the UVF had led the way in the north, recruiting, arming, parading and creating a mass movement that could be replicated in the south.

The prologue to the Rising of 1916 was thus an Ireland with a variety of organisations and movements, sometimes with conflicting aims, personalities and visions of the future. This was why deception and secrecy played such an important role in the organisation of the Rising. IRB treasurer Tom Clarke and secretary Seán MacDiarmada fomented the plans for a rebellion, and they persuaded others, including Éamonn Ceannt, the increasingly militant Patrick Pearse, and eventually labour leader James Connolly, that the First World War gave them an opportunity, due to England's obvious preoccupations elsewhere. In the summer of 1915 they established a military council of the IRB to secretly plan a rising. They were not preparing for failure, but those who eventually became involved in the events of 1916 did not all think alike or share the same philosophies, which is why there was so much confusion in the lead-up to the Rising. Eoin MacNeill did not believe a rising was justified unless there was an attempt by the British to disarm the Volunteers or significant help forthcoming from outside Ireland. He was conscious that public opinion would not be in favour of an unprovoked rebellion, but most of the leaders of the Rising were not concerned with public opinion. The essayist Robert Lynd made the point in 1917 that James Connolly, as leader of the Irish Citizen Army, believed it was necessary to align the labour and republican movements because in looking at Irish history, 'he saw insurrection following insurrection apparently in vain, like wave following wave, but he still had faith in the hour when the tide would be full'. In that sense, it was a certain mood of despair mixed with vague optimism within Irish republicanism and socialism that led to the Rising.

The original plan was to mobilise the Volunteers on Easter Sunday and then inform them a rising was about to take place. The idea was that this would be a nationwide rebellion, not just confined to Dublin. On Holy Thursday, when they had got wind of the secret plans, IRB member Bulmer Hobson and Eoin MacNeill confronted Patrick Pearse in his capacity as director of military organisation for the

Volunteers. Pearse convinced them military aid was imminent from Germany, as was the Volunteers' suppression by the British government. MacNeill relented, but the rebels' plans subsequently collapsed. The German supply ship, the *Aud*, was captured, as was Roger Casement who had sought German support. The British government wrongly believed they now had the main leader. MacNeill discovered that the document purporting to provide evidence of the Volunteers' imminent suppression was a forgery. He countermanded the order for the Volunteers to mobilise, while the British authorities decided to wait until after the Easter holiday to round up the suspects. On Monday, the rebels, numbering about seven hundred, decided to mobilise, by seizing prominent Dublin city-centre buildings, with the General Post Office (GPO) as headquarters. The stage was set. But nobody knew how long the drama would last or how the audience would react.

What happened in the five years after the Rising, until July 1921 when a ceasefire was called between the British crown forces and the Irish Republican Army (IRA), the successor organisation to the Irish Volunteers, is often referred to as 'the Irish Revolution'. In the most recent history of the Rising, historian Charles Townshend acknowledges that those who struck against the British Empire in 1916 were ready to act without majority support; in this 'they were hardly different from any revolutionary insurrectionist of the nineteenth or twentieth century'. He labels them rebels 'because it carries a charge of romantic glamour which was wholly appropriate to their minds'. Michael Laffan, in his definitive history of the rise of the Sinn Féin movement after 1916, makes the point that its greatest achievement in 1917 was 'the emergence of a sense of cohesion and common purpose among a disparate group of people who, until then, had often suspected or disapproved of each other'.

The Sinn Féin revolution brought down the quest for Home Rule that the constitutional nationalists had promoted since the nineteenth century; in its place the demand was now for an Irish Republic. Although the Easter Rising was crushed and its leaders executed, it led to a change in public opinion that saw Sinn Féin triumph in the general election of 1918, with Éamon de Valera, the sole surviving commandant from the Rising, as its president, and the commencement of a War of Independence in 1919.

The military conflict between British armed forces and the IRA consisted of sporadic guerrilla fighting overseen by the IRA's director of intelligence, Michael Collins. It was paralleled by the efforts of the self-proclaimed government of the Irish republic – the first Dáil (Irish parliament) assembled in January 1919 – to achieve an independent Irish Republic. In the midst of this, the Government of Ireland Act of 1920 created a separate parliament for the six counties of Northern Ireland, partitioning the island. The War of Independence witnessed assassination, reprisal and counter-reprisal. There was an attempt by Sinn Féin and the IRA to supplant the British administration in Ireland in the areas of local government and the administration of justice, with mixed results. There was also an intelligence war fought and a crusade to undermine the RIC, the country's armed police force since 1822. This war involved psychological, political and propaganda battles.

By the end of 1919, there were over 40,000 British army troops in Ireland. The British chief secretary, Hamar Greenwood, insisted that Britain had Ireland under control. The British prime minister, David Lloyd George, disingenuously referred to the IRA as 'a small murder gang', and in November 1920 announced 'we have murder by the throat'. The truth was that law and order had long ceased in Ireland and the conduct of the war from the British side was a disaster. Dublin Castle, the headquarters of British rule in Ireland, could not put together an effective, unified security command. As previously classified documents have become available, they have revealed a vast accumulation of frustration, error and confusion within the administration and its police force, and also within the British cabinet and army. In March 1920, the RIC was reinforced by the recruitment of British ex-soldiers and sailors, known as the Black and Tans due to their distinctive uniforms. By November 1921 there were almost 10,000 of them in Ireland. Although it is difficult to be precise about the numerical strength of the IRA, it is unlikely that more than 3,000 members were active as combatants.

But there were tensions within the IRA also, and differences of opinion. Despite the IRA's often effective use of guerrilla warfare tactics, historians in recent years have been more sceptical about the scale of the damage it inflicted and have highlighted some of the murkier aspects of the war, including the killing and intimidation of innocent civilians. There was often a pitiful shortage of weapons and communications problems between IRA headquarters and the regional brigades. There were chilling executions, anger about alleged spies and informers, and sometimes a resistance to the IRA when it was deemed not to be acting in the interests of the communities it claimed to represent. Many of the contentions in this book, originally published in 1948, about 'the unflinching support of a civilian population', about republican Volunteers coming through the ordeal 'with immaculate hands', will be disputed by professional historians as not withstanding objective historical research. It is a period of Irish history still much disputed, but a lot of the research to date has excluded the voices of the general population.

It was, like all wars, complicated and difficult, and the certainty expressed by so many in its aftermath was rarely evident at the time. There is much defiance and resoluteness on display in this book. There was a temptation after the events to simplify or romanticise what was a painful period for many, marked by pride, but also suffering and conflicting allegiances. This was overwhelmingly a revolution of the young and the inexperienced. Nonetheless, this book humanises the period and underlines the bravery and idealism that was evident. Many of those who fought in Dublin, as elsewhere, took huge risks for little or no reward, but the bonds of friendship and common purpose that they shared helped them in their quest. There were many resourceful women in Cumann na mBan, the women's auxiliary to the IRA, whose structures proved efficient and reliable and whose role in transporting dispatches was indispensable; they receive due recognition in this book as women who 'left their names indelibly' on the story of the Irish revolution.

This book, and others like it, also fulfilled a need in the 1930s and 1940s not just to allow the Volunteers to record their story in their own words, but to ensure a younger generation would be aware of their actions and of a time when, according to the book's contributors, there was a 'militant national insurrectionary spirit'. *Dublin's Fighting Story* captures the excitement and the immediacy of the Irish War of Independence and the belief that the leaders of the revolution did not urge people to take dangerous courses they were not themselves prepared to take. Many of their tragic ends are recorded here, and the book is also a reminder that some leaders are better remembered than others. Arthur Griffith, for example, the founder of the original Sinn Féin movement, and often neglected, is recalled here by Liam Ó Briain as 'the profoundest thinker of them all and one of the greatest men that Ireland ever produced'. There is also a concern expressed about what Seán McGarry referred to as 'a generation so lamentably ignorant' of the achievements of Michael Collins. This was an echo of a fear that had been highlighted in the 1930s by Fianna Fáil Minister for Education Thomas Derrig, who expressed his concern at a 'lack of knowledge of the 1916 leaders and of the events subsequent to 1916 displayed by boys with the leaving certificate'. With the passage of time, the certainties and emphatic assertions in this book about 'the destiny of an ancient people' and the righteousness of their course of action may appear to some as exaggerated, simplistic or even disingenuous. What cannot be disputed, however, is the contention that the source of their strength during the years 1916–21 'lay in their faith in their cause'. This moving and absorbing book allows the reader to understand why.

PROFESSOR DIARMAID FERRITER
BOSTON COLLEGE
MARCH 2009

FOREWORD

ALMOST THIRTY YEARS ago a small body of men engaged in combat with the armed forces of an empire. Militarily they were weak. Their strength lay in their faith in their cause and in the unflinching support of a civilian population which refused to be cowed by threats or by violence.

For almost two years these men successfully maintained the unequal struggle and finally compelled their powerful adversary to seek a truce. The battles in which they fought were neither large nor spectacular: they were the little clashes of guerrilla warfare – the sudden meeting, the flash of guns, a getaway, or the long wait of an ambush, then the explosive action, and death or a successful decision. And the stake at issue was the destiny of an ancient people.

Before the war years imposed a restriction upon newsprint, as upon other commodities, *The Kerryman*, in its various Christmas and other special numbers, told much of the story of these men, the men of the flying columns, the active service units of the Irish Republican Army. It now gathers these stories into book form together with others hitherto unpublished. First in the series was *Rebel Cork's Fighting Story*, the fighting stories of Kerry and Limerick followed, and now *Dublin's Fighting Story* is presented.

All the stories in these *Fighting Series* booklets are either told by the men who took part in the actions described, or else they are written from the personal narrative of survivors. The booklets do not purport to be a detailed or chronological history of the fight for independence, but every effort has been made to obtain the fullest and most accurate information about the incidents described. The publishers are conscious, however, that in the collection of data about such a period errors and omissions can easily occur and so they will welcome the help of readers who may be able to throw more light upon the various episodes related in the series. Such additional information will be incorporated into the second edition of the booklets which the present rate of orders would seem to indicate will be called for in the very near future.

The publishers believe that the younger generation who know about those times by hearsay only will find these survivors' tales of the fight of absorbing interest, while to the older generation they will recall vividly a memorable era and the men who made it. In short, they feel that *Fighting Story* series, the story of the Anglo-Irish War county by county, is a series that will be welcomed by Irish people everywhere. For that reason, so that the booklets may have the widest possible circulation, they are being sold at a price within the reach of everyone. To sell these booklets, with their lavish collection of illustrations of unique historical interest, at the very moderate price of two shillings, the publishers were content to reduce their own profit and to produce the booklet at little above the mere cost of production. They will be satisfied if the series serves to preserve in the hearts of the younger generation that love of country and devotion to its interests which distinguished the men whose doings are related therein.

ACKNOWLEDGEMENTS

Sceilg's stories of 1916 as given in this volume, are largely taken from his own articles published in the *Catholic Bulletin* soon after the Rising, when the *Catholic Bulletin* gave all the details that the military censor would allow. To Messrs M.H. Gill and Son Ltd., proprietors of the *Catholic Bulletin*, the editor of *Dublin's Fighting Story* expresses his thanks for permission to use the material; also to the directors of the Irish Press Ltd., for permission to republish material from the *Evening Telegraph*.

The Editor

HOW THE FIGHT BEGAN!

by PIARAS BÉASLAÍ

IT IS A curious reflection that, but for Sir Edward Carson and other bitter enemies of Irish freedom, there would have been no Irish Volunteers, and consequently no 1916 Rising, and the history of Ireland might have been entirely different. Had the carrying through of the Home Rule Bill of 1913 been allowed to take its normal legal course, we might have today a native government with severely limited local powers and those who then worked and hoped for an independent Irish state – a small minority – might be still ploughing a lonely furrow.

The Fenian tradition died hard, and in 1913 there was still a secret Irish Republican Brotherhood, but its membership was small, its activities restricted, and its existence hardly guessed at by the outside world. The hopeless failures of the attempted insurrections of 1848 and 1867 had disheartened most people; and two generations of what was called 'constitutional agitation', had weakened the old separatist tradition and created a new outlook. 'Home Rule', a limited control over certain local affairs, seemed to most people to sum up Irish national aspirations. Those who talked of 'physical force' or republicanism were looked on as harmless lunatics, the butt of many jests; and even the Sinn Féin policy of national self-reliance and passive resistance to English rule was regarded askance by the majority of the people as a cranky 'factionism' which disturbed the unity of the Home Rule movement, and weakened the position of its leader, Mr John Redmond. The advent to power, in 1906, of a strong Liberal government, pledged to Home

Rule, seemed to bring the success of 'constitutionalism' within sight. When, after two further general elections, the Liberals were returned to office in such reduced members as to give the 'casting vote' to Mr Redmond and his party – and when the power of absolute veto of the House of Lords had been altered to a power of mere temporary delay – then Irish people began to regard Home Rule as a certainty.

Then – from all quarters in the world – came a movement started by Sir Edward Carson and Mr F.F. Smith (Lord Birkenhead) and the British and pro-British die-hards to deal a fatal blow to Irish belief in 'constitutionalism' and bring back doctrines of physical force into favour. The 'Ulster Volunteers' were formed, and drilled, and armed, to resist a proposed act of the British parliament. They were told by political leaders – and heads of the Tory party – that 'rebellion was a sacred duty', that the government dare not interfere with the Ulster Volunteers although they were avowedly illegal, that generals of the British army would support their insurrection. The British government took no action, but gave signs of being intimidated by this noise and fury; there were whisperings of compromise, of plans for partitioning Ireland.

The Irish Parliamentary Party contented themselves with jeering at the 'Ulster Volunteers', but a number of their followers began to ask – 'If these men can arm to defeat Home Rule why should we not arm to defend it?' But this query met with no encouraging response from their leaders. Such was the situation, late in 1913, when the Irish Republican Brotherhood, headed by Tom Clarke and Seán MacDiarmada, saw in these doings an opportunity of establishing an openly armed and trained Volunteer force in the country. A government which tolerated 'Ulster Volunteers' threatening insurrection could hardly interfere with an army of Irish Volunteers. This point of view appealed to others besides revolutionaries. Professor Eoin MacNeill, vice-president of the Gaelic League, wrote an article in the official organ of that organisation advocating the formation of a force of Irish Volunteers. This was the first open lead given to public opinion. On 10 November 1913, Bulmer Hobson and Éamonn Kent came into my office – the *Evening Telegraph* – to instruct me to attend a meeting at Wynn's Hotel on the following night for the purpose of starting a body of Volunteers. Hobson was the 'Centre' of my circle in the IRB, and Kent was a member of the circle.

On 11 November I attended this historic meeting of a handful of men in a small private room in Wynn's Hotel. About half of those present were members of the IRB, but this was, of course, unknown to the others, who included The O'Rahilly and Seán Fitzgibbon. Professor MacNeill presided and opened the proceedings in Irish, but, after a while, it was pointed out by Seán MacDiarmada that some of those present did not know the language, and we turned to English. Our principal concern at the start was that the movement we were setting on foot should not be regarded as sectional or 'factionist'. To establish its broad national basis we decided to invite the co-operation of persons representing various interests and associations, and particularly of those identified with the Home Rule movement, who then represented the majority in nationalist Ireland. We were so far successful that, at the next meeting, a number of persons actively identified with support of the Irish Party – though none of them of much prominence – joined our Provisional Committee. Most important of these at this stage was Mr Laurance Kettle, brother of Mr Thomas Kettle, MP, who consented to act as joint honorary secretary with Professor MacNeill. The leaders of the Parliamentary Party, however, held sternly aloof and refused even to encourage our movement with a word of approbation; and the daily newspapers were equally unfavourable. Lord Mayor Lorcan Sherlock refused the use of the Mansion House for our inaugural public meeting.

Events moved rapidly. On 25 November, exactly a fortnight from the first meeting of the Provisional Committee, the movement was launched to the public at a crowded meeting held in the Rotunda Rink, then the largest hall in Dublin. Between those who filled the building, and those who attended overflow meetings outside, it is estimated that about 12,000 or 13,000 were present at the birth of the Irish Volunteers, and some 4,000 were enrolled as Volunteers.

The objects of the new body were declared to be 'to secure and maintain the rights and liberties common to all the people of Ireland', and to unite Irishmen of every creed, party and class for that purpose. It will be noted that there was no reference to Home Rule or the Ulster Volunteers. Within a few days drill halls were secured and opened all over Dublin. A great many ex-soldiers offered their services as drill instructors. Companies were formed and the city of Dublin was divided into four battalion areas – a division which continued up to the time of the Truce. In those early days we had companies and battalions and instructors, but no officers – the only officials being secretaries and treasurers, to keep the roll and collect subscriptions. Our company organisation and drill were based upon a British War Office manual *Infantry Drill, 1911*, which was already out of date as far as the British army was concerned.

The boys' military organisation of Fianna Éireann was already in existence, and young men who had been trained in this body – Liam Mellows, Con Colbert and Michael Lonergan – had secretly drilled members of the IRB. Five of these young men were on the Provisional Committee. Members of the IRB, Sinn Féin and the Gaelic League flocked to the drill halls, and so did many supporters of the Redmondite Party; but the attitude of the parliamentary leaders was one of contemptuous hostility. In spite of this the movement spread through the country and rapidly assumed large proportions. By May 1914, about 75,000 Volunteers were enrolled; and one member of the Parliamentary Party, Mr Tom Kettle, had joined the Provisional Committee. The British 'Home Rule' government, which had looked on passively while the 'Ulster Volunteers' armed against Home Rule, showed no such passivity in case of the Irish Volunteers. Within ten days of the Rotunda Rink meeting, on 5 December 1913, an edict was issued prohibiting the importation of arms into Ireland. A little later, in open defiance of this order, the 'Ulster Volunteers' landed at Larne and distributed a cargo of arms and ammunition, holding up police and coastguards at the gun's point. Again no action was taken by the British government. In fact a 'mutiny' had been fostered by high-ranking English officers at the Curragh, who had declared that they would refuse to take military action against the 'Ulster Volunteers'.

I have never seen a complete accurate list of the members of the Provisional Committee of the Volunteers in any publication, and it may be interesting to name them here. It may be noted that we had no official president, though Professor MacNeill usually presided at the meetings. The officers were: hon. secs Eoin MacNeill and Laurence J. Kettle; hon. treasurers The O'Rahilly and John Gore; members Seán MacDiarmada, P.H. Pearse, Tomás MacDonagh, Éamonn Kent, Joseph Plunkett, Con Colbert, Liam Mellows, Bulmer Hobson, Pádraic Ó Riain, Éamonn Martin, M. Lonergan, Robert Page, Peadar Macken, Colm Ó Lochlainn, Seamus O'Connor, Seán Fitzgibbon, Liam Gógan, Peadar White, Sir Roger Casement, Col Maurice Moore, T. Kettle, MP, George Walsh, M.J. Judge, Peter O'Reilly, James Lenehan and myself. This makes thirty in all – not twenty-seven, as has been erroneously stated in some publications; and of these sixteen were members of the IRB. Michael Lonergan went away to America early in 1914.

Mr Redmond, having tried in every way to discourage the growth of the Volunteers, became alarmed by their increasing strength and opened secret negotiations with Professor MacNeill and Colonel Moore with a view to gaining control of the organisation. Failing to secure this objective, he issued a letter to the press in June 1914, in which he declared that unless the Provisional Committee agreed to add twenty-five persons nominated by himself to their committee he would call upon his supporters in the Volunteers to break away from the central organisation and form their own county committees. Faced with the prospect of a split in the Volunteers, the majority of the members of the Provisional Committee decided to surrender to Mr Redmond's demand. Among this majority were Sir Roger Casement, The O'Rahilly and Bulmer Hobson. I was one of a minority of nine who voted against the surrender, and I think that subsequent events justified our attitude. The split was inevitable, but it only came after great harm had been done to the growing organisation.

The new departure was followed by a big increase in the paper strength of the Volunteers. Those interested in politics rather than military training flooded the drill halls and meeting places, apparently aiming at strengthening the party control of the movement – but the efficiency of the Volunteers was rather weakened than strengthened by these accessions. By the outbreak of war in August the Irish Volunteers numbered about 170,000 men.

It was at this time – June 1914 – that the first elections of company officers were held in Dublin – and the county followed suit.

It is not necessary to tell of arrangements made under the new regime, since all these were to be 'scrapped' in less than three months time. The only activity of historical importance – the supplying of arms to the Volunteers – was one in which no member of the Parliamentary Party had any part. These secret arrangements to purchase rifles in Antwerp and 'run' them to Ireland, which resulted in the landings at Howth and Kilcool, were initiated before Mr Redmond's nominees joined the Provisional Committee. Among those concerned in these activities were Sir Roger Casement, Darrell Figgis, Erskine Childers and Bulmer Hobson. On Sunday 25 July, some nine hundred German Mausers, the famous 'Howth rifles' were landed at Howth, along with a large quantity of ammunition, and, on the night of the following Saturday, 1 August, an additional six hundred rifles were landed at Kilcool, County Wicklow.

The events attending the former landing are of historic significance. A body of about eight hundred Volunteers was marched out to Howth; most of them being under the impression that it was only an ordinary route march. As they arrived, a yacht sailed into the harbour laden with the guns. The rifles were served out to the men, but no ammunition was given to them. At Clontarf, on their march back to Dublin, the Volunteers were confronted by Mr Harrel, the assistant commissioner of the Dublin Metropolitan Police, with a body of about two hundred policemen and a company of the King's Own Scottish Borderers. Mr Harrel ordered the police to disarm the Volunteers. A scuffle ensued in which shots were fired, and some in the front ranks of the Volunteers and some policemen were slightly injured. A number of the police refused to obey Mr Harrel's orders. He then called back his police and commenced a parley with the leaders of the column.

Meanwhile the greater part of the Volunteers behind the front rank got away with their rifles, crossing gardens and fields, so that the attempted coup proved a ludicrous fiasco. But this episode had a tragic sequel. The company of soldiers, while returning to barracks, was followed by a hooting crowd. It is alleged that a few stones were thrown at the soldiers, who retaliated by bayonet charges. When they reached Bachelor's Walk the officer in charge, Major Haig, ordered his men to 'prepare to fire', whereupon they fired indiscriminately, point blank, at the people in the street. Four people were killed and thirty-seven wounded. All Ireland seethed with indignation over the two occurrences, and the different attitudes shown to the enemies of Irish freedom and its defenders but, inside a week, a new and unexpected situation had arisen with the entrance of England into a great European war.

A Home Rule Bill had passed the House of Commons, but was delayed by the Lords. Meanwhile pressure was being brought on Mr Redmond to accept an amending Bill, embodying partition. It was felt that the outbreak of war had given Mr Redmond a unique opportunity to enforce his full demands. All the people of nationalist Ireland, including even the separatists, and the entire force of the Volunteers, were prepared to support a strong stand by him. He had all the cards in his hand to play. What he did was quite the opposite of what was expected. Speaking in the House of Commons, without even consulting his own party, he pledged Ireland to an *unconditional* support of England in the war. He went further, and agreed to the suspension of Home Rule until the end of the war, when it was to be subject to an amending Act, embodying all the modifications and limitations which Carson and his party might demand. Meanwhile, he started a recruiting campaign in Ireland, and told the young men that their only duty was to go out to France to fight for England.

One might have thought that, after what had happened, such a campaign had not much chance of success with the Irish people; but the whole force of the Parliamentary Party, the daily press and almost every provincial newspaper was thrown into the effort. The country was flooded with propaganda, tales of German atrocities, and every lie and fallacious argument that perverted imaginations could devise. The greater part of the Irish people was swept off their feet by this campaign, in which all the leaders they had trusted seemed to speak with one voice.

On the executive of the Irish Volunteers the situation soon became impossible. When Mr Redmond told Volunteers (as he did at a review at Woodenbridge) that their place was in France, the majority of the members of the old Provisional Committee felt that it was time to take action. A meeting had been announced to be held in the Mansion House on 25 September, at which the English prime minister, Mr Asquith, and Mr Redmond would speak on behalf of recruiting for the British army. On the night before the meeting the headquarters of the Volunteers were seized by a body of picked men, and twenty of the original members of the Provisional Committee signed and issued a manifesto declaring Mr Redmond's nominees expelled from control. On the same night a body of armed men, of whom I was one, met in a room in Parnell Square, with the intention of seizing the Mansion House by force and preventing the holding of the meeting. James Connolly was the leading spirit in this enterprise, but most of those present were members of the IRB, including Tom Clarke and Seán MacDiarmada. It was discovered that the Mansion House was already held by English military and the attempt had to be called off.

The split in the Volunteers had now begun. In Dublin the great majority of the original Volunteers adhered to the Provisional Committee. In some cases whole companies stood firm, practically to a man, and there was no company of which a substantial nucleus did not remain. In the country it was different. At the time of the split the paper strength of the volunteers was about 170,000; but of these only about 12,000 followed the lead of the original committee. Our numbers, however, increased steadily from that until 1916, while the membership of the Redmondite Volunteers fell away rapidly. By 1916 only a handful of them were left. At the time of the Rising our forces in the whole country numbered about 18,000.

At the outbreak of the war the Supreme Council of the Irish Republican Brotherhood decided on an insurrection, and steps were taken to get in touch with Germany by means of John Devoy of New York and Clan na Gael, with a view to securing arms and ammunition. Meanwhile the work of arming the Volunteers went on steadily, and in Dublin most Volunteers possessed rifles by 1916. The plans for the insurrection were already being drafted early in 1915. In February of that year I was supplied by my commandant, Ned Daly, with the plans of the positions we of the 1st battalion were to occupy in Easter Week, 1916. The position of the Volunteer executive at the time was peculiar. The secretary of the Volunteers, Mr Bulmer Hobson, was an officer of the IRB, but he was known to be opposed to an insurrection, and therefore the preparations which were being made were kept a secret from him – a rather anomalous situation. Those members of the executive who did not belong to the IRB (and some others who did) were also kept in ignorance of what was intended.

There was another volunteer body in Dublin – the Citizen Army – whose leader was James Connolly. Before the war Connolly had been regarded as one whose outlook was rather international than nationalist, but from the outbreak of war he showed himself an ardent patriot and passionate advocate of insurrection. He was the moving spirit in the plan to seize the Mansion House which I have already reported. In January and March 1915, he gave very practical lectures on street fighting to the officers of the Dublin brigade. Not being a member of the IRB, he was not in the secrets of the military council, and feared that by delay they would let the opportunity for insurrection slip through their fingers. At a later date he even threatened to bring out his Citizen Army in an insurrection of their own. However, ultimately, in 1916, as will be shown, he came to work in the closest collusion and confidence with the military council, who made him commandant-general of Dublin during the Rising.

Another small military body who worked in sympathy with us

was the Hibernian Rifles, belonging to the 'Irish-American Alliance' of the Ancient Order of Hibernians – a very different body from the 'Board of Érin' AOH.

In November 1914, Robert Monteith, Captain of 'A' company, 1st battalion, was ordered by the British military authorities to leave Dublin. He went to Limerick and, later, made his way to New York and thence to Germany, to join Sir Roger Casement and later return with him to Ireland.

On Whit Sunday, 23 May 1915, the Dublin brigade visited Limerick and, while marching through the streets, were attacked by a howling mob, who vainly tried to break up their ranks – a striking illustration of the effects of Irish Party pro-British propaganda. On the same day a very fine parade of Kerry Volunteers took place in Killarney, and was addressed by Eoin MacNeill without any sign of hostility.

At the beginning of 1916, conscription was introduced into England. As a result of this a number of Volunteers from London, Liverpool, Glasgow and Manchester came to Dublin and remained there until the Rising, in which they took part. A camp for these men was established in Kimmage. Many of these played a prominent part in the subsequent fight for freedom, the most noteworthy of all being Michael Collins.

On 19 January 1916, James Connolly disappeared for three days. Different theories have been put forward to explain his disappearance. Without entering into controversy on the matter I can only record that immediately after his reappearance the date of the Rising was finally decided on. I was sent to Liverpool, with a cipher message giving the date, to meet Tommy O'Connor, a steward on an Atlantic liner, who was to convey the letter to Devoy. I also bore a verbal message with regard to the proposed landing of arms from a disguised German vessel at Limerick. It was not until a little later that Fenit was decided on as the landing-place. I mention these matters because inaccurate statements, considerably pre-dating these decisions, have appeared in print.

On St Patrick's Day 1916, the Dublin brigade paraded, over 3,000 strong, in College Green and made a great impression with their arms, equipment and discipline. Most of them had rifles – though of the most varied kind – and after two years of intensive and enthusiastic training they were far more efficient soldiers than the conscript troops of England – as they were to prove in little more than a month. A certain number – not a very large number – of these men were members of the IRB, and these had a good idea that an insurrection was due at a not very remote date. It is probable that a very large number of the others also suspected what was brewing; but it is safe to say that not one Volunteer in a hundred had the least inkling that the grand parades and field manoeuvres announced for Easter Sunday were to prove, in fact, the beginning of a fight for Irish independence. The secret was well kept.

Neither Eoin MacNeill nor Bulmer Hobson – nor, indeed, other members of the executive – had any suspicion of what was intended until Holy Week. On Wednesday 19 April, Hobson ascertained that an insurrection was planned for the Sunday and informed MacNeill. Pearse was approached and openly admitted his intentions. MacNeill declared that he would do his utmost to prevent the Rising, and drafted an order as chief-of-staff countermanding the Sunday manoeuvres, and another depriving Pearse of his command. Next day, however, Tomás MacDonagh and Seán MacDiarmada had an interview with MacNeill and came away apparently satisfied that they would meet no more opposition from that quarter. What transpired at the interview is unknown, but there was evidently some misunderstanding.

Next day came bad news from Kerry. The German ship, the *Aud*, laden with rifles, machine-guns and ammunition, having successfully 'run the blockade' and reached Tralee Bay, had been captured by a British cruiser; Sir Roger Casement had landed from a submarine at Banna Strand with two companions, Monteith and Beverley, and had been arrested by the Royal Irish Constabulary; and three Volunteers, who had been sent from Dublin to carry out work in connection with the Rising, had been drowned at Ballykissane pier when their motor took a wrong turning and ran into the sea.

On Saturday night Beverley was captured – and next day informed his captors that a Rising had been planned for that day. The English authorities received the news with scepticism. They believed at the time that the Easter Sunday manoeuvres had been cancelled, and that, if any danger had existed, it was over.

This impression was due to the publication that morning in the *Sunday Independent* of a notice signed by Eoin MacNeill as chief-of-staff, rescinding 'all orders given for tomorrow', and announcing that 'no parades, marches or other movements of Irish Volunteers will take place'.

A meeting of the military council was hastily called together in Liberty Hall on Sunday morning, to decide what was to be done in face of this unexpected development. The leaders agreed to prevent isolated actions by confirming MacNeill's cancelling order, while at the same notifying officers to hold themselves in readiness for a fresh mobilisation. Messages to this effect were sent to Volunteer units all over the country. A few hours later, after much consultation and examination, and the receipt of various reports, it was decided that the insurrection would take place on Easter Monday at noon – and a fresh batch of messengers was dispatched to various places in the country with new orders to that effect. Those 'in the know' in Dublin were notified, but the general body of Volunteers was only informed by a 'surprise' mobilisation on Easter Monday morning. There had been many 'test mobilisations' before, and things worked smoothly enough. Messengers on foot and on bicycles went to the houses of Volunteers and told them to report at their battalion headquarters at ten o'clock. A great many Volunteers had left Dublin for the day, or the week, and the number who appeared on parade at noon was only about one-third of what would have been present had the Sunday 'manoeuvres' not been cancelled; yet it proved a sufficient force to start an insurrection that was to alter drastically the history of Ireland.

THE GREAT DUBLIN STRIKE AND LOCKOUT, 1913

by SEAMUS O'BRIEN

The man who will sacrifice anything for a principle gets rarer and rarer ... I am literary man, a lover of ideas, but I have found few people in my life who would sacrifice anything for a principle. Yet in Dublin, when masters issued that humiliating document asking men – on penalty of dismissal – to swear never to join a Trade Union, thousands of men who had no connection with the Irish Transport Workers – many amongst them hostile to that organisation, refused to obey. They would not sign away their freedom, their right to choose their own heroes and their own ideas. Most of these men had no strike funds to fall back on. They had wives and children depending on them. Quietly and grimly they took, through hunger, the path to the Heavenly City ... Nobody has praised them, no one has put a crown about their brows. Yet these men are the true heroes in Ireland today, they are the descendants of Oscar, Cuchulain, the heroes of our ancient stories. For all their tattered garments I recognise in these obscure men majesty of spirit.

Extract from a speech by George Russell (Æ) in the Albert Hall, London,
during the 1913 strike in Dublin

The story of the Dublin dispute of 1913–14 is meet subject for an epic poem with which some Irish genius of the future can win an immortality as great as did the humble fighters who, in it, fought the Battle of Labour.

James Connolly writing in The Irish Worker, *28 November 1914*

THE DUBLIN OF the first decade of this century was a Dublin of literary glamour and superficial display. The Irish literary movement had already made itself felt among the middle and professional classes; Dublin Castle and the vice-regal lodge attracted the landlord and wealthy commercial classes. The papers told of their goings and comings, their balls and hunts and concerts, and occasionally the activities of the Gaelic League, the Abbey Theatre and the Irish Party. Nowhere was there any mention of the masses of the people. Behind this façade of show and pomp and display there existed a silent, bitter, grumbling mass of people, living in the most abominable hovels of any European city, working for a mere pittance, only sufficient to keep body and soul together, without the right or the power to demand any decent conditions or any protection from the harshest and most overbearing accumulation of masters ever gathered together.

The average weekly wage of the labourer of the times was 16/–, though many worked for 12/– and 14/–. Women and girls were employed at about 5/– per week. In the largest factory employing women the wage of the majority was only 3/6, and on one occasion a Labour member of the Dublin Corporation accused an employer of paying a wage of 1/– per week to his female employees. The hours of work were 60 to 84 per week. Dismissals took place without any reason being given. Foremen and managers used their position of power to the utmost and many ugly stories were told of the manner in which men and girls were victimised because of their opinions or their independence. On the docks men scrambled for the day-to-day jobs offered by the stevedores. The unemployed labourer turned to the riverside for the chance of a few hours' work. Wages were paid in the snugs of the public houses in the vicinity – the stevedore collecting his rake-off from the publican for the trade secured by his patronage. Woe betide the man who dared to turn away and bring his wages home in full to his wife and family. He was black-listed by the stevedore and he walked the quays until he learned the lesson that he must leave a portion of his wages in the public house. Is it any wonder that in many cases the docker found himself with little or nothing to bring home at the end of a day's work?

Like other cities, Dublin suffered occasional crises of depression and unemployment. There was no unemployment assistance, no employment insurance, and the Poor Law Boards, controlled by the large rate-payers, gave little heed to the hunger and want of the unemployed worker and his family. Even National Health Insurance, as applied to Irish workers, was opposed by the Irish Party representatives in the House of Commons. It was carried only by the pressure of the few British Labour members and the British Liberal Party. Is it any wonder, then, that the Dublin worker felt himself abandoned, unprotected, despised; the prey of every petty master 'clothed in a little brief authority'? If he became a lickspittle, a grovelling slave, brutal to his wife and family, such slavery and brutality expressed the extent of the ravages of his conditions of life, on his body and soul. But he had his moments of brightness and gaiety, too. When the bands played and the flags waved, and the orators talked of Irish freedom, and the 'old house in College Green', the Dublin worker was always there to cheer and to applaud, to signify his desire for Irish freedom, a freedom that meant very little in his own life except a change of masters.

Into his city, seething with discontent, with bitterness and slavery, came Jim Larkin in 1907. As organiser for the National Union of Dockers in Glasgow and Liverpool, Larkin was also asked to keep an eye on Irish ports and to try to organise the workers. Larkin had himself sprung from the docks and knew all about the hardships and slavery of the work. He had little regard for formulae or rules. When he saw a condition of affairs to be remedied he set about the job. He did not willingly brook delays in awaiting the sanction of his executive in England before taken action. In Newry and Dundalk he called out the dockers without sanction, and his trade union secretary, Mr Sexton, bitterly complained to the Trade Union Congress of this unofficial action. In Belfast docks in 1908 he called a strike which cost the headquarters of the union £5,000, and over £8,000 in all. Again in 1908 he called a strike of the Dublin shipping and riverside workers, and in the same year the dockers in Cork fought for fourteen weeks. The English headquarters of the union resented this assumption of authority on the part of Larkin. They refused to support the Cork strike, and Larkin was suspended from his position of organiser on 7 December 1908.

Larkin refused to accept defeat. He felt that he had a purpose in life – the uplifting of the Irish workers – and he set about the formation of an Irish union without any control or any hindrances from outside the country. On 20 January 1909, the Irish Transport Workers' Union was formed in Dublin. It is told that its assets consisted of a table, a chair, a billy-can, a candle and two bottles. Its first office was in Townsend Street.

At a later period in the columns of *The Irish Worker*, official organ of the Irish Transport Workers' Union, Larkin's attitude on the subject of Irish versus English unions is well expressed: 'Whilst I agree that the formation of the English Labour Party was and is the best thing the English workers have ever done, so, too, the formation of an Irish Labour Party would be the best day's work ever attempted by Irish workers. The world cannot allow the Irish nation to be obliterated. Internationalism means internationalism, not ONE nationalism. We of the Irish workers are out to claim the earth for the world's workers, and our portion, as Irishmen, is Ireland … We are determined to weld together the common people of the north, the south, the east and the west.'

The new union had its early difficulties, its birth pangs and growing pains. Some of the early pioneers are forgotten today, but men there were who sacrificed 1/–, 2/– and 2/6 per week of their miserable wages to set the union on its feet and keep its offices going. Not least of the difficulties was the hostility of the English union, the National Union of Dockers, to Larkin. A charge of misappropriation of funds connected with the Cork strike was brought against him, and he was sentenced to twelve months' imprisonment. An application for a new trial was refused, and in June 1910, Larkin went to serve his sentence. The fact that the jury was entirely drawn from the employing class, that the summings-up of the judges in both courts were obviously against him, that any funds involved were used in the interests of the men on strike, and the ferocity of the sentence, created strong feelings against the decision. Meetings of protest were held and the viceroy, Lord Aberdeen, accepting the view that Larkin was not 'morally culpable' ordered his release, after he had served three months of his sentence.

It was during this period, July 1910, that James Connolly returned to Ireland from America. Connolly had already made contact with the Transport Union, and Connolly's paper, *The Harp*, the organ of the Irish Socialist Federation in America, which Connolly had founded, was transferred to Dublin. After a number of issues *The Harp* went out of existence owing to the threat of five or six libel actions. Connolly was invited to return for an organising tour on behalf of the Socialist Party of Ireland. He had been following events in Ireland closely and immediately on his return took a prominent part in speaking at and organising meetings demanding Larkin's release and in helping to build up the new union. At this time, 1910, the union became affiliated to the Dublin Trades Council and to the Trade Union Congress. Early in 1911 Connolly was appointed Ulster organiser and brought his family over from America. The die was then cast for the accomplishment of great things in Ireland during the next five years.

The union gained some big victories within the next two years. In Dublin the dockers joined up almost to a man; the system of payment in public houses was abolished after a campaign in which the abuses on the riverside were fully exposed. Larkin was always a great advocate of temperance. Neither he nor Connolly ever drank intoxicating liquor, and they realised that the manhood and courage of their members was being sapped as much by the excessive consumption of drink as by the abominable conditions under which they lived and worked. A story is told that one day Larkin and a union delegate, who liked to gaze on the beauty of a frothy pint, were making a number of calls on premises in the city where minor disputes had arisen. The day was warm, and after walking about for some hours Larkin turned to his companion and asked him would he like a drink. His companion, with the thoughts of a pint of 'plain' in his mind, said he would. Much to his surprise they walked on, passing by a number of licensed houses, without any disposition on Larkin's part to go in. Finally they reached a small dairy. Larkin walked in, and ordered two pints of MILK!

In Belfast the dockers were also the backbone of the union, and Connolly had considerable success in securing better wages and conditions for the members. In Cork, Waterford, Wexford, Tralee, Sligo and Galway branches of the union were formed. The union also enrolled members amongst the farm labourers in County Dublin. The prestige of the union far exceeded its enrolled membership. Its continuous activities, its exposure of every form of abuse and corruption, its fighting qualities, established it in the leadership of the trade union and labour movement in Ireland. It met with severe resistance from the employers. In Wexford, after a fight of several months, in which the employers refused to recognise the union, Connolly secured a settlement by the formation of the Irish Foundry Workers' Union, affiliated to the Transport Workers' Union. In June 1911, the Dublin Employers' Federation Ltd was formed. This was a direct challenge to the new unionism, or to 'Larkinism', as the bosses preferred to call it. Every effort was made to divert the workers from the union. Every interest, even religion, was appealed to to discredit the leaders in their eyes. The story was whispered that Larkin was the son of Carey the informer. The labour agitator was an anarchist, a syndicalist, an atheist, anti-Christ in disguise. But the strength and power and prestige of the union grew.

In August 1913, a strike at the Dublin Steam Packet Co. precipitated the conflict. About the same time the workers employed in the dispatch department of the *Irish Independent*, then owned by William Martin Murphy, were asked to give up their membership of the union. The men employed in the Dublin Tramway Co., also controlled by Murphy, were asked to sign the following pledge: 'I hereby undertake to carry out all instructions given to me for or on behalf of my employers, and, further, I agree to immediately resign my membership of the Irish Transport and General Workers' Union (if a member); I further undertake that I will not join or in any way support the Union.'

Hundreds of tram workers were immediately locked out for refusal to sign this pledge. The union accepted the challenge. All goods going to or from firms involved were black-listed, and the members refused to handle them. This necessarily involved other firms, but for a few weeks there was no extension of the lockout. In the meantime meetings were held almost nightly in Beresford Place and elsewhere in the city, explaining to the public the issues involved in the strike. The columns of *The Irish Worker* were used to expose the purpose of the bosses and to instil into the minds of the workers their right and duty to themselves and their families to fight this issue, which, in effect, denied them the right to choose their own union and their own leadership. The whole trade union movement in Dublin, through the Dublin Trades Union Council, supported the Transport Union, and on the strike committee, which was formed, there were representatives of several of the skilled trades and crafts unions of the city.

It was evident very early in the lockout that the representatives of Dublin Castle were willing to take a hand on the side of the employers. Large bodies of the Royal Irish Constabulary were drafted from the country into the city to supplement the Dublin Metropolitan Police, although no disturbances of any kind had taken place.

The trams were kept running on a skeleton service by the use of men who were imported into the city and some tramway men who agreed to sign the form severing connection with the union, and by others who were not members of it. There were a number of scrimmages with those men, who were regarded as traitors to their class.

In *The Irish Worker* their betrayal was referred to in strong terms. One heading ran: 'A scab is to his Trade what a Traitor is to his Country' and underneath a poem commencing:

> Who shuns the face of the open day,
> Who wanders out in the gloomy grey,
> Who gets his price and sneaks away?
> THE SCAB.

The daily and evening newspapers on the other hand lauded the 'loyal' workers and placed all the blame for the disturbance of trade on the union and its leaders. Reports of meetings were either suppressed or the speeches made were distorted. William Martin Murphy owned the *Irish Independent* and *Evening Herald*, but the other dailies joined in the campaign of calumny and abuse which Tom Kettle, MP, bitterly referred to as 'gutter journalism'.

The arming of Carson's Ulster Volunteers to fight against Home Rule was a big political issue at this time, and at a meeting held in the last week of August, the fact that Carson was permitted to import arms with impunity was referred to, and the workers of the south were advised to do likewise. Notes of the speech were taken down by a policeman, and on Friday 28 August, James Larkin, Wm O'Brien, Thomas Lawlor, P.T. Daly, and W.P. Partridge were charged before Mr Swifte, the magistrate, with criminal conspiracy to hold a meeting for the purpose of inciting to violence, etc. The policeman note-taker was subjected to a searching cross-examination, in which he admitted that he had seen no disturbances during the strike. The magistrate returned the prisoners for trial on bail. On leaving the police court they were met by a huge crowd, carried shoulder high, and a big meeting was held.

That night (Friday), another meeting was held in Beresford Place, at which James Connolly, P.T. Daly, and W.P. Partridge spoke. Arrangements had already been made for a big demonstration in O'Connell Street on the following Sunday. This meeting was proclaimed by Mr Swifte, and a copy of the proclamation was burned at the meeting. Connolly and Partridge were immediately arrested. Larkin was also being sought, but he evaded the police. On Saturday, Connolly refused bail, and was sentenced to three months' imprisonment. In a speech from the dock, Connolly challenged the right of the representative of the British crown to try a citizen of Ireland. He said that when it came to a choice of what was legal and what was right they would choose what was right. The crown had no right in Ireland, never would have any right in Ireland and he refused to recognise the crown. He refused to recognise the king's proclamation when it was used against the Irish people. In other words, he refused to recognise the court. He was sentenced because of this speech rather than the charge that had been made against him. On that night the police batoned workers in all parts of the city. That the workers replied in kind by throwing stones and other missiles cannot be denied, but the brutality of the police towards many inoffensive people was proven beyond all doubt. James Nolan left his home to call at Liberty Hall to pay his weekly subscription. As he turned into Eden Quay he was set upon and batoned. Taken to Jervis Street Hospital he died early the following morning. Over two hundred people were treated in hospital for wounds received from police batons that night. John Byrne, after discharge from hospital, died a few days later.

The strike committee decided that in order to save the general public from further attacks by the police, the Sunday meeting in O'Connell Street should be called off, and arranged for a meeting in Croydon Park (which was the property of the union) instead. The Women Workers' section had arranged an outing to the Glen-of-the-Downs. On Sunday morning the centre of the city presented the usual Sunday appearance. At Beresford Place the brakes and sidecars lined up in preparation for the outing. They paraded up Eden Quay, turned into O'Connell Street, and made a bright and gay display as they drove through the street around the Parnell monument and down the other side to the Wicklow resort. About twelve o'clock police swarmed into O'Connell Street. One division took up positions on the south side of O'Connell bridge at the ballast office and *Independent* office. Another division was stationed in three sections on the east side of O'Connell Street between Eden Quay and the Pillar. A third on the Bachelor's Walk side of O'Connell bridge. A fourth was posted in sections at Middle Abbey Street and Prince's Street; a fifth had charge of the west side of O'Connell Street from Henry Street to the Rotunda, and a sixth from Earl Street to Parnell Street. Thus it will be seen that the street was completely occupied and controlled. The disposition of the police is important in view of what happened later.

Larkin was being sought by the police, but was missing from his usual haunts. Some workers who had not heard of the calling off of the meeting gathered in the street, but those were very few. The people in the streets were mainly those who were returning from Mass to their Sunday dinner. Suddenly, about 1.30 p.m., the balcony window in the Imperial Hotel was thrown open and a figure wearing a long black coat and a beard appeared. He said a few words and members of the crowd surged towards the hotel, instinctively recognising that the bearded man was Larkin.

Then commenced the most savage and brutal assault on innocent people ever recorded in the annals of the city of Dublin. Converging from both sides the police attacked without discrimination. Men, women and children were caught in the pincer movement prepared by the officers who had arranged the disposition of their forces. At Prince's Street the worst havoc was wrought. The people rushing to safety from the pursuit of the police at Abbey Street and the Pillar found their way blocked by the forces stationed within that side street. Batoning the people to the ground, and kicking them when prostrate, the police vented all their fury on the innocent crowd, pursing them into lanes and side streets, determined that none should escape. The street presented a scene of havoc and bloodshed. Bodies lay everywhere in pools of blood, unable to rise until the ambulances came along to remove them to hospital. Dublin had a number of historic Bloody Sundays, but none for brutality and savagery can be compared with Bloody Sunday 1913.

Not content with the sufferings they had caused during that afternoon, the police turned out that same evening, having been further inflamed with drink in the meantime, and entered the house of the poor slum dwellers in Marlboro Street, Gardiner Street, Corporation Street, etc., smashed their bits of furniture in their over-crowded rooms, pulled their pictures from the walls and trampled on them, and even the little sanctuaries and altars with the ever lit lamp that proclaimed the religious fervour of those simple people were not allowed to escape. Bloody Sunday 1913, may well be described as the slaughter of the innocents, but its effect on the workers of Dublin was to burn into their souls a fierce hatred of Dublin Castle and the employers on whose behalf it had wreaked vengeance. Over six hundred people were admitted to various hospitals for attention.

Larkin had spoken only a few words from the window when the police rushed in and arrested him. A British Liberal MP who was present in the smoke room from the window of which he spoke, in an interview, published in the papers, said that Larkin's words were: 'Comrades and friends, the police have forbidden a meeting to take place in O'Connell Street, today, but I am here to speak and will remain and speak until I am arrested.'

The meeting arranged for Croydon Park in the afternoon attracted huge crowds. Forming up at Beresford Place, the members of the union, headed by cars containing speakers representing several trade unions, marched out in orderly fashion to the venue. At this meeting the announcement was made that Keir Hardie, the well-known British Labour leader, would arrive in Dublin during the following week. This news cheered the workers. They felt that the British Labour movement would extend its help to their comrades in their fight.

With Larkin and Connolly in jail, the two recognised leaders of the union were locked away. Connolly declared a hunger and thirst strike, demanding his immediate release. At the end of a week, very much enfeebled as a result of his ordeal, he was released by order of Lord Aberdeen. During that week the lockout extended to several additional firms. On 1 September, the day following Bloody Sunday, one firm locked out six hundred workers, some because of their refusal to handle flour from a flour mill where a strike was in progress, and others because they refused to remove the badge of the Transport Union it was alleged.

The Chamber of Commerce met and congratulated Mr William Martin Murphy on his stand against the union. It must be said here, to William Martin Murphy's credit, that he paid reasonably good wages and that the conditions of his workers were far better than those of other workers in the city. In a speech to the employers, he told them that THEY by their treatment of their employees were responsible for the rise of the Transport Union. But, nevertheless, he accepted the position of the leader of the Employers' Federation and placed all his vast resources and his ability at their disposal in the effort to destroy the union. Four hundred and four employers bound themselves together to refuse employment to any member of the Transport Union. Firm after firm locked out their staff and tried to find 'free labour' to replace them. The issue was knit. From a mere few hundred originally involved, the lockout extended to 20,000 workers. Artisans and tradesman threw in their lot with the victimised labourers, carters and dockers in sympathetic action. It can never be forgotten, and must never be forgotten, that those 'aristocrats' of the trade union movement engaged in what are known as sheltered trades, sacrificed themselves and their families in an effort to assist their downtrodden and despised comrades.

Thirty-seven trade unions became involved. It was this very sympathetic action on which the fury of the propaganda of the employers was now concentrated. They could find no words strong enough to condemn the use of this weapon. They determined that they would starve every worker and his family into submission.

In an historic defence of the sympathetic strike which appeared in *The Irish Review* of October 1913, Connolly wrote:

> What is the Sympathetic Strike? It is the recognition by the working class of its essential unity, the manifestation in our daily industrial relations that our brother's fight is our fight, that our sister's troubles are our troubles, that we are all members one of another. In practical operation it means that when any body of workers is in conflict with an employer that all other workers should co-operate with them in attempting to bring that particular employer to reason by refusing to handle his goods. That in fact every employer who does not consent to treat his work people upon a civilised basis should be placed and kept outside the amenities and facilities offered by civilised communities. The ideal is not new. It is as old as humanity … The boycott of the Land League is one instance … One of the Wise Men of old when asked what was 'the most perfect State' answered, 'That in which an injury to the meanest citizen was considered as an outrage on the whole body.'

And the reply has come down the ages to us as the embodiment of wisdom.

The lockout had then attracted not merely local and national attention, but international interest. The corporation of Dublin demanded an inquiry into police brutality and the four MPs representing the city published a letter calling for the dismissal of the authorities responsible for Bloody Sunday. Pádraig Pearse wrote in *Irish Freedom*: 'I may be wrong, but I do hold it a most terrible sin that there should be landless men in this island of waste yet fertile valleys, and that there should be breadless men in this city where great fortunes are made and enjoyed.' After a description of the conditions of life of Dublin workers he says: 'Can you wonder that protest is at last made? Can you wonder that the protest is crude and bloody? I do not know whether the methods of Mr James Larkin are wise methods or unwise methods (unwise I think in some respects), but this I do know, that there is a most hideous wrong to be righted and that the man who attempts honestly to right it is a good man and a brave man.'

Tom Clarke writing of the brutality of the Irish cossacks, as he called the police, said: 'Needless to say, there was no justification. We saw little girls ten years old with hair clotted with blood from broken skulls, and an old woman of eighty-four with her nose smashed by a baton.'

Larkin was released on 12 September on bail, after a legal battle. Connolly had already returned to the fray and in a speech from Liberty Hall called for the organisation of the workers into battalions, companies, squads under their own elected leaders, so that they would be in a position to present a disciplined front to police attacks. The *Evening Telegraph* published his speech under the heading 'Larkin's Lieutenant calls for Battalions'. Keir Hardie promised the assistance of British Labour movement in a speech to the Dublin Trades Council. Ships arrived in Dublin harbour containing food for distribution to the families of the workers involved. A kitchen was set up in Liberty Hall, of which Countess Markievicz took charge. Here the workers' wives were fed before being given food to take home, as it was found that many of them were denying themselves so that there should be more for the children. The lord mayor prepared a memorandum containing the basis on which a conference between employers' and workers' representatives could discuss the dispute. They met on two occasions at the Shelbourne Hotel, but the employers left the conference and refused to return. A Citizens' Peace Committee was formed, in which the lord mayor, Mr Tom Kettle, MP, and other prominent men took part, but again the employers refused the overtures. The British government sent over a commission, under the chairmanship of Sir George Askwith (who had considerable experience in industrial disputes in England) to inquire into the whole matter and secure a settlement. At this Commission of Inquiry, Mr T.M. Healy, KC, represented the employers and used all his gifts of bitter wit and caustic oratory to vilify the workers and their leaders and to laud the actions of the employers.

But the findings of the commission were definitely on the side of the workers. In one paragraph they said: 'Whatever may have been the intention of the employers, this document (referring to the pledge demanded) imposes upon the signatories conditions which are contrary to individual liberty, and which no workmen or body of workmen could reasonably be asked to accept.' They laid down a basis of settlement which was briefly: (1) Recognition of the IT and GWU; (2) One month's notice of strike or lockout; (3) An impartial tribunal to investigate breaches of agreement. The workers' leaders accepted these terms, but again the employers refused. In an article describing the efforts of the peace committee towards securing a settlement, Tom Kettle was moved to pay this tribute: 'The suffering has been great but the spirit has been greater. Brush aside all the deplorable personal abuse, all the gutter journalism with which this struggle has been muddied and there flashes out, clean and hard as steel, the courage of the workers.'

Days and weeks passed by and the suffering of the workers and their families increased. The Citizens' Peace Committee, angered by the actions of the police, changed its name to the Citizens' Defence

League. Capt. J.R. White, who was a member, was asked to approach the union leaders and suggest the formation of a citizen army. The idea, already mooted by Connolly, was taken up with acclamation. The workers responded and soon bands of men went daily to Croydon Park to be drilled by their own officers. Whether the fear of being faced with well disciplined and determined forces deterred the police, or that the Castle authorities did not desire a clash which might involve them in a minor revolution, the police now contented themselves by merely attending subsequent meetings as silent watchers. Throughout England meetings were held at which Larkin, Connolly, Æ, George Bernard Shaw and prominent men in the Labour movement spoke. At Albert Hall, London, Connolly moved a huge audience to a high pitch of excitement, and to exclamations of anger and dismay, by his description of the conditions in Dublin city. In an open letter published in *The Irish Times* on 7 October, Æ, addressed the masters of Dublin, reviewed the whole strike situation, and concluded:

> It remained for the twentieth century and the capital city of Ireland to see an oligarchy of 400 masters deciding openly upon starving 100,000 people, and refusing to consider any solution except that fixed by their pride. You, masters, asked men to do that which masters of labour in any other city in these islands had not dared to do. You insolently demanded of those men who were members of a trade union that they should resign from that union; and from those who were not members you insisted on a vow that they would never join it.
>
> Your insolence and ignorance of the rights conceded to workers universally in the modern world were incredible, and as great as your inhumanity. If you had between you collectively a portion of human soul as large as a threepenny bit, you would have sat night and day with the representatives of labour, trying this or that solution of the trouble, mindful of the women and children, who at least were innocent of wrong against you. But no! You reminded labour you could always have your three square meals a day while it went hungry. You went into conference again with representatives of the state, because dull as you are, you know public opinion would not stand your holding out. You chose as your spokesman the bitterest tongue that ever wagged in this island, and then, when an award was made by men who have an experience in industrial matters a thousand times transcending yours, who have settled disputes in industries so great that the sum of your

petty enterprises would not equal them, you withdrew again, and will not agree to accept their solution, and fall back again upon your devilish policy of starvation. Cry aloud to Heaven for new souls! The souls you have got cast upon the screen of publicity appear like the horrid and writhing creatures enlarged from the insect world, and revealed to us by the cinematograph.

You may succeed in your policy and ensure your own damnation by your victory. The men whose manhood you have broken will loathe you, and will always be brooding and scheming to strike a fresh blow. The children will be taught to curse you. The infant being moulded in the womb will have breathed into its starved body the vitality of hate. It is not they – it is you who are blind Samsons pulling down the pillars of the social order. You are sounding the death knell of autocracy in industry. There was autocracy in political life, and it was superseded by democracy. So surely will democratic power wrest from you the control of industry. The fate of you, the aristocracy of industry, will be as the fate of the aristocracy of land if you do not show that you have some humanity still among you. Humanity abhors, above all things, a vacuum in itself, and your class will be cut off from humanity as the surgeon cuts the cancer and alien growth from the body. Be warned ere it is too late.

This letter was typical of the emotions aroused by the struggle. Literary men, artists, writers and journalists united in their admiration of these humble men and women of the Dublin slums. The employers could find no man of principle or standing to support them. They were driven to hire an English writer, named Arnold Wright, to bring forth a distorted and coloured account of the lockout. Just prior to Christmas 1913, British Labour representatives who had come to Dublin presented the following suggested settlement to the employers. This document was sponsored by Archbishop Walsh and endorsed, although reluctantly, by the union leaders: 'That the employers undertake that there will be no victimisation, and that employment will be found for all workers within a period of one month.' Again the employers arrogantly refused these terms, satisfied that the starvation and destitution which they had brought upon one half of the city's population would succeed in bringing the workers to their knees.

Gradually men and women drifted back to work. No questions were asked by the employers, and no documents or pledges were placed before them for signature. They were embittered and discontented but proud in the knowledge that they had put up a great fight and only the sufferings of their children compelled them to end it. In January 1914, the lockout was over. 'It was a drawn battle,' wrote Connolly. Victimisation there was, but the employers found that they could not carry on their business or their industries without the assistance of men who remained faithful to the union and continued their membership. And the union remained heavily in debt, denuded of large bodies of members, but still there to rebuild itself and to stand up again as the bulwark and strength of the onward marching Irish working class. And with the union remained the Citizen Army, to mould and to inspire and to become the spearhead of the Irish nation in its battle towards freedom.

THE IRISH CITIZEN ARMY

by R.M. FOX

As FAR BACK as 1913, at a meeting held outside Liberty Hall during the great Labour struggle which divided the city into two camps, Larkin – the strike leader – made a speech which voiced the Citizen Army idea. Thundering defiance at his enemies, he cried: 'If Carson has a right to arm his men in the north then you men in Dublin have a right to arm to protect yourselves from police attack!' He went on to say that they would arm and return blow for blow. In consequence of this speech he was arrested but released, pending trial. It was decided then to hold a monster Labour demonstration in O'Connell Street. This meeting was proclaimed but Larkin declared that he would be there 'dead or alive'. Thousands of police were mobilised but Larkin outwitted them all by appearing on the balcony of the Imperial Hotel disguised as a bent old invalid. In revenge the police attacked the huge crowds in O'Connell Street, using their batons to such effect that five hundred people were injured.

After this happened, a 'Peace Committee' – composed of professors, writers and others sympathetic to Labour – held a meeting at which the police action was denounced. By this time two men had been killed in baton charges on the quays and the city was in a state of uproar. Captain J.R. White, DSO, who was a member of the committee, first brought forward the idea of forming a Citizen Army among the strikers. He was the son of Sir George White, defender of Ladysmith, and had much military experience. A well-made, dashing young man, he had plenty of energy, passion and enthusiasm. His idea was approved at a meeting of the committee held in the Rev. R.M. Gwynn's room at Trinity College. Professor Houston, of the Royal College of Science, was appointed treasurer and received the first cheque, handed over by Captain White, to equip the army with boots and drill staves. At this meeting, however, there was no idea of establishing a military force.

Captain Jack White was ready to put his experience and boyish enthusiasm to this service so he went to Larkin and Connolly and suggested that he should organise and drill this Labour Defence Force. The leaders, and Captain White himself, made stirring appeals to the men who gathered outside Liberty Hall every day while the struggle went on. Names were handed in and men enrolled. At Croydon Park – the union grounds – Captain White began to drill and discipline the new recruits. Broom handles and hurleys took the place of guns and the men marched, wheeled and manoeuvred to the captain's orders. Soon union parades and meetings were under the protection of this defence force. Police bullying and brutality were checked. A stalwart squad, swinging hurleys, protected the band instruments which on earlier occasions had been smashed. It must be remembered that at this time 'Larkinites', as the strikers were called, were regarded as outlaws by those in authority and all the tenement dwellers were treated as 'enemies' by the police, who entered their homes, smashed their furniture and beat them up. Often these victims of attack had nothing whatever to do with the strikers, though a third of the city was involved. These facts were established at an official inquiry into the disorders held in response to pressure from the general body of citizens. The Citizen Army was composed of people who were denied elementary rights of citizenship and so had to protect themselves.

When the men failed to attend regularly on parade Captain White was angry and complained to Connolly about them being dragged off to meetings. But, like Connolly, he had a great pride in the Citizen Army. Seán O'Casey became secretary to the Citizen Army Council when it reached the stage of being an organised body, while Madame Markievicz was also an active member. At one time, too, Francis Sheehy-Skeffington served on the council, but this was before there was any idea of its functioning as a military force. In the main it was confined to trade unionists though, at a later stage, Dr Kathleen Lynn was their medical officer on active service. An early red letter day for the army was when, in June 1914, a contingent went to Bodenstown to take part in the annual Wolfe Tone commemoration. This was arranged by Tom Clarke, chairman of the Wolfe Tone committee. The tall, broad-shouldered Jim Larkin led his Citizen Army men and his reputation as a strike leader added to the interest they aroused along the route. Recently a contingent of Citizen Army veterans in uniform took part in the 150th anniversary commemoration of Wolfe Tone in Dublin.

During the first phase of Citizen Army activity – its period of labour struggle – Jim Larkin was a fitting symbol of the force. Although it was equipped with hurleys it relied chiefly upon flesh and blood, upon passionate appeals to humanity, those qualities of loyalty, solidarity and sacrifice which Larkin expressed and knew how to evoke. The Citizen Army was the first organised Volunteer force to spring up south of the border in answer to Carson's truculent challenge, for it was formed in October 1913, a month before the Irish Volunteers and from the first it accepted the republican teaching of Wolfe Tone. In the spring of 1914 the Citizen Army had its distinctive uniform, dark green serge tunics with big slouch hats, often fastened at one side with the Red Hand badge of the union. From the beginning, women members had equal rights and duties with the men. The Starry Plough banner made its appearance and the Dublin Trades Council officially approved of the Citizen Army on 6 April 1914.

On 26 July, the Howth gun-running operation was successfully carried out by the Irish Volunteers and, as a result, the Citizen Army armoury was greatly augmented. The hedges around Croydon Park were very convenient for dumping rifles when British soldiers made their appearance and the Volunteers later decided that the Citizen Army should keep their windfall of rifles. Until then there had been one Lee-Enfield rifle used for practice at Croydon Park though revolvers were more plentiful. When war broke out in August 1914, the spirit of the army began to quicken. Membership fell away at the end of the strike when it no longer functioned as a labour defence force. But in the new circumstances it expressed militant national feeling against imperialist war and the threat of conscription.

Connolly now came forward to typify the second phase, the militant national insurrectionary spirit, though the army, as always, had its distinctive Labour outlook. Connolly and Larkin were to the front in a determined demonstration against the Asquith recruiting meeting held in the Mansion House. At first they had hoped to capture the Mansion House and stay in possession. But this proved impossible. They held the meeting at Stephen's Green. Citizen Army men turned out armed with rifles and bayonets, though the rifles were unloaded for ammunition was scarce. The Citizen Army made a defiant stand. From then on armed groups of Citizen Army men and women carrying out route marches became a familiar sight in the Dublin streets. On 24 October 1914, Jim Larkin made a speech of farewell at Croydon Park before leaving for America. In a message to the Irish Citizen Army (*Irish Worker*, 24 October 1914) he said: 'In my absence Jim Connolly will take command.' Connolly's leadership resulted in closer co-operation with the militant section of the Irish Volunteers. Michael Mallin, a keen and resolute soldier, with early experience in the British army, became his chief-of-staff. He helped to shape the army as a fighting weapon and also helped to gather arms. Connolly worked unceasingly to bring about an armed rising. Liberty Hall became an arsenal, with men and women making bombs in their spare time. Work was also put in on the construction of a light machine-gun.

Open propaganda for revolt was the foundation of Connolly's method and his chief instrument was the Citizen Army. He chalked on the board at Liberty Hall directions for Citizen Army marches, 'Attack on Dublin Castle' or 'Capture of Magazine Fort'. By degrees he familiarised his men with the idea of attacking all the enemy strongholds. Leaders of the Irish Volunteers were alarmed lest Connolly should betray plans for a rising prematurely and so bring the British forces down on them. Connolly, for his part, feared that there would be conspiratorial whispers in corners without any real attempt at revolt. During the period of misunderstanding, the Citizen Army leader was kidnapped by the Volunteers and detained in a house for three days while the Volunteer leaders discussed matters with him. When he returned to Liberty Hall he had little to say about what had happened. But it is quite clear that the Volunteer leaders convinced him that they meant business, for he became a member of the military council – along with those leaders – responsible for planning the Rising. It has been said that Connolly 'captured his captors' and events proved that the Connolly line – which was the line of the Citizen Army – was followed. Connolly interviewed each man of the Citizen Army individually and asked if he was willing to fight alone, if the Volunteers did not take part. It says a great deal for the courage and resolution of these Citizen Army men that they were willing to fight, if need be, without help from the Volunteers.

As the time drew nearer, feeling became more tense. Police and detectives swarmed round Liberty Hall but they dared not enter. Once, in a raid for 'seditious papers', they came into the newsagent's shop adjoining Liberty Hall. Connolly was sent for. Coming through the doorway leading from the hall to the shop he saw a policeman pick up a bundle of papers behind the counter.

'Drop those papers or I'll drop you!' said Connolly sharply, levelling his revolver.

The man dropped the papers. Connolly then enquired if they had a search warrant and on being told they had not, he said they had no business there unless they got one. They left, muttering threats about what would happen when they returned. As soon as they had gone, Connolly returned to his office and made out two hundred and fifty urgent mobilisation notices for men to report at once, fully armed, to Liberty Hall. James O'Shea of the Citizen Army took out these notices and they were delivered round the city – in shops, offices, warehouses, on building works, along the docks and to carters in the streets. The effect was immediate. Citizen Army men left their work, left horses and carts standing, dropped their occupations and, grabbing their weapons at mobilisation centres, converged on the hall. Before their arrival, the police came back with their search warrant which was read out to Connolly. He insisted that this was confined strictly to the shop. 'The first man who tries to enter Liberty Hall will be shot!' he announced, standing in the doorway, swinging his revolver! 'We have no desire to enter Liberty Hall!' said the inspector.

'I don't doubt it!' retorted Connolly, grimly.

Soon after this incident, groups of men came hurrying in – building workers with clay and cement on their clothes, carters with sacking about their shoulders and whips in their belts, dockers, clerks and shop-assistants, all carrying rifles and bandoliers. Passers-by looked at them with amazement. A policeman left his point duty to stare. The mobilisation was a great success. It showed how quickly they could act and how high was their spirit. After this it was decided that Liberty Hall should be under armed guard by the Citizen Army day and night.

In June 1915, an incident occurred which proved the efficiency of the army. Two Citizen Army squads entered into competition for a drilling championship to be decided at Tullow, County Carlow. Groups of Volunteers from all over the country had entered. Michael Mallin had set his heart on winning and the men were given intensive training at Croydon Park. At Kingsbridge station they encountered their first obstacle. An attempt was made to keep them off the train on the plea that there was no room. Mallin gave a sharp order to some of his men to proceed at the double with fixed bayonets and to mount guard over the engine. 'This train will not go without us!' he told the stationmaster. The railway official threatened to bring the police and Mallin advised him to bring the army too. 'If you don't decide to take us soon,' he said, 'I will order a couple of my Citizen Army men to drive the train!' Two extra corridor carriages were then found and hitched on without further trouble. At the competition, the Citizen Army squads were judged far and away the best. They were both under command of old soldiers, Captain C. Poole and Captain R. McCormack.

A highlight of Citizen Army activities – a fortnight before the Rising – was the hoisting of the flag. The army formed into a square outside Liberty Hall. Connolly was in command, assisted by Mallin, his chief-of-staff, and Madame Markievicz. With great ceremony the buglers took up their positions. The colour bearer – Miss Mollie O'Reilly, a member of the Citizen Army – received the flag, the guard presented arms. She bore the flag up to the top of Liberty Hall, to the parapet. There was a breathless hush and then thousands of people packed about the quays and on the bridge, saw the green flag of Ireland with the golden harp upon it, fluttering in the wind. This may not seem much today, but at that time it was an inspiration to all who stood for Irish independence. By some it was regarded as the first blow in the Rising.

As to the part played by the Citizen Army in the Rising, history has long since recorded that. Everyone should know now that when there was division among the leaders of the Volunteers, Connolly, the Citizen Army commandant, sent out messengers to the leaders for the final military council meeting at Liberty Hall on Easter Sunday, where it was decided to go on with plans for the Rising next day. This meeting was held under Citizen Army guard. Connolly was appointed commandant-general of all the republican forces in the Dublin area. He told his own men on the eve of the Rising that 'now there is no more Citizen Army and no more Volunteers, there is only the army of the Republic'.

Liberty Hall was the storm centre. In this place where the Citizen Army began, the final dedication of their lives to the national struggle was made. Neither Connolly nor the Citizen Army ever renounced their distinctive social outlook. In 1915, Connolly sent a squad of the Citizen Army, fully armed, down the quays to the offices of a shipping company to assist pickets who complained of police intimidation. Citizen Army men and women gathered at Liberty Hall on Easter Sunday for the final mobilisation before the Rising. Here Connolly gave each a last opportunity of drawing back. No one availed themselves of this chance. 'I never doubted ye!' Connolly told them, his face shining.

During Easter Week the Citizen Army men and women were steadfast under fire, just as were their comrades of the Volunteers. The

Citizen Army was strongly represented at two points – the City Hall, where a handful of men and women stood against overwhelmingly superior British forces – and at Stephen's Green, under the command of Michael Mallin with Madame Markievicz as second-in-command. Seán Connolly had command of the City Hall contingent and was one of the first casualties after the building was seized. About two hundred and twenty members of the Citizen Army were out in Easter Week. Casualties were heavy. They fought against tremendous odds. James Connolly and Michael Mallin were executed for their part in the Rising and Madame Markievicz was sentenced to life imprisonment. Many of the rank and file were imprisoned too. Torch-bearers of the Larkin movement in 1913, these Citizen Army men and women held up a greater torch in 1916 when the leaping flames in O'Connell Street bore witness to their stand. The Starry Plough banner waved above the Imperial Hotel, for Connolly sent it over during the week. Connolly himself was badly wounded but he had his bed wheeled to the front line and stayed in the fight.

Following Easter Week the Citizen Army had no independent existence for a time. But it rallied again under Commandant James O'Neill. The only work open to the army at first was that of caring for the wants of prisoners, arranging receptions and welcomes, trying to keep the old spirit alive. The tide turned with the release of Madame Markievicz in 1917 when the whole city turned out to welcome her home. As the forces of resurgence gathered again, the Citizen Army organised afresh and raised itself up from the ashes of military defeat. Two battalions of the Citizen Army operated, one on the north and the other on the south side of the city. During the Black and Tan period the force was active. Because they were ordinary civilian workers they were able to spring into action and melt away quickly when the operation was completed. Army members, too, were invaluable in securing arms, smuggling them off boats along the quayside or inducing British soldiers to part with them.

THE 1916 RISING

THE MAGAZINE FORT RAID

by John McCann, TD

THE PHOENIX PARK had its regular coterie of football fans, streaming in their hundreds, football boots and jerseys tucked under their arms going in the direction of the famous Fifteen Acres. Those going by the Islandbridge gate would have to pass the Magazine Fort, stoutly fortified British arsenal, containing large quantities of explosives, surrounded by a network of barbed wire and surmounted by a castellated terrace around which a sentry paced his monotonous 'Two hours on-two hours off'. Close by the footballers played; and it was not an uncommon sight to see the sentry in conversation with them.

The Irish Volunteers knew all this. Knew, also, every nook and cranny of the interior, for, within, a special intelligence officer had been employed for some time previously as a tradesman. On Easter Monday 1916, he was the officer-in-charge of a section composed of Irish Volunteers and boys of the Fianna, whose job was to capture the Magazine Fort and to destroy the ammunition and equipment it contained. Altogether the little band numbered about thirty. The mobilisation was for the immediate vicinity of the fort, on the side facing the Fifteen Acres, and there the attackers were to 'gang-up' with the numerous footballers in order to avoid the least cause of suspicion. Plans worked as arranged. The ball was kicked about and the group manoeuvred until in front of the sentry at the ground entrance. Then the football was rather carelessly kicked into the fort. A few approached and asked the sentry 'Would you mind throwing out that ball, please?' As he turned to do so the gate was rushed, the sentry overpowered and the whole party was inside in a couple of minutes, each man to do his appointed task. The soldiers in the guardroom were taken completely by surprise. The sentry on the terrace was disarmed; not, however, before he received a dangerous wound, of which he died subsequently. The Volunteers had information that all keys were usually to be found hanging on a board in the guardroom. Upon this board, however, the key to the main high explosive stores was not to be found. The officer-in-charge of the raiding party opened the ammunition room and had a fuse trail laid.

Within a few minutes, the boys and men left with their booty, a large number of rifles and ammunition. A hackney car was commandeered outside the park upon which some of the rifles were loaded, while the Fianna boys carried others away with them. The whole section was then dismissed, each member having received orders to report to his own company in the city. Thus the hackney car, well guarded, went off with its much-needed treasure, while a Fianna boy cycled behind for further cover. This scout was forced to fire on a young fellow in the vicinity of the officer's house at Islandbridge, to prevent him from raising the alarm. Proudly, the hack went by the Royal barracks on the quays (now Collins barracks) with its load of ammunition and armed men, and on the way passed some soldiers who were carrying wounded comrades. They got safely through to the barricade in King Street, and served for the remainder of the Rising in the area commanded by Commandant Edward Daly.

THE SOUTH DUBLIN UNION

by Sceilg

THE 4TH BATTALION, Dublin brigade, mobilised at Emerald Square, Dolphin's Barn, at 11 a.m., Easter Monday, fully equipped as far as they had reported. About 11.30, Comm. Kent with a dozen cyclists, followed by thirty men on foot, proceeded by the Back-of-the-Pipes along the canal bank to Rialto bridge, where they entered the South Dublin Union by a small door at the corner of Brookfield Road, took possession of the keys, and cut the telephone wires, to the astonishment of the officials, who first regarded them as engaged in weekend manoeuvres. Inside, the bulk of the men were sent from the sheds at the back of the Union right across the interior towards the gate of James' Street about half-a-mile distant; and the commandant, having entrusted nine men under a Volunteer officer with the defence of the Rialto gate and given them the necessary instructions, followed the main body. The battalion had a roll of about 1,000: fewer than 50 fought within the South Dublin Union, where they covered themselves with glory; the muster in the whole battalion area has been stated as between one hundred and fifty and two hundred, three-fourths of them cut off early.

A second group proceeded by Grand Canal harbour and Ervingstown Lane, passing into the Union by the front entrance, James' Street. The remaining parties proceeded respectively to the Jameson Distillery, Marrowbone Lane; to Watkins' Brewery, Ardee Street; and Roe's malt-house, Cromwell's quarters, Mount Brown. As the main Union garrison, entering by the front gate and back door, met in the courtyard inside the James' Street gate, the strains of a military band could be heard from Richmond barracks. 'They do not yet know,' Comm. Kent remarked to an officer standing by, but the sudden cessation of the music showed that the military had just got the alarm. It transpired that a telephone message had been sent at 12.15 p.m. to military headquarters, and Comm. Kent then intimated that – to take the place of the music – they might expect the no less thrilling tones of an explosion from the blowing up of the Magazine Fort, Phoenix Park: it was burnt out without the explosion. Forthwith, the front gate of James' Street was taken over, and the night nurses' home, which had been vacated, ultimately turned into headquarters.

This South Dublin Union, largest outlying group of buildings in the west side of the city, derived special strategic importance from its proximity to the Islandbridge and Richmond barracks; the Royal

Hospital, British military headquarters in Ireland, and the Kingsbridge railway terminus, serving the Curragh and kindred outposts. Though the northern James' Street frontage of the Union seems relatively modest, the southern wall flanking the Grand Canal is almost half-a-mile long, and the total area of the institution is over fifty acres. Internally, it has all the features of a town: streets, alleys, courtyards in every direction, halls, churches, dormitories, sheds and other buildings, accommodating over 3,280 souls during Easter Week, exclusive of the staff and fighting forces. The officials remained at their posts during the entire week; and, where necessary, the inmates were removed to safer positions, some buildings in the more dangerous quarters being entirely cleared. There was free access to provisions and victuals, and the bakehouse was kept going in the usual way. Red flags were displayed from the windows of the buildings not occupied by the Volunteers, and were used also when officials had to cross the grounds. The chaplains, Fathers Dillon and Gerhard, were in attendance throughout.

The whole Union, it may be well to state here, is on the left-hand side of the long highway running almost due west from the Trinity College front and linking College Green with Inchicore. Looking to the right or due north, from Trinity, we see the GPO, headquarters of the republican army, O'Connell bridge lying midway between. At the back of Trinity is Westland Row railway station with Boland's Bakery and kindred posts in the neighbourhood. Looking to the left – due south – from the Trinity front, Grafton Street links the college with Stephen's Green and the College of Surgeons, headquarters of the Citizen Army. Parallel to Grafton Street, the next highway to the left from Dame Street – not far from the Trinity front – leads to Jacob's factory. Proceeding along the direct College Green–Inchicore highway – still on the left – Dublin Castle and the City Hall, which saw their share of fighting, link Dame Street and Lord Edward Street, while Thomas Street, scene of Emmet's execution, links Lord Edward Street with James' Street, of which the northern walls of the South Dublin Union form part. To revert: running parallel to the College Green–Inchicore highway from O'Connell bridge is the Liffey, on either bank of which are the Four Courts and the Mendicity Institution, forming very natural links between the GPO and the South Dublin Union. Due north from the GPO and O'Connell Street through Glasnevin, Botanic Road and Ballymun Road lead to Ashbourne. Thus the entire area was planned and occupied with the utmost economy if only the mobilisation had materialised as anticipated.

The other boundaries of the South Dublin Union require to be defined too, as they get frequent mention through the whole fighting. Mount Brown, which is a continuation of James' Street, slopes down into a hollow towards Kilmainham Cross, and the highway again rises to some eminence at the Richmond barracks which, too, are on the left. On the right, that is north of the highway, are Kilmainham prison, and, slightly nearer the city, the Royal Hospital, both on comparatively elevated ground; on the right also are Roe's malt-house and part of Guinness' Brewery. At the very opening of the fight, Easter Monday, British troops marching by Mount Brown towards the city were driven back, and retreated round an angle to the left, which led them by the western boundary of the Union and Watery Lane to Rialto. Having a relative superabundance of men, they posted them in various buildings here, and gradually entered from this and from the south side. The east or city side of the Union was regarded as impervious to attack, being covered by high walls, except at the basin end, which was held by five Volunteers. However, their position having been revealed to the military, they were taken in the rear, and had to retire. This area was largely the scene of Emmet's Rising.

James' Street entrance gives access to the main group of Union buildings, and the grounds of the institution are bisected by several acres of open fields stretching southwards from James' Street to the canal at the rear. These are known as the Orchard Fields, the Master's Fields, the MacCaffrey Estate, and so on. On entering the Union, Vice-Commandant Cathal Brugha posted two parties of Volunteers in the MacCaffrey Estate which flanks the south side of the thoroughfare at Mount Brown; the more advanced picket – an officer and four men – near some cottages at the foot of the hill on the highway to Kilmainham Cross and Richmond barracks: an officer with eight men behind the road hedgerow higher up the hill near the Union gate. At the top of the hill in the back window of the nurses' home inside the Union gate a few marksmen were also stationed. Thus, the long line of communications from James' Street to Rialto was held by fourteen men unacquainted with the grounds, and hence excellently laid plans strategically conceived could not be put into effect owing to the unforeseen paucity of men, while a similar paucity – due to the conflicting instructions from Volunteer headquarters – proved the paralysing weakness of every brigade area. At no time does there seem to have been sixty Volunteers within the Union; hence, despite the utmost valour, they were often driven back with irreplaceable losses.

Half-an-hour after entering the institution, as indicated, Volunteers fired on a column of soldiers passing into the city by Kilmainham Cross, Mount Brown, James' Street, and compelled them to retreat. Shortly after noon also, a military party – probably part of the same column, retreating southward by Watery Lane – attacked the Union at Rialto. General Maxwell's dispatch says that the 3rd Royal Irish Regiment on their way to the Castle were held up by the rebels in the South Dublin Union. The strength of this British regiment in Dublin was eighteen officers, three hundred and eighty-five other ranks. Yet another account states that at 12.40 p.m. about two hundred men of the Royal Irish Regiment appeared at the foot of Mount Brown and approached the Union gate. Five of them, some one hundred and fifty yards in advance, were permitted to pass towards the city; but when the head of the column approached the top of the hill, they were met by a fusillade at point-blank range from the three Volunteer positions. They rushed to cover in the shelter of the wall, round the bend of the road, or into neighbouring houses. An officer, in advance, fell wounded; another tried, without effect, to rally the men who, in their retreat, bore away the wounded officer. Some of the soldiers stood for a moment and fired towards the hedges, fatally wounding John Owens, who, in a few hours, died where he fell, and wounding two other Volunteers.

The retreating military, now under cover at the foot of the hill, entered a long avenue ascending from the road to the Master's House. Thence, for two hours, they kept up a continuous fire which compelled the Volunteers to retire to the nurses' home. Volunteers at the inner side of the canal wall thus found themselves subjected to particularly heavy fire. Soldiers who had entered by the canal gate cut them off; others, who had entered hospital 2–3, took them later on the flank. From the further side of the canal, their position was dominated also at close range by a military party of fifteen men in the top rooms of Rialto buildings; and to this fire, it is thought, the Volunteer casualties were due. The fields were also swept by long-range fire from the Royal Hospital, with the inevitable result that the small party of Volunteers without adequate cover had soon to disperse. While retreating, Brendan Donelan and James Quinn lost their lives on Monday; and Richard O'Reilly, killed on the same day, was thought to have fallen in the fields, as was William MacDowell, who was not of this party but was thought also to have fallen between the nurses' home and the convent from the rifle fire of soldiers posted in the upper windows of hospital 2–3. Another of the party was desperately wounded, but removed later by a military ambulance. A military officer, severely wounded also, was removed by military stretcher-bearers.

This large double hospital No. 2–3 was the scene of many exciting and tragic incidents. About 2.30 on Monday, while two Volunteers were on the ground floor and six on the upper, a party of fifty military who had entered by the canal gate, Rialto, suddenly approached by the rear. Those on the upper floor fired on them, then, by using a pass-key, entered No. 3 hospital on the same floor. The two Volunteers on the ground floor, on going to the back, found themselves face-to-face with a large body of military, already in the courtyard. Instantly, one of them fired into the military group. Then rushing to an adjacent dormitory, and turning at intervals to fire, both reached the front, and flung themselves with difficulty onto the lawn. One unfortunately received a desperate wound in the stomach. 'Run on,' he shouted, 'I am hit.' The unwounded man lay for a moment on the grass, covering the angle round which the soldiers might appear. The first who rounded the corner retreated instantly before the fire, whereupon the Volunteer rushed towards the main group of buildings, but found his way barred by military who, however, disappeared at that moment into the building. Rushing past the convent, he reached the corner of the Protestant infirmary, where he found Commandant Kent standing by a badly wounded Volunteer.

Going inside, the commandant informed the Protestant matron that one of his men lay wounded outside. Instantly a nurse and two inmates bore the wounded man inside and, as he seemed to be dying, a girl was sent for the priest. Cut off by this sudden rush of the military, the commandant and his companion retreated by a cul-de-sac separating the Protestant hospital from the women's Catholic hospital, until they were held by a large wooden gate. Just then, an inmate appeared, and instantly got them a ladder by which they scaled the yard-wall of the Protestant hospital. Inside, the Volunteer now fixed the ladder, and, from it, with his levelled rifle covered the alley by which they had come. The commandant also held his pistol in readiness, but the military ventured no further. Consulting a map, Commandant Kent then decided to attempt to regain headquarters by rushing the open spaces with his unwounded companion. Covering their accoutrements with canvas from an outhouse, they made ready; and, at this critical moment, a gate was opened by a nun a short distance away. Thus they were enabled to reach the rear of the women's Catholic hospital, their retreat being covered by Volunteer fire from the back of the hospital and from a disused dormitory.

Gradually the British reached the upper storey of hospital 2–3. Meanwhile, the six Volunteers on the top floor having withdrawn to the east side of the building, Nurse Keogh and a companion on the west side were felicitating themselves on the fact that the military were not attacking it. 'Thank God,' said Nurse Keogh, 'there will be no bloodshed here.' Thereupon, shots rang out beneath them – the shots fired on the two men escaping from the ground floor. Nurse Keogh rushing down to aid anyone that might need it, was shot dead on the long stone stairway. At its foot, a porch and door opened at right angles into the side of a long corridor, now occupied by the military. Two soldiers kneeling back, out of sight, covered the open doorway with their rifles, and fired as the nurse entered the corridor, both shots entering her body. Her companion then rushed down. 'Are there any Sinn Féiners upstairs?' a British officer shouted as she entered. She had Nurse Keogh's body temporarily placed on a table in the corridor before removal upstairs. The wounded Volunteer lying outside was borne inside by another inmate, apparently in a dying condition. Thereupon a large party of military proceeded to search the hospital and, on reaching the top floor, obtained the pass-key. 'Hands up! Surrender!' they shouted, covering the door with their rifles. Entering, they rushed on the small group of Volunteers, clubbed them with their rifles, and took them prisoners.

It was about 5 p.m. on Monday, that fifty soldiers attacked the Women's Catholic Hospital, from which the patients had been cleared. Ward 17, intersecting Ward 16 at right angles, was occupied by the Volunteers. When the military entered Ward 16, they approached the closed door at the point of intersection, and called on the Volunteers to surrender, firing shots at the same time through the separating partition. As elsewhere, the commanding officer volunteered to count five before bursting in; and, as he proceeded to count, the Volunteers rushed to the other end of the ward, forced a door open by firing into the lock, and retreated through another vacated building, No. 4. They were pursued by the military who fired as they went. But the whole Volunteer party reached headquarters, while the military occupied both Wards – 16 and 17 – all Monday night. Early in the fight, the Volunteers had bored a hole through the wall of the rural district council's offices, James' Street and the nurses' home dominating Mount Brown was connected with the front by a hole bored through the yard-wall at the rear. Thus great freedom of movement was obtained along that frontage and the whole angle facing Mount Brown. The military, however, bored through the opposite side of the nurses' home, so that the belligerents ultimately met in the front hall where a desperate hand-to-hand conflict took place.

At Rialto gate on the south side, the outpost was held by the nine men left there at the outset by Comm. Kent, and another man left temporarily to assist. They occupied the long tin shed next to the gate, its sides and roof of thin corrugated iron. Some three hundred feet long by twenty-six feet wide, it was transversely divided by wooden partitions into six dormitories having narrow lateral corridors. It had been used for housing the male lunatic inmates, now transferred by the ward-master to a place of greater safety; and the Volunteers – finding it to be the only structure dominating gate and corner-walls that could be occupied in the interval at their disposal – entered it by the porch facing the Catholic church. Instantly, they barricaded the windows with mattresses, bedding and the like, and had not long to wait until the sound of the firing already described was heard from James' Street, followed immediately by the appearance of the military which was the signal for 'a brief but frightful combat', lasting a couple of hours. Within half-an-hour, John Traynor was killed by a bullet which penetrated the building near the porch. Fusillade after fusillade from the military now entered the tin walls at close range, and it became clear that they afforded no protection against rifle fire. Bullets passed clean through both lateral walls; even those entering the end walls passed longitudinally through all the separate partitions to the last dormitory. Fortunately, the inmates escaped injury, although a bullet pierced the ward-master's coat, while the iron tubing of the bedsteads was similarly perforated, as was the woodwork of the doors and windows.

Under these conditions, one party of the military entered the Union by forcing a small door near the large Rialto gate. Under cover of the wall, others crept around and, turning at the Rialto bridge, proceeded along the canal bank towards James' Street harbour. Working along the northern bank of the canal towards the Jameson Distillery, they entered the Union five hundred yards up, by forcing a large gate in the canal wall near the doctor's house. While sustaining many casualties through close fire from the Jameson Distillery on the opposite side of the canal, a considerable number of them entered the Union at this point.

Assisted by comrades, a few attempted to scale the canal wall, there about nine feet high; but, being met by Volunteer fire from the sheds, some were seen to fall, while one, who partially climbed a telegraph pole overlooking the wall, was shot down also, as was an officer. The Volunteer position, however, became untenable, so a messenger was sent to Comm. Kent for instructions, and brought back a written dispatch ordering a retirement. As this was now impracticable, the messenger was sent back to headquarters; but, the Rialto angle soon being completely cut off and the intervening fields swept by rifle fire, he found it impossible to regain the Rialto sheds. While the Volunteers at the sheds tried to retreat a short distance towards the male consumptive hospital, one of them got wounded under the arched gateway. One of two companions who carried him into the hospital was unable to rejoin his party, but the other Volunteers managed to regain the shed.

One of the first to lead the military attack at Rialto, Lieut Ramsay, RIR, had advanced but a few paces when, shot through the head, he fell mortally wounded on the roadway near the chapel. Taken into the women's epileptic hospital hard by, he died after an hour-and-a-half. Shortly afterwards, Major Warmington entered the hospital and, having exchanged a few words with the ward mistress regarding the fallen officer, he proceeded with a party to the interior of the Union. Passing under the Rialto archway, he had not proceeded far across the open fields when he was shot dead. His body was brought back, and laid next to that of Lieut Ramsay. Thus will it be seen that the open spaces and the interlacing passages of all kinds were danger zones equally for the experienced military and the inexperienced Volunteers. The military eventually, with a heavy lawn-mower, broke through the end door at No. 1 dormitory, and the Volunteers, thus rendered defenceless, were taken prisoners. Thereafter the Volunteer operations within the Union were restricted almost entirely to the group of buildings near the James' Street entrance, which were successfully held until the general surrender.

From daybreak on Tuesday, machine-gun fire from the Royal Hospital and steady military sniping literally sprayed the Union buildings. From the windows over the main dining-hall near James'

Street gate, military bullets passed clean through the front offices occupied by the Volunteers. A soldier who came within range at the east side of the hall was shot dead while standing between two inmates, and a woman residing in James' Street, opposite, was killed. As early as 7.30, a bullet from a military sniper concealed near the window of the maternity hospital, a few yards from the nurses' home, entered through a front window of the house, instantly killing W.F. Burke who, the previous day, had escaped unscathed from the severe fighting at Mount Brown. Although but a schoolboy at the Howth gun-running, William – on a holiday with relatives in Thurles – wired: 'Does my corps need me?' A card suspended over his remains had inscribed on it by Comm. Kent: 'Here a hero died for Ireland. May the Lord have mercy on his noble soul.' His body, with those of five others, as well as those of Nurse Keogh and a Belfast visitor fatally shot at Dolphin's Barn, were temporarily buried in the Master's Field, a request by Comm. Kent for a truce, Monday evening, to remove the wounded and bury the dead, being declined by the British.

We have met the Volunteer garrison at the Jameson Distillery in brisk action as the British military advanced in force along the northern bank of the canal to enter the Union from the south side at the doctor's house. This distillery at Marrowbone Lane was occupied at noon Easter Monday by about twenty Volunteers of 'A' company, 4th battalion. Reinforced on Monday night by the garrison of twenty from Roe's malt-house, Mount Brown and, on Wednesday, by Con Colbert's garrison, from Watkins' Brewery, they reached an aggregate of about one hundred and twenty men, well provided with arms and ammunition, as well as a large quantity of explosives. With them also were seven members of the Fianna and some twenty members of Cumann na mBan, related in many cases to the male members of the garrison, and always busy as dispatch carriers and in kindred services. The main post there was the malt-house, a fort of massive brickwork pierced with small windows, and projecting towards the canal and the rear of the Union. Early, Monday afternoon, they let a party of unarmed military accompanied by a band pass towards Robert

Street. On Tuesday morning, the military erected a barricade at the harbour near Echlin Street and, from that point, incessantly sniped the distillery; but the Volunteer garrison helped to stop the advance of British troops from Dolphin's Barn and Cork Street directions.

Early in the fighting, communication by this garrison with Comm. Kent was cut off, without abating their general activities. On Wednesday, a small party of military approached Marrowbone Lane, and, one soldier being shot down, the others beat a retreat. Con Colbert, stationed at Watkins' Brewery, Ardee Street – having learned on Tuesday that the men holding Barmack's factory, Blackpitts, had retired, and regarding his own position as somewhat ineffective – sent for instructions to Major MacBride at Jacob's. The major having directed him to reinforce the garrison at the distillery, it was augmented about 6 p.m. on Wednesday by Colbert's group of fifteen men as already stated. On Thursday, about 3 p.m., a party of soldiers advanced by the south bank of the canal under cover of supporting fire from the Union fields. As they drew nearer the distillery beside Forbes Lane, they were shot down at close range. Similarly, as elsewhere indicated, in the attacks by the military on the canal wall gate, on Monday and Thursday, several soldiers were shot by the distillery garrison, and removed by military stretcher-bearers.

After a temporary lull, there was a general attack on the Union on Thursday, under the command of Sir Francis Vane. He found Col Oates with a convoy held up by the Volunteers, his raw soldiers in a panic after a serve attack by the garrison in the distillery. So he brought fifty seasoned soldiers to the convoy's aid. Further, two of the four battalions of Sherwood Foresters sent from England had arrived at the Royal Hospital on Wednesday and, next day, joined troops from Belfast, the Curragh, Templemore, Athlone, and men in training at the RIC depot, Phoenix Park, in a concerted assault on the Union. So a hail of bullets struck the back of the nurses' home about 3 p.m., driving the Volunteers to cover. From the Rialto line, a large body of troops swept across in fan-like formation, advancing in files by sectional rushes, and pouring an incessant stream of bullets into all obstacles on their path.

Lines of fifty men followed each other, making the nurses' home their objective, so that the Volunteers at the back windows found it almost impossible to take cover while returning the whirlwind fire. Still, several soldiers were shot down in the fields and elsewhere, and were later removed by the military ambulance which entered at Rialto.

That the Volunteers were determined to contest the British advance to the very last shot was manifest from the defence set up at the nurses' home. The hole bored in the back wall there provided for a retirement from Auxiliary No. 1 to the front offices, where the final stand was to be made. Directly behind the hall-door here, in the interior of the house, a barricade was erected, which enabled the Volunteers to defend the front entrance – rather two barricades about five and seven feet high, one over the other and very firmly constructed – two hoardings of planks about a foot asunder, and having the interspaces closely packed with clay. The military, in reality, found it impossible to force this front door, though repeated attempts were made to do so: in one of these, Comm. Kent himself rushed into the open and shot down one of the assailants. So about 4.45, they rushed the ward-master's quarters beside the nurses' home by forcing the end-door of Auxiliary No. 2 adjoining. On boring from the ward-master's quarters into the nurses' home, however, they found themselves confronted by the barricade, which completely bisected the hall, separated them effectually from the Volunteers on the stairway, and proved the ultimate salvation of the Volunteer position.

The military, on entering the hall, loftily called for the Volunteers' surrender; a fusillade from the stoutly protected staircase came in prompt response. This was the signal for more terrific fighting at close quarters. Such soldiers as attempted to enter by the hole bored in the wall were fired on by the Volunteers, while such of them as otherwise reached the hall kept up an incessant fire in reply. Outside, from all directions, the converging soldiers poured volleys on the position of the heroic garrison; and the rattle of the rifles, the belching of exploding bombs and the uproar of infuriated combatants created a truly fearful din. The Volunteers felt it necessary to retire somewhat at intervals; but their steady fire from the windows and barricades continued to hold the military in check. So the soldiers began to throw grenades over the barricades, and it was then that the dauntless Vice-Commandant Cathal Brugha was severely wounded, and his iron will began to manifest itself. He went on firing until another grenade burst beside him and caused him dreadful injuries. So he was carried to a small yard in the rear, bleeding profusely; but, grenades cast over the wall having burst here also, he had to be brought back. Yet he continued earnestly to encourage and sustain his men, though he seemed really in a dying condition.

At this stage, Comm. Kent was at the other post. Feeling a growing need to consolidate his diminished force of forty-three men, divided between the nurses' home and James' Street, he desired to bring them all nearer the better-fortified position. His intention was misinterpreted and, in his absence, those in the real *bearna baoghail* withdrew in error to the upper rooms of Auxiliary No. 1, just when the English seemed almost to have won out. Thus Cathal Brugha, desperately wounded, found himself alone in the confusion, but in a position to cover the only hallway by which the British could advance. That hallway they entered with shouts of 'Surrender!' Cathal, all alone, answered them with defiance and a series of shouts to which they replied with volleys and grenades. For two awful hours he held them at bay until his comrades, missing him, thought him dead and their post lost. While the garrison was upstairs, the military reached the lower rooms and thence cast bombs which shook the whole building. About 5 p.m., six soldiers and two officers rushed across until they found themselves beneath windows occupied by the Volunteers. One of them, with an axe, tried to break through a partition; but, on showing his head through a hole he had made, the silent defender inside shot him dead. Other soldiers crept into an adjoining courtyard and, climbing to a barred window eight feet up, dropped a grenade inside. Eight or nine inmates were clustered by the fireside; and the grenade bursting caused fearful havoc, killing one, severely wounding the others. Meanwhile a Volunteer quietly reconnoitring overheard snatches of singing above the din.

Following his clue, he was astounded to find it was Cathal Brugha proudly singing 'God Save Ireland' with gusto, and still shooting to his last shot. Let a comrade unfold the substance of the epic narrated in *Cathal Brugha*, his eventful life in the language he loved:

> Cathal Brugha was vice-commandant of the 4th battalion, Dublin brigade, Éamonn Kent being commandant. Cathal led his men into the South Dublin Union, Easter Monday, to the strains of 'The Soldiers' Song': from that until Thursday midnight, he was always in the gap of danger, with never a thought of himself, yet always warning others never to be incautious. Night and day he was on the alert. Often at midnight – however gentle his approach – he startled a sentry; and, when challenged, he quietly answered with a smile: '*Tá go maith!* All's well!' A competent sniper himself, he studied the marks of the bullets on the walls to trace the direction whence they came, and thus rendering the enemy fire largely futile. He seemed to appreciate the advice of the latest recruit as he would that of any other: thus, his humility won him the affection of those around him, while his valour infused a new spirit into us all. He opened the day's work with public prayers, and always closed it with the Rosary. He and Comm. Kent further undertook that every man under their command would have the attention of a confessor as he desired it.
>
> Early on Thursday, Comm. Kent decided to consolidate the garrison at the headquarters post. He had not long parted with the vice-commandant when the enemy made a fierce attack on the Volunteer position with machine-guns, muskets, bombs, hand-grenades. Bombs tore gaps in the roof, but the Volunteers clung tenaciously to their position, Cathal urging them on by word and example in the midst of the inferno. After some hours of most undaunted fighting, he was dreadfully wounded with a grenade and a bomb. At that juncture, somehow, a mistaken order to retreat passed along, and was acted on. Cathal prostrate from his wounds was overlooked in the excitement and the din; yet, though lying alone and scarce able to move, he boldly challenged the foe again and again: 'Advance, you craven cowards! Advance, so that I can get one shot more at you!' Far away they kept, for another hour. Then the notes of 'God Save Ireland' having been heard by his comrades, a scout brought the incredible news that the vice-commandant – who was believed dead, and the position lost – was singing and still fighting. Comm. Kent at the head of his men, forced his way forward until he reached Cathal resting against a wall, his pistol to his shoulder, and he still keeping a watchful eye on the silenced enemy.
>
> Then came the great episode of the week – in love and sympathy. The two heroes laid aside their weapons; the commandant came

on bended knee the moment he saw the dreadful condition of his comrade – lying in a pool of his own blood four square feet in extent – embraced him, pressed him to his heart in a very passion of affection and tenderness. They exchanged greetings, very briefly, and the fond eyes of the commandant were flooded with tears. But, in a moment, the soldier-spirit asserted itself, and he was himself again.

'Let us all sing "God Save Ireland", Éamonn,' Cathal gasped in Irish, as he seemed to breath his last breath; 'let us sing it until the enemy is driven from here.'

'Driven out they will be anyway,' Éamonn answered. Soon the wounded hero was removed to the back of the building, and the defence resumed, to find the enemy entirely silenced by seven. By that time the flow of blood from his lacerated limbs was checked temporarily; but it was late into the night before his twenty-five wounds were dressed. The bullets and bombs had pressed his clothing through the wounds to the bone, so that he could be undressed only by cutting his clothing off his body.

During this long excruciating dressing, not a murmur of complaint was heard from him except that, once or twice, there seemed a slight tremor of the lips. Eventually, owing to the ebb of the blood, he was overtaken by a deadly thirst, and kept constantly calling for cold water. By Friday's dawn he was raving and in the very shadow of death until borne to the Union infirmary by noon under the direction of a Carmelite brother. Of his twenty-five wounds it was then announced that five were very dangerous having cut through arteries, nine very serious, and eleven not serious relatively. Such was the end of his fighting then: what wonder if those who knew him loved him. After the general surrender he was taken prisoner to the Castle hospital, pronounced incurable by the doctors there after some time, and ultimately released, a shadow of the all-round athlete he once had been. As he rallied, under the tender care of a devoted wife, he again threw himself wholeheartedly into the national struggle both on its constitutional and military sides, rightly reaching the most exalted position in the state – to find himself then tracked by blood-hounds, and sought night and day by the Black and Tans until, after six years, he fell fatally wounded in another desperate fight for the Republic, with the cry of 'No Surrender!' still upon his lips.

Little remains to be added. A party of soldiers approaching from the convent side after seven seems to have fired on their own men. Comm. Kent directed the Volunteers to man the windows and meet them with a cross-fire. 'Retire!' an officer called out; 'Retire, we are surrounded. Mind your flanks.' This won the Volunteers some respite, and about 9.30 the military withdrew in the direction of Rialto. The officers of a British party in the bakehouse seem to have felt themselves in a death-trap and so asked an official if they could possibly retire. Not until night did they attempt it. Then removing their boots, they rushed to a place of safety. A soldier was left behind, with the dead body of his companion. Next day, he made a sensational escape. Two coffins seem to have been brought to the bakehouse. In one of them the corpse was placed, the soldier entering the other, and when the coffins were removed from the hearse at Rialto, he arose from his resting-place to the consternation of those who witnessed it. Meeting some of the Volunteers at Richmond barracks later, he disclosed the whole story. British military, it may be added, occupied Guinness' Brewery as well as the malt-house at the harbour, and two officers, as well as two officials, were shot there on Friday. Thus ended the active fighting.

JACOB'S FACTORY

by Sceilg

IT WAS ABOUT 11.30 a.m., Easter Monday, that the 2nd battalion of the Dublin brigade mobilised at Stephen's Green West under Comm. Thomas MacDonagh. A section of the Citizen Army having arrived there later, the 2nd battalion proceeded to the positions assigned to them, their ultimate strength being about one hundred and fifty men, besides some members of the Fianna and a dozen members of Cumann na mBan, who joined them subsequently. The main body halted at Bishop Street, where they made Jacob's biscuit factory their headquarters. Some forty men under the command of a Volunteer officer proceeded by Kevin Street to Malpas Street, where they occupied Messrs Barmacks' and two neighbouring houses in Fumbally Lane. Four men occupied premises opposite Kevin Street police barracks, while public houses in Cuffe Street and Camden Street were also occupied on the way, and four policemen arrested, but all the outposts were gradually abandoned. Major John MacBride, though not notified of the Rising, had come into town, linked up with this garrison at Jacob's – though well aware of his fate should he fall into enemy hands – and naturally became second-in-command.

The factory was entered at Bishop Street by means of a ladder chained to an adjacent lamp-post, released and placed against the factory windows near the corner of Peter's Row. The windows were then forced and the premises entered. Concurrently, one of the main gates in Bishop Street, nearer Bride Street, was forced open with a sledgehammer and axe. A police sergeant and a constable, who intervened rather aggressively, were instantly covered by half-a-dozen rifles, and firmly ordered to quit the scene. Forthwith the Volunteers hastened inside, pickets being left outside to ensure order. Instantly, minor commands were arranged and positions of defence selected and fortified, all material at hand being utilised according to their convenience and utility: sacks of flour – not of sand – were placed at the windows to make cover for the marksmen.

Surrounded by narrow streets, the factory rises to great heights as compared with adjacent houses. Its frontages afford a very comprehensive outlook, and this is enhanced by the views from two immense towers. In these towers, marksmen had coigns of advantage from which they were able to cover the roof of Ship Street barracks, Dublin Castle, St Patrick's Park, Portobello bridge and other important enemy centres. The sharpshooters, aided by good glasses and scientific range-finders, were able to make their fire effective over very considerable distances, and the rank-and-file were alert also from the very outset.

Towards one o'clock on Monday, a picket of ten men in Bishop Street learned that a military party approached them through Camden Street. In a few moments, two soldiers of the advance guard passed by the factory, down Aungier Street, while, a short distance behind, were an officer and about twenty-five men. As they came into view at the corner of Redmond's Hill and Bishop Street, the Volunteers, who had lined up in readiness on the footpath and roadway, opened fire on them at close range. The officer and half-a-dozen men fell, the others fled, the wounded being taken away later by military stretcher-bearers. Meanwhile, a larger body of British troops with machine-guns were posted in Camden Street nearby.

According to Gen. Maxwell's dispatch, the Dublin garrison adjutant, on hearing of the outbreak shortly after noon, ordered all available troops in the city to concentrate on Dublin Castle. 'All the approaches to the Castle, except the Ship Street entrance were held by Sinn Féiners,' the dispatch stated. 'Between 1.40 p.m. and 2 p.m. fifty men of the 3rd Royal Irish Rifles and one hundred and thirty men of the 10th Royal Dublin Fusiliers reached the Castle by the Ship Street entrance.' It was further stated officially that there were three hundred men in Portobello barracks. Before the excitement of occupying their new quarters had well subsided, an official dispatch from republican headquarters, GPO, was received at Jacob's, as well as a copy of the Proclamation of the Republic there, with details of the early attack on the Lancers in O'Connell Street. In the course of the evening also, the dozen members of Cumann na mBan arrived, and they remained until the general surrender.

After midnight, in response to a request from Michael Mallin, twenty men were sent to relieve the Citizen Army in the Portobello area, and twenty to Stephen's Green where they occupied the Turkish Baths until driven out next day, when Comm. Mallin fell back from the Green to the College of Surgeons. About 2 a.m. Tuesday morning, a party of fifteen Volunteers was sent from Jacob's to Byrne's stores, Grantham Street corner, a party of six men under Councillor Richard O'Carroll being sent at the same time to occupy Delahunt's directly opposite. The function of those outposts was to hold the Portobello approaches to Jacob's. With the same object, outposts near the factory were established in Camden Street early on Tuesday. Next day, all those posts, despite a heroic defence, were in the hands of the enemy, and other post set up from Jacob's abandoned. At that juncture too it was that Con Colbert sought directions from Major MacBride as to abandoning Watkins' Brewery, Ardee Street as being of no practical utility.

On Tuesday evening, Francis Sheehy-Skeffington, who from the very outset had been engaged in humanitarian activities, was arrested by the military near Portobello bridge while on his way home, and taken to Portobello barracks, where Capt. Bowen-Colthurst soon irregularly ordered that he be handed over to himself. After ten o'clock, with a party of fifty men, the captain set out on a raiding exploit, his main objective being the tobacco stores of Ald. J.J. Kelly. They left the barracks by the Rathmines gate, accompanied by Sheehy-Skeffington, whose hands were bound together with a knotted cord, and who was being used as a hostage for the protection of military, with instructions that he be shot dead as a reprisal in the event of the raiding party being fired on. At the head of the Rathmines Road, the captain called a halt, and three young men who stood while the troops passed were accosted at the corner of Military Road. Passing Rathmines Catholic church, two boys were taken and one of them, named Coade, bashed by orders and shot dead by Bowen-Colthurst. At Portobello bridge, twenty men with Sheehy-Skeffington were left on guard, Capt. Bowen-Colthurst with the main body proceeding a few hundred yards further to Ald. Kelly's premises which were instantly riddled with bullets and bombed, the alderman escaping through happening to be on his way home. Meanwhile, Messrs Dickson and MacIntyre were arrested and, with Sheehy-Skeffington, brought as prisoners back to barracks. In the barracks yard next morning, Messrs Sheehy-Skeffington, Dickson and MacIntyre were shot dead, without trial, by a military platoon, and Bowen-Colthurst was subsequently excused on the convenient British plea of insanity.

Immediately after these callous military murders at Portobello barracks, a party of fourteen, including a man in naval uniform, came down by Charlotte Street, and attacked the two posts held by Volunteers since the previous morning: at Byrne's, Grantham Street, and at Delahunt's, Camden Street. Close behind was a body of about one hundred men, who remained in Harcourt Street, nearer the barracks. The advance party surrounded Byrne's at the street corner and, having ordered all pedestrians off the streets, fired repeated volleys until every room in the house was riddled. A hand-grenade thrown through the shop window left a chasm in the floor. The shop and upper windows of Delahunt's were also fired into, and an entrance forced by breaking the panes of the hall door with clubbed rifles, after which the military rushed upstairs. An automatic pistol, a shotgun and a rifle with some ammunition, were found on the premises. After the capture of Councillor Richard O'Carroll there, Bowen-Colthurst asked him if he was a Sinn Féiner. 'From the back-bone out' was the prompt and spirited reply. So he was instantly marched into the yard, and shot through the lungs, dying some days later, and leaving a widow and seven children to mourn his loss, the youngest but a couple of weeks old. Elsewhere, one of his daughters received two wounds in the left leg.

After these fierce conflicts, there was comparative calm in the immediate neighbourhood of Jacob's factory; but the sound of rifle fire and of machine-guns could be heard steadily from all directions. Small parties of Volunteers managed to pass, to and fro, between the factory and the College of Surgeons, reconnoitring, foraging, conveying arms, provisions, dispatches – generally late at night, or early in the morning. More than once, shortly after dawn, Major John MacBride – in civilian attire throughout – was seen to leave his headquarters by the lower windows in Bishop Street and conduct numbers of the garrison to new positions, thus maintaining the high courage and genial manner which won him special distinction and numberless friends in the Boer War. Occasionally at midnight too, armoured cars could be heard to rush by, and crouching soldiers with their rifles discerned, to be followed by instantaneous volleys from the factory windows.

On Thursday, a message from Comm. de Valera intimated that his garrison's supply of food was satisfactory, but the supply of ammunition running low; and, that night, came a report that military pickets were posted around Merrion Square. Comm. MacDonagh, with high hope in the future, decided to attempt to push through on the following Monday, May Day, and deliver the necessary ammunition. With this object he directed a party of fifteen cyclists, including their officer, to make a reconnoitring sortie from Jacob's at six on Saturday morning. All armed with Mauser rifles, their orders were to attack the pickets, endeavour to drive them in at Merrion Square and, if successful, to make contact with Boland's. Having proceeded by the south side of Stephen's Green, Leeson Street and Fitzwilliam Square, they dismounted at Fitzwilliam Street near Merrion Square. With the exception of a sentry outside a house on the north side of the square near Lower Mount Street, no military were visible here. The Volunteers took shelter on hall-door steps and by kneeling behind tram-posts. The sentry was shot, and the military in occupation of the house which he guarded, immediately opened fire, which was briskly returned for a short time.

This position being soon found untenable, and there being no hope whatever of reaching Boland's through Mount Street, the cyclists were obliged to return. When passing near the Red Cross hospital at Fitzwilliam Street, they were fired on from the left flank; but there was little else of moment until they approached the Russell Hotel at the south-west corner of Stephen's Green. Halting here for a moment, they rode quickly in open formation along the danger zone on the western side of the Green, which was under heavy military fire from the Shelbourne Hotel and the United Services Club. On reaching the corner of York Street, John O'Grady of the cycling party shouted: 'Dan, I fear they've got me.' Instantly, the officer-in-charge directed comrades riding on either side while continuing the retreat to support the wounded man who had been severely shot in the stomach. On reaching Jacob's he collapsed; and, a stretcher being procured, he was borne to the adjacent Adelaide Hospital. Having been attended by Fr Metcalfe, OCC, Whitefriars' Street, he passed away about four o'clock, at the age of twenty-seven and but eight months married. This raid, regarded by the Trinity College garrison as portending an attack from the rear, helped to relieve Boland's Bakery of anxiety about a contemplated onslaught from the Trinity direction.

As in the whole fighting area, there seemed a growing lull on Friday and Saturday, but Comm. MacDonagh remained cheerful and undaunted until disturbed by foreshadowings of contemplated surrender. Early on Sunday morning, indeed, over-confident soldiers in substantial numbers in St Patrick's Park were fired on from one of the Jacob's towers and dispersed with several casualties. The garrison's central position was one of exceptional strength, and afforded exceptional protection. This the military realised after a first attempt to take it, and so they practically abandoned the idea of reducing it by rifle fire. To take the place by assault would have been manifestly impossible, without recourse to artillery – an alternative which was seriously considered, ultimately decided on, indeed, had that proved necessary. The garrison, however, had made ample provision for a long siege, and their spirits were of the highest. The only sign of depression shown by Comm. MacDonagh was when the general surrender was announced to him. Even after the fall of the GPO, a military threat to shell the whole area if not promptly evacuated failed to obtain the acquiescence of leaders or men, who eventually yielded only to the personal entreaties of a very popular priest eager to prevent further bloodshed.

BOLAND'S MILLS
by Sceilg

COMPANIES 'A', 'B' and 'C' of the 3rd battalion, Dublin brigade, were mobilised at the new university buildings, Earlsfort Terrace, Easter Monday morning. Before noon, 'A' company under Captain Joseph O'Connor proceeded to occupy positions and dig trenches along the Dublin–Dún Laoghaire railway, take over the railway works and sheds, and establish posts in Grand Canal Street, South Lotts Road and other points. Gradually, snipers occupied most of the bridges and other vantage points. Those of 'B' company who responded to the call assembled early at the rallying point, with full equipment and a couple of days' rations. Ammunition brought there in a motor car was widely distributed, a goodly ration to the cycling corps. Their infantry left about 11.30, and by noon, a dozen of them had cleared Westland Row railway station, seized signal boxes, severed telephone wires, erected barricades, taken control of the main gate, and occupied vital points on the line. Simon Donnelly with some thirty-five men of 'C' company, having set out from Earlsfort Terrace, halted at Upper Mount Street, then marched to Boland's Bakery, Grand Canal Street, and occupied it. This bakery ultimately was chosen as headquarters, and Comm. de Valera with Capt. O'Connor were among the officers present at its occupation. It was used incidentally by those attending to the commissariat and by men relieved from the outposts who rested or slept there for brief intervals.

Thus Boland's Bakery, not Boland's Mills as generally thought, was the headquarters of this Westland Row–Merrion area. The 3rd battalion there quartered, under the command of Comm. de Valera, consisted of five companies comprising four hundred men at full strength, but hardly exceeding a hundred at any time during Easter Week. Their chief function was to defend some miles of railway as well as the other approaches from Dún Laoghaire to Dublin, and their task must have been rendered almost hopeless from the outset by the complete failure of Dún Laoghaire, Blackrock and neighbouring centres to mobilise. As set out, the main positions held consisted of Westland Row station, Boland's Bakery on the docks, Boland's larger flour mills, the Dock Milling Company's premises near by, the railway locomotive works, Barron Street: roughly, all these posts and more were linked with headquarters by the railway embankment.

The managers' houses, Grand Canal Street bridge, were also manned, as well as the last house of the street, which overlooked Beggar's Bush barracks. Entry to this house from the railway embankment was said to have been obtained by boring through a row of cottages at South Lotts Road, just as access was obtained from the Bakery to the Dublin–Dún Laoghaire railway by boring through a wall and erecting a gangway to the embankment. The gas-works on the city side of the canal were occupied for some time, as well as the dock bank, passing by the disused distillery to the Bakery. Guinness' store on this dock bank near the Bakery was occupied on Tuesday night, but evacuated next morning. This distillery near the gas-works was held by two men, and displayed from its roof a green flag with yellow harp. This was heavily bombarded and portions of its tower blown away. It also attracted the fire of the *Helga* from the Liffey; and though it had similar attention from a naval gun on a horse-lorry, the green flag was rescued on Sunday towards the very close of the fighting.

When opportunity offered, long-range firing was kept up over Grand Canal Street bridge from the railway embankment at the dock. This covered the line of the canal on both banks. The wall of Messrs Roberts' yard on the city side from Grand Canal Street to Clanwilliam Terrace, covering the canal Turf Bank opposite at short range, was manned by four Volunteers, three being posted on a low roof at Messrs Romes' gates, the other at Grand Canal Street corner. Soldiers who suddenly appeared in a cul-de-sac beside the Turf Bank were met by the fire of Volunteers on the wall and retired with some wounded. Two snipers, perched high on the cisterns on the roof of the railway locomotive works overhanging the dock, kept up heavy enfilading fire, and held the post until the general surrender on Sunday. Their high-roofed cover was screened at the end facing the docks, but open at the back, and afforded very insecure footholds. Their position seems to have been revealed at night by the flash of an over-heated gun, and one of them was fatally wounded: there was much difficulty in bringing him down a narrow stairway, and thence to hospital, where he died. Some soldiers who entered the yard beneath were driven back near Barron Street, taking their wounded, but leaving three rifles.

Grand Canal Street bridge was defended by a barricade formed of overturned bread-vans from Boland's yards. The low-lying walls of the Bakery facing the bridge were loopholed and manned, but only lightly like the other posts, many of which had soon to be abandoned. Trenches were dug across the railway line at points covering Lansdowne Road and Westland Row stations, and rails removed. Snipers at Haddington

Road bridge menaced the British garrison at Beggar's Bush barracks, a party of whom were resolutely driven from the line near Bath Avenue with considerable casualties, a sergeant-major being killed and the officer-in-charge badly wounded. In a conflict near Shelbourne Road, two British were killed and several Volunteers wounded. Judge Johnson's house near Lansdowne Road was the most distant of the outlying posts. True to tradition, on the other hand, British military were harboured at the Royal Dublin Society, Ballsbridge, and at Trinity College, cradle of alien ascendancy. The Volunteers held a house also at Grattan Street to cover Denzille Street, and another at the corner of Great Clarence Street, while Volunteer snipers at Westland Row were able to attend to British military at Lincoln Place. But the posts which covered themselves with real lustre were those on Northumberland Road, from No. 25 near the Ballsbridge end, to Clanwilliam House at the city end.

On leaving their mobilisation centre, the cycling section of 'B' company, 3rd battalion, halted at Merrion Square and passing by Mount Street Crescent halted again at Warrington Place close to Mount Street bridge. Thence George Reynolds, having conferred with Lieut Michael Malone, crossed instantly with a few men to Clanwilliam House at the city end of Northumberland Road, took possession, and ordered that any telephones there be disconnected. Lieut Malone then attended to the other squads at the bridge, sending some to the parochial hall further along the road, proceeding himself with three men to No. 25 at the other end of the road, of which he had taken possession at 12.30. This post became the spearhead of the defence against troops sent from England.

Northumberland Road, the city end of which was the scene of the battle of Mount Street bridge, runs from its intersection with Lansdowne and Pembroke roads in an almost direct line city-wards until it ends at the bridge; thence the highway continues towards the city as Lower Mount Street. At its midway intersection with Haddington Road, there is a slight bend. Here, as stated, the corner house, No. 25, was held by Lieut Malone, and from it the military advancing from Dún Laoghaire first became visible to the defenders.

Approaching the bend, they came at once under close fire from No. 25, duly followed by more distant fire from Clanwilliam House, Mount Street bridge. Almost midway between the two posts was St Stephen's parochial hall, in a recess, and commanding a narrow view right and left, but very valiantly held. The national school almost opposite but nearer the bridge, though occupied on Monday, was evacuated that night. The area thus held soon became a veritable zone of death during an engagement of terrific intensity lasting about nine hours.

Lieut Malone, while keeping in touch with the parochial hall and Clanwilliam House during Monday and, with his men, strongly barricading his post, helped in the evening to create one of the sensations of the Rising. In association with Volunteer snipers on the railway bridge, Haddington Road, they opened fire on an approaching body of military, who turned out to be 'The Gorgeous Wrecks', a West-British volunteer corps returning from manoeuvres at Ticknock, flaunting rifles, badges stamped *Georgius Rex,* but provided – it was said – with no ammunition. For their imperialist ardour, five of them lost their lives, and seven were wounded, while the survivors fled to the harassed British garrison at Beggar's Bush barracks at a pace which recalled 'the Races of Castlebar' and was appropriately dubbed 'the Leopardstown Races' which happened to be held in the neighbourhood that day. At the other end of the road, George Reynolds found that the slight garrison in the schools beside him had been withdrawn. During the night the spring silence there was broken only by the sound of distant fire, and even one member of the slender garrison at Clanwilliam House left.

At dawn, Tuesday morning, Lieut Malone calling at Clanwilliam House was instantly admitted. Having conferred with George Reynolds, he went at once to cut the electric tram wires – illuminating the area as the wires came sparkling to the ground – and then withdrew to 25 Northumberland Road. In the afternoon, five shots penetrated his post, as if military snipers had entered the house opposite, and the fire being returned – at twenty-five yards' range – firing ceased for the day. That same afternoon the lieutenant sent two junior comrades away, with certain directions; and with one companion, James Grace, heroically determined to hold the post. Throughout the night, they kept alternate watch, and heard firing in the Portobello direction. Wednesday morning, they sought to loophole the walls, but found they had no suitable tools. Soon a girl dispatch-carrier notified them that a large body of the thousands of British troops that had reached Dún Laoghaire was already at Williamstown, and, in a short time, they were seen approaching from Ballsbridge. The hour had struck for the garrison of two.

Side-views gave an oblique view of the approaches; a large-scale map of the area supplemented the view as far as necessary. The lieutenant had a high-power automatic pistol, with practically smokeless powder, his comrade a service Lee-Enfield, while rifles had also been left by the young men sent away. The advancing troops were permitted to come within close range – some to Haddington Road – before the garrison opened fire, which was supplemented from Charlemont House. Immediately the military took cover; but soon charged again and again, only to have several of their men shot even on the hall-door steps. Seeing rifle flashes from the windows, and thinking all the fire came from there, the military concentrated on the house, and almost from the beginning resorted to bombing: indeed, at five, bombs and grenades came in showers. The shattering of glass and woodwork destroyed such cover as the two heroes hoped to have to repel the assault; the fumes and the general din aggravated the situation. Soon, volleys from the belfry of the Haddington Road church swept the approaches to the stairs so that instant retreat seemed inevitable. A bomb through a back window fell on revolver cartridges and five hundred rounds of Howth ammunition wrecking the room the defenders had just left. Other bombs rendering the ground floor untenable, the defenders brought up the spare rifles, and fixed bayonets for a last stand at the head of the stairs should doors and windows be driven in.

Already, British troops moved more freely as far as the parochial hall. About 8 p.m., noise was heard in the parlour as if a party had rushed in at the front; but a few shots through the lock of the parlour door drove them from the house. However, another grenade attack enabled the assailants to get possession of the middle floor, and separate the two defenders, Lieut Malone being thus forced to the top, his comrade to the untenable basement. 'I am coming down,' the lieutenant shouted. Thereupon, a volley was fired into the basement, followed by a bomb to the coal cellar, and a second volley to the stairs, which must have proved fatal to the lieutenant. His valiant comrade watched for an opportunity to escape from the heavily barricaded kitchen. Noise in the basement drew a rifle-shot through a bomb-hole in the ceiling, but the kitchen escaped attention in the confusion, though all rooms overhead were searched. Later in the night, at the command: 'Clear the streets!' the soldiers left the house, and the hero in the kitchen, removing a network of obstructions, found his way into the garden, hid among the shrubs in the pall of smoke that shrouded the neighbourhood, and awaited a truly forlorn hope of escape.

'Later I entered the garden tool-house, and removed the key,' James Grace tells us in his own words. 'Hearing voices outside, I lay still. A further voice saying, "Perhaps there is someone inside!" I drew my revolver, which held my last four cartridges, and prepared to sell my life as dearly as possible. Soon someone grunted: "They must be all finished!" and the soldiers then retired. About 11 p.m., I got over the wall into Percy Lane; but, noticing sentries in the distance, returned to the garden. After three or four hours, a further attempt failed; but I got into another garden at the far side of the lane, and lay hidden there all next day. Late on Thursday night, I removed my boots, tied them over my shoulders, and crept to the canal end of Percy Lane with the wild idea of swimming the canal between the bridges and so entering the city. I was challenged by sentries and, not replying, was fired on. But I escaped in the darkness, rushed back into the lane, flung myself over a garden wall, and hid in a wooden shed until arrested next morning. I was taken prisoner to the parochial hall, thence to Ballsbridge, and finally to an English jail where I was detained for about eight months.'

The parochial hall, lying between No. 25 and Clanwilliam House, was held by four men: P.J. Doyle in command, Joe Clarke, William Christian and J. MacGrath. Standing well back from the footpath on the Sherwood Foresters' line of march, it had advantages and disadvantages. Though it afforded no view of the advancing troops, the four defenders poured volley after volley into them whenever they attempted to dash or to crawl past it, thus halting them until they were shot down by the marksmen of Clanwilliam House. As in the case of the more advanced post, no aid, no message reached them from Boland's Bakery. Withal, they held out until six o'clock on Wednesday. Having fired their last shot while they were being assailed with a very inferno of bombs, as well as revolver and rifle fire at close range, they retreated by the back to Percy Place. Here they were intercepted and seized by British troops, now practically in possession of all the approaches and exits. Joe Clarke on being searched was found in possession of his revolver, and placed with his back to a door, hands up. With his own revolver he was fired on, the bullet piercing the door just above his head. Immediately the door was thrown open, an indignant doctor rushed out, having narrowly escaped being shot as he attended one of a yard full of wounded British soldiers; and, after an almost miraculous escape, Joe was led away, his hands bound behind his back, his sympathies unalterably with the Republic for which he fought.

Clanwilliam House had a more eventful experience. The residents, who remained overnight, left early Tuesday morning, when the officer-in-charge proceeded to barricade the premises so that it would be impossible to enter from the street. Food was procured, pails filled with water, yet at no time did the Volunteers occupy the lower rooms, the upper windows affording an excellent view and a wider range of vision. Enquiries made at the school opposite the canal elicited the information that the small garrison there had been withdrawn; but a courier sent to headquarters for men and provisions got four men who remained to the end, bringing the garrison to seven. Mattresses were now placed on the upper floors, and furniture re-arranged to afford better shelter. Cartridges were placed near the guns and towels torn up for bandages. But there were no sand-bags, and the defenders were still dangerously exposed through the very high windows. News had casually come that Lancers had been shot in O'Connell Street, Volunteers in Stephen's Green; more intense firing was heard from the city, and the garrison watching all night had but snatches of sleep.

On Wednesday, as indicated, some 2,000 Sherwood Foresters advanced along the main highway from Dún Laoghaire, the officers frequently consulting maps, the troops halting at intervals. They were led by about eight hundred men, the others close behind, while a large body had halted at Ballsbridge. The advance section cautiously approached the danger zone at Northumberland Road, where it was engaged by Lieut Malone as already described. The next column advanced in turn, while the main body still remained beside Ballsbridge. The advancing column halted at Messrs Crampton's, close to Carrisbrooke House – occupied as early as Monday by a detail of a dozen military from Dún Laoghaire. While the middle column smoked or rested here, a revolver shot dispelled them. Other shots following, many of the soldiers fled back to the main body, or sought cover in side roads and Herbert Park. Others of them responded with random shots, and arrested on suspicion prominent citizens who, however, were soon released.

The column resting at Ballsbridge remained there for some time, and are said to have entered the city via Baggot Street bridge, while some of them there turned to the right and proceeded along the canal to reinforce by a flank movement the first detachment then attacking Clanwilliam House. They loopholed the walls of Beckett's yard near the bridge and used it as a sectional centre. At Northumberland Road, where the posts at No. 25 and the parochial hall had taken a fearful toll, 'flankers' on the footpaths – in Indian file at intervals of six feet – preceded the vanguard, who followed in fours and lay down at intervals as they advanced in parallel lines, on guard and with fixed bayonets. As they picked their steps under the devastating fire from Clanwilliam House, they continued to take such cover as the front gardens presented. A large local flank reserve was drawn up where St Mary's Road joins the Northumberland Road; but it was the advance column that took the main part in the terrible battle of Mount Street bridge and the posts leading to it.

Soon after noon on Wednesday, the three men at the side windows of Clanwilliam House overlooking Mount Street heard a volley that seemed quite near. Patrick Doyle hurried from the drawing-room:

'Now, boys, we are in action,' he said, 'for God's sake, keep cool.' In a moment, the officer-in-charge shouted: 'Up, Doyle, to the front room', thereupon placing two men at the middle window, one at the right, next to Mount Street, himself at the left. A rapid cross-fire was turned on the advancing troops, the men at the right firing to the left and vice versa. Almost immediately the order: 'Fix bayonets, charge!' was heard in the distance, and the attacking enemy troops rushed forward, officers leading with drawn swords, the rank-and-file with fixed bayonets. Fire was opened on them by the Volunteer garrison, and several soldiers fell. Up to this point, the destructive fire from No. 25 had prevented any soldier passing far beyond the Haddington Road intersection.

After half-an-hour another order: 'Fix bayonets, charge!' indicated that a frontal attack on Clanwilliam House was now intended, but the military were met by a devastating fire from all three angles. Soon, sixty of them charged along the road facing the bridge, others taking cover behind tree trunks along the way. When half-way up the road, they were mown down by the fire from the parochial hall, the last man dropping near the schools beside the bridge, the survivors retreating or taking such cover as presented itself. A mutual cessation of fire followed. During the lull, a woman with a jug, towels and other things was seen to cross the bridge and aid the wounded. The lull was brief. Three or four charges were made en masse in the first couple of hours, the last resulting in awful British casualties, so that the space in front of the bridge was strewn with dead and wounded, guns, knapsacks and other accoutrements lying everywhere in disorder. One soldier hit by a bullet fell into the canal, while an officer loudly urging his men to follow him fell as he reached the summit of the bridge. Soldiers tripping over fallen comrades lay still on the ground until they could seek cover. Not till late in the evening could Col Leslie-Neville, shot down early, be borne on a mattress from a neighbouring house.

No male civilian ventured near the bridge. But half-a-dozen men standing at Power's Court walked across it under very heavy fire, and assisted wounded soldiers into the nurses' home, Lower Mount Street. A priest rode on a bicycle to the nurses' home; later, an ambulance went amongst the wounded soldiers, assisted by a dozen nurses from Sir Patrick Dun's Hospital. Inevitably, there were civilian casualties. An elderly man carrying a parcel found himself surrounded in the afternoon by military engaged in a flank attack on Clanwilliam House. He remained for an hour at the corner of the lane facing the canal. At the first opportunity, he left the lane, halted a moment, and hastened for home along Percy Lane towards the bridge, but was shot by a volley from Baggot Street and fell dead near the school. A well-known resident of the Turf Bank was shot dead as he returned to his home, whence he had been sent away by the military.

The valour of Clanwilliam House remained unabated. The youngest of the small garrison, a boy of seventeen, 'was extended on a table' when his Martini, getting overheated, exploded, and threw him to the floor. Instantly, another rifle was placed in his hand, with the exhortation: 'Get up, for Heaven's sake, get up, and keep at them.' Frontal charges en masse having failed repeatedly, the idea of thus rushing the house was abandoned, and the conflict resolved itself into a sniping duel between the Volunteers and the troops cautiously creeping forward under every available form of cover. Early in the day, soldiers had rushed round the corner of Percy Lane opposite and into houses on the canal. From concealed positions they then sniped the windows of Clanwilliam House. Some seemed to come from the lane running behind the house held by Lieut Malone, so the Volunteer leader ordered those facing that direction to 'keep them off lest they cut off Malone's retreat!' At that moment a sniper's bullet fired across the canal through the fanlight of the corner house, Percy Lane, pierced the wall just over the head of a young Volunteer fighting with the utmost bravery. A comrade came downstairs with a ramrod to clear a jammed rifle: on returning, he found three bullet holes in the shutter that had been sheltering him. The situation had become truly tense.

Repeated flank attacks were now made by soldiers coming along both canal banks from Percy Lane and Baggot Street on the right. The canal embankment is here linked by an iron railing on a granite base twelve inches high. A line of soldiers crawled in the shelter of this base, their knapsacks often showing, so that they were said to resemble a long boa-constrictor crawling in the shelter. The knapsacks were often pierced by bullets from Clanwilliam House, and whenever the crawling soldiers rose even to their knees they were instantly shot down. At a break in the shelter, several of them were caught by the oblique fire. The first soldier having reached the bridge, the word of command was heard, and a dozen of them were on their feet, some of them to be shot down instantly, the others to rush across the road to cover. Those who went too far – towards the Turf Bank – were met by close-range fire from the Roberts' wall or from the cisterns in the distance, so that this line of possible advance was abandoned after many failures, a new obstacle being a more diversified defence than had previously been suspected.

Some soldiers also, as they approached from the Baggot Street direction, were shot down at Warrington Place or the city side of the canal. Two other soldiers were shot from Clanwilliam House as they stood on the steps of Miss Scully's home, occupied by herself and her maid. This house was subjected to a terrific attack by rifle, bomb and hand grenade, the military thinking it was occupied by Volunteers. Fifty bullets were in the ceiling of the front room; walls, floors, curtains, everything riddled; the two occupants arrested when the military entered and found them alone there, led to the bridge in front of Clanwilliam House then on fire, and released later in the night. A lady in the next house was shot through the hand. The military snipers who had taken up position in the Haddington Road church gradually commanded the Volunteer position here. Gradually, too, they entered surrounding houses and concentrated long-distance firing on Clanwilliam House. Most of the terrace on the opposite side of the canal was also taken as the day advanced, giving safe cover for an unremitting attack on the Volunteer garrison.

Thus, Clanwilliam House steadily became an inferno: window frames, shutters, everything blown away, the floors strew with broken pictures, mirrors, chandeliers; piano keys sometimes responding when fondled by bullets; all furniture in splinters; staircases threatening to collapse; water-pipes burst and threatening to flood the house; a hail of incendiary bullets through the frameless windows, smoke filling the rooms, the smell of burnt powder insufferable; beds, lounges, upholstering aflame, and all clamouring for attention. At 7.30, three Volunteers were still at the drawing-room windows, rapid-firing, their leader farther back, three others in the upper rooms. At last, the man at the centre window saw that his comrade on the right – firing while partially reclining on a chair – lay quite still. He shook him, to find him dead. Then, he observed the comrade on his left – firing also from a kneeling position – start slightly, and fall forward, dead. Turning backwards, he next saw the officer in charge drop to the ground, fatally wounded and bleeding profusely. The unwounded man called to his companions, who immediately rushed down. They bore the wounded officer to the landing, whence the four survivors escaped as if by miracle, the whole house being now aflame.

All back doors being firmly barricaded, they had to force their way through a small barred window, flinging themselves over the garden wall of the next house, to escape by a back-lane. Rifle fire having now ceased in front, the military threw several bombs into Clanwilliam House. Whilst removing Capt. Cursham, wounded by the rebound of a bomb, Mr Hutton, who was aided by Dr Marks, stood for a moment beside a soldier carrying a bucketful of hand grenades, and noticed that flames then burst forth from the whole front. The city fire brigade recorded in its annual report: '8.40 p.m., 1 and 2 Clanwilliam Place – Did not attend as the houses were being shelled by military.' Yet as late as 9.30 p.m., further casualties took place among the military from Volunteer snipers in the neighbourhood of the bridge. As late as Saturday, indeed, Dr Myles Keogh saw a sentry shot opposite his own house in Mount Street.

The remains have never been recovered of the three Volunteers killed in the blazing Clanwilliam House: Patrick Doyle of Milltown, Dublin; Richard Murphy of Dublin, who was to have been married in a week, and George Reynolds, a young Dublin silversmith, the officer-in-charge. That night, the remains of Lieut Malone were interred by the military in the garden of No. 25, the Rev. Fr Wall, of Haddington Road – later coadjutor-archbishop of Dublin – being requested to offer up the last prayers. He was buried in his uniform, just as he fell, his head and shoulders covered with a canvas cloth. A fortnight later, the unidentified remains were translated to Glasnevin. A record of the burial having been kept, a relative of the deceased officer, accompanied by some of his former colleagues, attended at the graveside, 12 June 1917, fourteen months after his burial, and fully identified his remains. *Beannacht Dílis Dé ar anamnaibh na gasradh ud uile.*

After the fall of Clanwilliam House, activities calmed down, especially as there was no conceivable hope of aid from general headquarters. Unfortunately a comrade, who in the excitement had lost his balance, shot Peadar Macken through the heart in the Boland Bakery area. Peadar, a Dublin-born painter, intimate with all parts of the country, was a fluent Irish speaker, an alderman of the corporation and, altogether, a citizen of great promise. When headquarters was ultimately transferred from the Bakery to a neighbouring chemist's shop, another Volunteer shot around him indiscriminately until stunned with a knock by Simon Donnelly to save his comrades. But the fight was maintained resolutely to the end; and the rumour finally got currency that Comm. de Valera expressed his conviction that the fight could be won if only the citizens came out and fought with knives and forks.

General Maxwell's official account of the advance of the British troops from Dún Laoghaire unwittingly confirms the entire story here narrated:

> Towards evening, he wrote, the 178th infantry brigade began to arrive at Kingstown; and, in accordance with orders received, the brigade left Kingstown by road, in two columns:
>
> The left column, consisting of the 5th and 6th battalions, Sherwood Foresters, by the Stillorgan–Donnybrook Road and South Circular Road to the Royal Hospital, where it arrived without opposition.
>
> The right column, consisting of the 7th and 8th battalions, Sherwood Foresters, by the main tram route through Ballsbridge and directed on Merrion Square and Trinity College.
>
> This column, with the 7th battalion leading, was held up at the

northern corner of Haddington Road and Northumberland Avenue, which was strongly held by the rebels; but with the assistance of bombing parties organised and led by Capt. Jeffares, of the bombing school at Elm Park, the rebels were driven back.

At 3.25 p.m., the 7th battalion Sherwood Foresters met great opposition from the rebels holding the school and other houses on the north side of the road close to the bridge at Lower Mount Street, and two officers, one of whom was the adjutant, Capt. Dietrichsen, were killed and seven wounded including Lieut-Col Fane who, though wounded, remained in action.

Mount Street battle: At about 5.30 p.m., orders were received that the advance to Trinity College was to be pushed forward at all costs, and therefore at about 8 p.m., after careful arrangements, the whole column, accompanied by bombing parties, attacked the school and houses where the chief opposition lay. The battalions, charging in successive waves, carried all before them, but, I regret to say, suffered severe casualties in doing so. Four officers were killed and fourteen wounded, and of other ranks, two hundred and sixteen were killed and wounded. The steadiness shown by these two battalions is deserving of special mention, and I understand the majority of the men have less than three months' service.

In view of the opposition met with, it was not considered advisable to push on to Trinity College that night, so, at 11 p.m. the 5th South Staffordshire Regiment, from the 176th Infantry brigade, reinforced this column and, by occupying the positions gained, allowed the two battalions, Sherwood Foresters, to be concentrated at Ballsbridge.

In connection with this fighting at Mount Street bridge, where our heaviest casualties occurred, I should like to mention the gallant assistance given by a number of medical men, ladies, nurses and women-servants who, at great risk, brought in and tended to the wounded, continuing their efforts even when deliberately fired at by the rebels.

Butcher Maxwell proved true to type and worthy of 'Protector' Cromwell; and it was not to be expected that he could conclude even a brief report without the traditional defamation of the Irish enemy, which almost over-reached itself in Emmet's day. A supplementary official dispatch states: 'There have been numerous instances of deliberate shooting on ambulances and those courageous people who came out to attend to the wounded. The city fire brigade when turned out in consequence of incendiary fires, were fired on and had to retire.' This, if written otherwise, would not represent England. Fortunately, none of the ambulance workers suffered the slightest injury, though unavoidably under fire the whole evening. One of them, Mr Hyland, parted with Dr Myles Keogh late on Wednesday night, both having exerted themselves to clear the wounded from the bridge. At dawn next morning, Mr Hyland was informed that the military intended to use artillery, and was advised to keep to the basement. Passing by the connecting door from his father's garden into his own, he was shot; but no Volunteer position overlooked the place. Clanwilliam House had been burnt out, and the other houses in the rear were then occupied by the military.

Dr Keogh, too, while helping to carry a stretcher, saw some soldiers advance behind him from Haddington Road. At once, he laid down the stretcher, raised his hand high, and called on the military to go back, just as they were peremptorily held up when wantonly seeking to shoot Joe Clarke. They had and have a scurrilous press, and they used it as they always will use it to defame those opposed to them. The 'incendiary' fires of Easter Week were caused solely by England's fire bombs and kindred means. It has been shown that the fire brigade could not attend the fire at Clanwilliam House for the reason that it was still being shelled by the military. The charge of cowardly conduct against the Volunteers was specifically denied in the press, even by the commander of the Sherwood Foresters, and the late Dr Con O'Brien of Merrion Square rendered one of his many national services by preparing a vivid statement of the fighting as it came under his own personal notice. From many, many sources indeed came tributes to the chivalry of the Irish Volunteers.

THE NORTH KING STREET AREA

by Piaras Béaslaí

Piaras Béaslaí was vice-commandant of the 1st battalion and second-in-command of the entire North King Street area during the rebellion of 1916. He is now the senior surviving officer of those concerned.

ALL OLD DUBLIN Volunteers who lived through those thrilling six days of Easter Week 1916, in the Church Street area, must have a vivid recollection of certain scenes witnessed and sensations experienced by them, but to reduce the whole to a coherent story is not so easy. The small body of men engaged occupied an area so widely spread across the city and were, necessarily, so little in touch with any save their own small units – especially in the latter stages of the fighting, when positions were cut off from one another by enemy attacks – that a great many persons should be consulted in order to obtain a clear and comprehensive view of the whole sequence of events.

Furthermore, to men who were practically without sleep for four or five days, and in a condition of severe tension, the recollection of occurrences is liable, at this time of day, to be a confused jumble of memories, in which some trivial things stand out vividly and events of major importance are almost forgotten. And many, in perfect good faith, make erroneous statements. The human memory, after a lapse of over twenty years is very fallible. I have heard extraordinary conflicts of testimony as to what happened on certain occasions from persons who were actually present, and have myself been told things by conscientious eye-witnesses which were entirely at variance with my own recollections.

Another complication is the fact that the Church Street of today is a very different place from the scene of the fighting of 1916. Revisiting the place where one had gone through such tense moments is a bewildering experience. A large area in Church Street which was then full of ruins, demolished buildings and waste ground is now occupied by streets of houses, and the same is true of the site of the Linenhall barracks in Lisburn Street. One's adventures of 1916 seem to belong to another century.

I shall endeavour to give a summarised account of the main events of that memorable week, directing my attention particularly to the fighting of the last two days. But to elucidate this it is necessary to start at the beginning of the week.

According to the plans of our leaders the 1st battalion was to occupy a line running from the Four Courts on the north bank of the Liffey (besides the Mendicity Institution on the south side) to Cabra, where it was to link up with the 5th battalion (under the command of Thomas Ashe). The Broadstone station, then the railway terminus for the west of Ireland, was to be occupied and the North Dublin Union was to be the battalion headquarters.

Had the parade announced for Sunday 23 April, duly taken place and the full strength of the battalion been available, this plan would have been carried out in every detail, but unforeseen circumstances compelled us to modify part of our plan.

When the Sunday parade was called off (for reasons which are well known) many Volunteers believed the parade to be postponed indefinitely, and the surprise mobilisation on Monday morning found them unprepared. When the 1st battalion left their headquarters in Blackhall Street at noon, it did not number one-third of its full strength. Many members joined up later, and we were also reinforced by men from other battalions, Fianna boys and quite a number of those who had come over from England.

The majority of the Volunteers who assembled in Blackhall Street had no knowledge, when they were summoned to parade, that they would be asked to go out in insurrection, though I think a good many had a shrewd suspicion, for some time previously, that an attempt of the kind was in contemplation. The order to go to fight for Irish independence must have come with startling unexpectedness to many of the small band assembled in the hall; yet none refused to obey the call.

No sooner had the men reached the Church Street area and commenced to take up their positions than shots rang out. I do not think that any unit in the city found itself in contact with the enemy sooner than 'C' company, though the encounter was entirely accidental. To this company, under the command of Captain Frank Fahy – later Ceann Comhairle of the Dáil – and Lieut Joe McGuinness, was deputed the task of occupying and holding the Four Courts. While engaged in this task, and erecting a barricade at the foot of Church

Street, a body of mounted Lancers, escorting an ammunition wagon, came along the quays, travelling in the direction of the park. The Volunteers believing themselves attacked, fired on the Lancers, killing one. A second Lancer galloped up Church Street firing wildly and was shot down after he had killed a child. The rest of the Lancers retreated to a building in Charles Street, on the eastern side of our position, where they remained prisoners throughout the week, afraid to venture out. After one unsuccessful assault on the building, we did not think it necessary to attack them again, beyond a little sniping to intimidate them, as they were penned up and entirely harmless.

Meanwhile 'D' company, under the command of Captain Seán Heuston and Lieutenant Richard Balfe, occupied the Mendicity Institution on Usher's Quay, on the south side of the Liffey, where they were soon attacked and put up a gallant fight against heavy odds. They were separated from the rest of the battalion by the Liffey, but were later reinforced by some members of the 5th battalion from Fingal.

Meanwhile the whole of Church Street and adjoining streets, as far as the North Dublin Union and Constitution Hill were occupied by our men, and barricades were erected and manned at various points in Church Street and the side streets running off it, such as May Lane (leading to the Jameson Distillery in Bow Street), Mary's Lane, North King Street and Brunswick Street. A number of houses in these last two streets were also occupied, and these posts figured largely in the fierce fighting of the last two days.

There exists a widespread impression, even among Volunteers, that the Four Courts building was a headquarters, but this is entirely incorrect. The Four Courts was one of the extremities of our position, and Battalion Commandant Ned Daly required a more central spot for his headquarters. On the Monday he took up his quarters in St John's convent in Brunswick Street, where he was received with enthusiasm by some patriotic Sisters of Charity, and here it was that he met the late Father Albert, OSF, and Father Augustine, OSF, both sympathisers. From Tuesday to the end of the week the Father Matthew Hall was used as our headquarters, as well as for the tending of our wounded by members of Cumann na mBan. It was only on Friday night, when we were compelled to abandon this position, that the Four Courts became our headquarters – not many hours before the order to surrender reached us.

The late Éamonn Duggan acted as adjutant and Éamonn Morkan as quartermaster to the battalion. The greater part of Church Street was occupied by 'F' company under the command of Captain Fionán Lynch, later Leas-Ceann Comhairle of Dáil Éireann, and now Judge Lynch, and important posts were held by Lieutenants John Shouldice and Diarmuid O'Hegarty, John S. O'Connor, F.X. Coghlan, Liam Archer, now chief-of-staff of the National Army, Frank Shouldice and Mortimer O'Connell, now chief clerk of Dáil Éireann. Martin Conlon was in general charge of the Father Matthew Hall. 'A' company was officered by Capt. Denis O'Callaghan (a Kerryman, who was given special commands during the week) and Lieut Liam Ó Cearbhaill, and 'G' company by Capt. Nicholas Laffan. There were other important posts held, but I do not pretend to give a complete list of these. In actual practice men from various companies, and even from other battalions, were mingled with one another in the various posts occupied.

Owing to our small numbers when we set out on Monday it seemed impossible to occupy the spacious Broadstone station effectively, and no attempt was made to do so. When, later, our numbers were reinforced, the station had been already strongly occupied by British military, and a daring attack, led by Denis O'Callaghan, was repulsed, one of our men being wounded.

Another officer of the battalion, Captain Frank Daly, who acted as engineer for the whole brigade, had been engaged from early on Monday morning on various demolitions, such as the blowing up of railway bridges and the putting of railway lines out of action. The battalion adjutant, Captain James O'Sullivan, occupied positions on Cabra Road and North Circular Road. On the Tuesday evening these positions were attacked by strong forces of British troops, artillery was used against the barricades and the defenders were compelled to evacuate them. Captain O'Sullivan then joined the GPO garrison.

Immediately beside our position in Lisburn Street stood the barracks, occupied by British soldiers, and, on Wednesday, a body of our Volunteers, led by Denis O'Callaghan, seized the building. It proved an easy task, as the soldiers surrendered immediately. The barracks were burned to the ground.

I think our position was unique in one respect – that whereas, in other parts of the city, buildings only were held, our troops were actually out in the streets in an area where a large civilian population resided, and our military problems were added to by problems of civilian administration. A good many of the residents were at first suspicious and hostile; but after we had been in occupation for a couple of days, they were impressed by our discipline and friendly attitude and became more favourable. We advised all who could, especially the women and children, to remove from the area to some safer quarter, but the majority preferred to remain where they were, despite the danger.

The fact that we occupied an important thoroughfare made things more difficult. For the first few days a constant stream of persons, seeking to pass through our barricades for various motives, had to be held up and questioned. Inside our position in North King Street there was a bakery in which bread was being baked daily, and, as other bakeries were closed, people from other parts of Dublin flocked there seeking loaves. Despite the danger to ourselves we admitted them, but had to form a 'food queue' and 'ration' them, limiting each person to two loaves.

In Church Street area most of the shops remained open for at least the first four days of the week, and there was not the least trace of an attempt at looting or any irregularity. The Volunteers preserved perfect order.

A number of minor actions occurred in the earlier part of the week in which the Volunteers sustained some casualties and inflicted a great deal more – notably an engagement with British forces at close quarters on Church Street bridge in which the late Peadar Clancy, then a lieutenant in 'C' company, played a daring part. Seán Heuston's gallant little band, cut off and surrounded by a large force, inflicted heavy losses on their attackers before they were compelled to surrender.

Despite the overwhelming superiority of the enemy, it was not until the Thursday that any attempt was made to encircle our whole position. A number of snipers took up posts on buildings in the neighbourhood of Capel Street, from which they kept our barricades under harassing fire. At this time, owing to the wastelands adjoining, a considerable portion of Church Street was exposed to their fire. By Thursday night we were practically cut off from touch with general headquarters in the GPO with which, up to this, we had been in constant communication. On Thursday night a considerable portion of O'Connell Street was in flames, and Church Street was lit up by the fires, rendering the men at the barricades a target for snipers. We had also buildings on fire in our own area and Volunteers had to work strenuously to prevent the spread of the flames, which originated from the burning of Linenhall barracks.

On Friday evening a fierce attack was launched on our position in North King Street from the direction of Bolton Street, supported by armoured cars. A handful of Volunteers under the command of Lieut John Shouldice occupied the house at the north-western corner of Church Street and North King Street – licensed premises which we afterwards nicknamed 'Reilly's Fort'. To these men it fell to bear the brunt of the attack which lasted many hours. North of this, at Brunswick Street, posts were held by Lieut Laffan and his men who also put up a spirited fight and, when, next day they were cut off from the rest of the battalion, they were the last to surrender. But the main British attack was directed against North King Street.

The British soldiers, under cover of an armoured car, first took up a position behind an unoccupied barricade on the opposite side of North King Street from 'Reilly's Fort', but they were met with such a withering fire from the defenders that they retreated in confusion leaving some dead behind. They fled down Beresford Street where they came under a cross-fire from Volunteers in posts on the east side of Church Street and were mown down. The men in 'Reilly's Fort' dashed out and seized the rifles which the soldiers had dropped, bringing them back triumphantly to the 'fort'. They found that their firing, which had inflicted such heavy casualties on the attackers, had also put several of their rifles out of action.

Later the attackers broke into houses in North King Street, from which they kept up a heavy fire for many hours at our positions, concentrating their attack on 'Reilly's Fort'. It was afterwards ascertained that these same soldiers murdered some young men whom they found in the buildings – men who were not connected in any way with the Volunteers.

At an early stage of the fight one Volunteer, Patrick O'Flanagan, was killed while entering the 'fort'.

The Father Matthew Hall, where we had our headquarters, was only about eighty yards from the position in North King Street which was being attacked. It contained a number of our wounded men and the members of Cumann na mBan who were nursing them, and was not in a position to be defended. Commandant Daly decided to transfer his headquarters to the Four Courts and Morkan and I proceeded to carry down the ammunition and explosives which were stored in the Father Matthew Hall. As we had no men to spare from the barricades we had to do it all ourselves and it involved a number of journeys up and down and the climbing over half dozen barricades while heavily laden. All this time the fight in North King Street raged with fury and the long street echoed with the sounds of the firing. The whole area was lit up as brightly as if it were daylight by the fires in O'Connell Street, and every now and then the ping of a bullet near one's ear showed that a sniper had just missed his mark.

All night long and next morning the fight raged in North King Street and the men at the barricades below, between them and the Four Courts, having to keep their thin line intact, could not be spared to go to the assistance of those holding the positions attacked. At length, after being about sixteen hours under constant fire, the men in 'Reilly's Fort', spent and exhausted, discovered their ammunition was practically finished. Seeing no prospect of relief they decided to evacuate the building. They made a dash across the street under fire, fortunately without a casualty, and retreated down Church

Street, rejoining their comrades at the barricade near the Franciscan church.

No sooner was the 'fort' in North King Street evacuated than the British soldiers occupied it and proceeded to pour a heavy fire down Church Street at the barricades. The men at the upper barricades fell back on the barricade at the corner of Mary's Lane. However, they rallied and returned to their former positions.

At this point I would like to pay a tribute to the coolness and courage of the late Joe McGuinness, then a lieutenant of 'C' company, who, arriving on the scene from the Four Courts where he was on duty, assisted the other officers in rallying the men.

And now occurred a piece of daring gallantry the memory of which thrills me still. In the very centre of the crossing of Church Street and North King Street we had planted a flag, using as flagstaff the lance of one of the unfortunate Lancers who had been killed on the Monday. All through the fighting this flag remained intact, and was still standing when the men in North King Street retreated. A Volunteer from London named Éamonn Tierney asked permission to 'fetch the flag', and, having obtained the sanction of Captain Lynch, walked up the street, exposed to enemy fire from both sides at close range, seized the flag, and walked coolly back with it, quite unhurt.

A daring charge up Church Street with the object of recovering lost ground, resulted in the death of one of our men, Seán Hurley, who had come over from London. Our line was now considerably shortened and the men on the far side of North King Street were definitely cut off from us and surrounded. They held out gallantly, and after Laffan was wounded his place was taken by Paddy Holohan, who only surrendered on the following day.

Immediately after the unsuccessful charge up Church Street, Commandant Daly called a conference of officers at which it was decided to make a fresh sortie that evening, and endeavour to recapture our lost positions. A daring Volunteer, Tommy O'Connor, undertook to try to bring a message from us to general headquarters, which we still believed to be in the GPO. We were not aware that building had been evacuated.

During our conference one officer called attention to the strange silence that had come over the city and remarked that evidently the enemy had suspended their attack for the present. After our ears had been deafened, day and night by the sound of constant firing, the silence seemed indeed unusual. We were not aware that a 'Ceasefire' order had been issued.

Later a priest arrived with news of the surrender, and finally Pearse's signed order to surrender was conveyed to Commandant Daly. He showed it to me and his eyes filled with tears. He had borne himself like a gallant soldier through the week of fighting. Again he rose to this fresh test of soldiership. He checked the murmuring of those who objected to surrender by an appeal to discipline. They must obey the orders of the commander-in-chief, however unwelcome. He impressed the English officers with his dignity. They permitted him to march at the head of his men as they brought us through the empty streets (where the few people we saw were those that cursed us) to where other bodies of prisoners were assembled in O'Connell Street. And when the English general asked: 'Who is in charge of these men?' – referring to his own officers – Daly proudly answered: 'I am. At all events I was.' – a remark which, he must have known, signed his death-warrant.

CITIZEN ARMY POSTS
by R.M. Fox

IF THE EASTER Rising had been on the scale originally planned, the occupation of Stephen's Green would have possessed a much greater significance. It could have served as a central transport base, with lines of communication, capable of being used as a means of linking up rebel activities throughout the city, taking supplies, munitions or men wherever they were needed. Lack of numbers prevented this plan from being carried out, for the small garrisons were largely isolated at the various points. Yet when the Citizen Army contribution to the

1916 Rising is assessed, a leading place must be given to the Stephen's Green operation, for here the Citizen Army had control. The garrison consisted of one hundred and four men and fourteen women or roughly half the total number which the Citizen Army had in the field.

Michael Mallin, who commanded this Citizen Army force, took over the Green on Easter Monday. A contemporary account speaks of this as 'one of the boldest act of the rebels' and talks of 'the systematic way in which they set about digging themselves in'. Outposts attached to the Stephen's Green command carried out subsidiary operations. Captain R. McCormack seized Harcourt Street railway station. Lieutenant M. Kelly held the railway bridge over the Grand Canal, while Captain John O'Neill took the railway bridge overlooking the South Circular Road. These flanking operations were intended to prevent interference with the process of 'digging in' at Stephen's Green. Later the men at the smaller posts helped to swell the Stephen's Green garrison.

James Stephens, in his *The Insurrection in Dublin*, gives an eye-witness account of the occupation. Civilians were bundled through the gates of the Green and men set to work immediately to dig trenches. Passing motors and carts were commandeered. Drivers were ordered at the point of the gun to bring in their vehicles where required, so that barriers were formed. Stephens speaks of an attempt to overturn a tram-car at the corner of Leeson Street to make a barricade. But this failed. In the Green itself, a first-aid centre and kitchen were established by a group of women under the command of Madeleine ffrench-Mullen.

Mallin selected houses round the Green for his riflemen to occupy. A man with a revolver in one hand and a hatchet in the other came out on the roadway and selected houses he wanted for his sharp-shooters. He smashed in the windows of the houses he selected and placed his men in the posts. While all this was being done with a garrison of around a hundred, there were hundreds of people, many of them hostile, gathered at as safe a distance as they dared. But the quickness, the resolution and the strategy of this Citizen Army force kept the Green in their hands.

If Mallin had had the men in sufficient strength to seize the Shelbourne Hotel he might have dominated the entire district. But he could not do this. From high buildings surrounding the Green, military snipers were able to take pot shots at the men who had not much protection. Casualties were fairly heavy. Mallin himself had a bullet hole drilled through his hat. The glittering cap badge – the Red Hand emblem of the union – drew the fire. He tore this badge off and gave it as a memento to Madeleine ffrench-Mullen. By Tuesday morning the British soldiers were able to get machine-guns placed in the Shelbourne Hotel from which they could rake the Green. It became imperative to evacuate this position so Mallin decided to take possession of the adjoining Royal College of Surgeons, which made an admirable headquarters. Countess Markievicz – who was second-in-command – took a leading part in the occupation in the college. It was an operation of no little skill and danger to evacuate the Green, to bring along the wounded in the charge of the first-aid girls, for everyone had to run the gauntlet of snipers as they entered the building. Bullets were striking the stonework around the entrance and one man was shot dead.

An early casualty on the roof of the college was that of Doherty who was hit by a full charge of machine-gun bullets and bled profusely. Although he was very badly wounded, Joe Connolly – afterwards chief of the Dublin fire brigade – managed to get him down through a skylight and away to hospital so that his life was saved. But he lost an eye and the use of one hand. Mallin soon saw that he would have to take the offensive if he wanted to hold the enemy in check. And it became increasingly necessary to raid for food and other supplies. He planned to seize Sibley's, a bookshop on the corner and to set fire to adjoining buildings which the military might occupy. Six men were given the task of raiding houses on the north side of the Green. There was a plan to attack the United Services Club which was a snipers' nest, but this would have meant advancing in the face of machine-gun fire which was not practicable without a counter-barrage.

Six men were chosen for a desperate sortie on Tuesday. They had to rest before they set out, for none of them had slept since the previous day. Madame Markievicz – dressed in an old tunic of Michael Mallin which she wore all the week – acted as guide. The party had to proceed along a plank stretched from the College of Surgeons' window to the Turkish Baths, with a thirty-foot drop underneath. Most of them, including the countess, went across on their hands and knees, but James O'Shea – a Citizen Army stalwart since the 1913 days – carried a big sledgehammer, a rifle and a load of bombs, so he had to run across. Connolly had many a time talked and written about house-to-house fighting. This method was practised by the Stephen's Green garrison with marked success. They entered houses, knocked a hole through the wall with the sledgehammer and proceeded onward cautiously. They were always careful not to leave a clear space or passage behind them along which the enemy could fire. The immediate object of their house-to-house fighting was to get food. They reached a pastry cook's shop which proved a treasure. But private houses also yielded results. Sometimes they found friends, as when two servant girls noticed the Rosary beads twined round the wrist of a Citizen Army man.

'Look!' said one of the girls, pointing to the beads. 'They're Catholics and I believe they're Irish!'

'What did you think we were?' cried the man indignantly.

'The lady told us you were Germans!'

When that misunderstanding was cleared up and they discovered they lived near each other, there was no difficulty about getting food.

Captain R. McCormack had charge of a party which succeeded in boring its way through about twenty houses and proceeded to South King Street. Margaret Skinnider – a member of the garrison – was severely wounded when she led an attack on an enemy outpost near the Russell Hotel. She was brought back to the College of Surgeons with blood pouring from her wounds. Before they could be dressed, her thick coat had to be cut away. Fred Ryan was killed during this sortie. Food supplies were the biggest problem. Women commandeered food from local shops and brought it in. This was a dangerous task for sometimes they were followed by yelling mobs. Lily Kempson held up a bread cart at the point of a revolver and brought it to the Green. Mary

Hyland did the same with a milk cart. Some of the women – including Elizabeth O'Farrell and Julia Grenan – made a perilous journey to the GPO in search of food. To do this they had to circumvent the military barriers and snipers in their path.

On Tuesday morning Chris Caffrey and another girl got through to the GPO and explained the position to Connolly. Sacks of bread and a supply of tinned food were issued to them. But they were unable to manage the heavy loads. Francis Sheehy-Skeffington, who was outside the GPO, saw their plight and, calling two newsboys, gave them money and asked them to carry the sacks. They kept their bargain and landed the food at the College of Surgeons. The same evening Chris Caffrey set off again with a dispatch from Mallin to Connolly, but failed to get through. She was detained by the military for some hours and had to eat her dispatch to get rid of it. But she managed to get back safely. These sorties for food, house-to-house fighting and the task of holding the College of Surgeons, constituted the main operations.

During the week the College of Surgeons was under continuous machine-gun fire, while enemy snipers held posts around the building. But the garrison stood firm and continued their own flanking movements. By Thursday, communications with the centre were impossible as O'Connell Street was in flames. The spirit in the college was one of calm confidence. W.P. Partridge – a man of firm and resolute character – used to recite the Rosary each evening. Madame Markievicz wrote some verses, which give an impression of the scene within the college on these occasions. One verse reads:

> The great hall fades away into the gloom
> As tremendous night falls slowly from above
> Merging us each in its tender love;
> One shadow marching towards one doom.
> On our rough altar, white flowers shine and bloom
> Intensifying dusky waves that move
> Around the tall, black cross.

The College of Surgeons was one of the last posts to surrender. That event took place on Sunday 30 April, at 2 p.m. Rumours of the surrender at the GPO had circulated the previous day. Mallin had the final order issued by Pearse, with Connolly's signed agreement for the men in the Stephen's Green command. The fight for the Green was over – for a time. Mallin called in his outposts, the first sign of disaster. The fighting spirit was still strong. Men wanted to hold out or to fight their way to the hills. Mallin discussed the position with Madame Markievicz, Partridge and McCormack. At first there was a disposition to regard the surrender order as an enemy trick. But later they were convinced that it was genuine. The leaders urged that they must continue to obey orders whatever the consequences and act to the end as a disciplined force. This decision was the hardest of the whole week. Mallin spoke to the garrison saying that he knew he would be shot but he would accept his fate as an Irishman should. No one wanted to take the first step in the surrender. But the sturdy Captain McCormack went up to the roof, lowered the tri-colour and put up the white flag. He had proved himself as a fighter. Now he proved that he could take defeat.

Many thought they would all be shot and buried in the big quick-lime graves which, it was said, were waiting for them. There was a feeling of general despondency when Captain McCormack told them that, if he were one of those to be shot, he would call for three cheers for the Irish Republic! At that moment this seemed very far away, but it had the effect of raising their spirits. If anyone had told them then that their stand had helped to bring the Republic within reach they would have dismissed the notion as a good-natured attempt to comfort them. But it was the literal truth.

They marched out of the College of Surgeons to the lower Castle yard. From the Castle they were marched to Richmond barracks. Here Mallin was separated from the rest and they did not see him again. But they remembered their commandant, the gay companion of so many Citizen Army route marches, who had so often played a tune for them on his flute. He had played a tune in Irish history that will not be forgotten. He was sentenced to death and shot. Madame Markievicz was also sentenced to death but this was commuted to imprisonment for life. It was a desolate time for them all, though the countess met it, as always, with a spirit of gay defiance. She cared little whether she lived or not when her friends were dying. Others of the garrison received long sentences. Many could have escaped at the end if they wished. Their stand indicated the spirit and fighting quality of the Citizen Army.

The Citizen Army was represented in practically every garrison during the Easter Week fighting. It had forty members in the GPO where its great leader, James Connolly, was in command. But, apart from Stephen's Green, the occupation of the City Hall and the fighting in adjacent outposts was the only other operation carried out substantially by Citizen Army men and women. The City Hall was a tiny affair, in numbers, as compared with Stephen's Green. There were, in fact, only ten men and ten women forming the garrison of the City Hall though – on the Monday night – when they were hard pressed, Connolly sent eight men from the GPO as a reinforcement, with the message that men were scarce everywhere and they were to hold on as best they could. The leader of this reinforcement was George Norgrove. He had two daughters in the City Hall garrison, Annie and Emily. The latter afterwards married John Hanratty, commandant of the Citizen Army during the Civil War period. Norgrove also had a son in the GPO.

Seán Connolly – who commanded the City Hall detachment – first led the attack at noon at the gate of Dublin Castle. An armed policeman and a sentry barred the way. Connolly ordered the policeman aside but he sprang forward to close the gate. So Connolly fired and the policeman fell dead. Six Citizen Army men dashed forward to capture the guardroom and the guards fled. The six men were: Tom Kane, Philip O'Leary, Tom Daly, George Connolly, James Seerey and Christopher Brady. This audacious attempt to bottle up the British forces in the Castle succeeded at first, for they remained for some hours in undisputed possession of the guardroom and enjoyed the meal which the guards had left cooking on the fire. Three guards were taken prisoner and tied up with their puttees. This action created panic in the Castle as was revealed at the later Commission of Inquiry and it has been said that the Castle itself could have been taken. With the few men available this was plainly impossible. The only purpose in seizing the guardroom was to impede the British forces and prevent interference with the occupation of the City Hall.

Leaving his six men at the Castle entrance, Seán Connolly led his main body into the City Hall where they took control. After placing his garrison, Seán Connolly went out on the roof where he was killed almost at once by a sniper's bullet fired from the clock tower at the Castle.

Soon, in response to frantic telephone messages, troops were pouring into the city from the Curragh. A cavalry column numbering 1,600 arrived at Kingsbridge, a composite battalion of infantry came from Belfast, with an additional 1,000 from the Curragh. All available troops from Portobello, Richmond and Royal barracks were ordered to proceed at once to the Castle. They were well equipped with armaments and a battery of four eighteen-pounders was ordered from Athlone. The impressive list of soldiery is given in *The Administration of Ireland* by 'I.O.' (Philip Allen) published in 1920. Evidently this was compiled from official sources. After staying in the guardroom for some hours, the six men pulled aside a press which revealed a door opening onto Castle Street. Left to their own resources – after Seán Connolly's death – they decided to retire, as otherwise they would have been trapped. They proceeded to Lahiff's shop, going along Castle Street. Here Kane hid the membership roll of the Citizen Army in the chimney of a disused room. He found it there, quite safe, a year after the Rising.

Almost at once the City Hall was subject to a terrific bombardment that seemed as if it would shake the building to pieces. Showers of plaster and bricks fell inside. A British nurse in the Castle hospital wrote an account, in *Blackwood's Magazine* (Dec. 1916), of the un-ending stream of soldiers pouring into the Castle yard. The nurses were warned not to be alarmed at the noise as machine-guns were going into action. Dr Kathleen Lynn and Helena Molony – two women members of the garrison – moved towards a window. At first they thought it must be raining outside. Then they realised that it was a rain of bullets. The tiny handful of civilian troops, who had never been under fire before, withstood this attack for hours. Eventually, when the building seemed to be rocking, an overwhelming body of soldiers rushed in with fixed bayonets. By this time it was quite dark though a beam of moonlight cut through the shadows. An officer with a revolver called upon the garrison to surrender and Dr Kathleen Lynn stepped forward and surrendered for the handful of women in the room. The men, blackened and weary, were on the roof or at the windows. Of the original ten men in the garrison, three were killed and two wounded. Of the eight sent as reinforcement, one was killed. For hours this little body of smoke-grimed men had kept an army equipped with machine-guns and grenades at bay. They stood in the path of the first onrush of British troops just as did the five Volunteers at Mount Street bridge. The City Hall contingent made just such an epic fight.

The same tenacity and determination to stand against odds was shown by other small groups of Citizen Army men in the vicinity. The *Evening Mail* office – close to the City Hall had a garrison of five men. Four of these were Citizen Army and one was a Volunteer. The British VAD nurse writes in her account: 'In the evening (Monday) we watched the men in the yard bombing the office of the *Evening Mail*. The noise was terrific but eventually the building was successfully stormed.' But although machine-guns and bombs were in action against the tiny garrison, the place was not taken until the early hours of Tuesday morning. Three men were at the Nicholas Street graveyard and three more were at the Synod House post. Fierce fighting also took place at the Henry and James' store, held by a small Citizen Army detachment consisting of seven. Here a boy named Charlie Darcy was shot dead on the roof, by a military sniper. He had given his days and nights to army activities at Liberty Hall in a spirit of devoted self-sacrifice. These small posts were held in connection with the City Hall command. Their purpose was to obstruct or impede British army activities from the Castle and so to enable the insurgents to dig themselves in everywhere. They carried out this purpose in spite of the overwhelming force flung against them. It was estimated, soon after the Rising, that Brigadier-General Lowe had an effective force of 4,500 men, when troops arrived from the Curragh. The odds were far too great to permit a military victory on the rebel side, but these Citizen soldiers left a record and a memory of which Dublin has a right to be proud.

One cannot conclude this brief sketch of Citizen Army military activities in Easter Week without a reference to the army's brave and resolute leader, James Connolly. In his final manifesto Pádraig Pearse said: 'If I were to mention names of individuals, my list would be a long one. I will name only that of Commandant-General James Connolly commanding the Dublin division. He lies wounded but is still the guiding brain of our resistance …' Although his ankle was shattered, Connolly insisted on staying in the firing line. He was one of the last men to be executed, the other being Seán MacDiarmada, a fellow signatory of the Proclamation. These executions were carried out in violation of a pledge given by Mr Asquith. Connolly was unable to walk so he was propped up in a chair and shot.

After the executions and imprisonments, a wave of resurgence swept the country. This found fitting expression in the verses of Maeve Cavanagh, a trusted friend of James Connolly whom he had described as 'the poetess of the revolution'. She was an active member of the Citizen Army and a dispatch carrier in Easter Week. Her finest collection of poems *A Voice of Insurgency* was published on Christmas Eve, 1916. In 'Éire – After the Storm', she wrote:

> Defiant still, though scarred by War's fierce passion,
> In glorious unrepentance Ireland stands,
> Her ruins stark, repelling all compassion,
> Her broken sword still clasping in her hands.
> Failure? Not so – no sigh her great heart troubles,
> No tears her brave eyes mar – Hope still reigns there.
>
> This day and hence, her lust for Freedom doubles,
> E'en now she stoops to build up and prepare.

Though round her feet her martyred dead are lying,
See from their blood her soul new life drinks in
Stronger she'll rise from this last crucifying
In Fate's despite she'll fight again and WIN!

The Dublin men and women who fought in the Stephen's Green garrison, in the City Hall, in the GPO and all other outposts of freedom during Easter Week had planted something that was destined to bear fruit.

THE BATTLE OF ASHBOURNE
by Colonel J.V. Lawless

THE CENTRING OF the fighting in the city, as described by others, tended at the time to obscure anything which happened outside the city, and in consequence the action of the Fingal Volunteers at Ashbourne has not been so well known or appreciated as the very effective part that it was of the whole Rising. The following account of 'Ashbourne' is written as a purely military study; apology being made for the inclusion of tedious statistics and map references, as being necessary for the understanding of the action from this viewpoint.

Previous to Ashbourne, the column, about forty-five strong, all mounted on bicycles, had been engaged during the week in a series of lightning raids upon RIC barracks and communications in the area, with the threefold purpose of collecting some much needed arms, hampering enemy movements, and drawing some enemy attention away from the hard-pressed Volunteers fighting in the city. Originally we had had twenty more men, but this number had, on orders from James Connolly, been sent to the city from our camp, at the time at Finglas. These twenty also gave a good account of themselves in the fighting in O'Connell Street and the Mendicity Institution, where one of their number was killed.

It may be well before proceeding to the description of the actual fight, to give some kind of picture of the organisation and equipment of the Volunteer unit, so that the reader may more readily grasp the significance of later details. The Volunteers of North County Dublin, or Fingal as the territory is known, constituted up to 1916, the 5th battalion of the Dublin brigade, but like most Volunteer units of the time was never near battalion strength. In fact, if my memory serves me right, I think the area was only able to muster a strength of about one infantry company at best, at that period. Due, however, to the confusion of cancelled orders on Easter Sunday and other causes, little more than half the numbers answered the mobilisation call by reporting; which meant that we had there just so many individuals and no useful tactical formation.

On detachment on Tuesday from our camp at Finglas of twenty men to the city, as already mentioned, and the arrival in camp of five or six stragglers from city units, the urgent need for reorganisation of our force arose. We had also, at this time, received orders from Connolly at the GPO that our activities were to take the form of diverting enemy attentions and troops if possible, from the city, and a rapid survey of the situation resulted in throwing overboard the old British infantry organisation, upon which we had been trained, and the adoption of a scheme made to fit the numbers available and the tactical requirements of our mission.

The arrangement adopted, which incidentally was quite sound from a tactical viewpoint, was to divide the entire force into four more or less equal sections of ten to twelve men, each section under the command of an officer, and with the remaining four senior officers constituting the headquarters and command staff.

The operation procedure adopted at the same time was that each day one section was detailed for foraging duty with the job of protecting the camp during the day and night, and also locating and procuring food supplies for the column. The remaining three sections, proceeding on the daily raid or other mission, moved always with the sections so spaced and detailed that the leading section constituted the advance guard, and was responsible for all the duties of such. The rearmost section was similarly arranged as a rearguard, while the commanding officer with his staff moved normally with the main body, which was the section between. The sections changed over duties daily.

The commander and staff of the column were a fortunate combination, and were largely, if not entirely, responsible for the successful exploits of the unit, including the Ashbourne battle. Thomas Ashe, the commander, was a fine physical specimen of manhood, courageous and high-principled. Something of a poet, painter and dreamer, he was perhaps in military matters somewhat unpractical. Early in the week, however, we had the very good fortune to be joined by a few stragglers from a city battalion amongst whom was Dick Mulcahy. Mulcahy was known already to the other members of the staff, and it was soon apparent to everyone that his was the mind necessary to plan and direct operations. Cool, clear-headed and practical, and with a personality and tact that enabled him to virtually control the situation without in any way undermining Ashe's prestige as the commander. My father, Frank Lawless, acted as quartermaster, and, because of his wide local knowledge of the country and the people, was of great help in arranging operations and movements, as well as the essential matter of supplies. Dr Richard Hayes was the other member of the staff and he also, in addition to his medical duties, was a valuable voice in the staff councils, and was always available for intelligence duties and the like. To come, however, to the engagement at Ashbourne we must skip other incidents from the mobilisation on Easter Monday to the morning of the Friday of that week.

The column had bivouacked late on Thursday night at a derelict farmhouse at Borranstown, abut three miles south of Garristown; and that evening, or some time during the night, information had come in that considerable bodies of troops were preparing to move from Athlone to Dublin per MGW railway. It was, therefore, decided that it was our job to cut the railway line, and thereafter to harass the troops which might arrive at the breach in the line. With this object in view, the column left the bivouac area between ten and eleven o'clock on

Friday morning, the immediate objective being the MGW railway line beyond Batterstown, about twelve miles away.

As we moved out that Friday morning at about 10.30 a.m., it occurred to someone that the Ashbourne RIC barracks, which was on our route, might not have been evacuated, as others had been as the result of our raids. Scouts sent out returned with word that the barracks was in a state of defence, and that a barricade was in the course of erection across the main road in front of the barracks. The advance guard, therefore, moved carefully forward, and the two men forming the point of the advance guard challenged and, after a slight scuffle, captured two RIC men who were working upon the barricade, and disarmed them, the prisoners being marched to the rear where they remained under guard. The remainder of the advance guard section, leaving their bicycles stacked on the by-road north of the crossroads, took up a position along the ditch south of the main road and in front of the barracks, while Ashe climbing up onto the road and in full view, called on the police to surrender, to which they replied by firing on him, though fortunately without effect. Up to this time the other two sections (the 4th section having remained in camp at Borranstown) had remained halted on the by-road about three or four hundred yards north of the crossroads, and were unaware of what was happening when the firing started.

About this time instructions were received from Ashe that the 2nd and 3rd sections were to take cover along the ditches facing the rear of the barracks, and await further orders. Accordingly the two sections, one of which was my own command, moved into the ditch shown at 'A' on the accompanying sketch, having stacked our bicycles on the road adjoining. We observed from this position that the barracks had no windows facing north, and therefore there was no purpose in opening fire from our position; but the barracks was under continual fire in front from our first section who were firing at a range of less than one hundred yards. The police inside were replying to the fire through loopholes of the iron-shuttered windows, and for about half-an-hour showed no sign of capitulating, though it was afterwards evident that their morale was considerably shaken from the first burst of fire. An

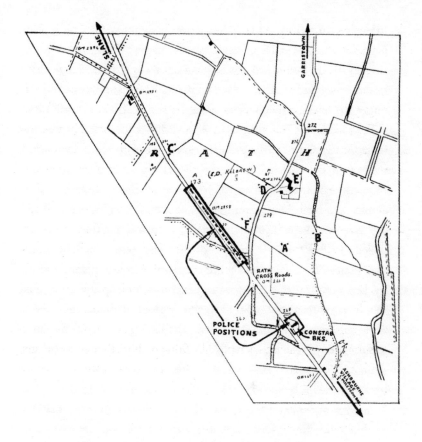

attempt was then made to throw one of our two homemade grenades at the barracks in the hope of breaking the door, which though locally splintered by bullets still held firm. This, however, fell short of its objective and exploded in the garden in front, doing no damage other than to the flowers and vegetables, but the noise of the explosion was apparently all that was needed to finally break down the resistance; for shortly afterwards a white flag or handkerchief fluttered from a window indicating the willingness to surrender.

Before, however, the beleaguered garrison had time to march out and hand up their arms, a new factor entered the situation, which encouraged them to change their minds and continue their resistance. This was the arrival of some twenty-four motor cars laden with police reinforcements.

It will be remembered that Nos 2 and 3 sections were still in the position 'A', and, not having received any further instructions, were more or less in the dark as to what was going on. I might here remark that the country around is entirely flat, and the high banks and thick hedges prevent any extended view beyond the length of a field except along the main road. The first indication we had that something unforeseen had happened was when we heard a heavy burst of fire from the north-west side of the crossroads, some of which passed in our direction. Going towards the crossroads to investigate, I met two very scared Volunteers of No. 1 section running along the ditch towards me. Their story was, when I could get them to talk coherently, that they had been detailed to watch the main road north-west of the cross, but becoming more interested in what was going on at the barracks behind them, they never noticed the arrival of the police reinforcements until the first car was within fifty yards of the crossroads. They then fired their rifles at the leading car, and one of the rifles having jammed (a Martini Carbine), they fled towards us to inform us that 'hundreds of police had arrived'. Actually I believe the number was about sixty or seventy, with three officers; one county inspector and two district inspectors.

The situation was definitely serious, the surprise of our force being complete, and presumably superior enemy forces in close contact. Knowing that Ashe and Mulcahy, who were with No. 1 section in front of the barracks, would by now know as much or more of the situation than we did, I moved the two sections into the ditch at 'B' facing west, and prepared to abandon our bicycles on the by-road now facing us, and to fight a retiring action eastward. A runner having been sent in the meantime to get in touch with No. 1 section on the south-east side of the barracks, and having failed to return, I then went on this mission myself, leaving the No. 2 section commander in charge of my section.

I had not got very far when I noticed Mulcahy, who was evidently looking for us. He was then about the original position we had just left at 'A'. Hailing him, he waved his arm to indicate that he required our men to advance to the by-road where our bicycles lay, and headed in that direction himself. The intervening field was ploughed, and we had been observing the strike of stray bullets in the dry clay. Nevertheless, the example of Mulcahy walking unscathed across it encouraged us to move across at once at the double and without seeking the shelter of the ditches.

Arriving on the by-road, Ashe appeared and, after a hurried consultation with him, Mulcahy assured us that the police had not a chance of success, and that we were going to rout or capture the entire force. His words had the immediate effect of inspiring confidence and making us feel ashamed of our previous apprehensiveness. He proceeded to outline the plan of attack, briefly summarising the situation, which was as follows: it seemed that the police had been unaware of our presence until surprised by the fire of the two men at the crossroads, which was followed very quickly by fire from the remainder of the section at the barracks. Jumping from the cars, which pulled up on the left of the road at intervals of ten to twenty yards, they sought what cover was available in their immediate vicinity, and were mostly in the deep ditch along the north-east side of the main road, and as far as the cars extended. Some few did in fact seek a fire position in the drain cuttings of the bank on the opposite side of the road, but these were all killed or wounded in the early stages of the fight.

The position then was that, though we had been surprised by their unexpected arrival, the police were equally surprised by our presence there; but whereas we had now a fair idea of their numbers and position, they were quite in the dark concerning our positions and strength.

Mulcahy seems to have been the first to grasp this fact, and his plan of attack was to make full use of the morale factor by driving home a vigorous assault, with all possible force, from the vicinity of the crossroads, and encouraging the impression in the enemy mind of superior force on our side by fire from the rear. He told me that he was taking No. 3 section, reinforced by half the men of my section, to support the main attack of the No. 1 section from the crossroads, and that I, with the remaining six men of my section, would be conducted by Ashe to the rear of the police position on the main road, where we would not disclose our position until the main attack was made. Our job was to cut off any attempt at an enemy retreat, and for this purpose one of my men carried the one remaining canister grenade, with the idea of blowing up any car that tried to pass. The 4th section of our force, which had been left in camp that morning, had been sent for, but up to this time, about 13.30 hours, had not arrived.

We proceeded under Ashe's guidance to our position, marked 'C' on sketch, in the rear of the last police car on the main road moving in cover of the hedges north of the road, and here Ashe left us, returning the way we had come. The place we now found ourselves in was the junction of a deep ditch bounding the north-east side of the main road, and a ditch running at right angles to it, the rearmost police car being about seventy yards from here in the direction of the crossroads.

Having noticed a motor cycle standing on the opposite side of the road, I then observed a man in civilian dress crouched near it in the hedge, and was about to fire on him when he saw me, and stood up with his hands raised. He said his name was Quigley, and that he had been trying to get in touch with us, to warn us of the coming of the police convoy. Actually I did not believe him, and somehow, perhaps because he was a very tall man, I thought he was connected with the police, but there was a doubt in the matter. I told him to leave his machine where it was, and to clear off across the fields. I afterwards learned that Mr Quigley was the county surveyor of Meath, and a good nationalist, and supporter of the Volunteer movement. Having posted the men in what vantage points there were, I then decided that it would be a good idea to reconnoitre the opposite side of the road and, crossing over some little way back, I came up in the field on the other side to a point opposite our position. I found, however, that the bank was so high and steep from that side that it did not offer a good fire position, but I had satisfied myself that there was no enemy on that side.

All this time there was sporadic firing between our men around the crossroads and the police, and when I rejoined my section I found that one of them had received a bad scalp wound, and another man (incidentally the man with the grenade), had taken him back to the dressing station. This left me only four men with myself, and as nearly an hour had elapsed since our arrival in the position, and there was still no sign of the promised attack, I was again beginning to get rather anxious. One of the men with me was a very young lad and had only a shotgun, so I put him to watch the main road in our rear, that is north-westwards, while I with the others began re-arranging our positions with a view to bringing our fire to bear on the police positions. While doing this, another man had his clothing perforated by a bullet, which convinced us that our position was observed by the enemy, and so we decided to open up on our own account. Lying on the roadside I was sheltered by a low bank between which and the high bank with the hedge on it, some police were sheltering lower down the road. I was, therefore, able to bring an enfilading fire to bear on this, while the others raked the deep ditch behind the hedge, where most of the police were.

The act of opening fire was a great relief from the continual wait-ing, and we became emboldened to creep closer to the police and so get better effect from our fire. A bullet strike to the road in front of my face, however, blinded me with sand and I had to get back to get my eye cleaned out, one other man keeping up occasional shots. Suddenly the man I had put to watch the rear called out that men were advancing upon us from behind along the roadside, and were then almost upon us. Running along the bottom of the ditch towards him I peered over the edge of the bank to see the flesh colour of faces through the bushes, of men creeping rapidly and purposefully towards us. Leaning over backwards I fired my rifle at the faces but slipped down before I could fire again. A volley from this party then raked our position, but without doing any damage and to which we replied, firing as rapidly as possible. Suddenly I made the sad discovery that my rifle ammunition was all expended and the others were nearly as badly off. Only one man still had good supply, but as his rifle was a 9m/m Mauser, he could be of no help in this way to the rest of us. I was, however, also armed with a service Webley revolver, and for this I had about twenty or thirty rounds which I proceeded to use up, instructing the others to clear out down the ditch in the direction we had come, while I and the man with the Mauser kept up the fire to cover the retreat.

It should be remembered up to this point we had seen no one except the faces through the bushes, though bullets were burrowing into the banks around us pretty thickly. One of the lads moving back down the ditch then shouted that someone was moving towards us on the field side of the road ditch, so running back to him I peered cautiously over the brink of the ditch, just in time to see a pair of boots disappear behind a furze bush about sixty or seventy yards up along the road ditch. I emptied my revolver a couple of times towards this bush, urging the others to hurry. Finding they had halted I went to the leading man, to find that he had come to a gateway crossing the ditch, and was nervous to expose himself to cross this obstacle, so jumping up myself and calling on the others to follow I dived headlong into the ditch on the other side. No one else followed, though I called on them to come on, and suddenly the firing stopped and there was a lot of confused shouting from which I concluded that the position had been rushed and the other men captured. As my ammunition was now all expended I couldn't do anything about it anyway, so I ran down the ditch, taking the first ditch which turned to the right and so made my way back to the by-road from where we had started. (At 'D' on sketch.)

Here I met the No. 3 section commander who had received a slight wound in the eye, and had come back to the dressing station at the house 'E'. I got five or ten rounds of rifle ammunition from him and in consultation with Dr Hayes and Ashe who came along just then, we decided, with the help of another man who was further up the road, to move the bicycles and Dr Hayes' car, which lined the road from within a few yards of the crossroads, back as far as the house at 'E' so that we might have some chance of saving them in the retreat which we thought was then inevitable.

Ashe proceeded towards the crossroads to order the retreat, and did in fact give the order, which was in the process of being carried out, when Mulcahy appeared on the scene. Being told by Dr Hayes what was afoot, he then informed us to our great surprise and my considerable discomfiture, that the force we had thought to be enemy reinforcements and exchanged shots with, were, in fact, our 4th section with my father, who had come up from the camp at Borranstown and were being conducted to our position at 'C' by himself, whose face in the bushes I had fired at.

It seemed that they had been equally at sea in the matter. Mulcahy knew that we should be about there, but owing to the lapse of time he could not count on what might have happened in the meantime, and our fire was so furious that they felt sure we must be an enemy group and could see them.

However, whether from the excellence of the cover or bad marksmanship, no one had been hit in the exchange, and Mulcahy rushed off after Ashe to have his retreat order countermanded. Apparently there had been considerable difficulty in getting the Volunteers out of their positions at the crossroads, owing to fire which was being kept up by the police, and fortunately as it happened, this had slowed up the business, so that when Mulcahy got there he was in time to get them all back in their original positions without our intention having been disclosed to the enemy. Moving on towards the crossroads myself, I found one of our men at a gateway on the right about the position 'F' having a duel with some police who apparently were in the ditch on the opposite side of the field. He had just then been wounded by a bullet through the forearm, so sending him back to get it dressed I took up the firing until, after a little while, there seemed to be no reply to my shots, when I returned to the cottage to try and borrow some more ammunition.

A man there, who had been left to guard the two prisoners captured in the beginning of the action, was helpful in this matter, and with ten more rounds in my magazine, I once more headed for the crossroads, accompanied by another man who was similarly circumstanced regarding ammunition.

I was again approaching the gateway through which I had previously been firing, and I think my attention must have concentrated on the road ahead, for the man following me shouted a warning and jumped for the cover of another gateway beside him. I got the fright of my life to see a policeman crouched on the bank of the ditch on my right, and about twenty yards from me. I had my rifle slung on my right shoulder, and there was no time to seek cover, so I realised somehow when I had got him covered that I should have been shot thrice over but for some reason, and then I noticed that he was standing up with his hands over his head. Calling on him to keep his hands up and come out on the road, I was further startled to hear a chorus of voices behind him in the ditch shouting: 'We Surrender'. With no little feeling of suspicion and fear of some surprise move, I called to the man behind me to keep them covered, while putting on a bold tone I ordered the police out on the road.

Eleven burly RIC men, a few of them wounded and all badly demoralised, lined up on the road. In reply to my question, they informed me that they had thrown away their rifles further up the field, but they had a plentiful supply of ammunition which was a Godsend to us just then.

We marched the prisoners back to the dressing station, where their wounds were attended to by Dr Hayes, and being relieved of their belts, ammunition pouches, etc., were left there under guard of two men, while I hastened towards the crossroads once more to convey the good news that the police were surrendering. I got as far as a point about fifteen yards from the main road where I found another of our men firing across the rear of the cottage on the right. He told me he had succeeded in getting one constabulary man who had tried to get through a window into the cottage, and he thought there were others in bushes above the cottage. With my fresh supply of ammunition I joined him in raking every possible bit of cover there, and then crept on, on my hands and knees, towards the main road.

It was difficult to attract the attention of our fellows who were firing up the main road from both sides of it, east of the crossroads; though I shouted to them that I wanted to come across. However, before I had decided to creep under their fire, I saw the fellows nearest me leaping across the hedge onto the main road, and running towards the police.

I noticed that they had their bayonets fixed, so rapidly flexing my own I doubled around the corner to meet an amazing sight.

In and out among the cars drawn up on the side of the road, and along the edge of the bank, and wedged into channel cuttings, were numerous dead and wounded police and drivers; while from out the ditch on the north-eastern side of the road, the remainder of the police were climbing and walking on to the road with their hands over their heads. My father with our 4th section was coming down the road towards us driving the police from along the ditch in front of them. The explanation of the final phase was as follows: when, during the incident of our firing upon each other around the position 'C', I had exposed myself to cross the gateway in the ditch, the Volunteers who were firing on us realised their mistake, and hastened to make themselves known to the other men who had been with me. I, however, having mistaken the significance of all the shouting, had run pretty fast, and Mulcahy realising that it was likely that I would convey a wrong report to the others, followed me, leaving the new section to occupy my old position.

When he had managed to make contact with Ashe and had the retreat order countermanded, he made his way by the fields on the south-western side of the main road, back to the section at 'C'. This section, leaving some men at 'C', then crossed the main road and moved down along the road ditch in the field where they were protected from the road by the high bank. Coming to a point about midway in the line of cars on the road, they could hear the officer commanding the police, County Inspector Smith, shouting at the police to get up and fight. He was standing on top of the bank on the opposite side of the road brandishing his revolver and reviling his men for their passivity. Climbing up the bank my father shot him down, but not before he had fired at and shot dead one of our men who was behind my father. Smith was undoubtedly a brave man, and the only one of the police who showed a fighting spirit. His death was the signal for a general collapse of the police resistance.

All that remained was to collect the arms, ammunition, and other items of equipment that were of use to us, and attend to the wounded, some of whom were in pretty bad shape. Ashe then paraded the remaining police under the one unwounded police officer who was left, and telling them they might return to their homes, he warned them of the consequences should any of them be found again in arms against us. Whereupon we returned to our camp of the night before and to well-earned food and rest, taking with us the captured arms and other material.

THE GPO
by Sceilg

FROM LIBERTY HALL near the Custom House came the first group to the GPO, James Connolly at their head, P.H. Pearse at his right, Joseph Mary Plunkett at his left; behind them a composite column of Volunteers and Citizen Army units, all now transformed into republican soldiers. Later, George Plunkett led about fifty men from Kimmage; from the north side came some twenty others under Frank Thornton. About one hundred and fifty men in all mobilised for general headquarters here, and their wide range of weapons constituted no negligible burden: rifles in some variety, sledgehammers, pickaxes, what not. Two drays followed with a further variety of rifles, shotguns, pikes, improvised bombs, while a cab came with additional war material. In due course came The O'Rahilly, with all the arms his car could carry: he had been to Limerick to call off the Rising, and, though returning with an aggravated and feverish cold, thus set out for the GPO when informed that the call to action had gone forth. From the beginning, more than half the entire garrison were urgently engaged in seizing surrounding posts; the others, in taking over the General Post Office, where the ordinary noon day duties for a bank holiday were in progress, and the public freely moving about their business.

In the post office, from the outset, we find five of the signatories of the Proclamation of the Republic: Thomas J. Clarke and Seán Mac-Dermott, as well as the three already mentioned: James Connolly, P.H. Pearse and Joseph Mary Plunkett. Naturally, we also found all the men busy with the internal defence and the general safeguarding of the building. Immediately on realising the situation, officials, civil servants, the public generally, women young and old, hastened outside, many of them considerably alarmed. Windows were smashed with rifle-butts and fortified, doors barricaded, all positions of note tested. In this, James Connolly's was the voice of command. As a party rushed upstairs, shots were heard, and a group of seven soldiers there, under a sergeant – but with no ammunition for their rifles – surrendered at once. A few policemen downstairs made a hasty exit with the others, while a lieutenant of the Royal Fusiliers, who had been making himself offensive, was tied up in a telephone box beside the Nelson Pillar. For the first day, graphic news of the preliminary activities was carried all over the city by those who happened to witness them, the most practical men exercising direction around the entrance to the GPO being Diarmuid Lynch – deeply involved in organising the Rising – and Diarmuid Ó Laoghaire.

By one o'clock, the Proclamation of the Republic was read aloud by P.H. Pearse – one of the most edifying documents associated with our struggle for national liberty: its chilling reception by those within earshot saddened the hearts of listeners and of spectators who longed for Irish freedom and appreciated all sincere striving for human liberty. It was posted both inside the building and outside, and its message deeply pondered:

Poblacht na hÉireann
The Provisional Government of the Irish Republic
To the People of Ireland.

Irishmen and Irishwomen: in the name of God and of the dead generations from whom she receives her old tradition of nationhood, Ireland, through us, summons her children to her flag, and strikes for her freedom.

Having organised her manhood through her secret revolutionary organisation, the Irish Republican Brotherhood, and through her open military organisations, the Irish Volunteers and the Irish Citizen Army, having patiently perfected her discipline, having resolutely waited for the right moment to reveal itself, she now seizes that moment and, supported by her exiled children in America and by her gallant allies in Europe, but relying in the first on her own strength, she strikes in full confidences of victory.

We declare the right of the people of Ireland to the ownership of Ireland, and to the unfettered control of Irish destinies, to be sovereign and indefeasible. The long usurpation of that right by a foreign people and government has not extinguished the right, nor can it be extinguished except by the destruction of the Irish people. In every generation the Irish people have asserted their right to national freedom and sovereignty; six times during the past three hundred years they have asserted it in arms. Standing on that fundamental right and again asserting it in arms in the face of the world, we hereby proclaim the Irish Republic as a Sovereign Independent State, and we pledge our lives and the lives of our comrades in arms to the cause of its freedom, of its welfare and of its exaltation among the nations.

The Irish Republic is entitled to, and hereby claims, the allegiance of every Irishman and Irishwoman. The Republic guarantees religious and civil liberty, equal rights and equal opportunities to all its citizens, and declares its resolve to pursue the happiness and prosperity of the whole nation and of all its parts, cherishing all the children of the nation equally, and oblivious of the differences carefully fostered by an alien government, which have divided a minority from the majority in the past.

Until our arms have brought the opportune moment for the establishment of a permanent National Government, representative of the whole people of Ireland and elected by the suffrages of all her men and women, the Provisional Government, hereby constituted, will administer the civil and military affairs of the Republic in trust for the people.

We place the cause of the Irish Republic under the protection of the Most High God, Whose blessing we invoke upon our arms, and we pray that no one who serves that cause will dishonour it by cowardice, inhumanity or rapine. In this supreme hour the Irish nation must, by its valour and discipline, and by the readiness of its children to sacrifice themselves for the common good, prove itself worthy of the august destiny to which it is called.

Signed on behalf of the Provisional Government:
Thomas J. Clarke, Seán MacDiarmada, Thomas MacDonagh,
P.H. Pearse, Éamonn Ceannt, James Connolly, Joseph Plunkett.

By this hour, the British had sent most of the available troops to the relief of Dublin Castle – from the Royal barracks, the Richmond barracks and Portobello – while a company of Lancers, in the pomp which they thought would confound the natives, was dispatched to the centre of the city. As they reached the Nelson Pillar from the Rotunda, Irish Volunteers on the roof and at the upper windows of the General Post Office prematurely opened fire, killing three of them and fatally wounding a fourth. The instructions were to withhold fire until the Lancers had come to the other end of the building, but – in the ardour of the hour – they were misunderstood, and so the Lancers, thus warned, swung round, with the valour of the race, and back towards the Rotunda as the second volley rolled out, never drawing rein until they reached their barracks after the 'Leopardstown Races', as the stampede was appropriately named – typical revival of 'the Races of Castlebar'. It was at this stage indeed that the Volunteer detachment from the Rathfarnham area reached the post office, past Jacob's, by Dame Street, College Street, Butt bridge, Lower Abbey Street and across the main thoroughfare to Prince's Street. 'Who are you?' cried a voice from the post office. Before entry can be obtained for them a lad of sixteen falls wounded on the pavement; and a Volunteer, wounded in the stomach, drops beside him. But they are soon admitted.

Inside, barricading and general preparations go on briskly, but not without inevitable accidents. Soon Liam Clarke has a most painful and dangerous face wound from a mishandled bomb. On the ground is another man with a badly gashed knee. 'Those windows,' says an ambulance man, bandaging up another Volunteer, 'have done us more damage then the entire British army.' But Cumann na mBan nurses and Volunteer ambulance men are already treating those in need of attention. Withal, the place steadily assumes ship-shape. Most of the men are in their ordinary attire, their arms of miscellaneous range; while a miniature munition factory is contrived for the repair of arms, the manufacture of bombs, and such kindred purposes as the distribution of ammunition. The commissariat also had due attention, and the pretty ample supplies on hand, to which the Hotel Metropole next door paid its contribution, are entrusted for preparation and administration to the good offices of Cumann na mBan.

In the interval, the occupation of other positions in the area went on apace. In Talbot Street, a strong barricade was erected, a tram car being used in its construction, while The O'Rahilly advised as to its defence. A tailor's shop on the second floor at the corner of North Earl Street had its windows mattressed while another tram in the street nearby was used as a barricade: with this post the name of the gentle Gerard Crofts is linked. The Ship restaurant, extending from Sackville Place to Lower Abbey Street is promptly occupied, and great rolls of *Irish Times* printing paper are among the materials used in erecting a formidable barricade from the Ship across Lower Abbey Street to J.J. Keating's cycle and motor factory beside the Royal Hibernian Academy and the rooms of the Celtic Literary Society. Hopkins and Hopkins at the southern side of this block – corner of Eden Quay and O'Connell Street – was taken over by Seamus Robinson with five men. Thus what may be called the whole Clery side of O'Connell Street from the Pillar to the bridge, is being occupied strategically while another party establishes itself over Kapp and Peterson's on the opposite or post office side of the street, and yet another nearer the bridge. Sniping parties among these had instructions to fire only on armed British troops approaching by Westmoreland Street, so an ammunition convoy, escorted by Lancers, was permitted to pass by Eden Quay, and held up only at Church Street bridge beside the Four Courts.

In the GPO, in time, a telephone connected the ground floor with the roof, so that all movements on the streets could be promptly reported. The operators were asked to be in readiness to erect an aerial over the wireless school when darkness permitted. J.J. Walsh, who had come from North Frederick Street with a score or more of the Hibernian rifles, sought to exploit the whole telegraphic system and, by representing himself as superintendent, transmit such information to the country as was thought desirable, while trying to obtain all that was feasible. More practical: an early code telegram was sent via Kenmare to Tim Ring at the post office, Knightstown, Valentia, conducted by his aunt; delivered thence to him at the neighbouring cable station and transmitted by him to New York as pre-arranged with Seán MacDermott. The message was to the effect that *John has been successfully operated on today*, and the cable was subsequently traced to Tim – to the detriment of the whole family – through a New York boast that news of the Rising had reached leaders there early Easter Monday through an obscure Kerry cable station. By 3 p.m., republican banners – green, white and amber – floated over the GPO. Hopes ran high in all areas at this stage, and rumours spread of promising responses even from places abroad. At night, wireless messages announced that Ireland proclaims Republic; but the arrangements courageously made in this direction were soon rendered inoperative. Meanwhile, came the viceroy's proclamation – generally regarded as a laughing stock:

> Where an attempt instigated and designed by the foreign enemies of our king and country to incite rebellion in Ireland, and thus endanger the safety of the United Kingdom, has been made by a reckless though small body of men, who have been guilty of insurrectionary acts in the City of Dublin.
>
> Now, we, Ivor Churchill, Baron Wimborne, Lord Lieutenant-General and Governor-General of Ireland, do hereby warn all His Majesty's subjects that the sternest measures are being, and will be, taken for the prompt suppression of the existing disturbances, and the restoration of order.
>
> And we do hereby enjoin all loyal and law-abiding citizens to abstain from any acts or conduct which might interfere with the action of the Executive Government and, in particular, we warn all citizens of the danger of unnecessarily frequenting the streets or public places or of assembling in crowds.
>
> *Given under our Seal, on the 24th Day of April, 1916. – Wimborne.*

In the city, early on Monday, looters – a truly degenerate class – had set to work, first by breaking plate-glass windows of confectioners' shops and stripping them of everything. It soon extended to boot shops, men, women and juveniles bursting through windows, and, though many of them brought scars and gashes, all freighted themselves with boot-wear while any such stock remained. The looting of the other shops followed until the Volunteers threatened the looters from the windows, even fired blank shots over their heads. Others rushed out and batoned them until they were cleared off, Seán MacDermott even limping across the street to implore them not to bring disgrace on the struggle for Irish liberty. In one of the toy shops looted, a fire soon broke out which required the attention of the brigade. The news, of course, was sent abroad that this rabble were the camp-followers and associates of the Irish Volunteers when, in reality, they had a liberal quota of England's 'separation allowance' folk, while the Volunteers – though placed in breweries, distilleries, hotels and like posts – came through the week's ordeal with immaculate hands. A non-Catholic police sergeant told a Donegal pastor as early as Easter Monday that the first thing the blood-thirsty Sinn Féiners did in Dublin was to seize the aged Archbishop Walsh on his way from his cathedral, knock him on the head and throw his dead body into a blazing cellar – before the eyes of his afflicted wife!

The headquarters garrison continued to fortify and equip their post in every feasible way. Seats, books, ledgers and such convenient lumber supplemented sand-bags to shield the open spaces; ammunition, preparations against possible gas attacks, revolvers, pikes, every available means of defence in the most appropriate and convenient place! On the ground floor, mattresses and beds were provided for the leaders; but sleep was rarely possible, sleeping draughts sometimes failing to induce it. Periodically in the beginning, the anxious leaders took counsel together while resting on barrels, boxes or other improvised seats. Here, as at every other post, the whizzing of bullets, the rattle of the machine-gun, the boom of artillery, assailed the ear from all directions and, to combatants as to non-combatants, the volume of distracting reverberation seemed to magnify, night and day.

Early on Tuesday, British machine-guns, backed by snipers, swept O'Connell Street and Beresford Place from Trinity College, Westmoreland Street, the fire brigade tower and the Custom House. From Tara Street also came heavy fire, directed rather on Liberty Hall while the military kept closing in; and, on Wednesday, heavier fire from the fire brigade station tower and the Custom House, as from the Tivoli Theatre, Burgh Quay, and from the British gunboat *Helga*. From the roof of the

Theatre Royal, Marlboro Street was swept along its whole length, while Abbey Street, Lower and Middle, was swept from the Custom House. At the Hibernian Bank, Lower Abbey Street, Captain Thomas Wafer of Enniscorthy died of terrible wounds, at the age of twenty-six, the place in which he fell being soon shrouded in flames. Menaced by encircling British troops, Seán Russell, Oscar Traynor and some sixty men at Fairview were withdrawn to the O'Connell Street area, where the posts at Hopkins and Hopkins and the opposite corner were lost. The strain, mental and physical, grows so desperate that a Volunteer at headquarters loses his balance, brandishes his gun, and threatens in a frenzy until Patrick Pearse has to have him placed under temporary restraint.

Flames continued to encroach more destructively, demanding more sleepless vigilance on the part of the entirely inadequate garrison. The story of Patrick O'Connor, who hastened from his brother's funeral at Rathmore, Kerry, to be received at the GPO Monday night by Patrick Pearse holding a lit candle, is typical of the average Volunteer's activities during the week. Later that night, he and some comrades crossed the street to Clery's. Tuesday, they spent largely in establishing lines of communication there, while on Wednesday they assisted the brigade in putting out fires in Clery's stables, Tyler's and adjacent buildings. Raging fires threatening their line of retreat on Thursday, they crossed Earl Street, and thence to Cathedral Place. Reconnoitring towards dawn, Friday morning, O'Connor made his way along Thomas' Lane, and never returned. Meanwhile, on the afternoon of Thursday, Patrick Pearse solemnly addressed the central garrison and, early next day, amplified his pronouncement in words which nobody could misunderstand:

Headquarters, Army of the Irish Republic,
General Post Office, Dublin.
28th April, 1916 (9.30 a.m.).

The forces of the Irish Republic which was proclaimed in Dublin on Easter Monday, 24th April, have been in possession of the central part of the capital since 12 noon, on that day. Up to yesterday afternoon, headquarters was in touch with all the main outlying positions, and, despite furious and almost continuous assaults by the British forces, all those positions were then still being held, and the commandants in charge were confident of their ability to hold them for a long time.

During the course of yesterday afternoon and evening, the enemy succeeded in cutting our communications with our other positions in the city, and headquarters is today isolated. The enemy has burnt down whole blocks of houses, apparently with the object of giving themselves a clear field for the play of artillery and field guns against us. We have been bombarded during the evening and night by shrapnel and machine-gun fire, but without material damage to our position, which is of great strength. We are busy completing arrangements for the final defence of headquarters and are determined to hold it while the building lasts.

I desire now, lest I may not have an opportunity later, to pay homage to the gallantry of the soldiers of Irish freedom, who have during the past four days been writing with fire and steel the most glorious chapter in the later history of Ireland. Justice can never be done to their heroism, to their discipline, to their gay and unconquerable spirit in the midst of peril and death. Let me, who has led them into this, speak in my own name, and in my fellow-commandant's names, and in the name of Ireland present and to come, their praise, and ask those who come after them to remember them.

For four days they have fought and toiled, almost without cessation, almost without sleep, and in the intervals of fighting they have sung songs of the freedom of Ireland. No man has complained, no man has asked 'Why?' Each individual has spent himself, happy to pour out his strength for Ireland and for freedom. If they do not win this fight, they will at least deserve to win it. But win it they will, although they may win it in death. Already they have done a great thing. They have redeemed Dublin from many shames and made her name splendid among the names of cities.

If I were to mention the names of individuals, my list would be a long one. I will name only that of Commandant-General James Connolly, commanding the Dublin division. He lies wounded, but is still the guiding brain of our resistance.

If we accomplish no more than we have accomplished, I am satisfied. I am satisfied that we have saved Ireland's honour. I am satisfied that we should have accomplished more, that we should have accomplished the task of enthroning, as well as proclaiming the Irish Republic as a sovereign state, had our arrangements for a simultaneous Rising of the whole country, with a combined plan as sound as the Dublin plan has proved to be, been allowed to go through on Easter Sunday. Of the fatal countermanding order which prevented those plans being carried out, I shall not speak further. Both Eoin MacNeill and we have acted in the best interests of Ireland. For my own part, as to anything I have done in this, I am not afraid to face the judgment of God or the judgment of posterity.

(Signed) P.H. PEARSE,
Commandant-General.
Commander-in-Chief of the Army of the Irish Republic
and President of the Provisional Government.

As a reflection of the mind of the commander-in-chief of the army of the Irish Republic, this was manifestly the beginning of the end. Later, the same day, however, the badly-wounded commandant-general, Dublin division, issued what was by contrast, a self-confident fighting address based manifestly on earlier information depicting a more hopeful general outlook. It read:

Army of the Irish Republic,
Headquarters, Dublin Command,
28th April, 1916.

To Soldiers:
This is the fifth day of the establishment of the Irish Republic, and the flag of our country still floats from the most important buildings in Dublin, and is gallantly protected by the officers and Irish soldiers in arms throughout the country. Not a day passes without seeing fresh postings of Irish soldiers eager to do battle for the old cause. Despite the utmost vigilance of the enemy, we have been able to get information telling us how the manhood of Ireland, inspired by our splendid action, are gathering to offer up their lives, if necessary, in the same holy cause. We are here hemmed in because the enemy feels that in this building is to be found the heart and the inspiration of our great movement.

Let me remind you of what you have done. For the first time in seven hundred years the flag of a free Ireland floats triumphantly in Dublin city. The British army, whose exploits we are forever having dinned into our ears, which boasts of having stormed the Dardanelles and the German lines on the Marne, behind their artillery and machine-guns are afraid to advance to the attack or storm any position held by our forces. The slaughter they suffered in the first few days has totally unnerved them, and they dare not attempt again an infantry attack on our positions.

Our commandants around us are holding their own. Commandant Daly's splendid exploit in capturing Linenhall barracks we all know. You must know also that the whole population, both clergy and laity, of this district are united in his praise. Commandant MacDonagh is established in an impregnable position, reaching from the walls of Dublin Castle to Redmond's Hill, and from Bishop Street to Stephen's Green. In Stephen's Green, Commandant Mallin holds the College of Surgeons, one side of the square, a portion of the other side, and dominates the whole Green, with all its entrances and exits.

Commandant de Valera stretches in a position from the Gas Works to Westland Row, holding Boland's Bakery, Boland's Mills, the Dublin and South-Eastern railway and dominating Merrion Square. Commandant Kent holds the South Dublin Union and Guinness' buildings to Marrowbone Lane, and controls James' Street and district. On two occasions the enemy effected a lodgment and were driven out with great loss.

The men of North County Dublin are in the field, having occupied all the police barracks in the district, destroyed all the telegraph system on the Great Northern railway up to Dundalk, and are operating against the trains of the Midland and Great Western. Dundalk itself has sent two hundred men to march on Dublin, and in other parts of the North our forces are active and growing. In Galway, Captain Mellows, fresh from his escape from an Irish prison, is in the field with his men. Wexford and Wicklow are strong, while Cork and Kerry are acquitting themselves creditably. (And we have every confidence that our allies in Germany and kinsmen in America are straining every nerve to hasten matters on our behalf.)

As you know, I was wounded twice yesterday, and am unable to move about, but have got my bed moved into the firing line and, with the assistance of your officers, will be as useful to you as ever. Courage, boys, we are winning; and, in the hour of our victory, let as not forget the splendid women who have everywhere stood by us and cheered us on. Never had man or woman a grander cause, never was a cause more grandly served.

(Signed) JAMES CONNOLLY,
Commandant-General, Dublin Division.

All that need be added here to these pretty full details is the graphic and sympathetic picture which a popular priest, since dead, has left of the week's activities in the GPO area, and the ultimate rescue of the bulk of the wounded before the evacuation and subsequent surrender:

My first visit to the GPO, he wrote, was paid on Monday night at nine o'clock in response to a request from Patrick Pearse. I went into an office at the back of the central hall, and was there engaged hearing Confessions until half-past eleven. During the ensuing two days I attended several men shot in the streets. The military began to close in on Tuesday evening, and machine-gun and rifle fire made it unsafe to be about. On Wednesday morning at eight, I said Mass at the pro-cathedral to a congregation consisting of a few women and the server. The bombardment of Liberty Hall and of other Volunteer positions began as if I had given the signal at the beginning of Mass.

Marlboro Street was swept from end to end by machine-guns posted on the roof of the Theatre Royal, and Abbey Street from the Custom House. Immediately after Mass, while on my way to attend two boys shot at 6 Lower Marlboro Street, I had some difficulty in persuading a crowd of people that I would be safer alone and that they would be safer at home. One poor man was so far from realising the seriousness of the situation that when I turned him back he objected and said he wanted to get to his work 'across the water'.

Subsequently I got down to Jervis Street and with several other priests had a busy day attending the wounded – both soldiers and civilians. Coming back by Parnell Street, I noticed some soldiers home on leave, standing about hallways with their friends. Though in khaki, and well within the danger zone, they did not seem to fear being shot at by the Volunteers. On my return, I found the church and sacristy pretty full of refugees from neighbouring houses and, as night fell, the fire which had been smouldering in Lawrence's at the corner of Cathedral and O'Connell Streets, blazed out afresh. A steady west wind swept sparks across the church roof. The brigade we were told in response to a call, would not be allowed out, and further fires might be expected before the week closed! We therefore spent the night preparing for the removal of books, registers and sacred vessels, feeling that if the fire spread along Cathedral Street, nothing would have saved the church. Luckily, the wind died away towards daybreak.

On Thursday morning, I said Mass at eight o'clock – again to the accompaniment of the guns – but, as we had closed the church, without any congregation. Two of my colleagues were on duty in Jervis Street Hospital, two away on holidays, and three of us remained in the pro-cathedral. About half-past ten, we were astonished to hear the hall-door bell ring. Responding, I admitted a young lady who had come from the GPO with an urgent request for a priest to attend a dying Volunteer. It did not seem a very reasonable request, considering that the way from the post office to Jervis Street Hospital was comparatively safe, and that we had stationed two of our priests there specially to meet such a contingency. However I accompanied the messenger back to the GPO by a very circuitous route via Thomas' Lane, Marlboro Street, Parnell Street and Moore Street. We experienced more than one thrill in Marlboro Street and while crossing by the Parnell Statue, in Moore Street, an old friend was shot down just beside me, and I anointed him where he lay. Some brave boys, procuring a handcart bore him to Jervis Street Hospital where, after a few days, he died. Proceeding on our errand, my guide and I ran across Henry Street, into Randall's hallway, upstairs and, through gaps in the walls of intervening houses, into the GPO.

On my arrival at the Volunteer's headquarters, I looked among the wounded for the patient to whom I had been called, and received a hearty welcome from as gay and debonair an army as ever took up arms. They evidently had felt their organisation incomplete without a chaplain and I immediately entered on the duties of my new position, which kept me pretty busy all day. My services were also in request for the soldier prisoners, one of whom was mentally affected by the unexpected events of the week. We had our first serious casualty about one o'clock, when James Connolly was brought in with a nasty bullet or shrapnel wound in the leg. He endured what must have been agony with grim fortitude. Soon I had another to anoint; and, though we had many minor wounds to attend to, these were the only two serious cases. As night fell, the fires along the other side of O'Connell Street – from Eden Quay to Earl Street – were a sublime and appalling spectacle.

Friday dawned to the increasing rattle of rifle and machine-gun. Early in the day, I succeeded in getting, through the *Freeman* office, into a house in Middle Abbey Street where I prepared for death a poor bed-ridden man whose house soon became his funeral pyre. In the afternoon – about four – the first incendiary shell landed on the roof of the GPO. A large hose was at once turned on, but the effect seemed to be rather to spread the flames.

All hands were then summoned to the front hall, and I asked what could be done for the wounded, of whom we had by that time fifteen or sixteen. Earlier in the day, a good number of the ladies who had volunteered to help the wounded and see after the commissariat had been sent away under a white flag, and reached their homes in safety. Some, however, remained. We were told we should be quite safe at the back of the building, which was newly-built of ferro-concrete, or in the crypt. But it soon became clear that we should have to find safety in flight.

While the wounded were being prepared for the perilous journey now before them, I stood for a moment discussing the situation with The O'Rahilly. When the word of command came for the charge into Henry Street, he turned to me, and kneeling down, asked me for a last absolution and my blessing. 'Father,' said he, 'we shall never meet again in this world.' Then he calmly and courageously took his place at the head of his men. The stretcher-cases were then taken in blankets through the walls of intervening houses, across a roof, up a ladder, and into the bar of the Coliseum Theatre. I am glad to be able to testify here that though that element of the Volunteer army, which would correspond to the 'Rough Riders', had been in possession of the Coliseum for nearly a week – a trying and nerve-racking week – not a single bottle of liquor had been disturbed or taken when we arrived on Friday night. There, on the deep carpet, our wounded were laid about 7 p.m. Meanwhile, the Volunteers had rushed from the central hall into Henry Place – whence they fought their way into houses in Moore Street. The military had set up two barricades – one at the end of Moore Lane and the other at the end of Moore Street – both in Parnell Street. They had, besides, an armoured car from which they poured machine-gun fire up Sackville Lane and Moore Street. Passing these streets in the front rooms of the Henry Street houses, we had to creep on hands and knees beneath the windows to escape the bullets. That no one of our Red Cross party was hit and that the wounded were got safely into the theatre was really remarkable.

Our first idea was to hang a Red Cross flag out of the roof of the theatre; but the storm of bullets and shrapnel that rained around the doomed building made it impossible to venture on the roof. The GPO was already ablaze, and it seemed quite certain that the theatre would soon catch fire too. We searched round for an exit – but all the doors were securely padlocked save one – the last we tried – which gave access to a passage. With a sigh of relief, we got by this passage to the collapsible gate leading into Prince's Street. Having again secured a pick-axe, we broke the lock of the collapsible gate and, still carrying our flag, made for the narrow passage leading into Middle Abbey Street. The entrance, however, was blocked by the barricade of paper on fire, so we found there was no course left but to select the lowest spot and jump across it. One of our stretcher cases – the boy I anointed the previous day – was still unconscious all this time. At the other end of the passage we encountered a further barricade before emerging into the battle zone of Middle Abbey Street, just then the scene of a warm exchange of rifle fire between the Volunteers in the houses and a military barricade at the dispensary entrance to Jervis Street Hospital.

In the fierce glare from the burning houses in O'Connell Street, our Red Cross flag was plainly distinguishable, and the firing on both sides ceased as our little procession made its way to the corner of Liffey Street. There we were halted by a command from the officer in charge of the barricade who evidently feared a stratagem. After five or six interminable minutes, he shouted down the street that the bearer of the flag and one other might advance for a parley. I at once went forward, accompanied by the British officer in khaki, who had been taken prisoner and had humanely given his services to our wounded. Twenty paces or so from the barricade we were halted again and, covered by the rifles of the men behind it, we were examined by the officer. He refused point blank to let us pass the barricade; but I explained that our objective was the hospital, which we could enter by the side door without crossing his men or upsetting his sand-bags. After a long conversation with a monocled major, he fetched two of the students from the front of the hospital in Jervis Street. Their recognition of me quite satisfied him and, having asked who and how many we had in the party, he allowed me to call the rest up from Liffey Street. It was within an hour of midnight when the good nuns and nurses in the hospital received us all weary and well-nigh exhausted. Next day, Saturday, the male members of our Red Cross party were marched off to the Castle, the ladies being permitted to return home. The wounded all recovered, and neither they nor anyone concerned are likely to forget the experience of that terrible night.[*]

As already indicated, James Connolly had been twice wounded – first in the left arm, more seriously later, above the left ankle. Having given Seán MacLoughlin, a young Fianna officer from the Mendicity Institution, instructions to resist any British advance from the south side, and just seen him off with some comrades towards Middle Abbey Street in a hail of fire, he was struck on the shin by a bullet as he returned, and lay unconscious in an isolated spot from which, for a considerable time, he was unable to crawl back to the GPO. This was his second wound. His first had been secretly dressed lest his men's confidence might be shaken; the second involved an operation in which Doctors O'Mahony, RAMC, then a prisoner, Ryan and MacLoughlin assisted. To dull the agonising pain even for brief intervals, he had to be given injections of morphine. Sleep was practically impossible, yet, despite his inevitable weakness from dreadful pain, loss of blood and want of rest, it was while in this condition that he sent for his secretary, Miss Winifred Carney, and dictated to her the manifesto already published here. This showed him somewhat at variance with Commandant Pearse who, having made the protest in blood, is said to have openly expressed the view that the Republic, having held out for three days, would be entitled to representation at the post-war Peace Conference.

---

[*] See the *Catholic Bulletin*, August, 1918.

There is little incentive to dwell upon the evacuation of the GPO – already seen in progress so far as the wounded were concerned – or the insufferable conditions that rendered it necessary. The entire surroundings had become a very inferno long before the first incendiary bomb exploded on the roof about 4 p.m. on Friday, and the flames seemed but to spread when the hose was turned on to extinguish them. From this stage almost until midnight, the wounded, with the exception of James Connolly, were being borne under seemingly insurmountable difficulties to the Jervis Street Hospital.

Since noon, petrol shells and incendiary bullets had been finding their way into the building, and the water, used to nullify them, over-flowed in all directions. This was aggravated by the perforation of pipes, the shattering of the sewerage and a stench which made it practically impossible to remove explosives stored in the cellars. Volumes of smoke and flame, with crashing staircases and debris drove the snipers reluctantly from the roof. In the inevitable excitement of the garrison, shots went off unexpectedly, as elsewhere. Thus Volunteers got wounded, and the order was promptly given to unload, and hold the muzzles of the guns up. A dozen British soldiers, some officers and a Metropolitan policeman, were released by orders of The O'Rahilly, who was ultimately placed in charge of forty men to fight their way to Williams and Woods factory and convert it into a new headquarters. But he and his North Kerry neighbour Patrick Shortis were killed in a hail of lead in their courageous onset on strongly barricaded British positions at the head of Moore Street and Moore Lane. Truly the possibility of an early surrender was not then, or at any time, among his thoughts.

Encouraged by Joseph Mary Plunkett, Patrick Pearse, Seán Mac-Dermott and Thomas Clarke, as far as encouragement was feasible, the remainder of the garrison rushed across Henry Street through spasms in the leaden hail, James Connolly being borne on a stretcher. Joseph Plunkett, indeed, ordered a van to be drawn across a lane as a shield against the machine-gun fire which wounded about a dozen of the Volunteers while rushing across to Henry Place to fight and gradually hew their way to the grocery store, 16 Moore Street, which became the new headquarters while the republican standard still floated over the blazing GPO.

THE SURRENDER
by Sceilg

TWO LIFE-LONG DUBLIN-BORN friends, Miss Elizabeth O'Farrell and Miss Julia Grenan, were among the forty members of Cumann na mBan in the GPO, and have left their names indelibly on its story. They were amongst the first to enter it, Easter Monday, and were the last to leave it when evacuation became inevitable. On Thursday evening, by orders of Commandant Pearse, the devoted women members of the garrison with three exceptions – those named and Miss Winifred Carney, secretary to James Connolly – left the building. By 8 p.m. Friday evening, the place being entirely in flames, all retreated with the intention, some thought, of joining Comm. Edward Daly at the Four Courts. In three sections, under very heavy enemy fire, they crossed Henry Street from a side entrance, into Henry Place, and thence into Moore Lane where there was a somewhat ineffective barricade. Miss O'Farrell was in the last section. P.H. Pearse, having assured himself no one was left in the flaming building, was said to have been the last to leave, though the distinction is also claimed for Tom Clarke, Diarmuid Lynch and others.

When Miss O'Farrell entered Gogan's, corner of Moore Street, she found members of the Provisional Government in the parlour there, the house well barricaded, and James Connolly lying badly wounded on a stretcher in the middle of the room. There he and some of the seventeen men wounded in the retreat were placed on mattresses, and Miss O'Farrell spent the night in nursing them, helping also, on the morning of Saturday 29, to cook for the Volunteers who, through the night, had burrowed from house to house towards the Parnell Street end of Moore Street. After breakfast, James Connolly and the other wounded men – followed in time by all the rest – were taken through these openings to 16 Moore Street, where Connolly was put to bed in a back room. T.J. Clarke, P.H. Pearse, Seán MacDermott and Joseph Plunkett were also there, as was William Pearse, three wounded Volunteers and a badly wounded prisoner, the three members of Cumann na mBan dutifully attending them.

After an early council of war, Miss O'Farrell carrying a white flag left 15 Moore Street about 12.45 on Saturday, with sublime courage and a verbal message from Commandant Pearse to the commander of the British forces to the effect that he wished to treat with them. As she waved her small white flag, the military, ceasing to fire, called her to the barrier at the head of Moore Street, entering Parnell Street. When passing Sackville Lane, she saw The O'Rahilly's hat and a revolver on the ground. On giving her message to the officer-in-charge, he asked her how many girls were down there. When she answered 'Three', he advised her to go down and bring the other girls out. But, while he seemed intent on sending her back, he suddenly changed his mind. 'You had better wait,' he said, 'I suppose this will have to be reported', and he thereupon sent another officer with her towards the Parnell Statue. They found the officer-in-command at 70 or 71 Parnell Street, and he came out.

'The commandant of the Irish Republican Army wishes to treat with the commandant of the British forces in Ireland,' said Miss O'Farrell.

'The Irish Republican Army! The Sinn Féiners you mean? …Will Pearse be able to travel on a stretcher?'

'Commandant Pearse doesn't need a stretcher.'

'Pearse does need a stretcher, Madam.'

'Commandant Pearse doesn't need stretcher.'

'Take that Red Cross off her, bring her over there, and search her as a spy.'

The Red Cross was cut off arm and apron, and Miss O'Farrell taken into the hall of the National Bank, at the corner, where she was searched, and nothing more dangerous found on her than two pairs of scissors, some sweets and cakes. She was then taken across the street to Tom

Clarke's well-known shop, where Brig.-General Lowe called after a total delay of an hour and a half and behaved like a gentleman. Having repeated her message, she was told by Gen. Lowe that he would have to take her to Moore Street, and she was to go and tell Mr Pearse that Gen. Lowe would not treat with him until he surrendered unconditionally. Moreover, she was to be back in half-an-hour. The officer who first met her wrote a note to that effect by order of Gen. Lowe, and both accompanied her to Moore Street.

As she passed back by Sackville Lane about 2.45, she saw the dead body of The O'Rahilly lying on the kerb a few yards from Moore Street. She gave both the written and verbal message to P.H. Pearse and, the situation having been duly discussed, she was back with the reply in just half-an-hour. 'Go back and tell Mr Pearse that I will not treat at all unless he surrenders unconditionally and Mr Connolly follows on a stretcher. It is Connolly that is wounded,' he said apologetically, 'not Pearse.' He added that unless Pearse came back with her in half-an-hour hostilities would be resumed. Miss O'Farrell bought back that message and, after another brief conference, Commandant Pearse decided to accompany her back to Gen. Lowe.

It was about 3.30 p.m. when they met at the top of Moore Street, and an officer who had been prisoner in the GPO failed to identify Comm. Pearse who then handed up his sword to Gen. Lowe.

'The only condition I will make is to allow the other commandants to surrender,' said Gen. Lowe. 'I understand you have the Countess Markievicz down there.'

'No, she is not with me,' Commandant Pearse replied.

'Oh, I know she is down there.'

'Don't accuse me of speaking an untruth.'

'Oh, I beg your pardon, Mr Pearse, but I know she is down there.'

'Well, she is not with me, sir.'

It was decided to detain Miss O'Farrell for the night so that she might take Comm. Pearse's order for surrender to the other commandants next day if she so agreed. 'Will you agree to this?' Comm. Pearse asked her.

'Yes, if you so wish,' she replied.

He then shook hands with her, without speaking, and with Gen. Lowe's son and another officer, was taken along O'Connell Street in a motor car, preceded by another carrying Gen. Lowe and Capt. Wheeler. 'It would be interesting to know how many marks that fellow has in his pocket,' said one of a number of officers standing round as he was driven off.

Miss O'Farrell was taken in charge by Capt. Royall, who took her back to Tom Clarke's shop, and procured her tea about 4.15 p.m. Gen. Lowe soon returned with Comm. Pearse's written order to surrender, and some half-dozen typed copies, one of which was signed by Comm. James Connolly for his men in the GPO and Stephen's Green areas. Gen. Lowe then gave Miss O'Farrell two orders – for the republican troops in Moore Street and those at the Four Courts respectively. A note with the order to Moore Street laid down the manner of surrender:

> Carrying a white flag, proceed down Moore Street, turn into Moore Lane and Henry Place and around the Pillar to the right-hand side of O'Connell Street; march up to within a hundred yards of the military drawn up at the Parnell Statue, halt, advance five paces, and lay down arms.

Having delivered the orders at Moore Street, Miss O'Farrell, proceeded with difficulty by Parnell Street and Capel Street to the Four Courts, being halted by several officers on the way, and roughly turned back by one, so that she had to return to Moore Street, whence a military guard escorted her to the barricade in Little Mary Street. Having crossed the barricade, she proceeded by East Arran Street and Chancery Street until meeting Fr Columbus of Church Street who, on hearing of her mission, took the white flag and accompanied her past Charles Street into the side entrance to the Four Courts. To contact Comm. Daly it was necessary to go around to the quays, corner of Church Street, where they found him strongly entrenched, but very much disappointed on receiving the order to surrender which, however, he accepted in the spirit of a loyal soldier of Ireland. He accompanied the bearers back to the side, where several republican officers awaited them, the news having already spread. Miss O'Farrell then returned to O'Connell Street by the same route, when she was again handed over to Capt. Royall, who was held personally responsible for her safety!

Before 8 p.m., the republican troops from the Four Courts marched up O'Connell Street, and were lined up by the Institute for the Blind, the Moore Street troops coming immediately after, to be lined up by the Gresham Hotel. About this stage, Miss O'Farrell was again taken over to the National Bank, and provided with supper as well as a bedroom in the top of the building. Looking through the window at dawn, Sunday morning, she saw some four hundred Volunteers on the plot of grass in front of the Rotunda Hospital, and with them Miss Grenan and Miss Carney, all wet and cold. She was no sooner dressed than she was summoned downstairs by Capt. Wheeler to take the surrender orders round to the other commandants. All the Volunteer arms and ammunition were piled at the Parnell Statue.

Capt. Wheeler now took Miss O'Farrell by car to the middle of Grafton Street, and, amid a hail of bullets, she had to walk under her white flag to the College of Surgeons, Stephen's Green. Comm. Mallin being resting when she entered there by York Street, she gave the order, with the slip containing directions for surrender at St Patrick's Park, to Countess Markievicz, second-in-command; and the countess was quite surprised at this development. Comm. Mallin Miss O'Farrell saw later. On returning to Capt. Wheeler in Grafton Street, she reported that Comm. Mallin had nothing to say. Having called for a few minutes at Trinity College, Capt. Wheeler next took her by College Street, until interrupted by the barricade, and by Tara Street, to Butt bridge in the effort to get as near Boland's Mills as feasible. Here he parted with her and, under her white flag, she set out again – first for Westland Row – and truly carrying her life in her hands every pace of the way.

At Westland Row, military screamed at her to turn back, but she waved her flag and papers, and a soldier was sent to escort her to Clare Street, whence an officer sent another soldier to pass her through the military lines at Holles Street under almost constant fire. By Wentworth

Place, Harmony Row, under the railway bridge Brunswick Place she passed, calling on the Volunteers and getting no reply; nor could she enter the gas works or the old distillery, where some of them were said to be. Crossing Ringsend Road bridge towards Boland's Mills she called at the Bakery and, again getting no reply, she went by Barrow Street towards the railway bridge where some Volunteers at last recognised her and said she would find Comm. de Valera at Grand Canal Street dispensary.

Retracing her steps, she crossed Grand Canal Street bridge amid terrific fire, where a man was shot half a yard behind her, and taken to Sir Patrick Dun's Hospital. On passing to the dispensary, the Volunteer on duty sent her round to the back. The barricade had to be removed, and she was lifted through a window into a small room. Comm. de Valera on meeting her there thought the surrender order a hoax and, when she was identified, he said: 'I will take orders only from my immediate superior officer, Comm. MacDonagh.' So, as in Stephen's Green, she drew a blank here – on Sunday. Then she returned towards Trinity College, by Holles Street, Merrion Square and Clare Street, where she met Capt. Wheeler in his car, and gave him Comm. de Valera's reply.

'We will go up to Jacob's, and see Comm. MacDonagh,' he said, and they proceeded by Dame Street and the Castle yard, where he made a brief call, Ship Street, Bride Street, in the middle of which he stopped the car, leaving her to go alone through the firing line – Golden Lane, Whitefriar Street and Peter Street to Jacob's, practically a repetition of her previous unnerving experiences.

Knocking at 15 Peter Street to inquire for Comm. MacDonagh, she was blindfolded; and, having thus walked for five minutes, she heard the commandant's voice. When the bandage was removed, she gave him the order from Comm. Pearse, and explained the whole situation. He 'would not take orders from the prisoner', he said. 'He was himself next in command; and he would have nothing to do with the surrender until he had conferred with Gen. Lowe, the members of the Provisional Government already prisoners, and the officers under his command.' The interview arranged by Fr Augustine, took place outside St Patrick's Park about three. Thence Comm. MacDonagh went to Marrowbone Lane Distillery to consult Comm. Kent. After this consultation, he agreed to surrender, returned, called his officers together, and then told the men they had decided to surrender. The men being very much against it, he said: 'It is not my wish to surrender; but, after consultation with Comm. Kent and other officers, we think it the best thing to do in the circumstances now confronting us. If we do not surrender, they will show no mercy to those who are prisoners.'

He then gave prompt orders to get ready for the surrender. Thereupon two of the Volunteers placed some money in the custody of Miss O'Farrell – one of them £13 in gold, as he had been on the eve of getting married. While she waited later with the countersigned surrender order at the corner of Bride Street and Rose Road where Comm. MacDonagh was to surrender, he came and complained to the military that a soldier had broken into Jacob's and fired indiscriminately at his men as they prepared to leave. An officer went back with him, and the soldier was placed under arrest. By six, Comm. Kent and his followers came to the same point and surrendered with his men and the members of Cumann na mBan attached to his command. When both sections were disarmed, Capt. Wheeler took Miss O'Farrell away in his car. It grew dusk as they drove to Trinity College; but being no longer necessary to take Comm. Pearse's order, countersigned by Comm. MacDonagh to Boland's Mills – Comm. de Valera having surrendered in the meantime – he took her to the Castle hospital, introduced her to the matron, said she was to remain as a guest by Gen. Lowe's orders and that he, Capt. Wheeler, would call for her next morning, May Day.

She was provided with supper and taken upstairs, where she slept tolerably well. But she found, next morning, that her clothes had been taken away, as well as the money of which she had the custody, and was informed they had been taken by a doctor. She protested against the removal of her clothes while she was a guest; and, when she mentioned the missing money to an inquisitive officer, he said with a sneer: 'Going to be married, indeed! He looted some safe.' When dressed, after her clothes had been returned, they brought her downstairs and across the Castle yard – to the provost marshal.

'What did the provost marshal say?' one asked the other in crossing.

'Oh, lock her up, and keep her there for the day.'

She protested against being made a prisoner in violation of Capt. Wheeler's leaving her there as a guest.

'You are very much a prisoner,' one of them observed, in spite of Gen. Lowe's promise to the contrary. 'You won't be lonely,' he continued. 'Your friends, with Miss Molony, and all the rest, will be here in a few moments.' And they were.

After 'dinner', she referred again to Gen. Lowe's pledge. 'Don't be silly,' another officer replied, 'I know for a fact you shot six policemen yesterday.'

Immediately they were taken to the Richmond barracks. While they were being told they were going to Kilmainham, Fr Columbus appeared, and promised he would go to Gen. Lowe. At 4 p.m., they were marched to Kilmainham, where women searchers stripped and examined Miss O'Farrell. 'Dinner' came in due course: awful stuff. Miss O'Farrell was called out, and there – most apologetic – was the man who had taken the money, and put her into Ship Street barracks. Captain Wheeler awaited her. Gen. Lowe had been informed by Fr Columbus, and was coming to apologise. Capt. Wheeler, with a nurse, drove her to O'Connell Street, thence to the Castle about 6.15 p.m. While she took some dinner, Gen. Lowe appeared, apologised handsomely, and offered to take her home. Thereupon, she protested against the indignity of being stripped and robbed while a guest.

'What about my money?' she asked.

'What money?'

'£16 taken out of my pocket here.'

'Who took the money?'

'That man there.'

'Where is the money?'

'The provost marshal has it.'

'Go get it immediately and restore it to this lady.'

The officer brought back the money; Gen. Lowe then bade goodbye and left, in due course, while the matron accompanied Miss O'Farrell to the Castle gate, Dame Street. So ended her epic part in the most dangerous and critical part of the struggle. Let her life-long friend, Miss Julia Grenan, briefly supplement it.

Miss Grenan had given Miss O'Farrell Rosary beads as she set out from Moore Street with Comm. Pearse, and felt convinced she could not escape being shot – so manifestly so that James Connolly called Miss Grenan to his bedside, and said: 'Don't weep for your friend; they won't shoot her.' All, men and women, were terribly upset over the surrender, and Miss Carney, kneeling at James Connolly's bedside, anxiously asked: 'Is there no other way?'

James replied that he could not see his brave boys burned to death, and there was no other way.

When Miss O'Farrell returned with the directions as to the manner of surrender, a considerable section of the rank and file, Miss Grenan declares, had not got over their objection to the idea. 'They spoke to Tom Clarke … who said he was satisfied, and they should be, adding that there were good reasons for believing that Ireland would be all right for the future.' The Rosary was then recited, after which the wounded were taken out into Moore Street. The others then marched out, up Moore Lane, Henry Place and around to the Pillar – the GPO still burning fiercely – up the right-hand side of O'Connell Street, Willie Pearse leading with the white flag. At the Gresham Hotel the ambulance corps were ordered to remove their red badges. Soon Tom Clarke was identified and called out of line, while a number of British officers came to have a look at him. 'You have cripples in your army too,' said another, pointing to Seán MacDermott, who gave him his appropriate answer.

The names and addresses having been recorded, they were taken across O'Connell Street to the green plot in front of the Rotunda. Including the Four Courts section, there were some four hundred prisoners here, in a space which would have seated about one hundred and fifty. With night came a severe cold, and both Seán MacDermott and Joseph Plunkett felt it extremely. So Miss Carney spread her coat and that of Comm. James Connolly, which he had given her in

Moore Street, on the grass to get them some little warmth. At dawn, Brian O'Higgins knelt down, and all followed his example, to say their morning prayers. Soon detectives began to arrive, and a DMP official came to say gratefully to Seán MacDermott: 'We wish to place on record the leniency you and your colleagues have shown during the Rising to the DMP, and we assure you that whatever we can say on your and their behalf will be said.'

A detective and military officer later took Tom Clarke away, searched him, told him his whole life-story, took everything he had, and then permitted him to return.

At 9 on Sunday, they were marched to O'Connell Street, thence to Richmond barracks. Joseph Plunkett fainted on arrival, and had to be borne in; and Seán MacDermott, unable to march, reached Richmond barracks three-quarters of an hour after the others, tottering, exhausted, almost ghastly. Miss Grenan and Miss Carney were taken from the ranks, and removed to a room where they were soon joined by members of Cumann na mBan from the Four Courts, accompanied by Fr Columbus, Church Street. Soon they were again removed, and joined after a while by Madame Markievicz and Miss ffrench-Mullen.

'Remove that woman,' an officer shouted as the countess shook hands with the others; and so they saw her no more. The others were then marched to Kilmainham jail at dusk, four placed in every cell, and surrounded by military until two female warders arrived from Mountjoy. Other members of Cumann na mBan were brought in during the week.

Wednesday morning, 3 May at dawn, they were awakened by the shots that executed Tom Clarke, Patrick Pearse and Thomas Mac-Donagh. Morning after morning they prayed fervently, listened for the volleys, and heard them four times. After ten days, some of them were released, Tuesday 9 May.

THE EXECUTED LEADERS

by JOHN BRENNAN

FIFTEEN SENTENCES OF death were carried out in Dublin following the Rising. The execution of Thomas Kent in Cork and Roger Casement in London brings the total of those who suffered death following trial for participation in the Rising to seventeen.* In all one hundred and sixty sentences were passed by British courts martial. These tribunals passed ninety-seven death sentences of which sixteen were executed. Seven sentences were commuted to penal servitude for life, twenty-three to penal servitude for ten years, three to penal servitude for eight years, fourteen to penal servitude for five years, and thirty-four to penal servitude for three years.

Five were sentenced to penal servitude for life. Of these three had their sentenced confirmed, one had it commuted to penal servitude for ten years, one to penal servitude for five years. Six were sentenced to penal servitude for twenty years. The sentence on one was confirmed, four sentenced were commuted to penal servitude for ten years, and one to penal servitude for five years. Two were sentenced to penal servitude for fifteen years. Both these sentences were commuted to penal servitude for ten years. Nine were sentenced to penal servitude for ten years. Three of these sentences were confirmed, three were commuted to penal servitude for five years, three to penal servitude for three years. Eighteen were sentenced to penal servitude for five

---

* Series Editor's Note: Fourteen men were executed in Dublin making the total executed for involvement in the Rising sixteen.

years. All these sentences were commuted to penal servitude for three years. Three were sentenced to penal servitude for three years. These sentences were confirmed. Seven were sentenced to two years with hard labour. One sentence was confirmed, three were commuted to one year with hard labour, three to six months' with hard labour. Thirteen were sentenced to one year with hard labour. In each instance the sentence was confirmed. These figures do not take into account the numbers who were captured in Dublin and those arrested throughout the country who were interned. It is, however, to the leaders who died before British firing squads in Dublin that the mind invariable turns whenever the Rising is mentioned and the following biographical sketches will help readers to visualise the manner of men they were.

PÁDRAIG PEARSE

AN ANONYMOUS DUBLIN poet, in verses written shortly after the execution of Pádraig Pearse, relates how he heard an Englishman say contemptuously of him: 'What was he after all – a schoolmaster!' To which the poet replied that Pearse had become 'schoolmaster of all Ireland' – a master 'who had taught Irish boys the way to live, and Irish men the way to die'.

What sort of man was this schoolmaster of all Ireland? Of him one of his pupils said: 'Not to have known him as a teacher is not to have known him at all.' Pádraig Pearse was a man a little over medium height, broadly built, with dark hair, grey eyes, and pale complexion. When in repose his face had a rather serious expression, as though he were deep in thought, and his habit of bending his head when in conversation gave the impression that he pondered over everything said. His photographs reveal a magnificently shaped head, with broad, high forehead, eyes well set apart and firm mouth. His features portrayed the man of action who found kindred spirits in such revolutionaries as Tom Clarke and James Connolly. But the grave, almost stern expression caught by the camera, does not reveal the Pearse that was as much a schoolboy as were his own pupils. To glimpse that side of his character one must turn to the following description of him written by one of his ex-pupils in 1913. The fact that it appeared during Pearse's lifetime makes it the more valuable, for in it comes to life the beloved master, rather than the hero of Easter Week: 'I have listened to him expounding the Elizabethan drama, seen him strip to take a class in drill, and have on occasions been called into his study to report myself on the complaint of an assistant master. Under all these circumstances I have found the headmaster of St Enda's very human, very interesting and very boyish. He sometimes seemed to me (and I have heard others say the same thing) to be more shy in my presence than I was in his; yet he could cast aside this shyness and talk with a deep and earnest gravity or with a terrible concentrated anger as the occasion demanded; and always there was the possibility of his lips twitching into a smile. When I left school and began to mix with members of the Gaelic League, nothing surprised and amused me more than the prevalent notion of Mr Pearse as a person of profoundly grave, not to say saturnine temperament. To us one of his main characteristics on and off duty was an almost irresponsible gaiety. Humour would break through his most serious discourses and his sternest rebukes. Although he could command and lead us, he seemed almost as much a schoolboy as we were ourselves.'

St Enda's school for boys which Pearse founded in 1908, and St Ita's school for girls, which he founded a few years later, were then the only two Catholic lay schools in Ireland; they were also the first in which a bilingual programme was used. Pearse had set out in life with three ambitions: to edit a bilingual newspaper, to found a bilingual school, and to fight for the liberation of Ireland. In a speech before the British court martial in 1916 he told how, as a child of ten, he had gone on his knees and promised God that he would devote his whole life to an effort to free his country, and added: 'I have kept that promise.' His brother Willie, as is now known, joined him in that solemn vow, though Pádraig did not say so before the court martial as Willie was also in the hands of the enemy. The solemn pledge explains his whole life. He kept steadily to his purpose from the time he left the Christian Brothers' school at Westland Row. First he acquired a deep and exact knowledge of the Irish language, of which he became an authority of the standing of Dr Douglas Hyde, Cathal Brugha and Dr Kuno Meyer. He took his first Irish lessons in the Gaelic League, after which he went to the Gaeltacht where, in the poor cottages of Connacht, he learned to converse in it with the fluency and idiom of a native speaker. Having graduated from University College (now the National University) he was called to the bar, and, though he never practised as a barrister, his readings for the law influenced his writings on historical subjects. He had pledged himself to fight for the liberty of Ireland, but 'liberty' and 'freedom' were terms that had to be defined. Accordingly, when he treated of history, he examined the motives, the lives, the teachings and the achievements of the great apostles of Irish freedom of other generations. Then he would sum up, and pass judgement. Among the Irish patriots, Wolfe Tone was the one from whom he drew most inspiration. Tone's ideals had for Pearse the force of dogma. 'God spoke to Ireland through Tone and through those who, after Tone, have taken up his testimony,' he wrote. Was it chance or affinity that made both Tone and Pearse 'forsake the foolish wig and gown' for the dangerous and glorious career of an Irish revolutionary? For God spoke to Ireland also through Pearse, and He endowed him with great gifts for his apostleship. His writings, whether in Gaelic or English, prose or verse, whether merely passing comment or of a major character, provided all the elements of pure literature. As an orator, he was superb. To natural gifts of expression and a glorious speaking voice he added the art of declamation, which he had studied as a barrister and which imparted rare dignity to his speech.

Before he was twenty-five years of age he had already achieved the first of his ambitions; for in 1903, he became the editor of *An Claidheamh Soluis*, the bilingual organ of the Gaelic League, and in his hands it became a stimulating and forceful paper. Pearse was an able controversialist and he used the columns of his paper to ridicule the 'Fan go fóill' (Wait a while) who wanted to see Ireland liberated, but by 'our children's children'. He poured scorn on those with 'the counting-house mentality', a characteristic which he abhorred. His work for the Gaelic League and on *An Claidheamh Soluis* made him the leader of a militant group in the organisation, which included among its numbers Éamonn Ceannt, Peadar Macken, The O'Rahilly, Brian O'Higgins, Seán MacDiarmada, Thomas MacDonagh, Cathal Brugha, Seán T. Ó Ceallaigh, Éamon de Valera, Liam Mellows and many others of high idealism and unflinching purpose. Known but to few outside the Gaelic League and the Irish-Ireland movement, they were well-known to Pearse, who saw in them the men who would make Ireland 'not free merely, but Gaelic as well: not Gaelic merely, but free as well'. Within a few years they were all by his side in the Rising of Easter Week.

Pádraig Pearse, militant champion of the Gael, was born in Dublin on 10 November 1879, of an Irish mother and an English father. James Pearse, his father, was born in Devonshire, and his mother Margaret, came of Gaelic stock from County Meath. Writing in *Poblacht na h-Éireann,* in 1922, Pádraig Pearse's mother said: 'Now and again Pádraig was taunted with being an "Englishman", but he always answered that he was proud of the fact that his father was English.' Little is known of that father, beyond the facts that he was an advanced radical, that he held a deep affection for his adopted country, and that he wrote a pamphlet in support of Irish freedom. By trade he was a monumental sculptor, and his son Willie inherited his artistic gifts; perhaps it was from him, too, that Pádraig brought his literary talents. The influence of his radical father may account partially for Pádraig's faith in and love for 'the great, splendid, faithful, common people'. His sympathies were with the workers during the great strike of 1913. 'My instinct,' he wrote at the time, 'is with the landless man against the lord of lands, and with the breadless man against the master of millions.' The Pearse who could thus speak and write attracted kindred souls like Constance Markievicz and James Connolly. They had a common aim for which they fought together three years later.

Pearse spoke of the Irish educational system of his day as 'the broad arrow on the back of the Irish people'. Planned to enslave the nation, its measure of success in that direction could not but have pleased its designers. Pearse was fully alive to the fact that until it was replaced by a system more favourable to his plans, there was little hope of freeing Ireland. So with his assistant master, Thomas MacDonagh, who shared his political and cultural ideals, he had made the beginning of a new system in St Enda's. The two men worked in joyous comradeship.

If Pearse's preoccupation with Irish education won him many new friends, it also made him enemies. Because of some educational clauses of which he approved in a Home Rule Bill, he spoke in support of it at an O'Connell Street demonstration. For that he became classified as a 'Home Ruler' in the minds of a certain narrow section of the Irish Republican Brotherhood and as one with whom they would not be associated.

The proposal was made several times in IRB circles in Dublin that Pádraig Pearse be asked to join the organisation; but it was rejected on the grounds that he was a 'Home Ruler' and not a republican. Pearse, like many others of the leaders, such as The O'Rahilly, Plunkett, MacDonagh and James Connolly, had a strong dislike of secret societies, and he was outspokenly critical of IRB methods. He was co-opted a member of the IRB executive in 1913, a few months before the Irish Volunteers were founded, and Thomas MacDonagh and Joseph Plunkett were later co-opted, because their military knowledge made their co-option necessary when the Rising was being planned. Pearse told Frank Fahy shortly before the Rising that he intended to leave the IRB, if the fight was successful, as he did not believe that a secret society of its kind would be necessary in a free Ireland.

He never used his gift of oratory to sway the emotions of a crowd or to urge dangerous courses that he was not himself prepared to take. His celebrated oration over the grave of O'Donovan Rossa was spoken in a voice which though quiet and gentle, could be plainly heard by all in the vast gathering. It was not merely great oratory; it was a public manifestation of his faith, and it had the effect of a call to arms. Several speeches which he made to the Volunteers during the weeks which preceded the Rising had, said Cathal Brugha, 'set his hearers literally panting for the word'. His speech before the British court martial came to light under curious and romantic circumstances which were related when it was published in *The Irish Press* of 16 August 1946.

He was executed on 3 May 1916.

JAMES CONNOLLY

EVEN A BRIEF outline of the life-story of James Connolly will reveal him as a man of genius, nobility, courage and firm purpose. Born on 6 June 1870, in County Monaghan, he was the son of a poor labourer, who emigrated to Edinburgh in 1880, when James was ten years old. The father had obtained work as a dustman for the corporation, and when James was eleven and his brother a few years older, they both had to go to work to supplement the meagre family income. They found it in the printing work of a local paper, *The Evening News*, where James, the diminutive 'printer's devil', was put on a stool behind the case when inspectors arrived, so as to conceal the fact that he was under working age. Finally, an inspector, more sharp-eyed than the others, noticed the little lad, and he lost his job. He next found employment in a bakery, where the work was so heavy that his health broke under the strain and he had to give up work for a period. When he recovered, he got a position in a mosaic tiling factory, where he remained for two years.

Leaving home at eighteen, he roamed through Britain, sometimes as a tramp, sometimes as a pedlar, sometimes as a navvy. Then a message from home told him that his father had had a serious accident, and would be unable to work, and he had to return to Edinburgh, and take up his father's work as dustman.

Connolly was an entirely self-educated man. Beginning his studies during this period of grim poverty, he carried them on during his life. Later he recalled for his children how, at a time when the family budget would not allow him a light or a pencil, he lay on the floor close to the fire, and wrote by fire-light with a piece of burnt stick for a pencil. He was passionately fond of reading, especially Irish history, and had studied the *Autobiography of Wolfe Tone*, and John Mitchel's *Jail Journal* until he had them almost off by heart. With his uncle, a Fenian, he used to attend meetings of the Social Democratic Federation and listened there with rapt attention as its chief speaker, John Leslie, spoke of plans for improving the lot of the workers. Leslie, who had written a sympathetic pamphlet on Ireland from the point of view of a socialist, became Connolly's hero, and in order to take part in the discussions at the meetings, he set himself the difficult task of correcting a serious impediment in his speech. This he did by patient endeavour, although to the end of his days there were some words which he found it hard to pronounce. Curiously enough, one of these word was 'socialist', which he always rendered as 'solist'. Through speaking at Leslie's meetings, Connolly developed into a public speaker for the Socialist Party in Scotland.

His father, to whom he was devoted, had a great influence upon him. He often spoke to James of the hard lot of the workers, and this first roused his interest in social questions. His father also exacted from his son a solemn promise that he would never take alcohol. Among his friends and fellow-workers in Edinburgh and in Ireland he had seen many a good man go to pieces through drink. James Connolly kept that pledge all through his life, abstaining also from smoking. His father, believing that he would never break his word, was shocked on one occasion to see him at a party with what appeared to be a glass of whisky in his hand. As the result of a stroke, the father had lost his power of speech, but his eyes, filled with anguish, stared alternately at the face of his son and at the glass in his hand. Suddenly James realised the cause of his agitation; he walked across to his father and let him smell the contents of the glass. It was lemonade! The old man's face broke into a happy smile. James had not broken his pledge.

During a visit to Dublin when he was twenty-one, James Connolly met Miss Lily Reynolds, a native of County Wicklow, and shortly afterwards they were married in Perth. It was an ideally happy marriage, although they went through many years of penury and hardship, for Connolly, who was not a mere theorist about the equality of the sexes and the emancipation of women, practised as far as he could those theories in the home. This kind and compassionate trait in his character, which made him the idol of those who worked with him and fought under him, is well exemplified by a story told by one of his daughters, Nora. When choosing a new house, he went first to the kitchen and examined it very carefully. 'You see,' he said to his daughter, 'the family is so big that mama will have to spend most of her time in the kitchen. You and I will be at work most of the day, so the kitchen won't matter to us, but it will matter a lot to mama. So as we are picking a house for her to live in, and as she is not here, and if she were she wouldn't think of herself, we've got to think of her.'

And Madame Markievicz, who was one of his closest friends and colleagues from 1910 to 1916, gives a description of Connolly in his home and in Liberty Hall which reveals why he won such personal devotion. Her friendship with him began through her appreciation of what he had done for the Belfast branch of the Fianna. When she went north to lecture for the organisation, she was invited to the Connolly home, 'a nice little house, high up on the Falls Road, with clear, open space around it, and a green field sloping down behind it … He was full of life, full of hope, and he had the happy knack of making friends of the best of those men and women he came across in a day's work … I came to look upon their house as my Belfast home, stopping there whenever I was up north. Their's was a delightful home, Mrs Connolly was a charming hostess. I remember pleasant and interesting evenings spent there listening to James Connolly and his friends talking. The conversation covered a very wide ground – history, politics, economics, social systems, class distinctions, culture, revolutions; and everything discussed led back to the same question – how can we work out Ireland's freedom? … When he began to organise the Irish Citizen Army he brought me along, treating me, as he got to know me, as a comrade, giving me any work that I could do, and quite ignoring the conventional attitude towards the work of women. This was his attitude towards women in general; we were never, in his mind, classed for work as a sex, but taken individually and considered, just as every man considers men, and then allotted any work we could do. When he appointed Commandant Mallin as his first staff officer, he appointed me as his second, with the rank of lieutenant.'

In 1896 Connolly brought his family back to Dublin, and shortly afterwards founded the Irish Socialist Republican Party, the programme of which embodied his twin gospels of national freedom and working-class emancipation. His now well-known works on Irish history, which stress the social background of Ireland's struggle against England, began to appear at this period. Written in an easy, lucid style, they reveal not only the deep study he had made of his subject, but his consuming love for his country.

Connolly never allowed himself to be hampered by lack of funds. *The Workers' Republic*, issued in 1898, was revived in 1899, printed on a hand-press, and chiefly written by himself. A complaint from the Dublin Typographical Association that he and his supporters were 'blacklegging' by printing the paper themselves, brought from Connolly the characteristic retort: 'Is the private use of razors blacklegging on barbers?'

In the Irish demonstrations against Queen Victoria's jubilee in 1897 and during her visit to Dublin in 1900, James Connolly took a very prominent part, which brought him into contact with such famous figures as the old Fenian, John O'Leary, with W.B. Yeats and Maud Gonne. Together they figured in many stormy scenes, during one of which, in a mock funeral of the British Empire, the 'remains' were cast into the Liffey and Connolly, who drove the brake, was arrested.

Following a lecture tour in 1902, which brought him to England, Scotland and the United States, he decided he would settle in the latter country, and emigrated in 1903, his family following in 1904. In later years he regretted having taken this step, for during his seven years in America new forces and personalities came into prominence in Ireland, and he longed to be there to take his part in what promised to be an Irish national resurgence. His opportunity to return home came when in Ireland on a lecture tour in 1910, he was offered work in Dublin at £2 a week. 'I love Dublin,' he said to his wife. 'I'd rather be poor there than a millionaire here.' Soon after he and his family were home once more, renewing old friendships, and finding new and stimulating personalities in the new Ireland that had sprung up during their absence. *The Harp*, a paper which he had started in America, had been transferred to Dublin, with James Connolly as its editor and Jim Larkin as its sub-editor, and in this way the two Labour leaders, whose names were so closely associated later, came into contact.

In 1911 Connolly moved to Belfast and was appointed secretary and Ulster district organiser of the Irish Transport and General Workers' Union.

The 1913 strike brought Connolly back to Dublin, and he was soon in the thick of the fray. Though a forceful and fearless speaker, Connolly was very far removed from being a demagogue. He never indulged in abuse of personalities, or picturesque invective, or used his powers as an orator to rouse the passions of a mob. On the contrary, in public speech or in conversation, he would often calm angry tempers and soothe ruffled feelings by a quiet, well-spoken word, or by a well-told humorous anecdote. But the brutal ill-treatment of the Dublin workers in 1913, both by the employers and the police, roused him to fury, as it did others with revolutionary ideals. George Russell (Æ) accused the employers in a trenchant letter: 'You determined deliberately and in cold anger,' he said, 'to starve out one-third of the population of this city, to break the manhood of the men by the sight of the suffering of their wives and the hunger of their children ...' To meet this crisis, food ships were sent by sympathetic trade unions in England, and Madame Markievicz opened a food kitchen in Liberty Hall. There, assisted by a number of her friends and political associates whom she had enrolled for the work, she was to be found daily, from early morning until late at night, preparing and serving meals to the locked-out men and their families. With Francis Sheehy-Skeffington, his wife Hannah and others, she also addressed meetings and collected funds for the strikers.

Connolly was arrested on a charge of 'inciting to riot' on the Saturday before Larkin's arrest at the historic proclaimed Sunday meeting, and was sentenced to three months' imprisonment. While on hunger strike to procure his release, he wrote to his wife these prophetic words: 'Many more than I (perhaps thousands) will have to go to prison, and, perhaps, the scaffold, before our freedom will be won. Nothing worthwhile can be won without suffering.' He saw in that tremendous industrial struggle in Dublin the first skirmish of the fight which was to begin in 1916. He welcomed, therefore, a suggestion made to him by an Irishman, Captain Jack White, who, after having won the DSO, had resigned his commission in the British army because of his pacifist views. White counselled the setting up of a defensive corps to protect the workers from the ferocity of the police during strikes. It would carry sticks, not firearms, but would be drilled and disciplined so as to be able to meet an attack.

The Irish Citizen Army which came into existence in October 1913, as a workers' defence corps, was very strong during the strike, but with the ending of the strike most of its members dropped out, leaving only about fifty on the rolls. In 1914, Larkin went to the United States, and James Connolly became acting secretary of the union and commandant to the Irish Citizen Army. In October 1914, under his leadership, serious work commenced. The men were taught the use of firearms and given target practice at Croydon Park by Michael Mallin and Madame Markievicz. Mallin, a member of the union, who had been for many years a soldier in the British army, instructed the Citizen Army in drill, feint attacks and night manoeuvres, while Connolly began their training in intelligence work. He was also busily engaged in surveying Dublin and making the military plans for the Rising which were later perfected in conjunction with those drawn up by Joseph Plunkett.

When the Irish Volunteers were holding their first meeting at the Rotunda Rink on 25 November 1913, a small group of foolish and irresponsible men from Liberty Hall attempted to howl down some of the speakers, and threw slap-bangs among the audience. Tom Clarke, very indignant over the incident, sent a messenger to Larkin asking him to repudiate the action of his followers, but Larkin refused to do so. This incident led to a certain amount of mutual suspicion between the two organisations, and as the war passed into its third year without the Volunteers going into action against England, Connolly began to fear that there was going to be a repetition of the story of the Irish Volunteers of 1782.

Writing editorially of Grattan's Volunteers and those of 1916 in *The Workers' Republic* for 8 January 1916, he said of those of 1782: 'If they were hostile to English influence, they were still more hostile to the vast mass of the natives of Ireland. They considered themselves as British subjects in the first place, and only as Irishmen in the second place … But the one certain mark to distinguish the Irish Volunteers of today from their forerunners is the fact that they set Ireland first. Given that, and all other things can be forgiven them. True, the presence on their executive of some of the men who voted the betrayal to John Redmond and his party is a standing invitation to suspicion and distrust. These men were either false to their trust or incapable blockheads. In either case, they should have been sent back to the obscurity and harmlessness of private life, to live under suspicion or pity the remainder of their days. To place them again in power was to forfeit the complete confidence of the people in a time when complete confidence was necessary. Yet we have heard demands for absolute trust and confidence in a body some of whose trusted members have already abused that trust so vilely.'

Unknown to Connolly, a secret military council, whose members were Tom Clarke, Seán MacDiarmada, Pádraig Pearse, Thomas Mac-Donagh, Joseph Plunkett and Éamonn Ceannt, had almost completed the plans for the Rising, and were anxious to keep them secret from those very members of the Volunteer committee whom Connolly distrusted. Fearing that this element would be influential enough to prevent the Rising, Connolly made it clear in his paper that if the Irish Volunteers would not fight, the Irish Citizen Army would go out alone. It was no idle threat. The Citizen Army had decided that if any one of their three leaders, Connolly, Mallin or Madame Markievicz were arrested, the Citizen Army would be brought into action by the others.

They were put to the test when Connolly disappeared on 19 January 1916, and was absent for four days. During this time the

Citizen Army and his friends and family were in a state of great alarm, fearing he had been secretly arrested and murdered by the British. Having failed to discover his whereabouts or get any reassuring news of him in three days' search, the council of the Citizen Army met, and decided to go into action without further delay. This decision was conveyed to Pádraig Pearse by Madame Markievicz, who met him by chance in the street. He turned very pale and implored her to stop the Citizen Army from taking this drastic action. She replied that it was impossible, that they had pledged their word to each other that they would fight in just such circumstances as had arisen. She returned to her home that evening to find Connolly there. When she asked him what had happened to him, he answered only: 'Madame, I have been through hell – but I conquered my conquerors.' In telling me this story in later years she said that she interpreted him as meaning that he had won over those who had been suspicious of him, and that they had all come to an agreement. Not even to his closest friends did he ever tell where he had been at that time, and it is very likely that, having been co-opted onto the military council, he took an oath not to divulge this secret, which would have betrayed the existence of the secret council. There is little doubt that he was kidnapped; but, as it would not have taken four days for mutual explanations to be exchanged, what started as a 'kidnapping' probably ended as a conference between the military leaders and their new colleague.

An account of Connolly's bravery in action was given in *An Phoblacht* for 19 April 1930, by a Citizen Army man writing under the pen-name of 'Veteran'. His unit, while stationed at Annesley bridge, had taken prisoner about a dozen British soldiers. When forced to retreat they brought the prisoners with them on the two-mile march to the GPO. One of the Citizen Army reported their coming to Connolly. He instructed them to avoid casualties from snipers by advancing to the GPO in single file and at the double. Unfortunately the khaki-clad prisoners looked in extended line like a formidable force charging on the GPO, and fire was opened on both captors and captured. Connolly realised what was happening. 'He rushed into the direct line of fire,' says the writer, 'with both hands raised above his head. His familiar figure was instantly recognised, and the firing ceased.'

The first shot in the insurrection had been fired by the Citizen Army against Dublin Castle. On 11 May, their commandant, who had been made commandant-general of the army of the Irish Republic, was a wounded prisoner in that same Castle, under sentence of death. At midnight, Mrs Connolly with her daughter Nora, had been brought there by ambulance to bid him goodbye. 'Hasn't it been a full life, Lily,' he said to his weeping wife, 'and isn't this a good end?' He had no fear of the judgement of his fellow countrymen; they would appraise and honour his deed. And Connolly the internationalist, who had seen many of the British socialists turned into raving jingoes during the war, knew what their verdict on him would be. 'The socialists will never understand why I am here,' he said to his wife. 'They will all forget I am an Irishman.' His forecast of them proved to be true even before his death. Captain Jack White, his colleague of former days, made an effort to save his life by rousing the British socialists to intervene on his behalf. He had written an article for this purpose which was actually set up in the Independent Labour Party paper, the *Merthyr Pioneer*. The paper appeared with the article blacked out – the leader of the ILP had wired from London forbidding its publication!

Before they parted, Connolly managed to slip into the hand of his daughter a document, which she smuggled out of the Castle. It was his speech before the field general court martial held at Dublin Castle on 9 May.

He was executed on 12 May 1916.

TOM CLARKE

ON 4 APRIL 1883, a young man called 'Henry Hammond Wilson', newly arrived from the United States, was arrested at his lodgings in London by Detective-Inspector Littlechild of Scotland Yard. A little over a month later, with three others, he was tried at the Old Bailey on a charge of being concerned in a Fenian dynamite plot, and on 14 June 1883, the four men were sentenced to penal servitude for life. Tom Clarke, for that was the real name of the young man who stood in the dock at the Old Bailey, had lost the first round of a struggle against English rule in Ireland that was to end only on that day in 1916 when he was sentenced to death by a British court martial.

Tom Clarke was fifty-eight years of age when he was executed, and the total number of years he had spent in Ireland was eighteen. He was born in an English military camp at Hurst Park, on the Isle of Wight, on 11 March 1858, the son of Corporal James Clarke, Irish Protestant soldier in the British army, and of an Irish Catholic mother. A year later, Corporal Clarke was drafted to South Africa, and there young Tom attended school until the family returned to Europe in 1865. On his appointment as sergeant of the Ulster Militia, James Clarke was stationed at Dungannon, County Tyrone, and in that place so full of historic associations, Tom grew to early manhood, becoming while still in his teens the leader of the young national element in the town. With his special friends Billy Kelly and Louis MacMullen, he had earnest discussions as to the best way of driving the English out of Ireland. The countryside was still full of living memories of the famine of Black '47, and all around them they saw the present evils of English rule – the evictions, the battering-ram, the blackened ruins of former homesteads and the abject poverty of the people. The Fenians had risen up against this and had been crushed, but songs in their praise were still heard at fairs and céilidhthe. Where such great men as these had failed, how could Tom Clarke and his two young companions hope to succeed?

The Dungannon district circle of the Irish Republican Brotherhood met, under cover, in the premises of the Catholic and Total Abstinence reading rooms and dramatic club, and of this club Tom was an active member. It was a favourite recruiting ground for the IRB, and, probably aware of this, Sergeant Clarke urged his son to give up the position he held as assistant master in the national school at Dungannon, and to join the British army. The sergeant, now a soldier of about thirty years' standing, must have been shocked at the violent way Tom resisted the idea.

In 1878, John Daly, with whom Clarke's fate was so closely linked for the rest of his life, visited Dungannon in his capacity as national organiser of the Fenians, and addressed a meeting of the IRB of the Dungannon district outside the town. Tom and his friends were greatly impressed with the young Fenian, and some time later, when they were in Dublin for the unveiling of the O'Connell monument, they were sworn into the organisation by Michael Davitt and John Daly. Fenianism had hardly been crushed when it had risen again!

In 1880, when several of his young companions, including Billy Kelly, were emigrating to the United States, Clarke decided to go with them. He slipped away without telling his parents that he was joining the emigrant ship at Derry. After a couple of years in New York he had, by hard work and efficiency, won a position of trust in the hotel business. No doubt there were letters home, filled with boyish pride at the progress he was making; then, after three years, he disappeared, leaving no trace. Only two men in camp No. 1 of Clan na Gael knew of his fate, and he was two years in prison before they were permitted to tell his sister, Maria, pledging her to secrecy, that Henry Hammond Wilson, the convict J464, was her brother Tom.

Shortly after they arrived in the United States, Tom Clarke and Billy Kelly had joined Clan na Gael, and soon after they had answered a call for volunteers for dangerous work in England. The Irish-American leaders were carrying on a war against England by sending over emissaries to dynamite public buildings, but the organisation was filled with English spies who kept Scotland Yard fully informed of the personnel and movements of the dynamitards, and many of them were arrested immediately on their arrival in England.

Tom Clarke, whose services had been accepted by the Clan, had temporarily shaken off his 'shadow' when the ship on which he was travelling struck an iceberg and sank. Rescued by a passing vessel and brought to Newfoundland, he gave his name as 'Henry Hammond Wilson', an Englishman returning to his native land. Given a new suit of clothes and a small sum of money to enable him to reach his home, Tom Clarke proceeded on his interrupted journey – and had, unknown to himself, been accompanied from the United States by an informer called Lynch. 'Henry Le Caron', an English spy (author of *Twenty-five Years in the Secret Service*) was high up in the councils of Clan na Gael. He had given due notice to his employers that the dynamitards would arrive in England by a certain date and, after they had sufficiently committed themselves, they were arrested, tried and convicted. With his companions, Dr Thomas Gallagher, John Curtin and Alfred Whitehead, Tom Clarke was sentenced to penal servitude for life, without hope of release until they had completed twenty years – and then each case was decided on its merits.

'I remembered,' wrote Tom Clarke in his book, *Glimpses of an Irish Felon's Prison Life*, 'with what relentless savagery the English government had always dealt with the Irishman it gets into its clutches, and the future appeared as black and appalling as imagination could picture it. But the worst my imagination could then picture was outdone by the horrors of Chatham prison that I was afterwards to experience.' Later he was removed to Portland prison where conditions were even worse.

John Daly, arrested a year after Tom Clarke, was his fellow prisoner during the great part of the fifteen years and nine months that he spent in this living hell. Every inhuman cruelty that the mind of debased man could invent was inflicted on the Fenian prisoners, whose ingenuity in finding ways of keeping themselves from breaking under the strain makes *Glimpses of an Irish Felon's Prison Life* an epic of human courage and indomitable will. Eventually two of them, Whitehead and Gallagher, became hopelessly mad, but were still kept in prison and savagely punished for any infringement of the strict prison rules.

After they had been five years in prison, John Daly and Tom Clarke had an opportunity of obtaining their release at the price of their honour. Charles Stewart Parnell, who had refused to plead on their behalf with the British government, was in danger in 1888 when the infamous Pigott case was being tried. First Pigot, then Inspector Littlechild of Scotland Yard, visited Clarke in prison and offered him money and freedom if he would appear as a state witness against

Parnell. 'I would rather rot in prison than dishonour myself,' was his answer, and he managed to warn Daly that he would probably receive a similar offer, which he did. Daly was even more outspoken than Clarke, and became so ill as a result of the brutal treatment he received that he was removed to the prison hospital where, on three successive occasions, he was given an overdose of the poisonous drug, belladonna … by mistake!

In 1896, Limerick forced the hand of the British government by electing John Daly MP, and this, together with the agitation carried on by the amnesty committee, led to the release of Daly on 21 August 1896, at the same time as Gallagher and Whitehead, who were insane. For nearly two years more Clarke, now without even the consoling presence of John Daly to help him, remained in prison, until he was released on 25 September 1898 on ticket-of-leave.

During a pleasant stay with John Daly, who had been elected mayor of Limerick on his release, Tom Clarke was made a freeman of the city, and was made much of by Daly's nieces and his seven-year-old nephew, Ned. Seventeen years later, Ned was to fall before the firing squad as Commandant Ned Daly. During that Limerick visit, Tom Clarke became engaged to Kathleen Daly, and later when he returned to the United States, she joined him there, and they were married in New York, on 16 July 1901. One of the witnesses of the marriage was Major John MacBride, also executed as a leader in 1916.

Clarke's experience of the American Clan na Gael leaders after his release would have made any other man turn from the Irish movement in bitter discouragement. Wanting the capital to restart his life, he applied to John Devoy to arrange a lecture tour, but met with a refusal. On reaching New York, he was given a post as a night-clerk at Clan na Gael headquarters at a weekly wage of fifteen dollars. This he supplemented by working in the daytime as a finisher at a pump works. When that job came to an end he tramped the streets of New York, applying without success for a position as a street-sweeper, and thinking that perhaps he had been better off in Portland prison! In 1903, mainly through his efforts, the *Gaelic American* was started, with Devoy as editor and Clarke as his assistant. In this position he remained until he returned to Ireland in 1907.

Early in 1908 he opened a newspaper and tobacconist shop at 75A Parnell Street, which was always filled with the young men and women whose names are now part of Ireland's history – among them, Pearse, Plunkett, MacDonagh, Countess Markievicz, MacDiarmada and Mellows. They came to exchange confidences and to seek the advice of this man who, with mind unwarped by his sufferings and heart still full of hope and courage, was already planning the next war against England. He was self-effacing and modest, and hated to be the subject of hero-worship; ready to serve his country, but he was unwilling to be regarded as a leader whose word was law. It was typical of him that when he was asked to deliver the oration over the grave of O'Donovan Rossa he replied: 'No, the young men must come forward,' and chose from among them Pádraig Pearse.

His story from the day of his return is the story of Ireland, and especially it is the history of the 1916 Rising. Miss Julia Grenan, of the GPO garrison, describes the scene at the Rotunda where the prisoners were being checked over by the British military accompanied by detectives:

> Later on a detective came up with a military officer, and brought away Tom Clarke under an armed guard. He returned after some time and told us they had searched him and taken away all he had, and that the record of his whole life had been read out to him. His life in prison, his conduct there, his life in the United States, even to the cut of clothes he wore there; his life from his return to Ireland up to the present day. 'Everything, they have everything,' he said.

This very complete dossier could not have been compiled from the files of the secret service in the United States, Scotland Yard and Dublin overnight.

In 1936 when Louis Le Roux was writing the *Life of Tom Clarke* he applied to the British Home Office for permission to see the files relating to the court martial of Clarke, but was refused. Too many valuable secret agents would have been exposed to light.

As they awaited court martial, Frank Fahy, one of Clarke's closest friends, was standing beside him. 'How do you feel, Tom?' he asked.

'Fine,' said Clarke, 'fine – it was great to see the devils run!'

Tom Clarke's last message to his countrymen were the words he spoke to his wife when she visited him in his prison cell a few hours before his execution: 'Make no mistake, freedom is coming, but not at once. Ireland will go through a very terrible time between now and the final blow. And there will be another big fight. We all believe this, and in that belief we die happy.'

He was shot on 3 May 1916.

SEÁN MacDIARMADA

WHEN SEÁN MACDIARMADA was fifteen years of age he ran away from home, and arrived in Glasgow in search of employment and with only a few shillings in his pocket. Like Tom Clarke, his great friend of later years, he had been a monitor in the local school, and it was a thirst for adventure which both men had in full measure that took them away from home. There the parallel ends momentarily. In 1884 when Tom Clarke had just completed one year of his sixteen years' torture in English jails, Seán MacDiarmada was born in Kiltyclogher, County Leitrim; the jail gates had not yet opened on Tom Clarke, when Seán was setting out on his first adventure. In Glasgow, MacDiarmada found employment with an uncle who was a gardener, but gave it up after a couple of years, and worked on the Glasgow trams for another twelve months. He then returned to Ireland and lived in Belfast, where he worked in turn as tram-conductor and barman. As a Catholic he inevitably joined the Ancient Order of Hibernians, then regarded by Ulster Catholics as the custodian of Irish nationalism. He did not remain long with the order.

Whilst working in Glasgow he had met some members of the Gaelic League, and soon after he settled in Belfast he enrolled in a local branch and later became a fine Irish speaker. In these circles he got in touch with such men as Denis MacCullough, Seán McGarry and Bulmer Hobson and they later recruited him into Cumann na nGaedhael, an open political organisation of advanced nationalism, of which they were leading members and which had been started by Arthur Griffith in 1900. His personal charm, sincerity and capacity for hard work made him an obvious choice for the position of organiser of the Dungannon Clubs, the foremost republican association in the north. His success in that position led to an invitation to join the Irish Republican Brotherhood in 1906.

He had already joined the Sinn Féin organisation, and in 1906 was sent to Dublin as one of the delegates from Belfast to the Sinn Féin annual convention. Although then but twenty-two years old, and of shy and retiring disposition, MacDiarmada made a deep impression on the convention. He was strikingly handsome, earnest, and spoke, not only with natural eloquence, but with a sincerity which held his audience. Gay and light-hearted, with a gift for telling a humorous story and a tongue that was witty without being malicious, he made an equally favourable impression off the platforms.

During the first parliamentary election contested by Sinn Féin, that in North Leitrim in 1907, MacDiarmada put in months of strenuous work and eventually the whole direction of the campaign devolved upon him. Night, noon and morn he canvassed from door to door and mile after mile he tramped over mountains and bogs in all kinds of weather; but his native county did not reward his work by returning the Sinn Féin candidate, Charles Dolan.

Before Tom Clarke returned to Ireland in 1907 he had been in correspondence with several young republicans who included Mac-Diarmada, and as soon as he opened his famous shop in Parnell Street, Dublin, one of Clarke's first visitors was Seán. It is hardly surprising that the friendship which sprang up between these two men at their first meeting should develop and endure to the death, for they were as one in their thoughts, desires, hopes and plans for Ireland. Tom Clarke commenced his dreary term of penal servitude when he was twenty-four years of age; and the wonder of it must have struck him that twenty-five years later another young man of twenty-four should be eager to finish the work he had begun. Shortly after they had met for the first time, Tom Clarke gave proof of the high opinion he had formed of MacDiarmada by asking him to become the national organiser of the Irish Republican Brotherhood. That was in 1908 when the organisation needed overhauling and new recruits, and Clarke had seen at once that in MacDiarmada he had the ideal man for the job. MacDiarmada made his home in Dublin from that year, and between then and 1911 he accomplished an incredible volume of work. It was not spectacular; a great deal of it was dull drudgery, routine business connected with committees and organisations. While other young men of his age were on the dance floor at céilidhthe he would stand at the door to collect the tickets; while others enjoyed a game at Croke Park, he would move patiently through the crowd to take down the names of likely new members for republican organisations. He carried out these inconspicuous tasks with such enthusiasm and driving force, and with such singleness of purpose, that he inspired others in the movement to a high sense of duty and a spirit of sacrifice.

With the foundation of *Irish Freedom* in 1910, with Dr Patrick MacCartan as editor and Seán MacDiarmada as manager, the fruits of MacDiarmada's work became evident. The semi-moribund IRB had come to life, and Tom Clarke was the real, though unacknowledged, leader of an organisation that within a few years was to enroll such new men as Pearse, Mellows, Plunkett, MacDonagh and Michael Collins. *Irish Freedom*, which was published by the IRB, had no paid contributors or staff. It contained excellent articles, and was read not only all over Ireland, but in Great Britain, the United States and in many parts of the British dominions. Its dispatch, a formidable task, was done entirely by voluntary help, and on publication day the office was always crowded with energetic workers.

The year 1911 was marked by a struggle for control of the secret organisation and of its paper. It was the year of the last visit of British royalty to Ireland – as distinct from visits to the six counties now partitioned. MacDiarmada had invited all republican and genuinely nationalist forces to co-operate in a series of demonstrations against the royal visit, and all over Dublin there were stormy meetings, baton charges, arrests, the tearing down of British emblems. MacDiarmada, whose fine and impassioned oratory was heard for the first time by the mass of the Dublin people, became recognised as a republican leader from that time. But it was the oratory of another man, Pádraig Pearse, which brought about the inevitable split in the IRB, which followed the annual Emmet commemoration concert in that year. Fred Allan, who at that time exercised the controlling voice in the IRB, having decided to curb the rising resurgent spirit in the organisation, gave orders that there were to be no 'political' resolutions introduced at the concert. Carried away by Pearse's speech on Emmet, however, Dr MacCartan jumped on the platform and asked the audience to pass a resolution which pledged them to refrain from participation in the pro-British demonstrations. Tom Clarke seconded MacCartan, and the resolution was passed and carried into effect.

As a result of the incident, the two IRB men were court-martialled by their organisation, and a determined attempt was made by Fred Allan and his supporters to have them expelled, and to take control of *Irish Freedom*. Before the matter was settled, and Fred Allan and his friends had retired in favour of Tom Clarke, MacDiarmada went through severe mental anguish, for he saw that if Clarke was expelled, the revolutionary movement would be nipped in the bud.

It was the strain of this period coupled with long years of over-work that brought about the illness which made him a cripple for life. Whenever I see his name written 'MacDermott' it recalls a story he told me when I visited him in hospital. He had given his correct name, Seán MacDiarmada, to the nurse, an English woman, who despite his repeated protests wrote 'John MacDermott' on his chart. Seán, who was suffering from infantile paralysis and unable to move, got another patient to bring him the chart which he tore into pieces as soon as the nurse had left the ward. Thereafter the nurse revenged herself by neglecting him as much as she dared. This angered the other patients so much that some of them spoke to the hospital authorities, and the nurse, unworthy of her profession, was dismissed. But such was the kind and gentle character of MacDiarmada that he actually appealed on her behalf.

MacDiarmada, though a cripple from that time onwards, worked with redoubled energy, confident and happy in the knowledge that under the guidance of Clarke the fight for a Republic would take place within his lifetime. He took an active part in the formation of the Volunteers, and as a member of its Provisional Committee, was one of the minority who voted against the acceptance of Redmond's nominees. Neither he nor Tom Clarke accompanied the Volunteers to Howth for the gun-running, lest their presence should rouse the suspicions of Dublin Castle to the fact that something more than a route march was intended. They were kept in touch with the operation by dispatch carriers, who reported great numbers of police and soldiers on their way to Howth. The two men set off in a taxi to meet the Volunteers, and transported a large number of the rifles to Clarke's house at 77 Amiens Street.

As a member of the military council which planned the Rising, Mac-Diarmada had a position of great importance and trust. All Volunteer officers, who were members of the IRB, received orders shortly before the Rising that they were to take instructions from Pádraig Pearse, and disregard orders from anyone else, 'unless such orders, signed by MacNeill or by Hobson were transmitted through MacDiarmada himself'.

During Holy Week, MacDiarmada and the other leaders made several efforts to win over MacNeill, who first agreed that the Volunteers should be called out to fight, and who later announced that he would oppose the step in every way, short of ringing up Dublin Castle. In a last minute effort to win his support MacDonagh, MacDiarmada and Pearse went to his house at Rathfarnham at 8 a.m. on Holy Saturday morning. MacDiarmada told him of the expected German arms, and he replied: 'In view of this landing of arms a fight is inevitable, and we are all in it.'

The news that MacNeill had issued a countermanding order was brought to MacDiarmada at midnight on Saturday by Thomas

MacDonagh. A hastily summoned conference, in which MacDonagh, Pearse, Plunkett and Diarmuid Lynch took part, continued until 2.30 a.m. on Sunday morning, and then as Ceannt, Clarke and Connolly could not be reached, it was adjourned and met again in Liberty Hall at 8 a.m. on Sunday morning. All the military council were at the second conference, which continued until 1 p.m. MacDiarmada, having snatched a few hours' sleep at Fleming's Hotel, was again at his desk that evening, to send dispatch carriers all over the country and to make the final preparations for the following day. Though ill and exhausted, he was supremely happy when he took his place with his comrades in the GPO, at noon on Easter Monday.

A description of the scenes which followed the surrender of the GPO garrison written by Miss Julia Grenan for *The Catholic Bulletin* of June 1917, tells how a Dublin Metropolitan policeman said to Seán MacDiarmada: 'We wish to place on record the leniency you and your colleagues have shown during the Rising to the DMP, and we assure you that whatever we can say in your and their favour shall be said.' Possibly some of these men did attempt to save MacDiarmada's life; for, although he was well-known in Dublin, he was not identified at Richmond barracks, and had been classed as one of those to be interned, when he was picked out as a leader by Detective Johnny Barton, who was shot dead in 1919 for his vicious anti-IRA activities.

THOMAS MacDONAGH

THOMAS MACDONAGH was the child of two teachers; a Roscommon man who had settled in Cloughjordan, County Tipperary, where Thomas was born in 1878, and his Dublin-born wife. It was from his mother that he inherited his love of music and art, but it was his father who implanted in him a deep and lasting affection for the countryside, and for the traditions and folk-songs of its people. The MacDonaghs were a large and talented family, whose precocity found an outlet in running little manuscript magazines, and composing humorous songs about rural romances and eccentric local characters. Out of that home came Thomas MacDonagh, poet, playwright, teacher and soldier; Joseph MacDonagh, Sinn Féin TD from 1918 until the Treaty, and director of the Belfast Boycott of 1920; John MacDonagh, playwright, who fought in Jacob's factory in 1916; and Terence MacDonagh, who became a celebrated musician in England.

Eight years of Thomas MacDonagh's young manhood were spent in Rockwell College, Cashel, studying for the priesthood, but finding he had no vocation, he left the seminary, and went to France to continue his studies for his chosen profession of teaching. He taught for some years in St Kieran's College, Kilkenny, and St Colman's College, Fermoy, his subjects being English, Latin and French. He had not at that time even a smattering of Gaelic. Later, when he had become a Gaelic language enthusiast he told the way in which he had been drawn into the Gaelic League. He hated prejudice and bigotry, and when some of his colleagues sneered at the Irish language revival, he determined he would attend a meeting which was to be addressed by Dr Douglas Hyde and hear the other side of the story. From that time on he was a close student of his native language, and brought to its study and teaching his own gifts and specialised knowledge, so that he became an accomplished Gaelic scholar and one of its most popular and successful teachers. Like Pearse, he studied the language among the native speakers, spending long periods in the Aran Islands, where, because of his personal charm, his easy manners, his wit and gaiety he was a welcome guest at the firesides of the people. He had a good singing voice and a repertoire which included French folk songs and Irish traditional ballads. The people of Aran still remember his fascinating conversation, his singing, and his humour. 'Fear an Rothair', they called him, 'the man with the bicycle', because MacDonagh's bicycle was the first one they had ever seen in the islands. All those who knew him even casually, whether they were simple country folk or learned professors, were so impressed by his vivid personality and brilliant talk that they can still remember the very tones of his voice, his animated gestures, and his merry, ringing laughter.

When Pádraig Pearse opened St Enda's College at Cullenswood House in 1908, Thomas MacDonagh was one of the first to join him. Pearse, sometimes depressed and worried with the cares of the school, turned with relief to his light-hearted assistant master, who could always transmute the most dismal experience into laughter. MacDonagh's classes were immensely popular with the boys, for there was nothing in him of the pompous professor. He would use a country story, a satiric French folk-song, or the strange English of the American comic strip to illustrate the subject on which he was lecturing.

Later, when St Enda's moved from Cullenswood House to the Hermitage, Rathfarnham, MacDonagh went to live at a little gate lodge attached to the house of his great friend, Professor David Houston, which soon became a Mecca for all the poets and writers of the period. Pádraic Colum, James Stephens, Joseph Plunkett, Seamus O'Sullivan, George Russell and many others climbed the steep road to Grange House Lodge where he kept his bachelor house.

Thomas MacDonagh's literary work includes several books of verse, two prose works, *Thomas Campion and the Art of English Poetry* and *Literature in Ireland*, and a play, *When the Dawn is Come*, produced at the Abbey Theatre in 1907. This drama dealt with a future period, with an Irish army, its command vested in a council of seven captains, fighting against England. Nine years later MacDonagh himself took his place on just such a council of seven captains. When the dawn *did* come, he was commandant of the Dublin brigade. The plot of this play, written so long before the Irish Volunteers had come into existence, shows that MacDonagh was already thinking of the future fight against England. In 1907 or 1908 he decided to join the French army in order to get military training, but finding that the foreign legion was the only branch open to foreigners, he gave up the idea. In 1909 he took his degree as MA at the National University, and in the same year became a lecturer there in English, expressing the hope to his friends that from among the students would come the revolutionary forces that would liberate Ireland.

From 1911 on he was associated with the *Irish Review*, to which he was a constant contributor, and in which a great deal of the work of

Pádraig Pearse and Joseph Plunkett also appeared. With the foundation of the Irish Volunteers in 1913, the magazine devoted a great deal of its space to the work of the Volunteers.

Though their Volunteer activities absorbed so much of their time, MacDonagh and Plunkett embarked on a new venture in 1914. In association with Edward Martyn, they launched the Irish Theatre in Hardwicke Street, Dublin. Its directors were Martyn, Plunkett and MacDonagh, and its stage manager was John MacDonagh, brother of Thomas, who also took part in some of its productions. Two Irish Theatre playbills extant, one for November 1914 and one for June 1915, give an idea of some of their work for the drama at this period. *The Dream Physician*, a play in five acts by Edward Martyn, was produced for six nights and a matinee on 2 November 1914, among the cast being Eric Gorman, now a well-known Abbey actor; Úna O'Connor, who has become famous as a film actress in Hollywood; Máire Nic Shiubhlaigh, the former Abbey actress, whose portrait hangs in the Abbey vestibule, and who was in charge of Cumann na mBan in Jacob's factory; John MacDonagh, also of Jacob's garrison; and Nellie Gifford, Thomas MacDonagh's sister-in-law, and later of the College of Surgeons' garrison. In June 1915, the Irish Theatre produced *Uncle Vanya*, by Anton Tchekov, and among the cast were Willie Pearse, Blanaid Salkeld, the distinguished poet, Máire Nic Shiubhlaigh and Nellie Gifford.

Thomas MacDonagh had begun as captain of 'C' company, 2nd battalion, but soon became director of training of the Volunteers. He was in charge of the marshalling arrangements at O'Donovan Rossa's funeral in 1915, and showed his great ability as an organiser on that occasion. In the years leading up to the Rising 'Fear an Rothair' became a familiar figure at all Volunteer rallies. During Holy Week, a period of confusion and deep depression in Dublin Volunteer circles, his influence was tremendous in bringing order out of chaos and hope out of despair. 'Who will ever forget the visits of Thomas MacDonagh to the various companies under his command?' wrote 'Veteran', in *An Phoblacht* for 19 April 1930, 'and who hearing him address his men during that week had any doubts as to what the future held for us? He met the officers of his command on Holy Saturday evening, and sent us away with hopes as high and cheery as his own.' And while he was rallying the men, he was also working incessantly with his fellow commandants, trying to undo the mischief which had been done by the countermanding order.

'We may all go down, but we have done the right thing,' he told his brother John during Easter Week. Only one sorrow clouded his mind – the thought that he might never again see his wife and children. He had been married in 1912 to Muriel Gifford, and he was a devoted husband and father. Miss Elizabeth O'Farrell, who had brought him Pearse's order to surrender, was standing beside him when they were about to march out of Jacob's factory. 'I would give anything to see Muriel just once more,' he said to her.

'Will I go and fetch her?' said Miss O'Farrell.

MacDonagh looked sadly round at the scene of defeat and said, 'Ah, no ... I would not like her to remember – *this*!'

His speech before the British court martial was taken down in shorthand by an officer of the court who had formerly been a journalist. Someone to whom he gave the notes had the speech printed at Maunsell's, where the *Irish Review* was printed. The firm was raided by the British, and many of the copies were seized, but it was reproduced again, and was distributed chiefly by Dublin newsboys, who hid it under their papers and sold it to sympathisers. In recent years it has been described by some historians as apocryphal because it contains the sentence, 'You have sentenced me to death'. It is pointed out that the sentence of death was not pronounced at the court martial, but later. The words were probably changed from, 'You may sentence me to death,' by whoever got it published, but there is no doubt whatever of its being authentic. His closest relations and most intimate friends recognise it as such, because it is in his literary style, voices the beliefs and ideals which he often expressed, and makes a reference to Savonarola, for whom he had a profound admiration.

Moreover, it is unlikely that anyone attempting to concoct a speech would have attributed it to Thomas MacDonagh who was not, like Pearse, a famous orator.

His last letter to his wife, written at midnight on Tuesday 2 May, from Kilmainham jail, reveals that he was tried that day, and was told at midnight that he was to die at dawn, 3.30 a.m. on 3 May. The British could not delay his execution for a few days, until it was possible for his wife to be brought from the Dublin suburbs to see him for the last time. His last letter was carried to her by Fr Aloysius, who had been unable to reach her within the three hours between his sentence and execution. It contained the sentence: 'I am ready to die and I thank God that I am to die in so holy a cause. My country will reward my deed richly ... I counted the cost of this, and am ready to pay it.'

ÉAMONN CEANNT

BORN IN GALWAY in September 1881, Éamonn Ceannt was the son of a Tipperary man who was a head constable in the Royal Irish Constabulary, and of a Cork woman, whose maiden name was Johanna Galwey. Soon after Éamonn's birth, his father was moved to Dublin, and there his son was educated at the Christian Brothers' school, North Richmond Street. He was an industrious and intelligent boy, and carried off many prizes and scholarships.

When Ceannt was seventeen years of age, the nation-wide cele-brations in honour of the '98 centenary were being held, and, in Dublin, processions, meetings, lectures, illustrated supplements in all the nationalist press, and the unveiling of memorials to the insurgents, roused once more public pride in the story of their gallant fight against the odds.

As the commemoration procession marched through Dublin, Ceannt took his place in the ranks, and was recruited from that moment into the service of Ireland. Within a few months he had bought a copy of O'Growney and had commenced to study Irish. In the Gaelic League, which he joined about 1900, he met Pádraig Pearse and Eoin MacNeill, and soon became so proficient in Irish that he was recognised as one of its best teachers. His success as a teacher was probably due to the fact that he was an excellent linguist, speaking French, German and Irish with a very pure accent. His efficiency and hard work were soon noticed in the central branch of the League, and he was elected to the governing body of the organisation.

He had a fine ear for music, and having learnt to play the war-pipes, joined Cumann na bPíobairí, and won two prizes for his performances at the Oireachtas in 1906. As secretary of the cumann, he insisted upon all the minutes being written and read in Irish – a regulation not enforced in the Gaelic League at that time.

In 1905 he married Miss Áine O'Brennan, who, with her sisters Kathleen and Lily, were so closely associated with the republican movement then and later. The marriage ceremony was in Irish, and, as there was no Irish coinage, he procured gold and silver French coins for the ritual gift.

Ceannt, a teetotaller and of a reserved manner, was a clerk in the city treasurer's office of the Dublin Corporation, and was regarded by most of his fellow employees as a staid, rather conservative type of man. But this was the impression he created only upon those with whom he had very little in common. He disliked what he called 'greenflaggery' and idle boasting, and as his mind was altogether taken up with thoughts of Ireland's future, he opened it only to his few chosen companions who thought like himself. In the central branch of Sinn Féin, which he joined about 1908, he found himself in company where he could talk on the subjects in which he was interested, and won a reputation as a speaker whose remarks were always pithy and worth hearing. He was not long a member before he was made secretary of the central branch, and soon after was elected to the national council.

But this young man who seemed so quiet, reserved and grave, had ideas far in advance of most of his associates in Sinn Féin. Already he had joined a rifle club, and was training for the day when he would stand behind a barricade and fight for his country. He was also studying social systems, including in his research the writings of such foreign revolutionaries as Marx and Engels, and when James Connolly returned to Ireland in 1910, Ceannt lectured on a few occasions at the Antient Concert Rooms, the headquarters of the Irish Socialist Party. But though he could discuss various social theories very intelligently, his ideal for Ireland was the kind of republic envisaged by Pearse – 'Not free merely, but Gaelic as well; not Gaelic merely, but free as well.'

In 1908 he accompanied a group of Irish athletes to Rome, where they were competing at the jubilee celebrations in honour of His Holiness Pope Pius X. While there he refused to speak a word of English, and made his way through the Eternal City by using French, Latin, and broken Italian. When the Irish athletes stepped onto the field, headed by their piper, a young man with a magnificent figure and a soldierly bearing dressed in Irish kilts, the Roman population succumbed to the splendour of his appearance and to the strange, wild music of his pipes. Word of him was brought to His Holiness, who summoned Ceannt to perform in his presence. With the Irish pilgrims, who were assembled at the Vatican for the occasion, were many old Irish priests, long exiled from Ireland. When in the distance was heard the skirl of the pipes coming nearer and nearer, and the tall Irish piper entered dressed in the costume of the eleventh century, and marched up the room playing 'The Wearin' of the Green', the emotion of some of the old priests was so great that they burst into tears. His Holiness looked on sympathetically, though probably surprised that such wild music should draw tears from their eyes.

Ceannt had taken an active part in the stormy meetings in Dublin which were organised to protest against the British royal visit in 1911, and in the following year, with Pádraig Pearse, The O'Rahilly, Brian O'Higgins and Peadar Macken he started an Irish language paper called *An Barr Buadh*, to preach the doctrine of an armed fight against England, but it was short-lived through lack of funds. Ceannt wrote well, with a clear and incisive style, and was a constant contributor to *Irish Freedom*. He was also one of those Volunteers who helped Seán MacDiarmada with dispatch and other work connected with the paper.

On the organisation of the Volunteers, Ceannt was one of those summoned to the inaugural meeting at Wynn's Hotel and to the Rotunda meeting afterwards, and subsequently he joined the 4th battalion at Kimmage. He had now come into his own. In the estimate of Seán Fitzgibbon, who was his colleague in the corporation, and who knew him as an Irish Volunteer, he, more than any of his comrades in arms, was by nature a physical force man – one who would have made a fine commander of an army in a free Ireland. He was quickly promoted, first to captain of 'A' company, and then to commandant of the battalion, the position he held in Easter Week.

He took an active and important part in the gun-runnings at Howth and Kilcool, and through strict discipline and intensive training had brought his men to that high standard which they showed in the Rising. Kevin O'Carroll, one of the 4th battalion, writing in *An Phoblacht* for 19 April 1930, told how, after a parade and manoeuvres in the Pine Forest about a fortnight before Easter Sunday, Ceannt delivered a short but significant address to the men. 'He requested all men to hand in the names of their dependants to their adjutants during the coming week,' said O'Carroll, 'and to obtain full equipment as soon as possible – the quartermasters would meet half their expenses.'

All those who fought under Ceannt unite in describing his great bravery, his coolness, and his splendid bearing all through the fight. Throughout the week, under the inspired leadership of Ceannt and Brugha, the 4th battalion made a magnificent stand. When, after a conference with Commandant Thomas MacDonagh, he agreed to surrender, he advised his men to surrender as soldiers. An eye-witness, writing in *The Catholic Bulletin* for July 1916, said: 'I saw him lead his men to the place where they laid down their arms. His bearing was noble, magnificent. I felt proud of him in my heart, and the soldiers looked on in wonder. Some day I hope to tell much that is inspiring of his last moments and his glorious death, with my own crucifix in his grasp.'

And in his last letter to his wife, written an hour before his execution, he left this message for his countrymen:

I leave for the guidance of other revolutionaries who may tread the path which I have trod, this advice, never to treat with the enemy, never to surrender at *his* mercy, but to fight to a finish. I see nothing gained but grave disaster caused by the surrender which has marked the end of the Irish Insurrection of 1916 – so far at least as Dublin is concerned. The enemy has not cherished one generous thought for those who, with little hope, with poor equipment and weak in numbers, withstood his forces for one glorious week. Ireland has shown she is a nation. This generation can claim to have raised sons as brave as any that went before, and in the years to come Ireland will honour those who risked all for her honour at Easter in 1916. I bear no ill will towards those against whom I have fought. I have found the common soldiers and the higher officers human and companionable, even the English who were actually in the fight against us …

I wish to record the magnificent gallantry and fearless, calm determination of the men who fought with me. All, all were simply splendid. Even I knew no fear nor panic and shrunk from no risk, even as I shrink not now from the death that faces me at daybreak. I hope to see God's face even for a moment in the morning. His will be done …

He was executed on 8 May 1916.

JOSEPH MARY PLUNKETT

JOSEPH PLUNKETT, THE eldest son of George Noble, Count Plunkett, was the youngest of the seven signatories of the 1916 Proclamation, and was born into a cultured and learned Dublin home in November 1887.

A delicate child who became a semi-invalid as the years went on, Joseph received his early education at Belvedere College, where he was discouraged from playing games; but in that fragile body was an iron will, and the story of his short life is one of intense activity, both physical and mental.

From Belvedere he went to the Jesuits' English house at Stoneyhurst to take a course in philosophy, and there he passed some happy years in study. A member of a family that had always been intensely loyal to the Catholic faith, and who gloried in the fact that they were kinsmen of Blessed Oliver Plunkett, the memory of that martyr who died for the faith must often have given inspiration and courage to Joseph when the time came for him to fight against his own ill-health, and against the intrigues of those who were trying to wreck the plans for the Rising.

Before he was twenty-four he had already travelled in Italy, Sicily, France and Malta, and was a master of many languages, including Arabic. He could draw and paint well, play the violin and piano, and was a talented actor. Dancing and roller-skating were his two favourite physical exercises, and he became so skilled at the latter that when he was in Algiers in 1911 he was offered a post of teacher in the largest rink in Cairo. These journeys abroad were made for reasons of health, and ended with his stay in Algiers in 1911. From that date, except for his trips to Germany and the United States on Volunteer business, all his time was absorbed in revolutionary activities.

His friendship with Thomas MacDonagh had commenced during the year 1910 when he was studying Gaelic under him at St Enda's in preparation for his matriculation examination at the National University. Pupil and teacher had many ideals, tastes and characteristics in common. They were both poets and scholars; both gay and humorous; both devoted to the arts, especially the theatre and literature; both devoted to the Catholic faith and to the cause of Irish liberty. MacDonagh at thirty-two found this boy of twenty-three, with his witty tongue, his widespread learning and his love of the arts, a delightful companion. They discussed the future of Ireland, and agreed that the fight against England would come in their generation, and that they must prepare the way for it. Plunkett added to his other studies with MacDonagh that of military tactics.

By 1911 Plunkett was already recognised as one of the best of the younger poets, and a collection of his verse under the title *The Circle and the Sword* appeared in that year dedicated to Thomas MacDonagh. On his return to Dublin from Algiers he helped to found and worked on *The Irish Review*, in association with David Houston, Pádraic Colum, James Stephens and Thomas MacDonagh. It was a literary magazine of very high order, and often contained stimulating articles on current Irish affairs and social questions. An article which appeared in its issue for July 1913, gave a new orientation to Irish political thought. It was entitled, 'Ireland, Germany, and the Freedom of the Seas', and was written by Sir Roger Casement, under the pen-name, 'Shan Van Vocht'.

It set out to prove that England's position of mistress of the seas had had disastrous results for Europe and the world and rested on her occupation of Ireland. Casement claimed that Ireland should, in the event of a war between Britain and Germany, act as a friendly neutral and enlist the sympathy of Germany. She should seek international guarantees that would make her an independent neutral state – 'an Atlantic Holland, a maritime Belgium'. This article was an answer to one which had recently appeared in *The Fortnightly Review*, from Sir Conan Doyle, in which Doyle advanced the familiar argument that the fate of Ireland was bound up with that of England, that she was under the 'protection' of the English fleet, and that 'no sword can transfix England without the point reaching Ireland behind her'.

Casement's article was re-issued as a pamphlet, and a copy of it was dispatched to Dr Kuno Meyer, an eminent German philologist and Gaelic scholar, who had returned to his home in Berlin. Meyer, who had given great service to the Irish Language movement during his years in Ireland, was a close friend of Dr Douglas Hyde, Pearse, MacDonagh and others who were playing a leading part in the language revival. At the outbreak of the 1914–1918 war, Dr Kuno Meyer decided to translate the pamphlet into German, and had just got it ready for publication when Casement arrived in Berlin. Dr Meyer, who had never before met Casement, learnt from him that he was the author of the pamphlet. When Dr Meyer visited the United States shortly after Casement's execution in 1916, he told the present writer that Casement's mission in Germany had been very successful until John Devoy, through whom alone Ireland had contact with Germany, wrote to the German government warning them not to trust Casement. 'We did not know what to think,' said Meyer; 'he (Devoy) gave us the impression that he was a spy, and our Government was afraid that we were walking into a trap.'

In a second article in *The Irish Review* Casement had suggested the raising of a Volunteer force to defend Ireland's neutrality if war broke out, and this idea, enthusiastically taken up, led to the organisation of the Irish Volunteers in November 1913. Joseph Plunkett, one of those present at the inaugural meeting in Wynn's Hotel, was elected to the executive and was an active and enthusiastic member. His mother, Countess Plunkett, allowed the Volunteers to drill in the grounds of Sandymount Castle, and in Larkfield, Kimmage, when they were finding it very difficult to get drill halls, on account of the opposition of the Irish Parliamentary Party to the organisation.

There was a widespread belief in those days that, though an Anglo-German war was inevitable, it would not come for many years. M.J. Judge, one of the standing committee of the Irish Volunteers, recalled in an article published in *The Irish Nation* for 9 September 1916, a conversation he had with MacNeill and Casement early in 1914. 'They considered war inevitable, but considered it could be averted for five or ten years,' he said. Casement had been sent by the Volunteer executive to the United States in July, 1914, to raise funds and support for the Irish Volunteers and he went from there to Germany.

On hearing of the outbreak of war, Casement predicted that England would 'drag in the whole world' and said, 'I can protect Ireland from being an innocent victim in this conflict; Germany is not Ireland's enemy.' According to MacGarrity, it was a meeting of New York nationalists – not Clan na Gael – which made the arrangements for Casement to get to Germany.

The Dublin leaders may have been aware that things were not going smoothly between Devoy and Casement, and in April 1915, Joe Plunkett was sent as their emissary to confer with Casement in Berlin. Having taken the precaution of destroying all photographs of himself (which accounts for the fact that only a poor snapshot photograph is now in existence), he set off on his perilous journey through warring Europe, changing his name to 'James Malcolm'. On his way, he grew a little moustache and imperial beard, which effectively disguised him. He passed through Spain, Italy, Switzerland and into Germany, finding himself at one time alone in a railway carriage full of German soldiers, who might, if their suspicions had been aroused, have given him short shrift as an English spy – for he could not speak German. But he reached Casement and together they visited Limberg camp to see the Irish Brigade. Casement, who as a result of warnings, was being treated with suspicion and coldness by the German government, was very dispirited. When Plunkett informed him that a Rising was planned to take place in the autumn of 1915, he spoke strongly against it unless it had the backing of a great continental power. He said, however, that if they were bent on it, he would join them, if the Germans would send him over. Before Casement set out on his fatal journey for Ireland, he wrote a last letter to St John Gaffney, the American ambassador in Munich, who was his great friend:

> I go tonight with Monteith and one man only of the boys, and am quite sure it is the most desperate piece of folly ever committed. But I go gladly – it is only right, and if these poor lads at home are to be in the fire then my place is with them.

Some months after his return from Germany, Plunkett was sent to America to tell Clan na Gael that the date of the Rising had been fixed. Back in Ireland, once more, in spite of the fact that his health was growing steadily worse, he worked indefatigably at the preparations for the insurrection with his great friend, Rory O'Connor. They began making munitions. Plunkett had studied wireless telegraphy, and an experimental station was built at Larkfield, where Con Keating, who had been a ship's wireless operator, was chief engineer. In Easter Week a wireless station at Reiss' in O'Connell Street was actually broadcasting to the world the news that Ireland had risen. Plunkett was a member of the military council who had made the preparations for the Rising, and when he showed James Connolly the plan of the insurrection on which he had been working for years, Connolly, who had made a special study of this subject, considered Plunkett's draft plan excellent, and they perfected it together.

On 19 April, Alderman Tom Kelly, at a meeting of Dublin

Corporation, read a paper which had been given to him by Francis Sheehy-Skeffington. This was the famous document repudiated as 'bogus' by the British government. Sheehy-Skeffington's interest in having it made public was that its provisions might not be carried out. Too long to give in detail here, it outlined 'precautionary measures' that would have led to a massacre, the wholesale arrest of the leaders, followed by military raids for arms, occupation of 'dangerous' houses, and the isolation of others. One of the places that was to be isolated and cut off from communication was 'premises known as Archbishop's House, Drumcondra'. The original document was in code, and after decoding by Joe Plunkett, it was set upon a hand-press at Larkfield, Kimmage, by Colm Ó Lochlainn and George Plunkett, a younger brother of Joseph. The name of the Archbishop's Palace in the original was given as 'Ara Coeli', which is that of the cardinal's house in Armagh. Noticing this while they were printing it, Jack Plunkett went to the nursing home where Joseph was lying ill, to consult him about this error. Joseph is reported to have said: 'Make it Archbishop's Palace', as it obviously was intended to be, since all the operations were to be carried out in Dublin. Out of this has been built up a fable that Joseph Plunkett deliberately forged the document in order to stampede the country into rising.

Meanwhile, we can test the rival theories by checking certain dates. If the document was forged to bring the Rising to a head, the delivery of arms from Germany would have to be speeded up. It was read in the corporation on 19 April. Joseph Plunkett's sister, Philomena, arrived in John Devoy's office in New York, on 14 April, and delivered to him an urgent message in code, which he was to transmit to the German government. It pressed the Germans to postpone the date of landing the arms in Kerry. Devoy decoded and transmitted the message which read: 'Arms must not be landed before night of Sunday 23rd. This is vital, etc.' This was postponing the landing from the date originally selected, 'between April 20 and 23' and would have deprived the insurgents of the use of the expected arms for several days.

The confusion between the names of the cardinal's house in Armagh, and the Archbishop's Palace in Dublin is the more easily accounted for if it is assumed that the document was British. The Plunketts were a leading Catholic family and, living in Dublin where the Archbishop's Palace was situated, they would not have been likely to confuse it with the primate's house in Armagh.

Joseph Plunkett had given instructions to the committee who were to publicise the document that they were to bring it to the notice of Dr MacRory, then bishop of Down and Connor (later cardinal), and to Maynooth College. Is it credible that he would have had the effrontery to try and palm off a forgery on the hierarchy of the church of which he was a devoted son?

He had been engaged to Grace Gifford since December, and it had been arranged that they would be married on Easter Sunday. MacNeill's orders countermanded not only the Rising, but also their wedding, and they agreed that if he was arrested, Grace would marry him in prison. Her brother-in-law, Thomas MacDonagh, had been executed in Kilmainham jail at 3.30 a.m. on 3 May; that evening at six o'clock, Grace was summoned to the same prison for her wedding. Until ten o'clock, when she was brought into the prison chapel, she walked up and down alone by a long wall, on the other side of which, she was told, Joseph Plunkett was waiting. The gas supply had failed and the prison chapel was lit only by a single candle, held by an armed soldier. Soldiers with fixed bayonets filled the little chapel, and as Fr Eugene MacCarthy read the marriage service, two soldier witnesses shifted their rifles from hand to hand as they assisted at the ceremony.

Immediately afterwards, the newly married couple were separated. Grace was taken away to lodgings found for her by Fr MacCarthy, and Joseph was led back to his cell. They met only once again; she was summoned to the prison just before his execution on the morning following their marriage. Fifteen soldiers with fixed bayonets stood by while they spoke in his cell. 'Your ten minutes are up,' said the officer in charge, glancing at his watch, and they parted forever.

As Joseph Plunkett waited with his hands tied behind his back to be led to the place of execution, he said to Fr Sebastian, who attended him, 'Father, I am very happy. I am dying for the glory of God and honour of Ireland.'

He was shot on 4 May 1916.

MAJOR JOHN MacBRIDE

Two cousins of the mother of Major John MacBride fought in the Fenian Rising of 1867, when MacBride was but a child of two. The major, who was born in Westport, County Mayo, on 7 May 1865, was a member of the Fenian organisation from early manhood. He was prominently associated with P.W. Nally and Michael Cusack in the early work of the GAA. Having spent some years in the study of medicine he gave it up to take a good position with Messrs Hugh Moore and Co., wholesale chemists. He was an active supporter of Charles Stewart Parnell, and after the 'Split' he attempted to revive the Fenian organisation in Dublin. In connection with this work he went to the United States in 1896, and while there his movements were closely watched by the enemy. On his return home British secret service agents suggested to his employer that the services of such a dangerous man should not be retained. Hugh Moore refused to dismiss him, but MacBride resigned his position and, after a period spent in London, went to South Africa shortly before the outbreak of the Boer War.

The British never forgave the Boers for the defeat they inflicted on them at Majuba Hill in 1881, and tension had been growing in South Africa, until it was obvious in 1898 that war was imminent. About seven weeks before war was declared, three Irishmen, Richard MacDonagh from Listowel, Dan O'Hare from Belfast, and Tom Byrne from Dublin, decided they would attempt to raise an Irish contingent to help the Boers. They sent their plan to John MacBride, then the most prominent Irishman in South Africa, and he eagerly agreed to help. Many of the Irish were miners, and the three men who initiated the scheme, having recruited others in the mines, held a meeting every Sunday to perfect plans. The existence of the Irish Brigade was kept secret from the Boer government until the outbreak of war, so that if hostilities did not break out, the Irish would not find themselves outlawed. About ten days before war was declared the brigade elected their officers. Their colonel was an old Indian-fighter from the United States, Colonel Blake, and their major was John MacBride. The Irish fought with great gallantry, often with captured British guns, and were personally thanked by General Joubert during his visit to their camp at Ladysmith.

On his return from South Africa in 1900, Major MacBride gave an interview to the press in which he said: 'The example of the brave Boers, and of the Irishmen who fought with them, should stimulate the Irish at home, and bid them not put their trust in cravings to the iniquitous British parliament, but lift up their heads, shoulder a trusty pike or musket, and fight like men. For I cannot believe that men of the same race as those who sent the English redcoats scuttling before them for dear life, like so many frightened rats, notwithstanding superior numbers, at Modderspruit and Colenso, could not do the same on their own soil and for their own land, any day they liked.'

MacBride was a good speaker, and often lectured to Sinn Féin audiences after his return to Dublin. There, too, he often spoke on anti-recruiting platforms following the outbreak of war in 1914. He was not a member of the Irish Volunteers, however, and the circumstances under which he joined the Rising are described by John MacDonagh, brother of Commandant Thomas MacDonagh of Jacob's garrison. Commandant MacDonagh's men were mobilised in Stephen's Green, and John MacDonagh, having noticed a man in civilian clothes marching in front, asked his brother, 'Who is that man in the blue suit?'

'That's Major John MacBride,' replied Thomas MacDonagh. 'He walked up to me and said, *Here I am, if I'm any use to you.* Of course I am delighted to have him.'

Major MacBride was made second-in-command at Jacob's factory, and during the week led out bombing parties.

In the course of his famous reply to General Sir John Maxwell after the Rising, the Bishop of Limerick, Most Rev. Dr O'Dwyer said: 'You remember the Jameson raid when a number of buccaneers invaded a friendly state, and fought the forces of the lawful government. If ever men deserved the supreme punishment it was they; but officially and unofficially, the influence of the British government was used to save them and it succeeded.' His Grace was hitting hard and hitting home when he addressed these remarks to Maxwell, who was himself one of the Jameson raiders. In the British House of Commons on 1 August 1916, Mr Matthew Keating (Kilkenny South) said: 'I do not know whether I have got my facts clear, but I am reliably informed that when the Jameson raid took place, General Maxwell was not unknown. Were the leaders of that raid executed? No, the leaders of that raid did not suffer the penalty of death ... Here you have martial law to follow all these things (the executions, prison sentences, etc.), administered by this gentleman who has been himself associated with a rebellion unless I am misinformed, and, if I am, I will withdraw gladly, because I do not wish to make an unfounded accusation.' But Mr Keating was not asked to withdraw, nor was any attempt made to answer his questions. And so by an extraordinary and dramatic coincidence the man who had fought with the Boers in their war of defence was executed by one of the buccaneers who had treacherously attacked them.

Major John MacBride died as he had lived, a soldier. He asked them not to bind his hands, promising to remain quite still. 'Sorry, sir,' replied the British soldier, 'but these are orders.' Then he asked not to be blindfolded and said to the priest who attended him: 'You know, Father, I've often looked down their guns before.' He stood perfectly erect until the fatal volley was fired.

He was executed on 5 May 1916.

MICHAEL O'HANRAHAN

SON OF RICHARD O'Hanrahan, who had to go on the run for his part in the Fenian Rising of 1867, Michael O'Hanrahan, was born in New Ross, County Wexford, on 17 March 1877.

When Michael was still a child the family moved to Carlow, and in the county town he was educated at the Christian Brothers' school and at the college academy. He had intended entering the civil service, but finding that entrance necessitated the taking of an oath of allegiance to England, he abandoned the idea.

During the 1898 celebrations in Carlow he first came in contact with the Gaelic League, founded its first branch in that town, and was its delegate at the second representative congress in 1900. He was an extremely enthusiastic student of the language, and often worked at it until two or three in the morning. He put the same hard work, in fact, into anything which he undertook.

'Cimarron', who contributed the GAA notes to *An Phoblacht*, writing of him in the issue for 11 April 1936, said:

> Micheál O'Hanrahan was one of the most unobtrusive of the men executed in 1916. His convictions were steady as a rock. They appeared to have been part of the man's mental and spiritual make-up. Outwardly he did not suggest any of the qualities which are usually, and often mistakenly, associated with leadership. The glow of the inward fire was felt only by those who were privileged to have had intimate relations with him. They were few, and perhaps for this very reason the writer of these notes particularly treasures the recollection of his intimacy with Micheál.
>
> We became acquainted in 1904, and that acquaintanceship ripened into close friendship. We collaborated in journalistic ventures, and often sat together at our little table far into the night. Reticent, slow and sparing in speech, Micheál confronted difficulties with great composure, surmounted them with marvellous perseverance. We recall an example. Fifteen thousand words had to be supplied to the printers. We had only one night to conceive and write. All through the night we worked on this truly stupendous task. Micheál's contributions were 'Aisling', 'A Grave in Glasnevin', and 'Notes for the Times'.

After he went to live in Dublin, he was for years secretary of the ard craobh of the Gaelic League, an active member of the Language Week organisation committee, and secretary of the Language Procession. He became the Irish reader at the Cló-Chumann Printing Works, and did a great deal of propaganda work on behalf of the language in the national journals. He was a constant writer for Arthur Griffith's paper, *Sinn Féin*, and, under the pen-name 'Art', contributed a humorous political commentary in dialect which was very popular. His novel, *A Swordsman of the Brigade*, won the praise of such a severe critic as Thomas MacDonagh, who afterwards became his great friend and was his commandant in Easter Week.

Though quiet and gentle, Michael was a man of great moral and physical courage. Once when a Sinn Féin meeting he was addressing in Newry was attacked by a mob, he found himself alone on the brake – the other speakers having fled – and continued the meeting unsupported.

He joined the Irish Volunteers immediately they were founded, and soon by ability, energy and enthusiasm had risen to the position of quartermaster of the organisation, a post he filled with great efficiency until the Rising. He had his office in the Volunteer headquarters, 2 Dawson Street, which were under constant police surveillance, and it is generally believed that it was because of his magnificent work as quartermaster that he was marked as a 'dangerous' man and executed. Michael and his elder brother, Henry, were devoted to each other, and fought side by side in the Rising. Henry was also condemned to death, but the sentence was later commuted to penal servitude for life.

Miss Sarah Keely, one of the Cumann na mBan ladies attached to Jacob's garrison, tells a story which shows the stuff Michael O'Hanrahan was made of. While they were exploring the building to check the supplies of food available, one of the Volunteers discovered a lot of useful foodstuffs such as cream, butter, etc., in a cellar which could only be reached by going in pitch darkness down a passage and a flight of stone steps. On his way down to inspect the supplies, O'Hanrahan fell on the stone steps and struck his head so heavily that he was momentarily stunned. On recovering, his first words to those around him were that they must not tell either MacDonagh or MacBride, lest he would be sent to hospital. Miss Keely says there is no doubt that he was suffering from concussion as a result of this accident. He was dazed, suffering great pain, and took no solid food all week.

He was deeply devoted to his family. When his sister Eily (now Mrs O'Hanrahan O'Reilly), who was in Cumann na mBan, came with a dispatch shortly before the surrender, he longed to accept her offer to stay. Then he thought of his duty. There was a dump in their house, and the guns had to be saved, so he sent her away to make sure that they were moved.

'He was one of the truest and noblest characters that it has ever been my privilege to meet,' said the priest who attended him at his execution. He told how, as Michael O'Hanrahan went out to the yard to be shot, he asked him to visit his mother and sisters and console them.

He was executed on 4 May 1916.

MICHAEL MALLIN

MICHAEL MALLIN was born in Dublin, and was about thirty-six years of age when executed. A silk weaver by trade, he had been secretary to the Silk Weavers' Union until an industrial dispute in his trade during 1913 brought him into contact with James Connolly, after which he joined the Irish Transport and General Workers' Union.

Following a youthful whim, he enlisted as a drummer-boy in the British army and spent many of his early years in India with his regiment. There, in an army notorious for its loose living, he retained his high moral standard and strong religious faith. Whilst in India he sent home for Gaelic text books and studied his native language. He held a high opinion of the Indians, and it was disgust and resentment of their ill-treatment by the British that first made of him a militant anti-imperialist. He told how, on one occasion, when he was present at an army gymkhana, an Indian standing close by him made an attempt on the life of a high British official and escaped. Another Indian, tried for the attempt, was convicted on the false testimony of thirteen British soldier witnesses and executed. Mallin, who was the only witness at the trial to testify to the innocence of the Indian, was also the only one of the witnesses who escaped the vengeance of the Indians.

Mallin, who had considerable musical talent, achieved proficiency on several instruments, and conducted military bands on occasions. On his return to Ireland he took a keen interest in Fianna Éireann, and helped with its organisation and with the training of the Fianna band. As a result of coaching by Mallin, Andy Dunne, the Fianna drummer, was asked to teach drumming to the officer's training corps in Trinity College, a job which he accepted in the hope of finding out where the OTC kept their guns. Having found that he was watched continuously, he gave up the job.

When preparing the plans for the Rising, James Connolly drew upon the military experience of Michael Mallin, who also carried out for him valuable intelligence work. As an ex-soldier Mallin mixed freely amongst British Tommies in Dublin, and learned from them the military strength and movements of the British. He trained the Irish Citizen Army specially for street fighting, and made of it a most effective unit of the republican forces.

Stories of Mallin by those who knew him before and during the fight show him to be a magnificent and fearless leader, never a bully, but nonetheless a rigid disciplinarian. J.J. Burke, writing in *The Torch* for 13 November 1943, tells how on one occasion Liberty Hall was quickly prepared for defence following receipt of information that it was to be seized by crown forces: 'Fifteen or sixteen men of the Irish Citizen Army fully armed, appeared as if by magic and took up positions in different parts of the building. No attempt was made, however, to seize the place, although a hundred or more policemen put in an appearance, and remained in the vicinity for an hour or so. Before I left for home that night Liberty Hall held a garrison of fifty or sixty men, under the command of Michael Mallin, chief-of-staff of the Irish Citizen Army, a splendid man and a great soldier.' And the men and women who fought under him in the College of Surgeons say that there was a quiet efficiency about him that set everything right when he was present; that he was as gentle, cool and brave during the fight as he was in times of peace.

Michael Mallin had the fortune to have fighting side by side with him in the College of Surgeons two of his closest friends – his vice-commandant, Countess Markievicz, and Councillor William Partridge. When Pearse's order to surrender was received the men at the outposts were summoned hastily and as each fresh batch arrived, it was the duty of Commandant Mallin to break the terrible tidings once more. The ordeal was repeated three times and all the while, Partridge, knowing what his chief was suffering, stood by with his arm about him.

Asked by a prison official in Mountjoy what her religion was, Countess Markievicz replied that she was a Catholic; that she had become a Catholic in the College of Surgeons. To a visiting priest she said that it was the example of Michael Mallin and Councillor Partridge that had made her a Catholic.

Michael Mallin was blessed to have his devoted friend Councillor Partridge with him as his fellow prisoner up to the hour of his death. In Mallin's last letter to his wife, written a few hours before execution, he said, 'I am satisfied I have done my duty to my beloved Ireland; but, oh, if only you and the little ones were coming too, we could all reach Heaven together … Mr Partridge, too, was more than a brother to me. He has held me close in his arms so that I might have comfort and warmth. Tell him I met my fate like a man. I do not believe our blood has been shed in vain …'

He was executed on 8 May 1916.

NED DALY

JOHN EDWARD ('NED') Daly, the youngest and only boy of ten children, born to Edward Daly and Catherine O'Mara, first saw the light on 25 February 1891, in Frederick Street, Limerick, six months after the death of his father. His father and namesake had been imprisoned in 1865 at seventeen years of age for his connection with the Irish

Republican Brotherhood. He was released in 1866, and took part in the Fenian Rising in 1867. As the result of ill-health brought on by his treatment in prison, he died at forty-two years of age. Ned Daly's uncle was the famous Fenian, John Daly, fellow prisoner of Tom Clarke, who was sentenced to penal servitude for life in 1884. After twelve-and-a-half years of imprisonment, during which several of his Fenian fellow-prisoners were driven insane by the brutal treatment meted out to them, John Daly obtained his release in a dying condition through a hunger strike. A deliberate attempt had been made to poison him in prison by giving him an overdose of belladonna, and his health, though normal for a few years, broke down completely in 1911, and he became a total invalid.

When Ned Daly, a little lad of seven, was leaving his infant school for the Christian Brothers, Tom Clarke, just released after serving sixteen years' penal servitude, visited John Daly in Limerick, and the fate of the two families was interwoven from that day. Soon after that visit Tom Clarke had married Ned Daly's sister, Kathleen, and Ned, with a Fenian father, a Fenian uncle, and a Fenian brother-in-law, was destined to be a Fenian also.

By the time Ned Daly was fifteen years of age, John Daly was the owner of a flourishing bakery in Limerick. As he intended to make the boy his heir, he sent him to Lemy's business school for a preliminary commercial training, intending afterwards to take him into the business and have him trained as a workman-baker. The rules of the Baker's Society, however, required that the sons of bakers only could be taken as apprentices, and Ned's uncle was forced to send him to a technical school in Glasgow in 1907 to get the necessary training. He returned in bad health, and it was decided that he was not strong enough for the bakery business, so he took up a commercial career, first in Limerick, and later in Dublin. In that city he lived from 1912 until 1916, working in May Roberts, wholesale chemists.

Tom Clarke had returned from the United States in 1907, and Ned Daly went to live with the Clarkes, and was in this way in close contact with Seán MacDiarmada and the other future Irish leaders.

He was one of the first to enrol in the Irish Volunteers in 1913, and told his sister, Mrs Tom Clarke, on the night he joined: 'I am at last what I have always wanted to be – a soldier.' From the first he showed a marked aptitude for the soldier's calling, and when, early in 1914 he was appointed captain of 'B' company, 1st battalion, Dublin brigade, the company which he had organised, he brought it to a high pitch of discipline and efficiency in a remarkably short time. The twenty-three-year-old officer had many men under him years older than himself, but he was as much loved and respected by them as though he had been a veteran.

His character particularly appealed to the Dublin men. He was gay, high-spirited and daring. He had a good singing voice, which was being trained by Dr Vincent O'Brien, and on route marches would help to keep up the spirits of his men by singing 'Eileen Óg', which became the regimental song of the 1st battalion. Handsome, with a fine figure that his Volunteer uniform set off to advantage, he was fond of social life and dancing, and when Volunteer dances, organised to raise funds for buying arms and equipment, became a feature of Dublin life during 1915–16, he was a constant patron and always the life of the gathering.

But though he could enjoy fun and social life, he never forgot to impress on his men that 'B' company meant 'Business'. This was his favourite slogan for 'B' company, and how well they profited by his slogan was shown at the Howth gun-running and at Kilcool.

Some of the fiercest fighting in the 1916 Rising was in the area where he commanded, and he had under him, as a result of MacNeill's countermanding order, less than half the number of men who were to have held the district. Yet this young and inexperienced officer won from James Connolly this special mention in a dispatch, dated 28 April: 'Commandant Daly's splendid exploit in capturing Linenhall barracks we all know. You must know also that the whole population, both clergy and laity of this district, are united in his praises.'

In attempting to excuse the murder of fifteen civilians by the Sher-wood Foresters in houses in North King Street, which was in Daly's area, Sir John Maxwell stated that it took twenty-four hours' fighting to capture the street, and that with the exception of the place at Ballsbridge where the Sherwood Foresters were ambushed, 'this was by far the worst fighting that occurred in the whole of Dublin'.

Tributes to the high discipline and gallantry of Daly and his men were paid by several of the enemy. Captain R.K. Brereton, JP, who was held in the Four Courts with ten other English prisoners for the week of fighting, said on 14 May 1916: 'What impressed me most was the international tone adopted by the Sinn Féiners. They were not out for massacre, for burning or for loot. They were out for war; observing all the rules of civilised warfare and fighting clean.' He went on to say that there was no drinking among them, though the Four Courts had a plentiful stock of spirits and wines, and continued, 'They treated their prisoners with the utmost courtesy and consideration, in fact they proved by their conduct that they were men of education, incapable of acts of brutality.'

But this brave, humane and chivalrous young man was to experience very brutal treatment when he was a prisoner in the hands of the English. The prisoners had spent the night in the open, in the plot of ground in front of the Rotunda Hospital. In the morning by the order of a British officer, Captain Lee Wilson, Tom Clarke and Commandant Ned Daly were taken behind a pillar in the Rotunda, stripped naked, and subjected to gross insults to their persons.

At about 11.30 p.m. on 4 May, Mrs Clarke and her sisters, Laura and Madge Daly, were taken by a military lorry to Kilmainham prison to see their brother. 'Relatives of Daly who is to be shot in the morning,' the jailors called out as they entered the prison – and that was their first intimation of his pending fate. 'Ned,' said his sister, 'looked like a young knight who had won some great victory.' He gave high praise to his men, and spoke affectionately of Thomas MacDonagh, Clarke and Pearse, who had gone that morning, adding: 'We shall have a glorious meeting in Heaven.'

He was executed on 5 May 1916.

CON COLBERT

CON COLBERT, WHO was born in Monalena and brought up in Athea, County Limerick, was just about twenty-three years of age in 1916. His father and an uncle had fought in the Fenian rising of 1867. This forged a great bond of friendship between himself and John Daly, the Fenian of later days, who had known Con's uncle, and Con never wearied of hearing stories about him. He was educated in the Christian Brothers' school, North Richmond Street, Dublin, and worked in Kennedy's Bakery, Parnell Street. One of the first members of the Fianna, Con threw himself whole-heartedly into the work of organising and training from the start. He was a deeply religious boy, and was never known to use strong language, so that a favourite Fianna joke was 'Colbert cursed last night – he called a man a pickaxe'. Although of a serious and determined nature there was nothing morose or priggish about him and he enjoyed a rough-and-tumble in camp or a practical joke as much as any other boy of his age. Like his friend, Seán Heuston, he spoke Irish fluently, was a great student of Irish history, and had thought much on past mistakes in his country's story. When any person quoted the saying that the Gaels, 'Went forth to battle but they always fell', he would reply fiercely: 'They won't the next time.'

Tom Clarke, Connolly, Madame Markievicz and Pearse held a very high opinion of Colbert, and he was as close as a brother to Liam Mellows. Liam, who had been deported to England shortly before the Rising, escaped and returned disguised as priest, making his way via Belfast to Dublin where he arrived unexpectedly at Frank Fahy's house at Chapelizod, and was not long there when Con came along, either by chance or pre-arrangement. Neither of the boys would be separated from each other, and in their joy at their reunion they spent the whole night playing tricks on each other, on the pretence that they were fighting for the one spare bed.

Con joined the Irish Volunteers at their inception, and was one of their first instructors in drill and musketry. Later, on Pearse's request, he acted with Mellows and Heuston as drill instructors to the boys at St Enda's, for which work they refused to accept any payment. He was one of the first on the Irish Volunteer executive, and voted against John Redmond's attempt to control the organisation, though great pressure was brought to bear on him by Hobson and others. Soon after he joined the Volunteers he was promoted to the position of captain of 'F' company, 4th battalion, commanded by Éamonn Ceannt, the rank he held in Easter Week.

He fought with great bravery in the Rising, taking over Watkins' Brewery with a very small force and holding it until dawn on Wednesday, when he joined forces with the Marrowbone Lane garrison. This garrison, with the others under the command of Ceannt and Brugha, won immortality both for bravery and strategy. They shattered and drove off large forces of experienced English troops, commanded by Sir Francis Vane, a humane and gallant soldier whose exposure of the murder of Sheehy-Skeffington afterwards cost him his command. By Thursday, there was a lull in the 4th battalion area, and the order to surrender came as a great blow. Con Colbert, whose youth and subordinate command could have saved him, stepped into the place of an older man who had dependants, and suffered in his place. Writing to his sister on the eve of his execution he said: 'Perhaps I'd never again get the chance of knowing when I was to die, and so I'll try and die well. I "received" this morning and hope to do so again before I die …' After asking his sister to have Masses said for him, he continued: 'May God help us – me to die well – you to bear your sorrow. I send you a prayer-book as a token.'

He was executed on 8 May 1916.

SEÁN HEUSTON

Seán Heuston, a Dubliner, was about twenty-five years old in 1916. Educated by the Christian Brothers, he took first place in Ireland in 1908 in the Great Southern and Western Railway Company's examinations, and was appointed as a railway clerk in Limerick. In that city he took an active part in the organisation and training of the Fianna, of which he was an officer. He always dressed in Fianna uniform when leading the boys on route marches, and for members who could not afford to buy uniforms and equipment outright, arranged that they could do so by paying small weekly sums. The result of this plan was that Limerick Fianna were always smartly turned out, and as they marched through the streets led by their pipers' band, they raised many a cheer and attracted many recruits.

Brilliant and excellently educated himself, Seán knew the importance of education in developing mind and character, and under his guidance the Limerick Fianna had a course which comprised not only drill, physical culture, signalling, general scout training and musketry, but also lectures on Irish history and Gaelic classes. Although of a happy disposition, he was deadly serious about work, and when the boys were in the ranks or on some special duty, he allowed no levity.

He was moved to Dublin in 1913 to a position at the traffic manager's office at Kingsbridge railway station (now re-named Heuston station), and was transferred to Sluagh Emmet of the Dublin Fianna. After a short time he was promoted captain of this sluagh, and later O/C for North Dublin. His fine character was quickly recognised by his comrades and by Countess Markievicz, commander-in-chief of the Fianna, and he was a constant visitor at her house in Rathmines. It was a gathering place for leading republicans, including members of the Fianna, among others Con Colbert, Éamonn Murray, Liam Mellows, Éamonn Martin, Andy Dunne, the brothers Fitzgerald, and Paddy and Garry Houlihan, all of whom later fought in the Rising.

Seán Heuston joined the Irish Volunteers immediately they were started, and was one of the Fianna who helped to train the men in the use of firearms. With Con Colbert and Liam Mellows he also trained the boys of St Enda's at the request of Pádraig Pearse. In the Volunteers Seán was appointed captain of 'D' company, 1st Dublin battalion, the rank he held during the Rising

The epic story of his great fight at the Mendicity Institution (now popularly called 'Heuston's Fort') has been recounted wherever the story of 1916 is told. He had been ordered by James Connolly to try to hold up British troops moving towards the Four Courts for two or three hours so as to give the garrisons there and in the GPO area time to establish their defences. On Monday he had occupied the building with about a dozen men and from the time the first shot was fired by Heuston's garrison at 1 p.m. on Monday, there was continuous hard fighting against besieging British troops between three hundred and four hundred strong. On Tuesday afternoon, in response to a dispatch, Connolly sent reinforcements from Swords. Fierce fighting continued, there were several killed and seriously wounded, and ammunition was running low. A dispatch was sent to the GPO, for further reinforcements. Connolly read it and was greatly moved; he had ordered these brave boys to hold the Mendicity for two or three hours; they had held it for nearly three days. Before reinforcements could be rushed to their help, the British had begun to set fire to the buildings around, and the garrison were forced to surrender. The total number of the garrison was between twenty and twenty-five.

Fr Albert, OFM Cap., describing the saint-like character which Seán Heuston revealed at his death, wrote: 'He was perfectly calm, and said with me for the last time: "My Jesus, Mercy". I scarcely had moved away a few yards when a volley went off, and this noble soldier of Irish freedom fell dead. I rushed over to anoint him; his whole face seemed transformed and lit up with a grandeur and brightness that I had never before noticed ...'

He was executed on 8 May 1916.

WILLIAM PEARSE

WILLIAM PEARSE, YOUNGER brother of Pádraig, was born in Dublin on 15 November 1881. He was a captain of the headquarters staff of the Irish Volunteers, and served in the GPO during the Rising. Shy, gentle and quiet, he was a sculptor by profession, and had attained distinction in the Dublin and South Kensington Art Schools. He was afterwards professor of art and other subjects at St Enda's College. He was a talented actor, and appeared in many productions at the Irish Theatre, Hardwicke Street, Dublin, and designed costumes and produced plays and pageants for St Enda's. In childhood, the two brothers had taken a mutual vow to devote their lives to the cause of Irish freedom, and if necessary to lay them down in that cause.

He was executed on 4 May 1916.

FRONGOCH UNIVERSITY – AND AFTER 1916–1919

by JOHN BRENNAN

THE UNCONDITIONAL SURRENDER of 1916 was the act of a disciplined force; in every Volunteer garrison there were many who wished to fight to a finish but who, having received Pearse's order, laid down arms. They had fought as an army, and as an army they surrendered, companies falling in behind their officers. Individual Volunteers could have escaped the British by the simple process of walking away before enemy forces got to close quarters with them. There were many whose thoughts must then have turned anxiously towards dependants and what would happen them should the head of the house fall before a firing squad or receive a long term of imprisonment. Others, frail men and women, knew that for them penal servitude could mean death in a prison cell. Yet, as they were escorted away to death or captivity, all bore themselves as soldiers should, heads held high, stepping proudly through the ruined streets of Dublin. 'A Soldier's Song' and other national airs were heard in the ranks, for the spirit of fighting Dublin was gallant and gay; it had survived defeat. Pearse, in his manifesto issued on 28 April gave this picture of Dublin in arms: 'For four days they have fought and toiled, almost without cessation, almost without sleep, and in the intervals of fighting they have sung songs of the freedom of Ireland. No man has complained; no man has asked "Why?" Each individual has spent himself, happy to pour out his strength for Ireland and for freedom.'

That was the resilient spirit which the Dublin men brought with them into jails and prison camps after the surrender. They had proved that they could fight and endure, and turn their sufferings into laughter and song. But ahead lay another testing time. Would the men who had fought so bravely with guns in their hands be as daring and defiant when stripped of their arms and placed behind prison bars? The future of Ireland depended upon the answer to that question, because those in captivity represented the best elements of Ireland's army; should their spirit be broken her fate would be sealed.

After the surrender, subsequent courts martial and executions, the scene quickly shifted to England, and there the Irish army in captivity gave its defiant answer to the question that was agitating the public mind. There the enemy was fought on her own soil; fought by men and women without weapons and behind prison bars. From the moment they became prisoners of the British, they were subjected to every conceivable indignity, insult and cruelty. Quickly realising what prison life was going to be, the Dublin men decided that if they had to endure a form of hell, it would at least be merry hell.

Pearse wrote in the *Irish War News*, issued from the GPO on 25 April: 'The populace of Dublin are plainly with the Republic, and the officers and men are everywhere cheered as they march through the streets.' As the Volunteer prisoners marched to Richmond and Kilmainham, however, there were few to cheer them; a sifting of the populace carried out by British military examining posts set up in the city resulted in few other than the wives of British soldiers and hangers-on of the enemy's army being abroad at the time. It is likely that the mob which gathered to curse and spit upon the prisoners as they were conveyed into the jails had been organised for that purpose by the British authorities. Seán MacGlynn, an Irish Volunteer who fought under Éamonn Ceannt in the South Dublin Union, gave this vivid picture which typified the contrasting experiences of the Volunteers that day:

As we marched through James' Street it was evening. All the dwelling houses were closed and the blinds pulled. Not a soul was to be seen; the centre of Dublin was still blazing and sporadic firing was still to be heard. The first encouraging word came on the North Circular Road as we marched along. A young girl wearing a shawl, she was hardly more than a child, ran out of a house, and with her breast pressed against the British bayonets, and her eyes blazing, shouted, 'Up the rebels! Up the rebels!!' We never knew who she was, nor did we see her again. At the Royal Hospital, Kilmainham, where soldiers' wives were lined up to see us arrive, we got a different welcome, as they almost spat in our faces, screaming, 'Shoot Them!'

Nellie Gifford, Jim Gough and Andy Dunne of the Citizen Army in the College of Surgeons' garrison, remember that as they stepped out as prisoners from the college, men and women on the street cheered and called out, 'God bless you'. Many rushed to them with presents of fruit and cigarettes. Some of the British officers, greatly perturbed when they saw that the people were not afraid to cheer the Volunteers, subsequently revenged themselves on their prisoners by mean and contemptible methods. Frank Fahy, the ceann comhairle, who was an officer under Ned Daly at the Four Courts, remembers the contemptuous exclamation of the British officer in charge as he handed over his prisoners at Richmond barracks: 'Here you are,' he said to the Richmond authority taking over, 'more for the manure heap.'

The surrender at Boland's Mills took place on Sunday, one day after that of the other garrisons. Joseph O'Connor, the vice-commandant, marched the men to the place appointed for them to join Commandant Éamon de Valera and lay down arms. People of the Ringsend area who had been very friendly all the week gathered to cheer the Volunteers in the bitter hour of defeat. 'At Grattan Street,' says O'Connor, 'Commandant de Valera took over command of the men. A couple of British officers were with him, and his order to ground arms was instantly carried out by all Volunteers.' As soon as the men had been disarmed the British took over. To quote O'Connor again: 'The British then assumed command and ordered all ranks to put their hands over their heads and march towards Lower Mount Street. At this point we were searched by the British and marched towards the showgrounds at Ballsbridge, which were full of cattle brought up for the spring show. The party I was in, consisting of between fifty and sixty men, was halted outside a stall containing a bull. Having removed the bull which had been there for about ten days, the British tossed out its bedding and thrust the whole of us into the filthy place. That was on Sunday afternoon. We remained in that stall until the following Tuesday morning.'

At Richmond barracks prisoners from republican posts were placed in rooms without bedding or furniture of any description, and some of the men, especially the wounded, suffered intensely from the cold. The aged Count Plunkett, unable to sleep on the floor, remained standing upright for a long time. Eventually, fellow prisoners managed to get from a soldier, an empty orange box on which he sat, with the overcoats of two Volunteers for covering. As a result of his sufferings he was visited by a military doctor, who having learned his name asked: 'Are you the father of Joseph Plunkett who was shot?' It was thus that Count Plunkett learned of the death of his son.

Even under the dreadful conditions which prevailed, the prisoners did not lose their ability to make light of their troubles. Whilst they awaited court martial, the Dublin tenor, Gerard Crofts, kept them in good cheer by leading in the singing of old Dublin ballads such as 'Cockles and Mussels, Alive, Alive, O'. To help avoid boredom they set up a mock court which tried de Valera on a charge of being pretender to the throne of Dalkey Island; but de Valera then expecting the death sentence from the British court martial, asked them to stop this game which was much too like grim reality. The chance happening which saved de Valera's life is told by Joseph O'Connor. Although born in the United States of America, de Valera had lived in Ireland from childhood and so did not qualify for the protection of American law as a United States citizen. 'After the surrender,' says O'Connor, 'de Valera's home at Morehampton Terrace was raided by British military. Mrs de Valera and her sister Brigid (Mrs Cotter) who were in the house, noticed that the soldiers appeared to be searching for something special. They returned a few days later and renewed their search, concentrating on de Valera's personal papers. The two sisters, speaking in Irish, discussed what the military might be looking for, and decided that it must be his birth certificate, which Brigid told her sister was safe in the family home in Munster Street. When the raiders had left, Mrs de Valera went to Munster Street, got the certificate and handed it to the American consul. She believes that this saved her husband's life.' In the event of execution, de Valera's case would automatically have been investigated in the United States. A great deal of publicity would have followed in the American press, and the British, determined to keep the true story of the Rising from the American people, had no alternative but to spare his life in order to avoid this.

The prisoners who had escaped summary execution were conveyed to England in the filthy and foul-smelling holds of cattle boats, and subsequently were placed in various English prisons in which the most appalling conditions prevailed. The meagre portions of food issued were of poor quality and no eating utensils were provided for the prisoners who were kept in solitary confinement for about three weeks. They were reduced almost to starvation point because of the poor diet which followed the severe food rationing necessitated during the fighting. Eventually, when the 'solitary' was terminated, the men elected their own officers who acted as their spokesmen with the prison authorities, and from whom alone they took orders.

At Wakefield, the prisoners' commandant, Joe O'Connor, instructed them to ignore a major general from the British war office who came to inspect them. Whilst that officer was present one of the prisoners suddenly dropped in a dead faint, and a warder was overheard saying contemptuously to another: 'Is that what calls himself a soldier?'

To which the other replied, 'If you were as hungry, you'd faint too.'

The incident cannot altogether have been lost on the representative from the war office, for soon afterwards the prisoners were allowed to receive food parcels from friends and to walk in twos during exercise. As they were not permitted to speak, O'Connor commanded them to do so, though three days bread-and-water was the stipulated punishment for breaking the rule about talking. As a result of this campaign the ban on talking was also removed. No attempt was made to have Mass celebrated for the prisoners, so following the third successive Sunday without Mass O'Connor decided to make a protest. He left the ranks during the first morning parade to make his complaint. The prison official in charge angrily ordered him to fall into the ranks, but he refused to do so, or to allow the prisoners return to their cells until the officer had promised that Sunday Mass would be provided in future. There was Mass on the following Sunday and hymns were played by Michael Lynch, organist of SS Michael and John's church, Dublin. 'I will never forget,' says O'Connor, 'how he played and we sang "Hail Glorious St Patrick".'

In Wandsworth, Douglas ffrench-Mullen, a talented musician who had been wounded at the South Dublin Union, presided at the organ, and the prisoners filing out after Mass were overcome with emotion when they heard the familiar strains of 'The Soldier's Song'. Although the warders did not know the song, it was not difficult to guess by the expression on the men's face that it was something 'seditious', and Douglas was not again allowed to play at Mass.

No charge was made against the majority of the 1916 prisoners in English jails, and they were never brought to trial. Instead, each had a document served on him or her (there were five ladies interned at Aylesbury), which conferred the right to appear before the advisory council, set up by the British government to deal with appeals against internment. Very few availed themselves of the facility. Even those amongst the prisoners who had been opposed to the Rising, had no desire to be classified as 'loyal' to a Britain which had just murdered in cold blood sixteen Irish prisoners of war, and which had sent many others without trial to penal servitude in convict prisons. Furthermore, the vast majority of the prisoners were soldiers who had gone into the fight prepared to meet death and who scorned to escape punishment by asserting that they had been 'led into it' by others. Never previously had a British government to deal with Irish prisoners of such calibre. The Fenians, members of a militant organisation, but not of an organised army, could be brutally punished individually as insubordinate convicts whenever they broke any of the prison regulations. It was extremely difficult, if not impossible, to deal similarly with the 1916 army, which, highly organised and disciplined, treated a jail fight as a military operation and planned and carried it out accordingly.

Frongoch detention camp in North Wales, in which untried Irish prisoners were interned, was described by Tim Healy in the British House of Commons as 'A Sinn Féin University'. It quickly became almost the equivalent of a military academy in which insurrectionary forces enlisted new recruits, and planned to re-arm, reorganise and resume the war against England as early as possible. At the outset, the north camp held eight hundred men and there were nine hundred and thirty-six in the south, which had once been a distillery. It had fallen into disuse and its grain lofts, in which the prisoners were housed, swarmed with rats which destroyed food and clothes. There was no proper ventilation, and the roofs leaked. Some time previously the building had been used as a camp for German prisoners of war. Conditions in the grain lofts were so bad that after a time the prisoners were transferred to the north camp. Batches of them were returned to the south camp at different periods for punishment.

It was obvious that the north camp had not been occupied pre-viously. If it had, the long grass about its new huts would have been trampled into a morass by the feet of the German prisoners, as it was soon to be by those of the Irish. In the opinion of William O'Brien, the Labour leader, who was one of the internees, the camp had been prepared specially before the Rising in anticipation of the wholesale arrests which the British authorities in Ireland had planned to make. The long grass was soon trampled underfoot, and as the place became a veritable quagmire the British authorities decided that they would build roads over it and that they would use the Irish internees as convict labour for that purpose.

When there was special work to be done, volunteers were called for by the Irish camp commandant, M.W. O'Reilly. One day he discovered that the British authorities had, without his permission, requisitioned internees to haul material to the north camp for the road-building.

Remembering that there was a trade union official on the spot, he consulted with William O'Brien as to what ought to be done. O'Brien's advice was that a certain number of men should volunteer for the duty and should then demand to be paid the full trade union rate of wages. That policy was carried into effect for every forced labour scheme. As a punishment, batches of the prisoners were put on bread and water and deprived of their privileges. Eventually, the ringleaders who included, amongst others, Seán T. O'Kelly (later president of the Irish Republic), M.W. O'Reilly, Seamus Robinson and William O'Brien, were transferred to Reading jail.

By the summer of 1916, feeling in Ireland was running high as a result of ill-treatment of the prisoners in England. 'Butcher Maxwell', who had been installed as absolute military dictator, was in control of the Irish police forces, and had about 130,000 British troops at his disposal. Public meetings were banned, and even members of the Irish Parliamentary Party were not permitted to address their constituents without having first obtained a licence from the police, or in other words, from Maxwell. Despite the rigour of these measures and a strict censorship of the press, people who could not be ignored indefinitely were beginning to make their voices heard on behalf of the prisoners. Priests, chairmen of public bodies, employers of labour, justices of the peace and others were deluging the Irish MPs with letters about their interned friends and neighbours. Laurence Ginnell, an Independent MP for North Westmeath, who alone had stood up fearlessly in Westminster to denounce the murderers of the 1916 leaders, earned for himself the affectionate title of the 'Member for Ireland'. He adopted the entire country as his constituency and questions of his in the British parliament revealed to the people of Ireland that their men were brought through British cities handcuffed and chained together in gangs, whenever they were transferred from one jail to another. Amongst those treated in this manner were ten boys whose ages averaged seventeen. Ginnell, using his privilege as an MP to visit the men in prison, smuggled out letters in the pockets of his frock coat, which duly became known as 'the Sinn Féin post office'.

Recruiting in Ireland failed completely after the Rising, and Irish propagandists immediately worked vigorously on American public opinion, which hardened against Britain and against entry into the war. In an effort to relieve the situation, the British government took the extraordinary step of bringing all the internees before the advisory council, as though they had appealed against internment. The council then pretended to 'examine' their cases, and although all refused to make plea for release, or to provide any information about themselves, numbers were set free. By August 1916 only 600 remained in Frongoch detention camp. Accordingly, about 1,136 Sinn Féin 'graduates' were sent home to Ireland where they immediately began to 'spread the light' amongst their compatriots. Those who still remained in Frongoch took a 'post-graduate course' under such competent tutors as Michael Collins, then about twenty-six years of age. Collins had worked in England for ten years, and in January 1916, he returned to Ireland to take part in the Rising, in which he fought in the GPO. In conjunction with a number of other Frongoch internees his long residence in England had made him liable to conscription. Internees liable for conscription had a foretaste of the shape of things to come in the treatment accorded three such Irish prisoners, who had been detained in London and whom the authorities had attempted to force into the British army. The three were the brothers Ernest and Seán Nunan and Thomas O'Donoghue. They refused to serve in the British army, and, as a result were thrown into prison and treated with savage cruelty until as a result public opinion was shocked to a point which compelled the authorities to release them. Seán Nunan, then of the Irish Volunteers, was later the Irish representative in Washington and Thomas O'Donoghue, then of the Citizen Army, became a priest on the English Mission.

Plans evolved by Collins to foil the efforts of the British authorities to round up those internees liable for conscription, revealed his farsightedness and the flair for organisation which he possessed. As the majority of the internees had refused to give the Advisory Council any particulars about themselves it was not possible for the camp authorities to identify them and consequently they merely represented so many names and numbers on the register. Accordingly, Collins divided them into two groups, one of which would answer their names and numbers and the second which would not. The men sought by the authorities for army service were amongst the latter. Punishment for men who refused to answer their names and numbers entailed transfer to the dreadful grain lofts in south camp, and the stopping of their food parcels, letters, cigarettes, newspapers and in fact the suspension of all privileges. As a result of the plans which Collins worked out, the men in the north camp who were not undergoing punishment were free to smuggle supplies from their own stores to the other group in the south camp. Collins himself took his place amongst the group which did not answer and which in spite of threats and a great display of military might maintained its attitude. The outcome was that the men sought after for conscription remained unidentified, and the British were thus thwarted.

There were moments of relaxation even in Frongoch. For instance there was 'Croke Park' in which many an exciting football match was played, and where Dick Fitzgerald, captain of the Kerry football team, could be seen in action. The admission charge to games was said to be 5/– and posters warned that wives and sweethearts should be left home! Amongst the internees were musicians, writers and other artists who provided a varied range of entertainment for their fellow prisoners. Douglas ffrench-Mullen gave classical recitals on the piano, and the magic fingers of Paul Cusack brought from the same instrument light music which set the whole camp singing. There was that versatile genius, Cathal MacDowell, musician and writer of popular songs, and Michael Lynch who played the organ so beautifully during Mass. The sweet singing of Gerard Crofts and Andy Dunne charmed everybody, even the enemy. Andy describes how the music-loving Welsh soldiers who guarded the camp were won over to friendship with the internees by Irish music and song. Whilst he was in hospital, Andy's singing of Davis' lovely 'Annie Dear' so charmed the medical orderly, Corporal Brett, that he was loth to discharge him and other Irish patients who were good singers. To keep them in hospital he would always delay the taking of their temperatures until he had first induced them to fever point!

Jimmie Mulkearns, better known as 'The Rajah of Frongoch' was another who contributed largely towards making life a little more bearable in that dismal detention camp. Prior to 1916 Jimmie was 'Rimlock' of 'Palmer and Rimlock', a team of amateur entertainers who performed in towns all over Ireland. In Frongoch he organised a minstrel troupe amongst the internees and put on shows which were as good as anything seen in the Dublin theatres. As Mulkearns, who was master of ceremonies at the first show, appeared in the flowing robes of an oriental, there was with him a humorous Dubliner named Peadar O'Brien who, whenever Mulkearns appeared on the 'stage', advanced before him in slow and stately movements, at the same time bowing and leaning after the Eastern manner. His salutation, 'Hail to thee! O Rajah of Frongoch', gave Mulkearns the name and character which passed into 1916 history. From that time he was never known by any name other than 'The Rajah of Frongoch'. Jimmie's personality and strong sense of humour quickly made him the idol of the camp. Soon his fame spread beyond it and later, when he was released, the fact that 'The Rajah of Frongoch' was billed to appear at a concert or céilidhe for Volunteer funds always attracted crowds.

The internees in Frongoch camp and Reading jail, but not the leaders in Lewes, were released at Christmas 1916, and the whole country turned out to welcome them with bonfires, bands and torch-light processions. Little over a month later many of them were marching triumphantly through the streets of Dublin, whilst riding on an outside car at their head was the man of the hour; the same man who wrapped in the coats of fellow prisoners had sat upon an orange box in Richmond jail, mourning the death of his son, executed after the Rising. Dublin was celebrating the great victory of Count Plunkett at the Roscommon election and the tenor of his message to the cheering crowd was carried by the words 'the fight will be made in Ireland and won in Ireland'.

The prospect of imprisonment did not deter the people of Dublin from making the first anniversary of the 1916 Rising an occasion for great public demonstration, even though General Sir Bryan Mahon, who had replaced Sir John Maxwell in charge of the British forces in Ireland, had issued a proclamation forbidding processions or meetings within the Dublin metropolitan area, between Easter Sunday and the Sunday following. An immense crowed assembled at Glasnevin cemetery on Easter Sunday. The Rosary was recited in Irish and the graves of the republican soldiers killed during the fight were decorated by Cumann na mBan. Helena Molony, who had been released at Christmas in 1916, planned a special commemoration ceremony, which was carried into effect by some of her comrades. As a result, copies of the 1916 Proclamation, with the added words 'The Republic Still Lives' were posted widely throughout the city, and the tri-colour waved over all the positions held in 1916.

Promptly at noon, Frank Jackson, a young sailor who was also a Volunteer, made his way along the narrow ledge on top of the ruined GPO, more than one hundred feet above the street. There was little grip for his hands or hold for his feet, and the crowd below watched fascinated as he approached the flagpole. Amidst deafening cheers he hoisted the tri-colour over the GPO, to the very moment that it had been hoisted a year previously. The event attracted at least 20,000 people into Sackville Street, as it was then known, and many of them cheered and sang rebel songs in defiance of the police. A constable ordered to remove the flag was unable to undo the intricate knots made by the sailor, and eventually the flag pole had to be sawn through. The flag which fell to the ground was carried away triumphantly by a section of the crowd assembled below.

Meanwhile, a scroll placed across the front of Liberty Hall by James Connolly's comrades to commemorate his murder by the British, was instantly torn down by the police. It was immediately replaced by another scroll similarly worded and made by Helena Molony. With Brigid Davis, Rosie Hackett and Jane Shanahan, three other Citizen Army girls, she went on the roof of Liberty Hall through an upstairs kitchen. Having fixed the scroll around the parapet, the girls returned to the kitchen, the door of which they barricaded with two tons of

Meeting of Dáil Éireann, 21 January 1919. TOP ROW: *R. Barton, R. Mulcahy, C. Collins, P. Shanahan, Dr Crowley, J. Burke.* MIDDLE ROW: *J. Sweeney, K. O'Higgins, D. Buckley, E. Duggan, P. Béaslaí, Dr J. Ryan, P. Ward, P.J. Moloney, R. Sweetman.* FRONT ROW: *J. O'Doherty, John Hayes, J.J. O'Kelly (Sceilg), Count Plunkett, Cathal Brugha, S.T. O'Kelly, P. O'Malley, J.J. Walsh, T. Kelly.*

Erskine Childers' yacht Asgard, *used in the landing of arms and ammunition at Howth in July 1914.*

Volunteers returning with arms and ammunition after the Howth gun running.

Jim Larkin, the impassioned orator.

Savage attack by police on Dublin public in O'Connell Street on the occasion of the proclaimed meeting, Bloody Sunday, 30 August 1913.

Arrest of Jim Larkin after he had spoken to the people from the balcony of the Imperial Hotel, Dublin, Bloody Sunday, 1913.

Citizen Army on parade outside Liberty Hall. Note the scroll, 'We serve neither King nor Kaiser, but Ireland.'

Citizen Army guard on the roof of Liberty Hall.

Ruined buildings in O'Connell Street (then Sackville Street), after the Rising.

General Sir John Maxwell, Commander of the British forces, at a review of loyalist volunteer corps in the grounds of Trinity College, after the suppression of the Rising. It was 'Butcher' Maxwell's secret court martial which ordered the execution of the Irish leaders.

Clanwilliam House survivors (left to right) standing: Willie Ronan and Jimmy Doyle; seated: James Walsh and Thomas Walsh.

Clanwilliam House in ruins, after the battle of Mount Street Bridge.

Troops in Trinity College during the rebellion.

In the GPO, 1916 – from the painting by Paget.

Ruins of O'Connell Street (then Sackville Street) after the ceasefire, 1916.

Pádraig H. Pearse surrenders his sword to General Lowe, 1916.

Group of officers of the Irish Brigade which fought for the Boers.
Major John MacBride is on the extreme right.

1916 prisoners under heavy escort marched to cattle boats, in the foul-smelling holds of which they were conveyed to England where the jails and prison camps awaited them.

Seán Treacy (left) and his friend and comrade in the struggle Dan Breen, TD.

British military in full battle-dress and supported by tanks and armoured cars, about to raid in Dublin for badly wanted IRA men.

First-aid for a civilian casualty in a Dublin Street.

Scene of the arrest of Kevin Barry photographed immediately after the ambush of British troops, in the course of which he was captured.

Yard in Kilmainham jail, where so many Irish patriots made the supreme sacrifice in the cause of freedom.

General Tudor, Commander of the Auxiliary Division.

IRA casualty at Custom House fight is examined by an Auxiliary.

Prisoners taken at Custom House fight guarded by an Auxiliary.

British soldiers on roof of the Four Courts.

Seán MacEoin (left) photographed with Seán Moylan during the Truce.

The demonstration by crowds outside Mountjoy jail attracted British military with armoured-car support.

6th Battalion Council, Dublin Brigade, July 1921
FRONT ROW *(left to right)*: *Capt. Niall MacNeill, Batt. QM; Commandant A. McDonnell; Vice-Comm. M. Chadwick; Capt. T. Cardiff, transport.* BACK ROW *(left to right)*: *Capt. J. Foley, 'F' Coy, Deansgrange; Capt. E. O'Brien, 'B' Coy, Barnaculla; Dr J.J. Loftus, batt. MO; Capt. J. Curley, 'A' Coy, Dundrum; Capt. L. O'Brien, 'C' Coy, Bray; Capt. W. Walsh, 'D' Coy, Dún Laoghaire.*

A unique picture: Arthur Griffith, Éamon de Valera, Laurence O'Neill, then lord mayor of Dublin, and Michael Collins, at Croke Park during the Truce.

coal. For some time the authorities believed that the Citizen Army had returned to the building in force and that night British soldiers and police from both city and county were mobilised to attack it. Eventually the surrender of the 'garrison' took place when police, begrimed with coal-dust, had dug their way through the barricade.

The Longford election of May 1917, was another victory in a series of Sinn Féin successes which helped to bring about the release of the remaining 1916 prisoners. Joseph McGuinness, the Sinn Féin candidate, was a prisoner in Lewes jail at the time, and his election posters which showed him in convict dress, carried the appeal to the electorate: 'Put Him In to Get Him Out'. Organised mob violence took place during the election as the unionists and the Irish Party joined forces against Sinn Féin.

The powerful Irish-American element also exercised an important influence on the release of the 1916 leaders. America had then entered the war and the British ambassador at Washington strongly advocated a conciliatory policy. It was his belief that the Easter Week executions had a disastrous effect on opinion in America. 'The Irish here have blood in their eyes when they look our way,' he declared. These circumstances contributed largely to the British decision, not alone to release the remaining prisoners, but furthermore about the same time to arrange a convention to 'settle' the Irish problem. It was a trick which Griffith's *Nationality* immediately saw and exposed thus in its issue for 2 June: 'Mr Lloyd George summons a convention and … is to assure the world that England left the Irish to settle the question of government for themselves and that they could not agree.'

Dublin was astir early on the morning of 17 June 1917, for the imprisoned 1916 leaders had been released and were coming home. By 4 a.m. Westland Row station was already densely packed with people, many of whom had been there all night. Vain efforts were made by police and the railway officials to move the people, who took orders only from the Irish Volunteers. At the request of the Volunteers they opened a passage for the relatives of the prisoners, but when the train steamed in, everybody immediately became a relative and rushed to embrace and kiss the men. Traffic was at a standstill as a solid mass of cheering people which stretched from Westland Row to the North Strand crowded around the 'brakes' in which the ex-prisoners rode in triumph. It was a memorable occasion. The events were repeated when Countess Markievicz returned on the evening boat.

Early in 1917 a start was made to reorganise and re-arm the Irish Volunteers. Sometimes the opportunity offered to buy rifles and ammunition from Irish soldiers home on leave from the British army. Many of these men who joined up in the belief that they were to fight for the freedom of 'small nations' were bitter about the treatment of Ireland by the British. Such opportunity to acquire arms came the way of 'A' company, 3rd battalion, when a Dublin Fusilier in Wellington barracks approached Seamus Murray, the quartermaster, and offered to sell rifles and ammunition. It was proposed that these would be handed out after dark through the barrack railings at a point on the Royal Canal, between two bridges. This offer was avidly seized upon. It was still winter at the time, and the gas-lamps along the canal were turned down by Volunteers, who watched from the bank opposite the barracks whilst one of their number, Kit Farrell, stripped off and swam across the ice cold water to the barracks' railings. Having got the rifles and received the 'all clear' from Volunteer collaborators, he made the return journey with rifles strapped upon his back.

One night during a similar operation whilst Farrell was in the water with rifles, a party of British soldiers arrived with their girls and loitered at the point where he had planned to emerge from the canal. They stayed some time until Seamus Murray eventually got rid of them by letting the air out of his bicycle tyres and pretending to work on imaginary punctures until the loiterers moved off because of his unwanted presence. Meanwhile Farrell had to remain in the water and the extreme cold brought on severe cramp so that he was barely rescued from drowning by Peadar O'Meara. When the rifles were landed by Farrell they were always wrapped in ground-sheets, and strapped on bicycles before being carried away to the dump. About fifty had been acquired by this method before it was altered to the less arduous but more risky plan to trade for arms at a small gate about twenty yards from the main entrance to the barracks on the South Circular Road. The initiative and daring of 'A' company resulted in their procuring about a hundred rifles and a substantial supply of ammunition before the garrison at Wellington barracks was transferred.

On 23 June, Sinn Féin won another by-election, this time in Clare, where de Valera, just released from jail, polled 5,010 votes to 2,035 by Paddy Lynch for the Irish Party. A month later Lloyd George's convention began its sittings in Dublin. As it was boycotted by Sinn Féin, by Labour and by William O'Brien's All-For-Ireland League it represented only such small sections of Irish opinion as the unionists, the Redmondites and the Carsonites. 'We must realise,' said the Archbishop of Melbourne, Most Rev. Dr Mannix, 'that this convention does not really represent Ireland.' 'Though I direct you to pray for it, I know,' said the Archbishop of Dublin, Most Rev. Dr Walsh, 'that this convention has no authority from the Irish people.' It was meant to fail, as far as Ireland was concerned, and it did fail.

Seventeen hundred delegates representing 1,200 clubs attended the Sinn Féin ard-fheis on 25 October. Éamon de Valera was elected president and enthusiastic approval was accorded the national programme, according to which: 'Sinn Féin aims at securing international recognition of Ireland as an independent Irish Republic. Having achieved that status the Irish people may by referendum choose their own form of government.' Two days later the Volunteers, who had remained independent of Sinn Féin, also elected de Valera as their president.

By the Conscription Bill, passed on 16 April 1918, the authorities were empowered to apply the Conscription Act to Ireland. The bill became law without the votes of the Irish Party, who opposed it at every stage, and who called it 'a declaration of war against Ireland'. The party furthermore informed the government that they would not answer for the inevitable conflict which would follow any attempt to enforce the Act in Ireland. Having said so, the members returned home to participate in the most solid front that had ever faced the British. Over a month prior to the passing of the conscription measure, John Redmond, the leader of the party, had died and was succeeded by John Dillon.

On 17 March, the following resolution was passed at monster Sinn Féin meetings held throughout Ireland. 'Here on St Patrick's Day we join with our fellow-countrymen at home and in foreign lands in proclaiming once more that Ireland is a distinct nation whose just right is sovereign independence. This right has been asserted in every generation, has never been surrendered and never allowed to lapse. We call the nations to witness that today as in the past it is by force alone that England holds Ireland for her Empire and not by the consent of the Irish …'

At the famous Mansion House Conference on 18 April 1918, Sinn Féin, the Irish Party, Labour, Independent MPs and William O'Brien's All-For-Ireland League pledged again to resist conscription. A delegation from the conference waited on the Catholic bishops who were in annual session at Maynooth on the same evening and their lordships immediately issued a strong pronouncement against conscription. A national defence fund, set up to finance the efforts to defeat conscription, raised a huge sum of money. On 21 April, hundreds of thousands signed the anti-conscription pledge at the doors of Catholic churches throughout the country. On 9 June, 'Women's Day', a great procession of women marched to the Dublin City Hall, where they signed a pledge to the effect that they would not fill the jobs of men conscripted into the British forces. The women's committee included amongst its members, Mrs Stopford-Green, Mrs Gordon (later Mrs Austin Stack), the Misses Agnes O'Farrelly, Alice Milligan and Sheila Humphries.

A trade union congress in Dublin, attended by 1,500 delegates, agreed to an Irish Labour Party proposal that trade unionists should carry out a one-day protest strike against conscription. The date appointed was 23 April and on that day the first general strike to be carried out in Western Europe took place. With the exception of Belfast, the order was observed everywhere throughout the country, from the largest factory to the smallest shop. Transport services were suspended, hotel guests served themselves, and even the Dublin cabby, though on the hazard, refused tempting offers to take visitors out of town. The stoppage was complete and demonstrated most effectively what would happen if conscription were enforced.

In the hour of national danger, Michael Collins, then serving a short sentence for a 'seditious' speech, was advised to pay the fine involved and come out of prison. Shortly afterwards, a friendly detective in Dublin Castle gave him a long list of Sinn Féiners whose arrest was imminent, and thus enabled him to warn many of them. Some disregarded the warning and were arrested; others who included Collins, Cathal Brugha, Harry Boland, Dick McKee and Rory O'Connor escaped the British swoop. In all, over eighty persons prominent in the revolutionary movement, and including Éamon de Valera and Arthur Griffith, were sent to prisons in England, and charged with being involved in a 'German Plot', a bogus affair invented by Lloyd George to justify the arrests. As a result of the arrests the anti-conscription movement placed a crushing burden upon those who remained at liberty, but they threw themselves with a redoubled energy into the work of resistance. Brugha crossed to England where he instructed Volunteers in that country to carry out reprisals there should British actions warrant them. Collins went to Liverpool to arrange for the shipment of arms and munitions to Ireland.

The general election of December 1918, gave the Irish people the opportunity to establish the Republic of Ireland, for which the men of 1916 had fought. The conscription threat, which had passed with the end of the war in November, was replaced by an even greater danger to the Irish nation, for Lloyd George had announced his intention to introduce a measure of Home Rule from which six of the Ulster counties were to be excluded, thus achieving the partition of the country. At the time, the majority of the Ulster Catholics were members of the Ancient Order of Hibernians (Board of Érin), a sectarian nationalist organisation, whose leader, Joe Devlin, had at one time wielded immense influence over the Irish Parliamentary Party. Devlin, a man of the people, had gained control of the politically very efficient AOH by reason of his dynamic energy and great personal charm. He strongly supported Redmond when the Irish Party attempted to gain control of the Irish Volunteers in 1914. Following the expulsion of the Irish Party nominees from the Volunteer Executive, in September 1914, the party set up a rival body called the National Volunteers, 28,000 of whom fought for the British in the war, and numbers of whom helped to suppress the 1916 Rising. Devlin became a bitter enemy of the Irish Volunteers, and hated Sinn Féin. About 10,000 Ulstermen of the National Volunteers who joined the British forces were killed in the war, and as a result Ulster grew low in manpower. While the threat of conscription prevailed, Hibernian hostility towards Sinn Féin abated; and the Irish Party, conscious of its own weakness, had absented itself from Westminster and thrown in its lot with the republican forces, in order to defeat the measure. It was hoped that the party would pursue a like policy in the general election. As the feeling of the country was obviously behind Sinn Féin, it was felt that the party should stand down and allow the people to express by their election of Sinn Féin candidates their protests against partition, and their desire for an Irish Republic. With a clear mandate thus obtained from the nation, representatives could demand that Ireland's case be heard by the Peace Conference. However, speaking at a United Irish League meeting in Dublin on 22 November 1918, John Dillon, leader of the Irish Party, made it clear that there was to be no co-operation with Sinn Féin when he declared: 'We will fight Sinn Féin with all the forces at our disposal.'

Both Sinn Féin and the Irish Party decided to avoid a three-corner contest in such Ulster constituencies wherein Catholics and nationalists combined had but a small majority. These constituencies were South Down, East Down, East Tyrone, North-West Tyrone, East Donegal, South Armagh, Derry city and South Fermanagh. In order to implement this policy, Cardinal Logue and other distinguished ecclesiastics proposed that the seats be equally divided between Sinn Féin and the Irish Party. Sinn Féin, on the other hand held that a plebiscite should be taken in the eight constituencies to decide whether the people wanted to be represented by a Sinn Féin or Party candidate. The Sinn Féin executive appointed Eoin MacNeill to act as its representative in discussions with John Dillon of the Irish Party and with the lord mayor of Dublin. MacNeill was given clear instructions by the executive that he was not to agree to any method of settling the question other than by a plebiscite. On the eve of nomination day, however, these three men announced that they had agreed that the eight seats should be equally divided, and left their allocation to the discretion of Cardinal Logue. Furious because of this unauthorised action, Sinn Féin at first decided to contest every Ulster seat, but following a public pronouncement by the cardinal to the effect that he had allocated the eight seats equally between the two parties, Sinn Féin reluctantly withdrew their candidates for South Down, East Tyrone, East Donegal and South Armagh, the constituencies which had been allowed to the Irish Party. Sinn Féin headed the poll in three of the compromise seats awarded to it by the cardinal, but in the case of the fourth, East Down, the Irish Party broke the agreement, put up a candidate, and a unionist was elected as a result of the split vote.

Sinn Féin fought the election under a tremendous handicap. It contested some eighty seats, of which seventy-three were won, although more than one hundred of its ablest men and women were in jail, and although Sinn Féin itself and every other national organisation was banned by the authorities. Forty-seven of the Sinn Féin MPs were in jail and many others were on the run. Robert Brennan, Sinn Féin director of elections, was arrested and sent to prison in England three weeks before polling day. The censor also lent his able assistance to the forces lined against Sinn Féin by deleting almost the whole of the organisation's election manifesto. He left in the words 'Sinn Féin aims at securing the establishment of that Republic'. Leaflets showered from aeroplanes which flew over many parts of the country warned the people against voting republican. Despite these tactics no fewer than twenty-six Sinn Féin candidates were returned unopposed.

It must be borne in mind that most of the printing houses in the country were at the disposal of the anti-Sinn Féin elements and that the majority of the newspapers supporting Sinn Féin had either been suppressed or were strictly censored. Election addresses of Sinn Féin candidates who were prisoners of the British were confiscated in the post, and the organisation had to fight the campaign by rushing its few available speakers from place to place, with little rest in between. The Irish Volunteers, under permanent mobilisation for ten days, were allocated all kinds of jobs, which even included the addressing of election meetings and the guarding of election booths and ballot-boxes. Sinn Féin election literature consisted of small hand-bills, printed secretly on hand-presses; picture postcards of the 1916 leaders; political cartoons drawn by republican artists; and topical ballads about election personalities and events. The number of candidates who were in British jails simplified publicity and posters for a number were standardised. 'Vote for the Man in jail' covered many constituencies.

Pending the general election, the British withdrew the order which prohibited the holding of public meetings without a permit. As a result, Michael Collins, Harry Boland, Cathal Brugha and other 'wanted' men enjoyed the experience of addressing election meetings in the presence of detectives and Castle touts who had been on their trail for months. Many priests, foremost amongst them Fr Michael O'Flanagan, worked and spoke for the Sinn Féin candidates. For the first time women were permitted to exercise the franchise and to stand for parliament, though that right was still restricted to those over thirty years of age. The women were enthusiastic supporters of Sinn Féin and their activities and support throughout the country during the campaign contributed in no small measure to its sweeping victory. Cumann na mBan, strong and well organised, took a prominent part.

The most exciting and enthusiastic election scenes in Dublin took place in the St Patrick's division, in which the Sinn Féin candidate, Countess Markievicz, was then a 'German Plot' prisoner in England. The Dublin workers had not forgotten her great work for them during the 1913 lockout and to a man and woman they turned out to help her. Thousands lined the streets which led to the election booths, and as the electors passed in they were greeted with shouts of 'Up the Countess' and even, in the excitement, 'Up the Duchess'. Countess Markievicz was returned at the head of the poll in a three-cornered contest, with a majority of 3,771 over the combined votes of her opponents. She thus became the first woman to be elected to the British parliament, and shortly afterwards she was chosen by President de Valera to be his minister for labour in the first Dáil Éireann.

The election results were announced on 28 December. They were published outside the Sinn Féin premises at 6 Harcourt Street, and a vast crowd assembled to cheer the victory, which few had hoped would be so complete. In Dublin, once the centre of British power in the country, unionists secured their only success apart from North-East Ulster, when, in a three-cornered contest in the Rathmines and Rathgar constituency, Sir Maurice Dockrell was returned with a majority of sixty-four over the combined Sinn Féin and Irish Party votes. Of one hundred and five seats in Ireland, seventy-three were won by Sinn Féin. Four of those elected sat for two seats each, viz., Arthur Griffith, Éamon de Valera, Eoin MacNeill and Liam Mellows, so that Sinn Féin returned sixty-nine members. The unionists won twenty-six seats and the Irish Party, which had eighty seats previously, was reduced to six in Ireland and one in Liverpool. Of the six Irish Party seats four were the 'compromise' seats in Ulster. De Valera, who defeated the Irish Party leader in Mayo, and who secured more than twice Dillon's votes in so doing, was himself beaten by Joe Devlin in the Falls constituency in Belfast. On the night of 28 December the crowds which gathered in Dublin to cheer the Sinn Féin victory were attacked by hundreds of British soldiers, armed with sticks. American soldiers, some of them in uniform, who were on the streets, joined forces with the Sinn Féiners and the streets were quickly cleared of the British.

Sinn Féin, having contested the election on an abstentionist policy so far as the British parliament at Westminster was concerned, quickly implemented its pre-election guarantee to set up in Dublin its own assembly, Dáil Éireann.

A private meeting of the first Dáil Éireann took place in the Mansion House on 7 January 1919. Six of the newly elected MPs, Seán T. Ó Ceallaigh, Piaras Béaslaí, George Gavan Duffy, Con Collins, J.J. Walsh and James O'Mara drafted a provisional constitution and a

Declaration of Independence and prepared the agenda for the first public session of Dáil Éireann.

The first Dáil Éireann assembled at the Mansion House, Dublin, on 21 January 1919. As President de Valera and Arthur Griffith were in jail, Cathal Brugha was elected acting president on the proposition of Count Plunkett. The huge Round Room was thronged and the galleries were filled with journalists and foreign visitors. Enormous crowds gathered outside to catch a glimpse of their new representatives, and to cheer them as they entered the building. The assembly possessed many impressive and dramatic features and all the proceedings were conducted in the Irish language. The opening prayers were recited in Irish by Fr Michael O'Flanagan, a young priest whose splendid oratory was first heard when he spoke during the lying-in-state of O'Donovan Rossa in the City Hall in 1915. He had since become well-known as a speaker on Sinn Féin platforms. The chairman, Cathal Brugha, had received so many wounds during the fight in the South Dublin Union in 1916 that the British were of opinion that he could not live, and so did not execute him. The roll call in Irish was read by Cathal Brugha and responded to in Irish also by Seán Nunan, one of the clerks of the Dáil. As the chairman called the roll of deputies the clerk responded, *Fé ghlas ag Gallaibh* ('Imprisoned by the English'), in the case of thirty-six who were still in British jails. Three other Sinn Féin TDs were in compulsory exile, and in all only twenty-seven were able to attend the first session of Dáil Éireann.

All who had been elected to Irish constituencies, whether members of the Sinn Féin, Unionist or Irish Party were invited to take their seats in Dáil Eireann. Their names were included in the roll call, but none attended other than the Sinn Féin deputies. Two men, whose names were answered as being present were in fact absent from the session. They were Michael Collins and Harry Boland, who had crossed to England to arrange for the escape of de Valera from Lincoln jail, and it was arranged that their names should be answered by other members so that their absence from Ireland would not be noticed by the British.

In his address Cathal Brugha said: 'We are now done with England;

let the world know, and those who are concerned bear it in mind.' An address to the free nations of the world was issued, and de Valera, Griffith and Count Plunkett were appointed delegates to represent Ireland at the Peace Conference. Cathal Brugha nominated the following as ministers: Michael Collins for home affairs; Eoin MacNeill for finance; Count Plunkett for foreign affairs; and Richard Mulcahy for defence.

The 'German Plot' prisoners in England were all released about a month after de Valera's sensational escape from Lincoln jail, and Dáil Éireann met in private for its second session on 1 April. De Valera was elected president, the title by which he was to be known for the next three years. He appointed a new ministry which included Griffith, Cathal Brugha, MacNeill, Count Plunkett, Countess Markievicz, Cosgrave, Barton and Ginnell. Collins became minister for finance, and Brugha minister for defence, while Dick Mulcahy was appointed chief-of-staff of the Irish Republican Army, as the Volunteers became officially styled. 'Our duty,' declared de Valera in the Dáil, 'is to make clear to the world the position in which Ireland now stands. There is in Ireland at this moment only one lawful authority and that authority is the elected government of the Irish Republic. Of the other power claiming authority, we can only say, adopting the words of Cardinal Mercier, "The authority of that power is no lawful authority".'

Dáil Éireann, elected by the free votes of the Irish people was, on 10 September 1919, declared by the British to be a dangerous association and was accordingly prohibited and suppressed. Thus was the issue knit and the way prepared for the fighting which was soon to commence. During the campaign of 1920 and 1921 the British vainly endeavoured to break the spirit of the Irish by all the force and frightfulness at their command. In subsequent pages, writers tell of the magnificent struggle and of the dramatic events which culminated in the Truce, for which the British asked, and which came into operation at noon on 11 July 1921.

SAVING OF THE BATTALION DUMP

by CAPTAIN T. SCULLY

ON SPY WEDNESDAY, 1918, our QM Jimmy Murray, set out on his cycle to North County Dublin for the purpose of taking back to the company dump a Lee-Metford rifle that was in possession of a Volunteer who had been transferred from 'A' company to another unit. As Jimmy was responsible to the skipper (late Major-General Seán Guilfoyle) for all arms belonging to the unit, Jimmy could not see his way to let this Volunteer's new unit have our Lee-Metford. Hence the journey into Fingal, where the rifle was collected.

No incident happened on the way home until Jimmy was almost at the door of the dump. Then out hopped a DMP man from the shadows and wanted an explanation as to why our quartermaster had not got a light on his cycle. Jimmy told all the lies in the calendar, but the cop did not believe him, even when the latter gave his name and address. So, to make sure, our quartermaster and his cycle were conveyed to the Bridewell police barracks, where he had to languish in durance vile for the night.

In those days the DMP were required to furnish all information in relation to arms, etc., to the British military authorities, and so it looked extremely blue for the 3rd battalion dump. We could do nothing and, in fact, were utterly helpless if the British, when the raid came off, found our dump. It would have been very serious, so we just crossed our fingers and prayed. We could, of course, have gone to the dump and made an attempt to move the stuff, but, knowing British tactics for what they were worth, we had no intention of being mouse-trapped; so the only thing that could be done was to wait until the British made their raid and trust to luck. This we did.

Then the British struck. Three companies of infantry, with machine-guns, etc., surrounded the district of Michael's Hill, High Street, St Augustine Street, the South Quays, etc., while the intelligence people and detectives turned out the domicile of our imprisoned quartermaster. Eight hours the British spent on the job and for their trouble were rewarded with one BSA 22-calibre rifle, while 43 single-shot Martini rifles, two hundredweight of gelignite, gun-cotton, revolvers, Mills grenades, .303 ammunition and other war material just stared them in the face.

Commandant Joe O'Connor, our battalion O/C, and his staff met to consider the position. At this period I was a squad leader, which rank is the equivalent of a corporal, and it fell to my lot to patrol with my squad the area in which the battalion staff were meeting. I met the skipper on his way to the meeting and, standing in front of him and at attention, I said: 'Sir, if you will allow me, I will make an effort to shift the dump.'

He looked at me, smiling, and said: 'If I do, how do you propose to carry it out?'

I answered: 'You are keen on strategy and tactics and as one of your pupils, who has taken in all your teaching, I have, I believe, found a way to do the job.'

He then said: 'Hang on here a few minutes' and went on his way.

After about fifteen minutes he came to the door and called me in before the battalion staff, and, having satisfied the O/C about the feasibility of the plan and its reasonable chance of success, I was asked how many men I would require to carry out the job. I answered, 'two and myself'. I chose Kit Farrell and Christy Murray, brother of our quartermaster, and, having arranged to meet my two assistants next morning, I handed over my squad to Seán Whelehan. My final instructions from the skipper were to report to him when and if the job had been completed.

I had now to get some place to store our dump, so I called on the late Pierce Walsh at his provision shop in East James' Street, and told him what I required. Not alone did he give me his cellar, but actually thanked me for, as he said, paying him a great compliment. His wife, the late Mrs Walsh, and their sons – Tom, Jim and Leo – were all delighted at the prospect of our attempt to save the dump – and, by the way, those are the famous brothers who defended Clanwilliam House in Easter Week until it was burned out.

Now for the transport. I could, of course, have obtained a motor car or other large vehicle, but that would have drawn the attention of the British military or their counterpart, the DMP, to our activities, so some other form of transport had to be arranged. At this time there was a lady residing in Irishtown who was of great assistance to our battalion. I remembered that she was having some addition made to her home by a firm of building contractors, and so I paid her a visit with the object of getting that builder's hand-cart, and some of his materials, to make our journeys look the real thing, i.e. three builder's labourers going on a job. Our friend here, when told what we wanted, said: 'Is that all you require? Why not bring your stuff here; no one would suspect this house.' I had a job to convince her that I had already arranged for a place to put our dump in. She seemed hurt that I overlooked her house, but was appeased when told that it would have to be in the city, where city units could get to it at short notice.

We went through the builder's gear and selected his hand-cart, ladder and other things, our friend undertaking to have them at my home by 10 a.m. next morning. I trust this lady will forgive me if I mention her name. She is Mrs Joe Cunningham, wife of the prominent Dublin commission agent; but it is so long ago I cannot remember whether she was Mrs Cunningham or Miss Fitzpatrick at the time. Well, she had the hand-cart and the other builder's gear at the spot appointed and at the correct time.

Everything was now ready for the attempt, so Christy Murray, Kit Farrell and myself, with our builder's hand-cart and other gear, proceeded on our way to the dump. At Christchurch Place we met

Jimmy's sister, May, who informed us that herself and her mother (the late Mrs Murray) had made a reconnaissance of the neighbourhood and all was clear. So far so good.

We entered the yard where our stuff was stored and proceeded to unearth it. We now became aware that our handcart, etc., would not be able to take it all in one or two loads, so we decided that, since Dame Luck had so far been kind to us, she would hardly desert us now, we would remove the lot. Our first load consisted of the forty-three Martini rifles, made up in bundles of five, and the two hundredweight of gelignite, which we unloaded safely in its new abode. In our next load we took all our .303 and other ammunition, together with some Lee-Enfield rifles; but our third and final journey was nearly a failure, for we got stuck in a traffic jam at the Grafton Street corner of Nassau Street. One of the hand-cart wheels had a tendency to come off and, to make matters worse, the policeman on point duty became very abusive and, as we moved away, shouted after us that he would report our boss (the builder) for employing kids to do men's work. The names this cop called us and our employer would lift the hair from your head, and, of course, we had to grin and bear it. Here were we with a load of war material, which included slabs of gun-cotton and Mills grenades, and a hand-cart with one wheel doing its damnedest to come off. Well, anyone with an elementary knowledge of explosives will agree that the other traffic and our poor selves would have been in a bad way had this hand-cart wheel succeeded in its object, for gun-cotton, coming into contact with hand-grenades or paving stones, is likely to make one hell of a mess of surrounding objects.

However, we got to our destination without any further trouble and, having unloaded the stuff, thanked our stars that the job was done – so we thought. I invited my two pals to have a well-earned meal at my home, but when we got there, sitting in the kitchen was the skipper, who said: 'Well done, lads', and at the same time informing us that Major-General Seán MacMahon had decided that the stuff was to be distributed to the units which comprised our battalion, and that, when I had finished my meal, I was to contact him at once and he would give me the details for the distribution. I contacted General MacMahon at Fitzgerald's shop in Pearse Street and received his warm congratulations, plus the details of the distribution of our dump and the longest screw-driver I have ever seen. This tool was used for removing the butts from the stocks of the Martinis. Well, the three of us completed the distribution of the dump and left Walsh's house at 2 a.m. next morning.

COLLINSTOWN AERODROME RAID

by PATRICK HOULIHAN

IN THE LATTER part of 1918, I was working in Collinstown Aerodrome for the enemy against whom I had fought in 1916, but keeping my eyes open to see what I could do to help the Republic to which we had pledged our allegiance. I was not long there before I discovered that there were several other Volunteers on the job, working away peaceably enough to all appearances, but awaiting an opportunity to further the cause which we all had at heart.

Collinstown Aerodrome was, at that time, a regular little arsenal, and, needless to say, it was well guarded by the British military. The choice collection of arms it contained excited our envy, as the Volunteers were badly in need of military equipment; so we decided to notify GHQ and await instructions. We gave GHQ details about the strength of the position, and were told to submit our plans for carrying out the proposed raid.

My comrades in Collinstown Aerodrome were Peadar Breslin, later killed in Mountjoy; Pat Doyle, later executed by the British; Seán Doyle, who died of wounds after the attack on the Custom House; and Christy O'Malley. I, at that time, held the rank of 1st lieutenant in the Volunteers. Summoned to brigade headquarters, I was told that our plans were approved, and that I was to be put in command of the raid. I was given the choice of what Dublin brigade men I wanted, and I decided that I would have men from 'A' and 'F' companies of the 1st battalion – men of the calibre of those whom I have already mentioned, and P.J. Ryan, Brian Kelly, George Fitzgerald, C. O'Malley, Phil Leddy, Mick Magee (later killed in an ambush), Barney Ryan (later executed) and Tom Merrigan.

As the work before us was of a very dangerous character I did not wish to call upon any married men to take part in it, but when Pat Doyle heard that he was debarred for this reason he became very indignant with me and threatened to leave the Volunteers if he was not included in the attacking party. I am glad to be able here to pay a tribute to that noble soldier, later to suffer on the scaffold for his country. He was the most devoted soul, and never shirked any risk or danger, although he had a young wife depending on him. Mrs Pat Doyle was one of those splendid and patriotic Irishwomen who sacrificed so much for their country during the War of Independence. She never complained, although her husband's life was so much given up to the fight for Irish freedom that they had both been reduced to poverty. Instead of trying to influence him to think of his own safety and her comfort, she stood by him and encouraged him all through the struggle to the day of his death.

Pat Doyle having overcome my objection to his accompanying us, it was arranged that we should meet at the Doyle's little home, at St Mary's Place, to get ready for the expedition. A final reconnoitre of the aerodrome showed us that we had dangerous opponents to meet, in addition to the soldiers, for two large and fierce Airedale dogs were kept outside the guardroom. These dogs, while they never attacked a man in khaki, would not allow any civilian to pass after nightfall. No attempt to coax or bribe them was of any use, for they seemed to say: 'You will get in here only over our dead bodies.' We soon saw that it was only over their dead bodies that we would be able to penetrate inside Collinstown Aerodrome. On the afternoon of 19 March 1919 (the night fixed for the raid), Seán Doyle and I, while we were at work, administered a large dose of poison to the Airedales, a dose which was calculated to kill them some hours later. This work was very unpleasant for us, but was absolutely necessary under the circumstances, for the whole success of our undertaking depended upon our being able to enter the grounds without an alarm being raised.

The raiding party met at Mrs Doyle's house, where they dressed in khaki, supplied by GHQ, and masks.

As we left town for the aerodrome at about 11.30 p.m., we were troubled to notice that there was a glorious moon, a silent enemy, which would greatly increase our difficulties in approaching the aerodrome unnoticed. According to plan we were to divide forces about four miles from Collinstown, and I appointed the party which was to attack the rear to Peadar Breslin, I myself taking command of the party which was to attack the front, the total number of those engaged being about twenty-five. The party which I was commanding had to reach the front of the guardroom without detection, so we had to crawl, lying flat on the ground, for about two miles. Peadar's squad had orders not to attack in the rear, until my squad was already in action in the front. All during the action, from the moment we entered the aerodrome grounds, we were to speak as little as possible, and never to address each other by name. Numbers were selected for each man beforehand, and every man knew that when he wanted to speak to a comrade he was to address him as 'Number One', or whatever his number was. These orders were carried out so strictly that later, the British reporting the raid, said that the men 'were as silent as mummies'. In order that there would be no need to fire shots we had brought with us a good supply of rope, and a kind of knuckle-duster weapon. We also carried some sledgehammers, which came in useful, as it will appear, later.

Tom Merrigan, who had been detailed to deal with the sentry outside the guardroom, waited until the sentry was at the point farthest from us, and then rushed at him from behind. He was taken completely by surprise, disarmed, and then forced into the guardroom, where the other sentries, about twenty in number, were treated in a like manner. When all of them were disarmed we proceeded to tie them up. We made sure that their arms and legs were securely roped, and swung them out of the cross beams of the guardroom.

While one section was engaged in dealing with the guard, another was busily engaged in collecting all the arms and ammunition, and getting ready for transport.

Our brigadier had arranged to send motors to carry the munitions, and two others in addition to convey the men back to the city. Willing hands loaded the rifles, bayonets and ammunition into the cars in record time, and got them safely away.

Our next precaution was to make our own retreat secure, and now the sledgehammers came into play. We paid a visit to the military garage, which housed at least twenty motor cars, all in perfect condition, and demolished them. We made sure that these cars would not be able to pursue us that night, and it is doubtful if they were ever able to go on the road again.

Our work being successfully done, we went to look for the two cars which were to drive us into town, but to our disappointment only one, driven by Pat MacCrae, was at the appointed place. This car, a taxi, had to carry thirteen passengers into town, and luckily it made the journey without any mishap. However, one of the cars transporting munitions was not so fortunate, and we had the alarming experience of it breaking down about three miles from our dump. The men in charge of this car, not daring to ask for help, had to get out and push the car for the remaining miles, unload it at the dump, and push it again until it was a safe distance away.

Sufficient credit can hardly be given to the men engaged on this raid for their coolness and daring. That the raid was well worth while can be shown when I mention that our 'haul' that night consisted of seventy-five rifles and bayonets, and 5,000 rounds of ammunition, the largest number of arms ever captured at one time from the enemy. In addition, we had no casualties and lost no prisoners.

Next morning we all turned in to work at the aerodrome, and as we passed into the gates we were surprised to see our late captives, the guards whom we had tied up, being led away prisoners under a heavy escort. We were sorry for the poor fellows, for they seemed to be having a run of bad luck. I am sure they little suspected that the men going into work, dressed as 'civvies', were no others than the masked men in khaki the night before. However, I fear that someone else did, as the Volunteers at Collinstown all lost their jobs shortly after.

ATTACK ON LORD FRENCH

by DESMOND RYAN

IT HAS BEEN calculated that in all some twelve attempts were made to ambush Lord French, all of which ended in disappointment. They were planned by the Dublin GHQ as a demonstration against the head of the British military administration in Ireland, and reports as to Lord French's movements were regularly submitted to the headquarters' meetings by Michael Collins. Seán Treacy and Seamus Robinson were told by Tomás MacCurtain, after the failure of the first attempt, that the only good thing about it was that he had been given a revolver, which he kept as a reward for his patience that morning and as something he had vainly tried to get before.

Seán Hogan, on another attempt on 11 November 1919, preserved a less welcome souvenir. The plan was to ambush the lord lieutenant as his car passed over Grattan bridge from the viceregal lodge en route to an armistice banquet in Trinity College. Seán Hogan had been informed of the actual moment French's car was due to pass, so within a stone's throw of Dublin Castle he drew the pins from his two hand-grenades and threw away his pins. The night was bitterly cold. Two hours passed while Seán Hogan held on grimly, but French failed to appear. Finally Hogan made his escape, still gripping the grenades, until he reached a palace of safety and secured new pins. He never forgot his walk through the crowded streets, his numbed hands, and the effort of will that alone saved him or some innocent civilians from being blown to pieces. Dan Breen and Peadar Clancy, according to Breen's account, on another occasion waited for two hours outside the door of a Merrion Square doctor whom French sometimes visited.

The last attempt on the life of Lord French was made at Ashtown on Friday, 19 December 1919. Paddy Daly was in command of the attackers, who included Seán Treacy, Dan Breen, Seamus Robinson, Seán Hogan, Mick McDonnell, Tom Keogh, Martin Savage, Vincent Byrne, Tom Kilcoyne and Joe Leonard. One of that ambush party was to be killed that day, and two others – Treacy and Keogh – were to meet violent deaths within two years in the Black and Tan struggle and in the Civil War. It was only by chance that Martin Savage came with them, although he was a lieutenant of the 2nd Dublin battalion. It happened that through his activities he met Seán Hogan at a city house and spent the night of 18 December there. Hogan told him about the expedition and lent him an automatic pistol when Savage insisted on joining the party.

Their information was that Lord French would arrive at Ashtown station on the north side of Dublin, some two miles from the city, leave the train there, and travel the short distance to the viceregal lodge by car. This was an easy and obvious route, as one of the gates of Phoenix Park is so near as to be named the Ashtown gate. About two hundred yards from the station, and one hundred yards from the Ashtown gate stood a country inn, 'Kelly's', or 'The Half-Way House'. The station was under observation by the ambushers for about half an hour before the arrival of the train, which was due at 11.40 a.m.

The plan to attack Lord French was animated by no personal feeling against him – indeed, the attackers without exception bore him no grudge afterwards for eluding, their bombs and bullets. 'I must say I am glad now that Lord French escaped,' said Dan Breen. Seamus Robinson in the same spirit declared: 'I am sure he was as delighted as we were disappointed!' What the eleven men were risking their lives for was to make a protest against the military occupation of Ireland by the British government of which the lord lieutenant was the highest representative. Why, they argued, attack the ordinary soldiers and political spies, and leave a viceroy immune, especially when that viceroy always went guarded by a considerable armed escort?

On this morning at Ashtown the attackers had only one advantage on their side: surprise, and as it turned out, only a brief and partial surprise at that. Against them were three cars, the occupants of which were well protected by rifles and machine-guns.

Daly's orders to his men were to arrive in pairs, enter the inn, and mix with the other customers as if ordinary cyclists on their way past. Shortly before the train arrived they were to line the hedge on the right-hand side for about thirty yards. Dan Breen, Tom Keogh and Martin Savage would then at the last moment block the road by drawing a country cart, which stood handy, right across the path of the approaching cars. This would slow down the cars, which invariably were driven at a very high speed. It was necessary that Dan Breen and the other two should carry out this last order with a slow and stupid air, as any haste might arouse the suspicions of the other people in the inn. The GHQ instructions, in addition, emphasised that casualties among the attackers and among the civilian onlookers were to be avoided. To guard against the second danger, some of the party were to be stationed at the crossroads to prevent anyone walking into the line of fire.

Daly also instructed the ambushers that the first car was not to be attacked. It was understood that Lord French usually travelled in the second car – his first car conveyed his armed escort invariably preceded by a military motor-cyclist scout. Behind French's car there was always a third car with the rest of his armed escort. Seamus Robinson was somewhat disturbed by Daly's order that the first car must be allowed a free run through. He had not time to argue the matter with Daly or point out to him at the last minute the danger of the escort in the first car opening fire on the attackers whilst they were in the thick of the battle with the second. Robinson decided when the time came to side-step these orders and withhold his own grenade until the second car had been dealt with.

Inside the 'Half-Way House' the cyclists, who had dropped in two by two, mixed with the small crowd inside, greeted each other as if the meetings were accidental, and talked of every subject imaginable, except, as Dan Breen records, 'politics'. Outside some members of the party kept a close lookout on the station, and nearer to the station still was Vincent Byrne on the watch to signal the arrival of the viceregal cars to the main body. As it happened, the train arrived some minutes ahead of time, and this was the first check to the attack, as the men had to take up their positions along the hedge at very short notice. At this moment, too, a policeman arrived from the viceregal lodge to keep the road clear for when Lord French's car should arrive. In the meantime Vincent Byrne duly gave his signal, and the three cars had already set out from Ashtown station.

Breen, Tom Keogh and Martin Savage had begun to pull the heavy cart slowly across the road and the policeman, quite deceived by their acting the parts of slow and innocent countrymen, rushed from his position at the crossroads to argue loudly with them that a passage must be 'kept clear for his excellency'. They stared at him obstinately and stupidly, and not wishing to offer him violence or hurt him, tried to meet the situation by swearing at him and telling him to mind his own business and go away quietly. The argument held up the work of barricading the road with the cart. One of the party lining the ditch now made an unhappy intervention. Instead of leaving the dispute to Breen, Keogh and Savage, he hurled a hand-grenade at the policeman's head and stunned him just as Lord French's motor-cyclist scout dashed by, fifty yards ahead of the first car. It was now too late to barricade the road, as the party had been thrown into confusion. To the best of Seamus Robinson's recollection, the hand-grenade failed to explode; according to other accounts, the grenade fell wide, exploded, and the force of the explosion knocked policeman and barricaders flat, fortunately without injuring anyone. The slight contradictions in these accounts are understandable because of the deadly explosions, rattle of machine-guns and flying bullets which assailed the ambushers within the next few minutes.

The second car took the full force of the ambushers' attack and was shattered by the rain of bullets and grenades concentrated on it as it came on close behind the first. Seán Hogan and Paddy Daly were thrown to the ground as a grenade slipped from Hogan's hand and exploded. They were smothered in mud but escaped injury. Daly was able to land a grenade into the second car. Seamus Robinson hurled his grenade at the first car, as it brushed past some slight obstructions which had been thrown on the road, but what effect his bomb had he never knew. Lord French's bodyguard, Detective-Sergeant Halley, who sat next to the driver, was at all events slightly wounded; Halley hurled a hand-grenade at random behind him in reply while the car tore ahead at full speed.

The ambushers' calculations were again upset: contrary to his usual custom, French on this occasion travelled in the first and not in the second car – fortunately for himself, as the second car had swerved and crashed into the ditch, and the driver staggered out of the wreckage made by the bombs. He had been the only occupant. Breen, Savage and Tom Keogh were protected only by the slight shelter of the cart behind which they crouched, their revolvers rattling as the road was swept with the terrific and accurate volleys opened upon them by the occupants of the third car – four soldiers with rifles and a machine-gunner.

Seamus Robinson has given a vivid snapshot of the scene: 'In the back of the car stood a soldier with his legs braced between the seats, his rifle held tight to his shoulder with the left hand, and his right hand working evenly, almost gracefully, on the bolt and trigger. This soldier was a sharpshooter. His first shot gave young Martin Savage his death wound; the second went through Breen's hat and the third hit Breen in the leg.' Breen, badly wounded, had to seek shelter in the 'Half-Way House'. Robinson took cover behind a milk cart on the main road. The rear car flashed away out of sight into Phoenix Park with a final burst of gun fire. The driver of the second car staggered towards the ambushers who had now come out on the main road, from Dublin to Blanchardstown. Beside the ditch lay the wrecked car, armour-plated like the other two now hurrying Lord French to safety. The third car had been an open one. The mass of splinters and steel beside the ditch was a closed one, and this misled the ambushers; curiously enough they thought that Lord French lay dead somewhere within, because surely no man could survive the fierce hail of grenades and revolver fire directed on it. It lay neglected on the road that curved away towards the park, the small narrow road in which they had fought. Martin Savage lay dead, killed outright by the bullet that had passed through his throat. Sadly his comrades looked down on him and abandoned the idea of carrying his body away. They looked at the trembling driver who came towards them with his hands up. He expected they would shoot him as they disarmed him, but to his relief and surprise someone said: 'We are soldiers too, and do not shoot unarmed prisoners.'

The ambush was over. At any moment reinforcements would arrive from the Phoenix Park. Martin Savage's body was carried into the inn. Dan Breen was already weak from his wounds, and his left leg was useless; he was helped onto his bicycle and Paddy Daly mounted his own. Daly supported Breen with one arm and eventually both reached Mrs Toomey's house in Phibsboro in safety. En route they met Frank Thornton and some others who helped them to finish the dangerous journey. Seán Treacy and Seamus Robinson remained behind until the others had gone. Treacy, like the majority of the ambushers, escaped without a scar. During the fight he was with the party on the crossroads, firing deliberately, unperturbed. Seamus Robinson mounted his bicycle, but had hardly started when one of the pedals struck a stone and snapped off. The bicycle was useless. Viewing the position most philosophically, Robinson threw it over a hedge and jumped on the step of Treacy's machine, holding on to Treacy's shoulders. Their progress was slow as the bumpy and uneven ground made Robinson press down on the rear mudguard. Just then a man came in sight wheeling a brand new bicycle. Treacy and Robinson knew that speed was a matter of life or death for them, and in this new bicycle they saw speed and safety. Very politely but very firmly they informed the astonished owner, an RIC pensioner, that they must have it, although they understood his indignation. They cycled away from him with the promise that the bicycle would be left for him at a certain place in the city at a certain time that evening.

The promise was later carried out. Treacy and Robinson sped to their friends, the Lynches at Dolphin's Barn. No one was more astonished than they when they read in the evening papers some very highly coloured accounts of the Ashtown ambush, and discovered that Lord French had, after all, escaped in that despised first car at which Seamus Robinson had thrown a disdainful bomb.

RAID ON THE KING'S INNS

DARING COUP IN BROAD DAYLIGHT
KEVIN BARRY'S PART

by DENIS HOLMES

ONE OF THE best-planned and most successful raids for arms carried out by the Irish Republican Army was that on the King's Inns, Dublin, on 1 June 1920. The daring nature of the coup, which was brought off in broad daylight, created a great sensation at the time, especially as the King's Inns was an outpost to the British military position at the North Dublin Union close by.

Our GHQ had learnt through the intelligence department that although the Inns were well guarded, military discipline was not so strict as it was in other outposts. It was possible for 'civilians' to get quite close to the entrance by the simple ruse of going into the green in front, and sitting down among the soldiers and their girlfriends, who were always to be found there at a certain hour on a fine day. This made it possible for us to get a good knowledge of the position from the outside, while the plans of the inside of the building were obtained, and studied by Dick McKee, our brigadier, and Peadar Clancy, our vice-brigadier.

The success of this attack depended chiefly upon careful organisation and discipline on our side, for it had to be carried out with the greatest speed possible, not more than seven minutes being allotted to us for the whole operation. Even after flawless preparation our attempt might have been marred by a rainy day, which would have kept the soldiers confined to the guardroom and building, and would have made it impossible for us to enter without a pitched battle. However, on 1 June the sun gave the decision in our favour, and a party of picked men from the 1st, 2nd and 3rd battalions, under the personal command of Peadar Clancy, left 46 Parnell Square at various intervals, and made their way to the scene of action.

The access to the King's Inns is by Henrietta Street, at the top of which is the gateway – the entrance to what is known as the Temple. It was here that the soldiers of the garrison would be found on a fine day on the green sward outside the Temple.

Each section of men had been instructed as to the special task they were to perform, for every act depended upon the success of the one that went before it and came after it. Had any of the men lost his head, or become confused in carrying out his orders, it would have been disastrous to the whole party. The action was opened by Joe Dolan, who had been instructed to approach the sentry, who was guarding the door to the building leading in from Henrietta Street, and distract his attention by enquiring the way to some office. When Dolan had engaged the sentry, the latter was surprised and disarmed, not a simple thing to do, for the soldier was a 'Distinguished Service' man, who had served at the front, and had a good British military record in the European war. The disarmed sentry was made a prisoner for the time being, and immediately a party under Section Commander Fitzpatrick came into action. These men had strolled into the green, where they were pretending to play cards, but working closer and closer to the soldiers who were there. When the sentry on guard had been disposed of, our men rushed the soldiers in the Temple Green, took them prisoners, to prevent their going to the assistance of the sentry, or raising an alarm, and marched them into the building. The girls, who had been with the soldiers, were placed under an armed guard outside for the same reason, and a man detailed for the work closed the gates, and stood by to prevent their being opened.

At that time I was a 2nd Lieut of 'C' company of the 1st battalion, and I was one of a party which followed close behind Dolan, holding up the occupants of the building, and disconnecting the telephones. Our party entered the front without any exciting incident, and meanwhile another section were making their way in through the back, to carry out the raid for arms on the guardroom at the left of the building.

One of this party was young Kevin Barry, who was a mere youngster compared to most of us, but who showed the courage and daring of a born soldier on this occasion. So far as I know, Barry had never been on an important operation before this raid, although he had taken part in many of the smaller actions, always with great credit to himself. I had drilled Kevin when, at an early age, he joined 'C' company of the 1st battalion in 1918, later transferring to 'H' company. All of us older Volunteers loved the boy, for he was gay and enthusiastic, and yet very serious in his devotion to the cause, and in his rigid attention to orders.

It was Kevin Barry who, in a moment of doubt, stepped forward and led the section into the building. Had it not been for his action in steadying one of the officers and leading the rush, the work of all the other men might have gone for nothing.

When the guardroom had been entered, the work of carrying away the arms and ammunition was done at top speed. I have a picture in my mind of Kevin Barry coming out of the guardroom with a Lewis gun hugged in his arms. His boyish face was wreathed in smiles, as he said to me: 'Look, Dinny, what I have got.' I could not help laughing even in the excitement of the moment, and, thinking that he looked like a child clasping a new toy to his breast.

While we were at work inside the building, a party in Henrietta Street, under Seán Prendergast, acting officer commanding 'C' company of the 1st battalion, was standing ready to protect the men on the raid. Section 8 Commander Paddy Kirk was in charge of another party, who formed a cordon across Henrietta Street, and who did not leave their position until all our men had got safely away.

Cars had been provided by GHQ for the transport of the munitions, which consisted of about twenty-five rifles, two Lewis guns, a large quantity of ammunition and other military equipment. The whole operation was carried out in less than the allotted time, being performed in five or six minutes, fortunately for ourselves as it appeared later. The transport parties were the last to leave, as part of their work was to prevent the alarm being raised and to cover our retreat, and about ten minutes after they got away the British military from the North Dublin Union closed in on the area, holding up all cars and searching all pedestrians. None of our men were captured, and the munitions were soon safe in IRA hands.

Part of the success of such a raid always depends upon the attackers being able to get clear away, which they were able to do on this occasion. We were always cautious about bringing any man with us who was physically remarkable in any way, as he would be easily identified afterwards by the enemy spies. One of our men, Seán Flood, who was very tall, had to be refused permission to accompany us to the King's Inns, a decision that grieved him very much. The raid on the King's Inns was of importance, not only on account of the munitions which we seized in that British stronghold, but because of the moral effect it had on our men, who had carried out this operation in daylight. On the other hand, it created a panic in British military circles, as the story of many successful ambushes shortly afterwards through the country, in which large parties of the enemy surrendered with hardly a fight, will show.

FIGHT AT FERNSIDE

by DESMOND RYAN

THE FLEMINGS' HOUSE in Drumcondra Road had been a centre for the Tipperary men 'on the run' ever since October 1919. Éamonn O'Brien and Jim Scanlon had hidden there after Knocklong. Dan Breen and Seán Treacy often made their way there. Michael Fleming had been connected with the republican movement ever since he had gone into Jacob's in 1916 and thence onwards into one of the fiercest fights of Easter Week with Richard Mulcahy and Thomas Ashe at Ashbourne. His friend, Rourke, had first put his elder brother, James, in touch with Éamonn O'Brien and Jim Scanlon in 1919. As the chase after Breen and Treacy grew hotter, they often stayed with the Flemings. Seán Hogan, Seamus Robinson and Dinny Lacey came there too. James Fleming knew that his house was being watched, and that it would some day or other become too dangerous as a hiding place. So, fearing that his house might be raided, and knowing that Breen and Treacy were coming, he went to his friend, Professor Carolan, of 'Fernside', Drumcondra, and told him the full facts, as well as he knew them, about their activities. Carolan at once declared that they were welcome to come to 'Fernside' at any time. So Breen and Treacy went there, accompanied by another member of the Fleming family, Peter. Professor Carolan gave them a key, showed them over the house and garden, with a special word on possible exits in case of surprise. He invited them to stay there any night they wished. They slept there several times.

Early in October 1920, Richard Mulcahy sent a very urgent warning to the Flemings after a raid on their house. It would be unsafe, he said, to shelter any wanted man, or have anyone who was active in the movement around the premises until suspicion had died down. This warning was phrased in the most emphatic terms, and Miss Fleming, who received it, took it very seriously. She had a suspicion that she was being shadowed by a man she noticed hanging around the neighbourhood; a 'man with a bow-tie', with a mean air and furtive look. But spy-mania was in the fashion, too much so, she thought, and she kept her suspicions to herself – until 11 October 1920. On that afternoon, Miss Fleming boarded a Drumcondra tram and went into the city to meet Mrs Éamonn O'Brien in O'Connell Street. Mrs O'Brien was in Dublin arranging with Michael Collins for papers and passports that would enable her to slip over to the United States and rejoin her husband, Éamonn O'Brien. Miss Fleming had just received the papers from Joe O'Reilly and the news that all arrangements had been made for this trip to America. Éamonn O'Brien's father had also come to Dublin and was staying with the Flemings; it was his second visit to the capital. On the tram behind her, Miss Fleming noticed the 'man with the bow-tie' again. But she forgot all about him when she met Mrs O'Brien at the Pillar.

Both ladies went into a picture house and had no sooner taken their seats when Dan Breen and Seán Treacy came casually in and took two vacant seats in front of them. Seán turned and recognised them. He and Breen had had a very mixed day. Breen had backed a lucky horse and drawn the winnings. Before that their fortunes had been bleak. Treacy told Miss Fleming that he and Dan were 'wall-falling' from hunger as they had tasted no food that day. They were in so exhausted a state that even when they had got funds they had not bothered to break their fast, but had slipped into the cinema to rest. Miss Fleming's one idea then was to take the two men to Drumcondra, give them a quick meal before curfew, and send them off to a safe place. She remembered Mulcahy's warning, but decided she could take the risk. Treacy and Breen accepted the invitation. As they were leaving some time later she noticed that the 'man with the bow-tie' was seated some distance behind her. She moved away from the group quietly, left by another exit and met the others outside. The man might be trailing her, but still she said nothing. She was afraid that both Treacy and Breen were too exhausted and, at any hint of danger that involved the Flemings, would make some excuse not to come. Treacy's phrase 'wall-falling' from hunger and his casual mention of a certain house from which they had set out very early that morning with no more substantial fare than a cup of milk had shocked her. Outside in the street she noticed the same man again, but still kept silent. She kept silent for a different reason now. She understood suddenly by Treacy's eyes and manner that both he and Breen knew that the spotters were again on the trail. (Breen afterwards in his account said that he recognised one of the Castle murder gang also on the watch.) Treacy restrained Breen with a look from drawing his gun and dealing with the spotters. Breen, too, checked an impulse to open fire, and fell behind the party; he knew that an exchange of shots would endanger the lives of Miss Fleming and Mrs O'Brien. The trackers disappeared. But only for a space.

Breen and Treacy took up positions at each end of the tram top to keep an eye for possible spotters. Once, before Drumcondra was reached, Breen and Treacy, with their guns ready, made a dash for the stairs – and a startled Castle tout jumped from the footboard and vanished down a dark side street. When the Flemings' house was reached, Éamonn O'Brien's father gave Treacy and Breen a great welcome, and they held a lively conversation in spite of Miss Fleming's open warnings of the dangers that dogged them. Treacy admitted that he knew quite well that they were shadowed when leaving the cinema. It was evident that Breen and he had other shadowers in mind besides the one suspected by Miss Fleming, but this gentleman was not to be long forgotten. Michael Fleming and Miss Dot Fleming next arrived and warned the party that 'the bow-tie' was outside the house again. The meal went on, and it was decided that Breen and Treacy should leave by the back exit which led into Botanic Avenue. Michael Fleming left by the front door in the hope of distracting attention, but he could discover then no signs of any watch on the house.

In the meantime, Treacy and Breen had made their way via the Tolka bridge to 'Fernside', some five minutes' walk away. The spotter had vanished, but it is believed that he still kept the house and its exits under observation, that he had tracked Treacy and Breen to Professor Carolan's door, returned, and rang up Dublin Castle from a neighbouring house. Otherwise, since Treacy and Breen had left the Flemings only just before the curfew hour, then at 11 p.m., it would be difficult to understand how the two men could be located, and Dublin Castle informed, at that late hour.

'Fernside,' Drumcondra, was a small two-storey house with a long garden at the back, opening at that time onto fields since built over, near Home Farm Road. Breen and Treacy arrived shortly after eleven, and entered quietly without disturbing any of the family, who were unaware of their presence. They made their way upstairs to the back bedroom on the first floor, which Professor Carolan had told them they could use at any time. The bedroom overlooked a small glass conservatory. A high wall separated the garden from the neighbouring houses, but the wall at the end of the garden was low.

Dublin Castle was astir. At last they had tracked down Breen and Treacy, whether or not they were certain of the exact identity of the men in 'Fernside' whom their spies had located; but Dublin Castle's armed forces were gathering to speed through the darkened streets, headed by Major Smyth. Professor Carolan was rudely awakened. He realised the danger to his guests and their presence in the house almost at the same moment ... the noise of lorries with their engines running after a swift halt at the gate outside ... an armoured car rumbling round the corner of Home Farm Road ... a hurried rush along the short path in front of 'Fernside' ... a raid breaking suddenly in the dark hours of the night. Even as the raiders hammered on the door, Professor Carolan rose quickly, tapped an abrupt warning on Breen and Treacy's door, and rushed downstairs. The glass panels of the front door went in with a crash; the angry voice of Major Smyth sounded in Professor Carolan's ears: 'The names of the men who are staying with you, quick who are they?' The commonest name in County Tipperary came to Professor Carolan's lips – it would leave the major no wiser than before and if he questioned the guests the name at least would match the accent: 'Do you mean the Ryans?'

The house was surrounded now, and through the windows of the small bedroom where Treacy and Breen were springing out of bed to dress hurriedly and secure their revolvers glared the powerful searchlight from the armoured car stationed in the rear. They slipped into socks, shirts and trousers. They had only time for a whispered farewell and a handshake, then gripped their guns. Treacy had his long parabellum ready, Dan Breen had a weapon in each hand – and none too soon … 'Where is Ryan? Where is Lacey?' The shouts of the raiders rang through the house … Two bullets crashed through the door of the little room. Treacy's parabellum and Dan Breen's German Mauser cracked in reply. Louder and louder rose the chorus inside and without in the garden: 'Where is Ryan? Where is Lacey?' The quick flashes from the raiders' guns lit up the garden beyond … Treacy and Breen replying … A death trap beyond a doubt … a ring around them … no escape. Already Breen was wounded and blood flowed from his right thumb … Cries of pain floated in through the half open door … the thud of falling bodies … Breen and Treacy feeling as if they were in some strange nightmare. Dan Breen dashed onto the landing … the group of raiders there scattered pell-mell and beat a hurried retreat to the floor below as he fired on them. Downstairs bullets were crashing through the glass door panels into the back room … the conservatory windows were riddled … the volleys were wild but had deadly intent, Breen returned to the bedroom … he thought Treacy's gun had jammed, and he shouted at him to stand back. But Seán had merely paused to re-load … he stepped back … just as he did so a bullet from without crashed through and buried itself in the wardrobe … Another … Treacy's parabellum volleyed into the dark … There was silence on the stairs and in the hall. This lull did not deceive them. They knew that the forces were regrouping for an overwhelming assault.

Breen was beside himself with rage and defiance, as he saw half-a-dozen soldiers creeping up the stairs. Point-blank he fired into them, and rushed forward with a fury from which all calculation or thought of safety had gone … in his excitement he did not feel his wounds, although several times the shots of the attackers had caught him. From the room behind came a peremptory summons from Treacy to return … Breen had emptied his gun with telling effect at the soldiers as they fled for safety down the stairs. He stumbled over two dead officers and a wounded Tommy as he made his way back into the room to Treacy … Major Smyth lay dead across the threshold … and his friend White … They had fallen in their first wild dash to get Breen and Treacy in their bed. Dan Breen staggered into the room, and he thought that his guns had jammed … He had forgotten to re-load … His wounds were telling on him …

Treacy's sixth sense – the old instinct that had saved the ambush party at Oola … at Rosegreen … in many a tight corner – had already told him the way out of this death trap. He pointed to the window and shoved Breen towards it, urging him at the same time to re-load. Breen swung down over the window-sill and crashed into the conservatory roof, cutting his knees and feet severely. Outside stretched the night … the friendly darkness … the long garden and the fields. In a trance from pain and shock … with blood flowing from five bullet wounds and numerous cuts, Breen groped his way towards the low wall at the end of the garden, stumbling over the dead bodies of two soldiers. He crossed the low wall and called out to Treacy in the darkness … there was no reply … Into his numbed brain came the thought that his comrade, Seán, was dead … no reply but the rifles … and the armoured car at which he blazed as he turned down Drumcondra Road … in desperation then – he knew not how – climbing the high wall of St Patrick's Training College … and so across the Tolka River towards a friendly lighted window and succour.

But what of Seán Treacy? He was not dead, as Breen had thought, nor had he yet quitted the house. When he pushed the half-conscious Breen towards the window, Seán dashed back onto the landing and emptied the parabellum over the stairhead at the soldiers who were stealing up once more. Then he returned to the room and followed

Breen through the open window. He lowered himself onto the broken conservatory roof and so to the ground, groping his way in the darkness towards the low garden wall … he, too, stumbled over the dead bodies of the two soldiers. Treacy called to Dan, but no answer came. He looked, but could not find him … the darkness had swallowed him up. Breen, he thought then, was dead somewhere in the garden or in the fields. Treacy crossed the low garden wall, and as soon as he recognised his surroundings, pressed on towards Finglas, dressed only in shirt, trousers and socks. There would be safety there at least in the house of Big Phil Ryan whom he knew and where he had stayed before … if he could find it in time. Treacy's hands and knees were bleeding from the broken glass of the conservatory. He staunched the blood with his handkerchief. He came to Phil Ryan's door at last and knocked. A woman's voice replied. Treacy answered that he 'was an Irishman who must get in'. Big Phil Ryan knew the voice and the door was opened. Seán Treacy was unusually silent. He told the company very little at first. His thoughts were with his old comrade, Dan Breen, dead in the Drumcondra fields … dead or wounded … probably dead. But Big Phil Ryan's questions drew him on and out of his mourning. They listened as he told them briefly of the fight at 'Fernside'. They acted promptly. It was settled that a messenger should be sent to the Flemings to tell them what had happened, and see what aid could be sent to Breen if he was still alive and free. Treacy's wounds were bandaged. He went into the room they got ready for him and sank into a deep sleep. It was now well into the early hours of Tuesday, 12 October 1920.

A presentiment of imminent trouble and danger for Treacy and Breen had kept Miss Fleming wide awake after they left the house. Just before 12.30, hearing heavy firing she rose and dressed. She knew that the firing was near enough to be at 'Fernside', and she had no doubt that 'Fernside' was being raided and that Breen and Treacy were fighting for their lives … And she knew, too, that the Flemings' house would very likely be raided before long. Her sister, Dot, woke and argued with her; shots were not unusual during curfew hours … but even as they argued, they heard the lorries rumble down the main road and stop. It was about one o'clock. There was the usual knocking, and the shouts for admittance, but this time there was an angry fevered note in the summons. From their badges and red hats and gold braid it was evident that some very high military officers had come out on this particular raiding party. James Fleming had hardly time to dress before the raiders were inside the door. He noticed that the hand of the officer who first spoke to him was shaking. 'I don't mind war,' cried the officer, 'but two of your men have shot two of our best officers in "Fernside".' The officer recovered himself and asked a question about Breen and Lacey. The question was reassuring: the raiders were uncertain of the identity of the men who had escaped, but it was equally certain that the Castle spotters had connected the Flemings and 'Fernside'.

The senior officer, after a sharp and very heated argument with James Fleming – who told him that he, James Fleming, could not answer questions until he was dressed decently – allowed him to finish dressing, and then asked for the key of the safe. Fleming gave it to him, but the result was disappointing. The search went on, and a most extraordinary search it proved. From the outset, the raiders seemed to be suffering from nervous shock, and were almost hysterical in their inconsequence and aimless violence. James Fleming felt a hand groping towards his pocket; he gripped the hand, jerked it downwards, and shot out his hip: an officer beside him cried out sharply. 'Do you see that,' protested Fleming to the officer in charge, 'why have you not ordered this man to search me before he tries to plant something in my pocket?' The would-be planter fell back, a silly dazed expression in his eyes. The senior officer snapped something at him and he left the room. The raiders were ransacking the house. A drunken or hysterical officer lurched against the wall, and half-a-dozen eggs broke in his pockets and oozed through the cloth. A third officer entered with a revolver and ordered James Fleming to sit down on a wicker chair. Soldiers stood with rifles at the ready at an open door. 'Sit down!' blustered the third officer with hell in his eyes. He backed to the door as James Fleming flamed up and refused with the invitation to shoot him standing, if they must shoot him. Fleming continued to defy him angrily. Miss Fleming rushed in and called for the officer in charge of the raid. He came down and assured her that her brother's life was in no danger. He sharply told the third officer to put up his gun and control himself.

Already Miss Fleming had learned much about the 'Fernside' raid. The raiders who dashed upstairs into the bedroom had been in the charge of an officer who assured them politely enough that they had nothing to fear. He sat down on one of the beds, almost weeping. Miss Fleming listened to his story and was sorry for him, he seemed so grief-stricken. Mrs O'Brien and Miss Dot Fleming refused to speak. But the sincerity of his words struck Miss Fleming at once; and even if they had not, what an extraordinary story he was telling! 'We have lost five of our best men,' he was saying, 'in the fight in "Fernside", including Major Smyth, my best friend. Smyth was the best intelligence man we had in Dublin.' The officer rambled on, telling and re-telling the story and asking odd questions, now and then, but not with any great malice, and not pressing them. He did not get any information from Miss Fleming, in spite of her sympathy for him, and her opinion that he was the best-behaved officer on the raid. He, too, was suffering from the shock of the encounter in the darkness with Breen and Treacy.

Like her brother James, Miss Fleming noted the thoroughness of the raid, the search for documents in vases, in and behind every article of furniture. She noticed the high rank of the officers – and, with the exception of the officer who mourned his friend, the evident thirst of the party: whiskey ran like water, provisions were scattered on the floor; the raiders rattled, angry, beside themselves. But before they departed, the full story of the 'Fernside' fight reached the Flemings under the very eyes and noses of the raiders, officers, sentinels and all. Miss Fleming saw a woman halted at the door by the guard. She looked up and said quickly: 'That's all right. That nurse looks in here from time to time when she wants brandy for a bad case.' Nurse Long came in.

Nurse Long, whom Miss Fleming knew only slightly – they differed in politics – was a messenger from Dan Breen, who was lying seriously wounded in a neighbouring house. Nurse Long passed the guard and managed to say to Miss Fleming, almost within earshot of them, quite calmly: 'Seán Treacy is dead in the fields behind Home Farm Gardens. Dan Breen is badly wounded in Holmes' in Botanic Avenue. He wants clothes, stimulants and help.' (The Holmes had admitted Breen after he had waded the Tolka and knocked at random on their door. Their political sympathies were unionist and pro-British, but they took him in and dressed his wounds.) Nurse Long made a second journey that morning to summon Joe Lawless, who made arrangements to remove Breen to safety, and inform Dick McKee. As Nurse Long was leaving with the aid which Breen had asked for, Mary Lawless arrived from Finglas, and was stopped by the guard. Miss Fleming spoke again, guided by a sure instinct that surprised her later: 'That's my aunt. Please let her through. She often comes in to see us.' Mary Lawless was the messenger from Seán Treacy. Dan Breen, she said, was dead or dying, somewhere near 'Fernside'. Seán Treacy was safe, though wounded.

Before the raiders left, the officer who had spoken to Miss Fleming first asked her if the women were remaining in the house that night. Her two brothers, James and Michael, were already under arrest, as well as Éamonn O'Brien's father. The officer advised Miss Fleming to close the shop, and take her sister and Mrs O'Brien away for the following night. His warning was vague and kindly, but he pressed it. She thanked him and the raiders went off at last, with wild looks and threats. Flemings' was a scene of utter confusion. The garden had been dug up. The inside of the shop was a wilderness of empty bottles, tumbled furniture and egg-strewn floors.

Gradually the full horror of the night at 'Fernside' came out. Professor Carolan was removed in a dying condition to a Dublin hospital. He sent for Miss K. Fleming and Miss Dot Fleming before he died and told the whole truth about the conduct of the raiders after the escape of Breen and Treacy. He said that he was ordered to stand with his face to the wall outside the room where Treacy and Breen had slept, and was then shot through the back of the neck. At first, a British military inquiry suggested that Carolan had been shot by Breen and Treacy's bullets. He made this statement not only in the presence of the Misses Fleming, but also to Mr Joseph Penrose, then on the staff of the *Freeman's Journal*. His account was published in the Dublin daily papers. No official denial was made, and the story that Treacy and Breen had been responsible dropped abruptly.

Bloodhounds had been employed by the raiders after the escape of Breen and Treacy. The waters of the Tolka had broken Breen's trail. But there are bloodhounds and bloodhounds. The second species, a human one, was still very active. Michael Fleming, after his arrest, was cross-examined in Dublin Castle. From the questions put to him, he guessed that the British authorities were still uncertain as to the identity of the men who had been in 'Fernside' the night of the raid. The intelligence officers in the Castle told Michael Fleming that it was quite useless for him to deny all knowledge of Seán Treacy, Dan Breen, Dinny Lacey or Seamus Robinson. He was treated with great politeness, and it was urged that he was very foolish to persist in his denials. He was offered wine and cigars, with all this good advice, but showed no enthusiasm for either. No threats were used, but the persuasion with a threat behind went on from day to day: if he would give information leading to the capture of Treacy, Breen, Robinson, Hogan or Lacey, any one or all of them, £10,000 would be paid into any bank in his name, a safe-conduct and passage to any part of His Majesty's dominions would be assured in addition; or, if he wished, the money could be collected by any friend or person he named.

When Michael Fleming refused, he was court-martialled and sentenced to three years' penal servitude; even on the eve of his court martial, and after sentence again, the offer was repeated; finally they despaired of changing him, and the sentence was reduced to nine months. James Fleming was taken to Mountjoy jail. There he was called into the governor's room, and interrogated under the Defence of the Realm Act about 'Breen and Lacey'. His interrogator was a Mr McLean, chief intelligence officer, afterwards shot on 'Bloody Sunday', November 1920. James Fleming was offered Egyptian cigarettes, much good advice, warnings about DORA, and many subtle questions. He refused the cigarettes, and for the rest, blandly fenced with the IO. Shortly afterwards he was released and went home to his business in

Drumcondra. He was a very lucky man that he found a home to go to, or that his house had not become even more famous than 'Fernside' in his absence.

On the evening of the raid a skull and cross-bones warning written on a telegram form had been thrust through the letter-box, and Miss Fleming again recalled the threats of the raiders as they departed: 'We are coming back!' – and the warning of the friendly officer, several times repeated. By the time the warning arrived, Joe Lawless was already in touch both with the Flemings and with Michael Collins, through Dick McKee. Collins had discovered through his sources of information that the Gormanstown Black and Tans had planned to descend on Flemings' and set fire to it and the whole block of buildings in which the premises stood. He told them to stand fast and sent an armed guard, fourteen strong, from the Squad. An elaborate ambush for the Black and Tans was arranged. Miss Fleming and her sister, Dot, waited with the party until near curfew. The hours wore on. As curfew drew near, Joe Lawless discovered through Dick McKee that the raid and the ambush were off, to the mixed relief and disappointment of the armed party.

Much earlier, Joe Lawless had removed Dan Breen to safety. Lawless always had a car ready at Collins' disposal, and acted as his driver. Miss Fleming sent Nurse Long to Lawless to warn him about Breen's plight. Lawless drove down to Holmes' in Botanic Avenue, where he found Breen lying on a mattress in the kitchen in great pain and semi-delirious. He communicated with Dick McKee, and returned with his car, accompanied by Maurice Brennan, Joe Vize and Tom Kelly – who had received word from Collins through McKee of the work in hand and the arrangements made to receive Breen in the Mater Hospital. They found Breen, semi-conscious, groaning from his severe wounds, and half-clothed, on the mattress; the gashes from the cuts made as he crashed into the glass roof of the 'Fernside' conservatory very evident. The brandy, which had been given him in default of an anaesthetic, had gone to his head, and as its first effects wore off he began to shout. By then, the car was well on its way towards the hospital, along Phibsboro Road. At Phibsboro Corner a policeman motioned to the car to slow down; it was to let a convoy of Auxiliaries pass through first. As they approached the Eccles Street entrance to the hospital, Dick McKee appeared and waved them ahead. He re-joined them when they stopped further down and warned them that police and military were already raiding the place. (The cause of this raid was the fatal accident to a Volunteer named Matt Furlong who had been rushed in from Dunboyne in a dying condition, following an explosion while he was testing a shell in a trench mortar.) The party drove away with Breen to wait until the raid was over. Breen's wounds were now aching painfully and he shouted aloud in agony.

A stop was made at a neighbouring public house, a bottle of brandy bought, and this violent anaesthetic again poured into him. The car cruised aimlessly around. As they crossed Dorset Street, they again met the Auxiliary convoy speeding past, and again escaped notice. Soon afterwards they met Mick McCormack who guided them to an old disused stable in Great Charles Street, which was then used as a dump by the 2nd battalion of the Dublin brigade. McCormack opened the door and the car drove right in. The door was closed, leaving the whole party in darkness. They waited there a long time. Every now and then Breen moaned with pain, and sometimes shouted aloud. Gradually he came to himself. Time dragged on in the dark stable. Vize, Lawless, Kelly and Brennan talked in low tones. Breen became more conscious. Suddenly there was a sharp knocking on the stable door. Seán Treacy was outside. He had cycled in from Finglas that morning to see Dan Breen once again. Mary Lawless told him of Dan's escape and the plans to remove him. Seán had traced him. He knew the old stable very well. Breen listened eagerly to Treacy's story and was overjoyed to find his old comrade alive and well. And while they waited, Treacy told them all his impressions of the events of that night in 'Fernside'. Outside the Mater Hospital small parties were on the watch. And after Pat McCrae – another member of the Squad – had told the waiting group in the dark stable that the road was clear, Breen was carried into the hospital on a stretcher. Seán Treacy helped to carry him in. He shook hands with him and went away. Dan Breen was never to see Seán Treacy again.

DEATH OF SEÁN TREACY

by DESMOND RYAN

THE 14 OCTOBER 1920 was a day of tragedies long remembered in Dublin. It was a day of intense police and military activity from noon onwards. The search for Dan Breen led to many raids on private houses, shops, the Mater Hospital, Beaumont Convalescent Home, which was connected with the Mater, Jervis Street Hospital, and also the Clarence Hotel. The raid on the Mater was the longest and most elaborate. The Black and Tan Auxiliary force from Beggar's Bush barracks and a strong force of military threw cordons round the building and its approaches, and for nearly three hours carried out a methodical search of every ward. It was the first raid on a large scale that this new force had carried out, although the Auxiliaries had already been on the streets. An armoured car was stationed on duty outside the Mater while other armoured cars patrolled the neighbourhood. Dan Breen saw Auxiliaries on guard as he looked down from the window of the nursing home attached to the hospital. The search did not extend to the nursing home, but it lasted long enough to rouse Breen's friends outside. The alarms spread through the city, and something like a general mobilisation of all available Volunteers began. The Beaumont Convalescent Home was also surrounded by Auxiliaries and soldiers, all patients were questioned, and the raid lasted over an hour. An ambulance arrived while this raid was proceeding, but left empty before the three lorries of Auxiliaries and soldiers drove off at 1.30. By this time, Michael Collins, Dick McKee and Peadar Clancy were sending out warnings and messengers in all directions.

From the last moment he had seen Dan Breen, Seán Treacy was pre-occupied with his comrade's dangerous situation. After he had parted with Dan, Treacy remained in the city and did not return to Finglas. That Wednesday night he spent in the company of Paddy Daly and other members of the Squad who met him in the Holland's house at Silverdale Terrace, Inchicore. Treacy slept that night at the Holland's. Bob Holland's mother was horrified at Treacy's condition. He was still suffering from the effects of the 'Fernside' fight. He was also footsore from his wanderings, and Mrs Holland insisted on bathing his feet and giving him a change of linen and fresh socks. Daly was anxious that Treacy should remain under the care of some members of the Squad. Treacy, however, was so tired that he remained in the house some time after breakfast and did not leave too early.

Shortly after leaving he met Daly, Joe Leonard and Tom Keogh at the Republican Outfitters. They were all armed and pressed him to come with them. He refused, saying that he had an appointment with Dick McKee and must wait around for him. The others left and Seán said goodbye to them. There was much activity going on, and Treacy went off to make several inquiries. When Daly and the others left him there it was still early. Later they regretted that they had not insisted on his coming with them as they were armed; and although Treacy was obviously shadowed, any attack on him would then have taken place under circumstances that would not have been so hopeless as the raid in which he was to be trapped.

Shortly after the rumours of the raids in the city for Breen had begun to circulate, Seán Treacy was calling in to see his friends, the Delaney's, at 71 Heytesbury Street. He stayed there for lunch and left shortly before two o'clock to go across to Peadar Clancy in the Republican Outfitters in Talbot Street. When Miss Delaney (who was engaged to Seamus Robinson) arrived just after Treacy left, she found her mother somewhat disturbed about Treacy. She believed that he was being shadowed, and she suspected that a man whom she had noticed hanging round the street while Seán was there was a spotter. This man had disappeared as Treacy left. Earlier that day Treacy had left a message with Mrs Maurice Collins in Parnell Street, to the effect that he wanted to see D.P. Walsh who he knew called in there regularly to collect dispatches left by Joe O'Reilly. Mrs Collins did not know Seán Treacy, but she gave Walsh the message when he came in almost immediately. Walsh had only met Treacy once before. When he returned to Mrs Collins, Treacy asked Walsh to get him a bicycle with low handlebars, and a waterproof coat.

At first Treacy suggested meeting him at the Republican Outfitters in Talbot Street to collect them, but changed his mind, and fixed Jim Kirwan's in Parnell Street as the place where the things were to be left. He also suggested a later meeting with Walsh in Phil Shanahan's at 4.30. Treacy seemed silent, abstracted and very obstinate. Walsh, who knew too well the danger Treacy was running in moving round so openly, urged him very strongly to lie low; the spotters were very active, and it was so soon after the 'Fernside' fight. Treacy hardly replied to Walsh's arguments. Walsh took the coat and bicycle to Kirwan's about 11.30, and enquired for Michael Collins who had just called in with Gearóid O'Sullivan and gone off at once. Walsh went away again, too, after leaving the new coat for Treacy on a hat rack upstairs. This small hat rack was at the top of a flight of stairs facing the street door to the left of Kirwan's public bar, onto which a door opened. From the flight of stairs there was a view of part of the street through the door fanlight.

When Jim Kirwan set up his business in Parnell Street in March 1920, all his staff were members of the Volunteers, and always had guns handy beneath the counters to repel a raid by force. Arms and ammunition were dumped and distributed from there. The house was a regular meeting place for the GHQ. Here Michael Collins often came to meet his intelligence officers and many others, in a snug or at the open counter.

Seán Treacy arrived in Kirwan's on 14 October some time after two o'clock and went straight upstairs through the door on the left of the public bar. For as long as he had known him, Kirwan knew that Treacy would never linger in the public bar. He was a strict nondrinker. Under his pillow every night that he slept at Kirwan's he placed a revolver – and the large crucifix found in his pocket after his death and a rosary beads. Kirwan met him on the first landing and pointed out the coat which Walsh had left on the rack for him. Treacy seemed preoccupied. He told Kirwan of his appointment with Walsh in Phil Shanahan's later, but Kirwan urged him not to expose himself in the streets so much, and to lie low for a while. He pointed out that there had been no raids on his own house. As he spoke he turned and saw through the small fanlight over the front door the tin helmets and rifles of British soldiers in lorries outside the door, moving slowly past. When Treacy heard this, he said, 'They have been after me all day!' Seán snatched the new coat from the rack and fitted it over the old one he was wearing. In his hurry he dropped a large silk handkerchief on the floor; it was still blood-stained from his wounds after 'Fernside'. He whipped out his parabellum, and turned towards the stairs. Jim Kirwan, to quote himself, 'like the amadán I was, went down the stairs in front of Treacy, a target for Seán and the expected raiders at once. But the spotters had not traced Seán to Kirwan's, and the soldiers passed on to raid a neighbouring house. With but a casual glance towards the raid in progress within a few hundred yards of Kirwan's, Seán Treacy vanished from the scene. He almost mounted his bicycle in the shop, moved swiftly out on to the pavement and away up Parnell Street, down Moore Street, into Henry Street, and towards the meeting with McKee and the others on which his mind and will were set. On his way he passed two friends, one of whom was anxious to delay him and discuss some important matter. Seán Treacy waved as he saw them and was gone.

The events in the Republican Outfitters immediately before his arrival some time around four o'clock are somewhat obscure. The small group within consisted of Dick McKee and Peadar Clancy, who had been on the move the whole day, Joe Vize and Leo Henderson. They were discussing the dangerous situation of Dan Breen, and the measures being taken to cope with it. Just before Treacy's arrival, Peadar Clancy left with a friend and went in the direction of the Pillar.

Frank Thornton and Tom Cullen had also left before Seán arrived. Somewhere in Talbot Street, Joe O'Reilly stopped them with an urgent message from Michael Collins to hurry to the Mater Hospital. Early that day O'Reilly had had orders from Collins to collect all the members of the Squad and all the Dublin officers he could find. Before he met Thornton and Cullen he called at the Republican Outfitters to find that they had left. As he cycled after them Joe O'Reilly noticed Seán Treacy on his way to the shop. The Republican Outfitters had been the meeting place of those who were determined that Dan Breen should not be taken. All day Peadar Clancy and Dick McKee had been active both at the Mater Hospital and in Talbot Street organising and directing the mobilisation of all the available Dublin men.

The experiences of Seán Brunswick, an active member of the Dublin brigade at the time, bring out very clearly the heated and almost reckless atmosphere that prevailed from the moment it was feared that the British forces were preparing to swoop on the hospital. Brunswick, more than most men, was to be an eye-witness of the events of that afternoon of 14 October in Talbot Street. He was one of the links between the Mater Hospital and the Republican Outfitters. He had been active most of the day bringing reports to Peadar Clancy in the Talbot Street headquarters. From two o'clock until nearly four o'clock, Brunswick noticed that the shop in Talbot Street was under observation. One man, whom he believed to be the intelligence officer known as Francis Christian, was walking up and down Talbot Street all that time. Sometimes pacing the pavement outside the Republican Outfitters, sometimes loitering outside the Masterpiece Cinema, sometimes outside Speidel's Pork Store. Brunswick noticed the loiterer's dress particularly – blue nap overcoat, velvet collar and cap. On the other side of the street another spotter in civilian clothes also sauntered and loitered. Brunswick was very uneasy, busy though he was with the work he had in hand, and several times warned Peadar Clancy, who was impressed by what he reported. In the shop during his frequent visits Brunswick noticed the Plunketts, Leo Henderson, Seán Kiernan (who worked under Peadar Clancy then as director of munitions), and other members of GHQ.

Brunswick was told to mobilise certain men, keep watch on the Mater Hospital, and report back at frequent intervals. When Brunswick started back on his last journey from the hospital, the meeting was ending in the Republican Outfitters. Only three members of the original party – Dick McKee, Leo Henderson and Joe Vize remained behind, conversing in a group near the door. Seán Treacy was standing at the counter midway up the shop, talking to the man in charge, Seán Forde. It was about four o'clock – or somewhat later, 4.15 according to Leo Henderson – when an armoured car, followed by two lorries full of armed soldiers and several plain clothes members of the Auxiliary division and intelligence officers, turned into Talbot Street from O'Connell Street and came at great speed from the Pillar towards Amiens Street. The noise of the approaching cars made the group in the doorway break up quickly. Dick McKee was nearest to the door. He looked out and then said: 'They are coming – Get out!' Seán Brunswick was now walking down Talbot Street. He saw Dick McKee come swiftly out. A moment later the armoured car and the two lorries stopped dead at the training college, Talbot House, and some of the soldiers, led by a couple of officers, rushed across the street towards the Globe Hotel and the Republican Outfitters.

In the confusion, Seán Treacy had taken the wrong bicycle, possibly one belonging to McKee who was a taller man than Seán. As Treacy tried to mount it beside the kerb he stumbled. The delay was fatal. He mounted a second time and had only gone a yard or so when two men in plain clothes rushed at him and knocked him off the machine. One of them, who had leaped from a lorry, seemed to know Treacy by sight. It was Francis Christian. He had gone off to join the raiders before Brunswick returned. He grappled with Treacy, now clear of the bicycle and with his parabellum ready. Treacy opened fire and drove off two other plain-clothes attackers who were rushing towards him, and fired twice at Christian who collapsed. In the struggle, they had moved up some yards towards the Masterpiece Cinema. Now two of his assailants fired at him at close range. As Seán turned to tackle one of them he was shot through the head at five yards' range and fell to the

ground – dead. One of his opponents, Price, was killed outright and
fell dead with Treacy. Before the fight ended Seán Treacy had left his
mark on at least three of the enemy, Christian, Price and another. But
he had done more than that. A sudden panic swept the military. From
the armoured car, one of the lorries, and the soldiers on the street,
came a tremendous burst of gun fire in the direction of the struggling
group, heedless of the safety of their own men or of the civilians on
the pavements. Seán Brunswick saw the scene – the street alive with
rifle and revolver volleys, and the more deadly rattle of the machine-
gun. He caught a glimpse of Treacy falling on the pavement outside
a shop which was then Speidel's … a glimpse, too, of the loiterer in
blue cap and blue nap coat – Christian, closing with Seán Treacy …
Christian falling … Shots… Stampede … and the struggle is shut
off from Brunswick's sight … He sees the panic-stricken pedestrians
stampeding and hears the rattle of the machine-gun and the volleys
which roll on for some minutes after Seán Treacy lies dead. Innocent
passers-by are killed: young Patrick Carroll, a messenger boy just
fifteen years old … the bullets catch him on his way up the street, and
he drops, dead; Joseph Corringham, who crashes from his bicycle to
the pavement, dying with three bullets in his stomach. A policeman on
duty is caught, too, as he seeks cover, and collapses with a bullet in his
right side and a broken right arm. The volleys are continuous for five
minutes and more.

Some in the crowd kept their heads and went to the assistance
of the struggling people, herding them into the shops and advising
them to seek shelter behind the counters, under desks, or to throw
themselves flat on the floors – anywhere and everywhere to dodge the
bullets that crashed through and speckled door after door, window
after window.

Seán Brunswick was caught in the struggling mass. He had one
determination: to get to Seán Treacy … to see if he lived … to save
the documents that he knew Treacy must have in his pockets. He
pressed forward and came nearer to the fallen men on the pavement
near the cinema. The firing ceased and the soldiers spread out along

the street, their rifles at the ready. Perhaps over it all the great spirit of Treacy lingered for a moment in a last farewell to the Dublin where he had suffered and fought, sending one last salute to the Tipperary scenes and folk, to his old comrades of Soloheadbeg, Knocklong, Drangan and Oola. For a moment or two a tension held the people and the soldiers still face to face … Anything might happen. Several men stepped forward and approached the officers in charge. They were trained ambulance men, and an officer told them to attend the wounded. One declared that he was a student who wished to give first-aid to the wounded. The officer let him pass. It was Seán Brunswick who hurried to Seán Treacy. Christian was dying … Another lay dead close to him … further off lay prone civilians. In the confusion Seán Brunswick bent down and saw that Treacy was beyond help. He quickly emptied Treacy's pockets, rose and slipped away in the excitement as the corporation ambulance came on the scene. The British officers told the ambulance men that the military would look after the bodies of the men killed in the fight. Christian and Treacy were lifted into separate lorries. The ambulance drove away.

TORTURE AND EXECUTION OF KEVIN BARRY

by JOHN McCANN, TD

THE CITY OF Dublin was up with the grey, murky dawn of All Saints Day, 1 November 1920. In fact, for hours before, people had been wending their way towards Mountjoy jail. People from the little streets and the big squares, women with shawls drawn closely about them; women well-clad and ill-clad. Men and boys well attired and some tattered, feeling the pinch of winter. The flickering sickly yellow gas-lamps of alley and avenue; the sizzling, great arc-lamps of the main thoroughfares served only to accentuate the gloom ushering in a day that was to be a tragic one indeed in Ireland's long years of sorrow.

A boy-soldier of Ireland, until recently unknown to the masses, but whose name was on everyone's lips that November morn, was to be executed by the British at eight o'clock. Already, outside the jail, thousands knelt in prayer for the last-minute reprieve or for the repose of the soul of Kevin Barry, medical student of University College, Dublin. All Ireland knew his story then. He had been captured on 20 September, when the company to which he was attached, 'H' of the 1st battalion, attacked a party of troops outside Monks' Bakery. Barry carried a Colt automatic. The gun jammed and he sought cover under a lorry to free the weapon. There he was surrounded and taken prisoner. In the engagement, the British lost one killed and two died of wounds. Two Volunteers were wounded. Kevin Barry was tried by court martial and condemned to death by hanging. He received his sentence with the courage and deportment befitting a soldier, having committed not a crime, but an act of war against his country's oppressors. Everywhere, the sentence was received with horror and few believed that the British would hang a youth of eighteen who had been captured in battle. Immediately that the sentence was made known, the Most Reverend Doctor Walsh, archbishop of Dublin and the lord mayor waited upon General Macready, who referred them to Dublin Castle. Scant courtesy they received there, but were sent further to the viceroy, Lord French, who assured them that their appeal would be forwarded to 'the proper authorities', the British government.

As it was plain that the British intended to go ahead with the despicable act, Dáil Éireann sent the following message to the 'Civilised Nations':

> The English government now proposes to set aside the high standard set by the Irish Volunteers and to execute prisoners of war, previously attempting to brand them before the world as criminals. Such an outrage upon the law and customs of nations cannot be allowed to pass in silence by civilisation. It may be in the power of England to hang an Irish boy of eighteen under such circumstances, but it is not in her power to prevent the conscience of mankind reprobating with horror such an action.

Hopes of a reprieve were entertained in many quarters. The Volunteers, however, decided to leave nothing to chance, and prepared an elaborate scheme for rescue. The original plan having been considered to be impracticable was abandoned, and the brigade went ahead with a new plan, to implement which the Volunteers had actually been posted at vantage points near the jail on the eve of the execution, when news from GHQ arrived that Barry had been reprieved. That was the rumour which circulated freely in the city on the night of 31 October, and that was the hope which was uppermost in the minds of all who kept vigil outside Mountjoy jail on the morning of All Saints. As time advanced slowly towards eight o'clock a great hush fell on the throng; for even then, the word for which they waited might come at any moment. But time passed mercilessly, and eventually a great clock struck the hour. With the first stroke came the sound of many voices in prayer; blessed candles were held high, a hymn to Mary Mother of Sorrows was heard in the harsh November morn … and a grand, clean soldier of Ireland went to meet his Almighty, fearless in the face of the miserable earthly tyrants who had offered him his life if he would inform on his comrades.

'Barry walked to the scaffold smiling,' came the word later in the day. 'Kevin died bravely.' His last message was: 'Tell my comrades to fight on for the ideal for which I am dying.' That message re-echoed throughout the land and thousands of young Irishmen, some even younger than Barry, joined the Irish Republican Army. His persecutors had hanged him 'as an example' to others. If they had troubled to read Irish history they would have known the consistent reaction to such example.

Bravely, indeed, had Kevin died. But braver still had been his last hours in which they tortured him to renounce his ideal and inform on his comrades. This was his solemn declaration, four days before his death:

I, Kevin Barry, of 58 South Circular Road, in the County of the City of Dublin, aged 18 years and upwards, solemnly and sincerely declare as follows:

On the 20th day of September, 1920, I was arrested in Upper Church Street, in the City of Dublin, by a sergeant of the 2nd Duke of Wellington's Regiment, and was brought under escort to the North Dublin Union, now occupied by the military. I was brought into the guardroom and searched. I was then removed to the defaulters' room by an escort with a sergeant-major. The latter and the escort belong to the 1st Lancashire Fusiliers. I was then handcuffed.

(2) About a quarter of an hour after I was placed in the defaulters' room two commissioned officers came in. They both belonged to the 1st Lancashire Fusiliers. They were accompanied by three sergeants of the same unit. A military policeman who had been in the room since I entered it remained. One of the officers asked my name which I gave. He then asked for the names of my companions in the raid or attack. I refused to give them. He tried to persuade me to give the names, and I persisted in refusing. He then sent the sergeant out of the room for a bayonet. When it was brought in the sergeant was ordered by the same officer to point the bayonet at my stomach. The same questions as to the names and addresses of my companions were repeated, with the

same result. The sergeant was then ordered to turn my face to the wall and point the bayonet to my back. I was so turned. The sergeant then said that he would run the bayonet into me if I did not tell. The bayonet was then removed and I was turned round again.

(3) The same officer then said to me that if I persisted in my attitude he would turn me out to the men in the barrack square, and he supposed I knew what that meant with the men in their present temper. I said nothing. He ordered the sergeants to put me face down on the floor and twist my arm. I was pushed down on the floor after my handcuffs were removed by the sergeant who went for the bayonet. When I lay on the floor, one of the sergeants knelt on my back, the other two placed one foot each on my back and left shoulder, and the man who knelt on me twisted my right arm, holding it by the wrist with one hand, while he held my hair with the other to pull back my head. The arm was twisted from the elbow joint. This continued, to the best of my judgement, for five minutes. It was very painful. The first officer was standing near my feet, and the officer who accompanied him was still present.

(4) During the twisting of my arm, the first officer continued to question me as to the names and addresses of my companions, and also asked me the name of my company commander and any other officer I knew.

(5) As I still persisted in refusing to answer these questions I was allowed to get up and I was again handcuffed. A civilian came in and repeated the questions, with the same result. He informed me that if I gave all the information I knew I could get off. I was then left in the company of the military policeman; the two officers, the three sergeants and the civilian leaving together.

(6) I could certainly identify the officer who directed the proceedings and put the questions, I am not sure of the others, except the sergeant with the bayonet. My arm was medically treated by an officer of the Royal Army Medical Corps, attached to the North Dublin Union, the following morning, and by the prison hospital orderly afterwards for four or five days.

(7) I was visited by the court martial officer last night and he read for me a confirmation of sentence of death by hanging, to be executed on Monday next, and I make this solemn declaration conscientiously believing same to be true and by virtue of the Statutory Declarations Act, 2835.

Kevin Gerard Barry.

Declared and subscribed before me at Mountjoy Prison, in the County of the City of Dublin, this 28th day of October, 1920.
(Signed) Myles Keogh,
A Justice of the Peace for the said County.

Kevin's mother visited him in his cell, to take a last farewell. Not even then did his courage fail, nor had he any regrets. Neither had that great, patriotic soul, as she bade her son goodbye. She had taught him to love Ireland, and then in her greatest time of trial she comforted him during his last hours. Broken-hearted, yet staunch to the end, through tear-filled eyes her last glimpse of Kevin as she left his cell showed him standing there, proudly erect, his hand raised in military salute.

And Barry was but the first of many who died on the scaffold for Ireland during the months which followed.

BLOODY SUNDAY

by ERNIE O'MALLEY

THE BRITISH INTELLIGENCE system in Ireland at the beginning of 1920 was divided into a number of practically self-contained compartments. There seemed to be no proper co-ordination nor any one controlling staff for the whole country. The RIC functioned as an espionage corps, which for years had methodically watched and as methodically reported on every rebel or potential rebel in their district. They noted the movements of any stranger who entered the territory controlled by their barracks. In Dublin the 'G' Division of the DMP was a specially trained branch who knew the city area thoroughly, its volunteer officers and important separatists, and, guided by RIC information, its officers followed all outstanding men who came up from the country. Each British regular army command had its own intelligence officers, guided both by RIC and DMP information, but they had little or no intimate personal knowledge of wanted men or of country districts. The British secret service, another force, worked in devious ways, made its own contacts, but used the general pile of information available at Dublin Castle.

By the late summer of 1920 the British intelligence service had become much less efficient, a good number of men in city and country were on the run, columns of fighting men moved around their own brigade areas, and as local spies had been executed, new officers unknown to the British had been elected to office. As well, the RIC had been driven in from many of their outlying posts. Their barracks had been attacked, their patrols ambushed, and individual police who had wounded or killed Volunteers and civilians, or those who had been specially active, had been shot down. The RIC were still of use to identify captured men, or to lead the military on raids, but their morale was being slowly shattered and they were forwarding less and less information to Dublin Castle. RIC men by this time were passing on both information and codes regularly, both to GHQ of the IRA and to local brigades.

In Dublin members of the 'G' Division had been killed, others were unwilling to report information, and a number of their men had established a special counter-intelligence system which tapped all available British secret information. The RIC and the 'G' Division were now scouts who had to operate in hostile territory. Local spies had been shot off, so that the once vaunted British boast that any Irish movement could be watched and destroyed by its own members was no longer accurate.

In England new recruits were raised to fill the gaps in the RIC which had been brought about by numerous resignations. The new recruits had no knowledge of police duties and no local knowledge, but as all had served in the First World War, they were a stiffening force, useful as terrorists and for shooting up undefended towns and villages. Another force, the Auxiliaries, recruited from ex-British army or naval officers, were also added to the RIC but they largely acted as independent companies. They were a formidable, well-trained, and a ruthless force, who were organising their own intelligence service.

The British military intelligence was never a serious problem. Their adamant psychology warped their judgment and side-tracked even their own information. Capture of documents in raids helped to add new names to their files and often gave them intimate and important information, but in a city like Dublin, IRA headquarters officers could slip through a foot patrol or bluff their way out of a sudden street hold-up.

The capital had now two governments and two rival army GHQs. The offices of Dáil Éireann were scattered throughout the city as were the offices of members of the GHQ staff and of the Dublin brigade.

The British, impelled by lack of information, decided to strengthen their secret service in Dublin and through this body locate the various civil and military offices of the Irish Republic. If they could capture, or kill, their enemy key men, then the movement would lose, they felt, both direction and impetus. Each secret service man worked through a group of contact men known as 'touts', or of minor spies, who could move around freely enough, whilst the officers themselves had to move carefully. Some of them came out only after curfew when their real activities began, for then the city was completely controlled by British armed forces.

In opposition to the variations of British intelligence was the IRA intelligence system under Michael Collins as director. Each brigade had its own intelligence officers who could make use of copious local information. At IRA intelligence headquarters there was no inter-lapping and no red tape. Information passed to and fro from the outside areas to Dublin and from Dublin throughout Ireland, but the effectiveness of the system was naturally dependent on its thorough organisation in any given brigade area. Indeed, every member of the IRA was an unofficial intelligence agent.

Liam Tobin was deputy director of intelligence and with him worked Tom Cullen and Frank Thornton. Under them was the Squad, which, as it consisted of twelve men, was known as the 'Twelve Apostles'. Tobin had his office in Crowe Street, about two hundred yards from one of the gates of Dublin Castle. Here enemy information and our own was catalogued and cross-indexed. Newspapers were gleaned for information, photographs of individuals were identified, and miscellaneous reports from hotel waiters, boat stewards, post office sorters and telegraphists, were fitted into this queer intelligence jigsaw puzzle. The 'Twelve Apostles' trailed touts and hostile agents, waited for an opportunity to shoot high-ranking officers and members of the Castle murder gangs or they watched for 'G' men. Tobin and Cullen had the hazardous work of interviewing agents who were anxious to meet Collins, supposedly to give him information or to work for him. Soon a number of these men had betrayed themselves, or 'G' men had passed on information about their real intentions, and as a result they had been shot on Dublin streets or in the country.

The basis of resistance to English power in the capital was the Dublin brigade, which had slowly developed under the command of Dick McKee and of his vice-commandant, Peadar Clancy, both of whom were also attached to GHQ; McKee as director of training, Clancy as director of munitions. The four Dublin city battalions had a very intimate knowledge of the metropolis, its lanes, by-lanes, alleys and back yards, its enemy barracks and the habits of its opponents. The men who worked on Michael Collins' intelligence staff had also come from the brigade, which in addition, had its own well-organised intelligence service. The government of the Republic could not have functioned in any one capacity save for the protection of and the security given to it by the city brigade.

The combined services of GHQ and brigade intelligence were directed towards locating the new enemy agents and 'touts'. A special group of about thirty friendly DMP men watched and noted British movements during curfew which began at ten o'clock and ended at five in the morning. Houses which showed activity at night meant enemy houses. Scraps of waste paper extracted from paper-baskets by maids were pieced together by Tobin and his men, 'touts' were followed and checked on, special agents known through photographs or by sight, were discreetly watched.

Some of these agents had already shot some men in Dublin. As well TDs had been sent death notices, and it was now a question of time only until a well-organised series of British raids would act against the Dáil, GHQ and brigade offices, with a gang in the background to shoot dangerous men. It was decided by IRA GHQ, that the important secret agents would be shot at a definite hour one morning. When information from miscellaneous sources was thoroughly tabulated, it was passed on to the cabinet, who, as was their custom, viewed the evidence before sanction would be given for an execution. Dick McKee and Frank Thornton attended a cabinet meeting in Upper Dominick Street where each name on the list was slowly checked. Cathal Brugha, minister for defence, had worked through the files of information but he was not satisfied with some of the evidence. Cathal Brugha was very conscientious and adamant in his judgment. If to his mind there was the slightest loophole for uncertainty about an agent or spy, then that individual could not be dealt with. About fifteen names were rejected at that interview. The Dublin brigadier was to use his men from each battalion whilst the intelligence squad was to help both in identification and in action. In addition, patrols in the neighbourhood of each lodgings flat or hotel, were to act as a protective force.

A week before the date fixed, Tobin and Cullen, who were sleeping in Vaughan's Hotel, were awakened by a gang of men at night. Some of the men they knew, amongst them Bennet and Aimes, who were on their list. Both Tobin and Cullen were able to persuade the raiding officers of their assumed identity after a long interrogation. In the end Cullen was talking freely about racehorses to some of them and giving them 'certain' winners, but the raiders were hard to convince and reluctant to leave. Some nights later on the raiders returned asking for Tobin and Cullen by name, having made sure of their identity in the meantime. There would have been only one end to the two men if there had been any doubt in the minds of their visitors.

The date for the operation had been fixed for Sunday 21 November at nine in the morning. McKee met Collins and some GHQ officers in Vaughan's on Saturday night. The hotel was raided shortly after McKee had left it. Collins had a more narrow escape, and a young man from Clare, Conor Clune, was taken prisoner. McKee and Clancy saw a number of men who were to take part on the job the following morning. They listened to detailed information about houses to be visited, the situations of rooms, descriptions of agents and routes of approach and of retreat. That night there was tension in Dublin where men of the brigade were screwing themselves up to shoot officers who were armed and who had all been trained in war.

Before the brigadier and Peadar Clancy left their headquarters, which was in the Typographical Society in Gardiner Street, word came that two of the officers had changed their lodgings and fresh instructions had to be issued half-an-hour before curfew. The two brigade officers had been delayed and at curfew they went directly to Fitzpatrick's in Gloucester Street. In this neighbourhood a sergeant-major of the military police had been suspect by some men in the second battalion. A company quartermaster, Brennan, had asked permission to have him shot, but Tom Ennis refused as the evidence of his activities was not sufficient. A number of Volunteers had been arrested nearby and it was thought that the raids were linked up with this policeman who was a brother of the famous Becky Cooper.

During the night there was a loud crash at Fitzpatrick's door. It was said later that a white cross had been marked on the door soon after curfew as a sign for raiders to act on. McKee had time to burn all his papers, including a list of the officers to be dealt with, before the raiders smashed in the outer door. Fitzgerald, McKee and Clancy arrived at Dublin Castle guardroom at three o'clock on Sunday morning. There were a number of prisoners sleeping on army blankets, amongst them Ben Doyle who had been doing some intelligence work for Collins. Doyle knew Clancy, who had rehearsed many times with him and others details of a proposed attack on the guardroom at the King's Inns. Clancy put his fingers to his lips and the gesture was interpreted to mean that he was not to be recognised or that he was using a strange name.

That morning squads from each of the four battalions were on the Dublin streets, waiting tensely for the agreed-on hour. The largest number of the British officers, who always wore civilian clothes, was around the region of Baggot, Mount and Leeson Streets. In this neighbourhood men from the Squad were with each group. The Squad had been accustomed to attack their wanted men on the Dublin streets, but the other Dublin men were more nervous, for this type of work, some of them regarded it as a dirty job which had to be done to safeguard their important officers and cabinet ministers. Each small section of men knew of the position of their next groups and their ways back so as to avoid any streets which had already been raided and in which they might meet enemy troops.

Second battalion men with Tom Ennis, the best officer in Dublin, had come across the Liffey by ferry boat into battalion areas not their own. These men ran an added risk for in case of trouble they would not be so intimate with the back-lanes of the foreign areas.

In Mount Street there were two officers: Mahon (then under the assumed name of Angliss), who was said to have been specially recalled from Russia to help to organise a section of South Dublin for his fellow agents, and 'Peel', who had been warned by Mahon to be extra careful as he knew they were being shadowed. Seán Hyde, attached to intelligence, had been observing Mahon's movements. He had got to know Mahon and as both were interested in horses they often exchanged information about 'good things'. Recently men had tried to shoot Mahon in a billiard room, but while they were holding up the billiard players the agent was upstairs drinking tea with the proprietor. Mahon was shot that morning, but 'Peel' had his door locked. He piled furniture against the door, but though the raiders fired through it, he was not injured.

About this time a tender of Auxiliaries in plain clothes left Beggar's Bush barracks to travel by train. Engine drivers at the time were refusing to carry men in uniform or armed men, and the Auxies were trying to avoid the train hold-up. As they drove down Lower Mount Street they heard a maid in No. 22 shouting for help for men were trying to burst into Peel's room at the time. The Auxiliaries tried to rush the front door but it was closed by a man inside as they had it half open. The other men decided to go out both by the front and the rear. Tom Keogh headed the front door party, using either hand quickly to shoot his way through to the street. Then his small party fought a rearguard action with the more numerous Auxiliaries, whilst Keogh by the accurate use of his Peter the Painter kept the ex-officers at a respectful distance. One of the Volunteers, badly wounded in the arm, was able to walk with his comrades.

Two Auxiliaries were sent to Beggar's Bush for reinforcements, but they were killed by outposts before they had gone any distance. Reinforcements, however, who had heard the shooting, came from the

Bush under General Crozier, and he was in time to stop a cadet who had given Teeling ten seconds to tell the names of the raiding party and was counting slowly before he fired. Teeling, who was in the lane at the back of Mount Street had been badly wounded. He was the only one arrested that day against whom there was direct evidence, but he escaped later with Simon Donnelly and Ernie O'Malley from Kilmainham jail.

The 2nd battalion men, who had done most of the shooting that morning, reached the Liffey ferry-boat which was waiting for them, and so avoiding bridges reached their battalion area. The 1st battalion had had no success. They had raided a house on the North Circular Road where the lieut-colonel in charge of British military intelligence lived, but he was absent that morning. A group from the 4th battalion were called off as they were ready to visit the Standard Hotel, as officers on their list had been moved to another lodging where they were found. In all, thirteen officers were killed, four wounded and two Auxiliaries were killed. Amongst the dead was an officer from the Royal Army Medical Corps in the Gresham Hotel who had been shot by mistake.

As reports came into Dublin Castle that morning, consternation turned to something close on panic as the list mounted up. Confusion was increased by the long processions of touts, spies, agents and their wives who came towards the Castle in hacks, motor cars and military lorries. The anonymity of quiet Dublin lodgings was no longer a secure shelter for men engaged in the attempt to destroy civil and military officials and the capture of Dáil Éireann offices. The Castle gates were difficult to enter that morning as fear and uncertainty had quadrupled the ordinary carefulness of its guards.

Repercussions of this excitement were echoed in the anger of Auxiliaries and intelligence officers who began again to question the prisoners from the guardroom. Prisoners were brought out one by one repeatedly. Threats and blows increased with each visit to the feared interviews in the intelligence room.

Outside, Michael Collins waited impatiently for a complete report from McKee and Clancy. When he was told that they had been taken prisoners early that morning he became suddenly quiet, for now he was thinking of their fate. McKee had always worked coolly, methodically and carefully. He had built up a fine intelligence system within the brigade and he had trained his officers carefully. On him GHQ could always depend for its special instructions being faithfully carried out. Without his co-operation and that of his vice-commandant, and their unit, the large enemy force held in the capital would have been released to reinforce British strength in other of our hardly pressed areas in Ireland. Peadar Clancy would be an equal loss. His energy, driving force, his thorough planning, backed by a gay humour, could not be replaced. When the men of the brigade learned of their arrests they felt the morning's operation had been a failure.

It was thought that the two officers were in the Bridewell. A party was quickly mobilised to attack the building, but later information proved that they were in Dublin Castle. The inside confusion there made it difficult for accurate reports to be passed out, nor could friendly 'G' men get to the prisoners to give them arms, as was suggested. MacNamara was able to drink with some cadets and officers in the canteen next to the guardroom. Excited and fairly drunk Auxiliaries were threatening vengeance as they hastily swallowed their drinks.

The twenty-six prisoners in the guardroom were lined up at two o'clock on Sunday for removal to another barracks. Two officers, with lists in their hands came down along the file; one of the officers limped. He was Captain Hardy, who had vicious fingers and an itching trigger sense. McKee, Fitzgerald and Clune were picked out. They were ordered to sit near the guardroom fire. A few minutes later the same two officers came back to the guardroom. Each prisoner was again asked his name. This time Clancy was picked out, but Fitzgerald was put back into the file.

McKee and Clancy must have passed through an agony of suspense ever since their arrest. They knew what would happen at nine that morning and they knew what would happen to themselves later. They must have been trying to strengthen themselves against their imaginative fears, for they knew too much information which the enemy badly needed; the addresses of GHQ officers, names of personnel, and of all the badly wanted men in their own brigade! The rising excitement of their captors was easy for them to understand, and when the three were left by themselves their tautness of will and courage must have been at snapping point. They knew why the other prisoners, who might have been able to piece together the subsequent story, had been taken away. The Castle murder gang prowled around the guardroom. Colonel Winters, known as the 'Holy Terror', began the new interrogation with the added menace of Captain Hardy, both of whom the two other officers knew by reputation and through photographs. Clune must have wondered why he had been picked on, but the only reason for his inclusion would seem to be his presence in Vaughan's on the previous night. Perhaps his captors persuaded themselves that he had come up from the country to carry out killings in Dublin. Shots were fired as questions became urgent, then bayonets were used on McKee. Finally the three prisoners were killed in the narrow courtyard leading from 'F' Company's quarters to the military guardroom.

In the meantime crowds were on their way to see a football match between Dublin and Tipperary at Croke Park. The grounds were patrolled by twenty-five men from the 2nd battalion who acted as stewards. Outside the gates Andy Doyle and Harry Colley met Seán Russell, who had come hurriedly to Jones' Road to get the match called off for he had news that British forces were on their way to open fire on the spectators. Word, it seems, had come from a police sergeant in the Castle that a meeting of officers there decided to carry out an immediate reprisal. Some wanted to burn O'Connell Street, others to attack the crowd at the football match. The issue had been decided by tossing a coin. Russell had great difficulty with GAA officials, who were either unwilling or unable to call off the match, but Russell ordered Andy Doyle to dismiss the stewards.

Already the crowd knew of the morning's shootings from successive stop-presses. As they watched the match an aeroplane circled the field and then fired a Verey light pistol. That must have been the expected signal, for machine-guns and rifles opened up from dominating ground.

RIC from the depot with fixed bayonets charged up the outside road, Auxiliaries and British regulars all joined in. The startled crowd inside rushed to the gates like frightened cattle whilst bullets swept up and down the playing field. Men and boys were trampled on by herds of stampeding human beings. The wounded lay on the ground whilst RIC and Auxiliaries kept back anyone who tried to attempt to staunch the blood. One by one the crowd were moved towards the gates with the help of rifle butts where they were patted by regulars for arms as they passed out. At times, British soldiers directed some of the emerging crowd away from streets which were held by Auxiliaries and RIC who were having a good time at the expense of the long lines who passed through them.

All prisoners inside had to keep their arms outstretched over their heads, but when they became tired of holding their hands up they were forced to put them up again. A small elderly priest walked out from a group of prisoners towards the Auxiliaries. A cadet, with an oath, shoved the old priest back into the crowd where he fell. A tall priest walked over to the Auxiliary, hit him a smashing blow on the face and then a surge of khaki and bottle-blue Auxiliaries battered the gallant maker of objections.

The result of the Croke Park attack was fourteen killed and sixty wounded.

The bodies of McKee, Clancy and Clune were brought to a small chapel in the pro-cathedral. At night Collins and some of the intelligence squad brought doctors who examined the bodies so that the minds of their comrades could be satisfied for they had not been tortured, as their imaginations had led them to think. The dead were then dressed in uniforms of the Irish Volunteers. Next morning Collins and Cullen, Thornton and Gearóid O'Sullivan, the adjutant-general, in spite of waiting intelligence agents, carried the bodies out to the waiting hearses.

A photographer had taken a quick photograph which appeared in the *Evening Herald*. It showed Collins and Tom Cullen at the head of the coffin. The intelligence squad and others quickly bought up all copies of the paper from newsboys, then they smashed the metal die in the newspaper office, a half-an-hour before a British intelligence group came to the office.

There was an immediate migration of agents and touts to England, but not all of them left, for next morning Seán Hyde's digs was raided, and on the raid was 'Peel', an Irishman. Hyde had time to lather his face and so was not identified. The British cabinet must have thought that the optimistic reports they had been receiving from Dublin Castle about their success in defeating the IRA were not so reliable as their plausible words suggested, for a little over a week later negotiations to consult leaders in Ireland began.

ESCAPE FROM KILMAINHAM JAIL

by SIMON DONNELLY

On Thursday, 10 February 1921, I was arrested in Dame Street and brought to Dublin Castle to be interrogated by British intelligence officers, where, after the preliminary interrogation, I was taken to the guardroom of the Castle. I was detained there until Friday 11 February, when I was summoned before the notorious Captain Hardy.

The captain was famous throughout Ireland at that time for his bullying and his brutal methods of attempting to extract information, and he tried his usual system on me, warning me that I was accused of being implicated in the shooting of British intelligence officers on Bloody Sunday, and giving me a pretty fair idea of what any of us were to expect if evidence could be found connecting us with the affair.

From the Castle I was sent to Kilmainham jail under a heavy escort. I was not long there, before I recognised a number of my old comrades, who were there awaiting trial on various charges. There was one among them I was sure I knew, yet I could not place him at first. His appearance was changed, for he had grown a heavy moustache, but I soon learned that 'Mr Stewart' was none other than Ernie O'Malley, without doubt one of the bravest soldiers who ever fought for Irish independence.

We had to be careful of our fellow prisoners, because it was quite usual for the British to place spies among us, who were supposed to be 'prisoners', in the hope that we would betray ourselves to them while we were off our guard.

When my comrades were sure that I was the man I represented myself to be they took me into their confidence, and told me that they were working on plans for escape. Among the prisoners who were in Kilmainham at that time were Captain Paddy Moran, Volunteer Thomas Whelan, NCO Frank Flood, Volunteers Thomas Bryan, Pat Doyle and Bernard Ryan, who were afterwards executed on 14 March 1921; Frank Teeling, wounded and captured on Bloody Sunday; and Ernie O'Malley.

There were so many of us there charged with 'murder' – for England did not recognise us as prisoners of war, although a state of war had been declared – that we used to talk about our part of the prison as 'Murderers' Gallery'. The soldiers of the republican army never shirked a sacrifice, in order to come to the help of their comrades who were in danger, and we had full confidence that the people outside would do everything in their power to rescue us from the enemy.

We knew the position outside, for we had established good communications with the help of two friendly soldiers. There were terrible difficulties and dangers to be overcome, for with the curfew order in force it meant almost certain death for anyone found loitering near the prison after nightfall, and, of course, the rescue could not be effected in the day-time. Then, Kilmainham was no easy place to penetrate, with its high walls, barbed wire entanglements, machine-guns mounted at every strategic position, and heavy guard of soldiers. At first the IRA had almost despaired of releasing us, but the news from inside the prison that we had found two friendly soldiers who were willing to help, brought the first ray of hope. The first plan, quickly abandoned as impracticable, was that a drug should be smuggled into us, and that we should administer it to the soldiers in their tea.

It was a shipyard worker who suggested the plan – and furnished the implement – which was successfully used to set us free. This man had used a bolt-cutter in the course of his work, and assured the O/C of the Dublin brigade that it would be just as simple to cut a prison bolt as any mere 'civilian' bolt. A bolt-cutter is an instrument as long as a pair of garden shears, and two difficulties arose before the instrument could be introduced into Kilmainham. First, a bolt-cutter had to be procured, and this could only be done by breaking into the Dublin dockyards, not a very easy thing to do with the curfew in full swing, and the military and Tans combing the streets for 'rebels'.

This operation successfully carried out, the next question was, 'How can such a big, unwieldy instrument be smuggled into the prison?' The soldier who had promised to do it had himself to run the gauntlet of the sentries, and in order to make it possible for him to carry in the instrument, the handles had to be sawn away. Without the handles the cutter would not have the necessary leverage, so two handles of tubular steel had to be procured, which would fit exactly on to replace those which had been taken off.

Now there was a right and a wrong way of fitting on those new handles, and when they were put on the wrong way the instrument was not workable, so the soldier had to be given many demonstrations as to the right way of adjusting the handles. At last he assured the O/C that he had caught the idea, and the bolt-cutter, handles and a number of revolvers were brought by the soldier into the prison from time to time for our use.

An alternative plan had been made in case the bolt-cutters should fail, and this was that a rescue party should take up their position close to the prison with a rope ladder and, awaiting an agreed upon signal, throw in the rope attached so that we could haul the ladder to our side of the wall.

As we were not sure of the bolt-cutter working, we were not counting upon more than one or two making their escape. Our principal concern was to save the life of Frank Teeling, as he had already been sentenced to death, the fate of the rest of us being so far uncertain.

Outside, 'F' company of the 4th battalion of the Dublin brigade, who had been detailed for the work, had to leave their homes every night while awaiting the signal, get outside the city boundary, in order to avoid patrols and make their way stealthily back along the railway lines to be ready at the jail gate when needed.

Inside, we had concealed our revolvers, until they should be required in an unoccupied cell convenient to ours, amongst a lot of old lumber and boxes. We planned to get out through a disused gate, on to a side road.

At last, our plans being perfected, we sent word to our friends outside and reached the gate, armed with our revolvers and the bolt-cutter, and were actually in sight of the rescue party. We soon found that our bolt-cutter would not work, and we whispered to our friends to throw in the rope attached to the rope-ladder, which they did. Here another disappointment awaited us, for though we had the rope in our hands, we could not make any headway at getting the ladder across. Harder and harder we pulled, but the more efforts we made, the more securely did the rope seem fastened on top of the wall. What had happened was that the rope had sunk into a joint in the masonry, and the more we dragged at it, the more it got locked. After a terrific effort, we got it loose, only to find that it had broken!

Very sad and dispirited, we had to bid goodbye to our comrades outside, not knowing whether we would ever see them again, and return to our cells in 'Murderers' Gallery'. In our disappointment over the failure, we were beginning to think that the soldier who had promised to set us free with a bolt-cutter was making a fool of us, and we doubted that such an implement could be of any use to us in jail-breaking.

The soldier, however, was quite sincere in his sympathy for us, and in his wish to help us, but he had forgotten his instructions, and had gone the wrong way about refitting the handles of the bolt-cutter. He was so ashamed of the muddle he had made that he went to the O/C again and told him that he was sure none of us trusted him, and that the O/C himself must think he was double-dealing. The O/C took him very kindly and patiently demonstrated again how the handles should go on in order to get the right leverage.

The soldier, in order to prove that he was honest, decided that he would cut the bolts for us himself, if we would make another attempt. Meanwhile, unfortunately for ourselves as it might have happened, we had been grumbling about the dirt of the prison and on Monday, whether by chance or design, the enemy decided to clean out the place – including the disused cell where we had stored our revolvers.

Naturally the news caused consternation amongst us, because the discovery of the revolvers would shatter our hope of escape.

At this point I adopted an unusual procedure for Irish prisoners in enemy hands, and volunteered that we should do fatigue duty and clean up the cells ourselves. Having secured our revolvers, we decided that the next attempt to escape should be made as early as possible after dark on Monday 14 February, so as to avoid running into the patrols around the jail and being held up on our way through the city.

We had reason to believe our jailers suspected that some plan had been made, and failed, for the papers were hinting the rumours of escape; but the situation of Teeling was desperate and that of Mr Stewart, when he should be recognised as Ernie O'Malley, would not be much better, and I was facing a murder charge. So we decided to risk everything and try to get away that night at about 6.30.

When the time had come, O'Malley and Teeling began to make their way down to the gate – a trying ordeal, for they expected every moment to run into a sentry and be bayoneted or shot. I remained behind for a few moments, trying to persuade poor Paddy Moran to accompany us, for he was also to be tried in connection with the shootings on 'Bloody Sunday'.

Moran was so sure of acquittal – for he had a clear alibi – that he absolutely refused to leave, saying that his trying to get away would be interpreted as guilt if he was captured. Poor Paddy Moran paid with his life for relying on British justice. Finding that I could not bring Moran with me, I began my hazardous journey after my two companions, and this time to our joy, the bolt-cutter did its work.

While this operation was being carried out, and when the gate was being opened, we had our revolvers at the ready, for we were prepared, if the sentry appeared, to shoot our way out and run for it. However to our great relief every thing was clear, not even a 'Tommy' in sight to bar our way. For this latter blessing, we learnt later, we had to thank our comrades outside, who had been hampered in their duty on the first occasion by the presence of some soldiers and their girls hanging around near the prison. With great foresight our comrades had put the whole party under arrest, and had carried them away to remain in custody until we were free.

So we three ex-prisoners walked very casually out of Kilmainham, hid our revolvers in a near-by garden, made our way around at the back of Richmond barracks, along the canal, boarded a tram at Rialto bridge, and parted company to report to our respective officers.

INCHICORE RAILWAY WORKSHOP OCCUPIED BY IRA

by JIM DONNELLY

TRAVELLERS ON THE Great Southern Railways are familiar with the sight of the company's great locomotive works through which the train passes after leaving Kingsbridge terminus. These works cover a large area between Sarsfield Road and Tyrconnell Road, Inchicore. This great industrial centre has many times sprung into prominence in recent Irish history, but never did it create such a stir as it did on the occasion when, in the height of the Tan terror and during the British military curfew, it was seized and held by the local unit of the IRA from 8 p.m. on 6 March until 6 a.m. the following morning.

About 6 p.m. on Sunday 6 March, I received an urgent message from battalion headquarters instructing me to seize or destroy a consignment of steel plating which had recently been delivered at the G.S. and W. Railway Works, Inchicore, for the construction of armoured cars. This order was accompanied by an invoice giving measurements of the different plates and other details.

'F' company, 4th battalion, Dublin brigade, was thoroughly trained and disciplined, each officer and NCO being capable of taking over any vacancy in the company, or even in the battalion. The company area, extending from James' Street fountain to Clondalkin and The Green Hills at Chapelizod left plenty of room for manoeuvres.

Duplicate keys of the entrance gates, stores, etc., at Inchicore Works were always available, and men could enter the works at any time during the night (provided they eluded the different watchmen) and billet in railway carriages and other places.

During 1920 and 1921 enemy raids were of frequent occurrence and were mostly carried out on the block system. People were turned out of their beds and lined up in the streets while the houses were being searched. Arrests were made and the prisoners marched off to Richmond. As a general rule the members of 'F' company were safely outside the cordon. Our men were practically unknown to the enemy and could go to and from their work during the day without any great danger of arrest. An entirely different situation presented itself at night. IRA men were not secure in their own homes. Precautions had to be taken for the safety of the company. After working hours the usual parades, classes, etc., were held, while an armed patrol was always standing to, ready to be moved to any point if required. Parades were usually dismissed about 9 p.m. After supper the lads would go to their different sleeping places. Port Leinster House, Blue Bell, was always open to members of the IRA. A few farmers in the neighbourhood allowed us to use their outhouses more for their own protection, I should think, than from patriotism. Railway carriages in Inchicore Works, as well as sheds, were also utilised.

I remember one night a few of us made use of a timber shed in the works. We had a duplicate key and locked ourselves in. Making a shake-down with our overcoats between piles of timber, we went to sleep. About three o'clock in the morning the watchman, with his lamp, came in, accompanied by a little dog. We kept perfectly still. After a cursory glance round he seemed satisfied and was going off. It was different with the dog. He started to growl. The man tried to coax him off, thinking it was rats were about. The dog led his master round. We saw there was no further use in concealing ourselves, so we stood up and confronted the watchman. After the usual explanation he assured us he would make no report and went off.

From a civilian point of view it might seem a very easy matter just to enter the works and remove the material required, but from a military point of view it required some thinking out. If the British military should be warned that a raid was in progress we could be surrounded by troops from Richmond barracks in a very short time and our line of retreat cut off. Therefore, it was evident that all civilians on night work should be placed under arrest and no one allowed out. To carry out this effectively in such a large works every available man in 'F' company was needed.

About eighty men paraded at 7.30. Officers and section commanders received final instructions. Arms were distributed. Three different parties were sent off under a leader to enter the works from three different points at a given time. For this purpose watches were synchronised. One party went off in straggling groups and took up a position near the main entrance gate facing Kilmainham, a second party marched through the fields and halted at Private Pass, a narrow pathway leading from the north side of the works to Sarsfield Road opposite the Ranch, and a third party went to a gate near the railway line on the Clondalkin side. A fourth party was kept in reserve as a working party.

At the appointed time the three sections entered the works, placed guards at the gates, dismantled the telephones and took possession of the general offices. Skirmishing parties from the three sections moved through the works, making prisoners of all watchmen and other workers. One powerfully built man, about six feet four inches in height, was taken prisoner by a small boy and marched to the room where the prisoners were housed. He was a pensioner from the Royal Garrison Artillery and often had a joke afterwards about this incident. Any time he met the lad he would say 'when are you coming back again, I want another night's rest'.

All who were not sent off for guard and patrol duties set to work on the plating. The smaller pieces were carried away and dumped. Sledge-hammers were brought to bear on the large plates but with very little result. A couple of motor lorries belonging to the railway company, were taken and loaded up. Everything was cleared about 3.30. We had decided to take the large plating away to the vicinity of Clondalkin but thought it better not to move off until after curfew which finished at 6 a.m.

We now thought of something to eat and soon found what we wanted. In a short time every man was provided with a good breakfast at the expense of the railway company. One man attached to our company, who took a prominent part in the raid that night, was a sailor on a liner which occasionally called at the North Wall. He brought a supply of small arms and ammunition on every visit, which will be the subject of another story later. He is now in the Dublin fire brigade. All men who could be spared and who could get to their homes without coming in contact with a curfew patrol were dismissed. Engine-men and firemen were allowed to get steam up and get ready for the road. Mostly all these men were favourable and could always be depended on to assist the IRA. At six o'clock the lorries were loaded with armoured plating and driven off. The large lorry broke down on its way to Clondalkin, at the Seventh Lock bridge. It was over-loaded. A guard, under G——, accompanied it. After fruitless attempts to get it restarted there was nothing left for them to do but heave the stuff into the canal. This stuff remained in the canal for a long time and some plates may be there to the present day. A party of British military drove up one day and commandeered some locals who were drinking in Mr Clair's public house to assist in removing it. The military soon got tired and gave this job up as hopeless.

There was consternation in Inchicore works the next day. Managers and officials were flying about. It seemed impossible that a large railway works could be occupied by the IRA from 8 p.m. to 6 a.m. with curfew in force and Richmond barracks only a stone's-throw away, Kilmainham a few hundred yards, Tallaght about two miles, and Baldonnel Aerodrome about three or four miles away. So once again had the men of Éire stolen a march on the Sasanaigh.

BATTLE OF BRUNSWICK STREET

by PHIL QUINN

IN 1921 SAINT Andrew's Club, 144 Brunswick Street (now renamed Pearse Street) was the headquarters of the IRA. To safeguard it from sudden attack a constant patrol was kept around the neighbourhood by the IRA, and, as it was known to be a district where many republican soldiers and sympathisers lived, it was equally well patrolled and searched by the enemy.

Headquarters was quite accustomed to the sound of firing close at hand, as ambushes of troops in the vicinity were frequent, so that when, at about 8.10 p.m. on 14 March 1921, the men in '144' heard the sound of a bomb not far off, no serious alarm was felt, and we might have been taken by surprise only for the prompt action of the patrols.

Inside the building some men of 'B' company of the 3rd battalion were handing in arms and ammunition, which had to be sent to another district. Outside on the street three sections of 'B' company were on patrol, one under Acting Captain Peadar O'Meara, one under Lieutenant Seán O'Keefe, and one under Section Commander Carass.

The battle of Brunswick Street opened at 8.10 p.m. when two lorry-loads of Auxiliaries, and an armoured car mounted with a machine-gun, drove up Brunswick Street, heading in the direction of headquarters, and it did not end until 5 a.m. the following morning. As the Auxiliaries' lorries passed the corner of Erne Street four men, under Carass, opened fire, and immediately the British went into action. They were attacked by the men in '144' and by the patrol in Sandwith Street, under Seán O'Keefe.

As the only IRA forces on the street were our ordinary patrols, we had to carry on the fight against tremendous odds. The enemy were well supplied with ammunition, and the machine-gun from the armoured car poured a deadly fire into our ranks, but the IRA, although outmatched, showed especial gallantry in this engagement.

I remember some heroic deeds which were done on that night. Early in the fight Martin O'Neill – later accidentally shot dead in 1922 – was seriously wounded at the point commanded by Seán O'Keefe, and O'Keefe carried the wounded man to safety under heavy machine-gun fire. One of the bravest soldiers we had with us was also one of the youngest. Vol. Bernard O'Hanlon, of Dundalk, a mere lad of seventeen, had been arrested in connection with the shootings on 'Bloody Sunday', and after a detention in Portobello barracks, had been released on account of his youth. He was not long home from the military prison, and was not on duty on 24 March, but getting word of the attack on headquarters, he rushed down to take part in the defence. He was shot dead very shortly after he had joined his comrades outside '144', and he lies buried in his native Dundalk, where he was brought by the men of his battalion some days after the fight.

Another splendid young Volunteer who lost his life on that occasion, was Leo Fitzgerald, who had seen active service in 1916, when he was only a Fianna boy. Fitzgerald's conduct in what was to be his last battle was so brave that, if he had belonged to any of the great imperial armies, he would certainly have been rewarded with an 'Iron Cross', 'VC', or some such distinction.

I can never forget the kindness and courage of the people when we were in trouble, for it took courage as well as kindness to help a hunted man to escape from his enemies, or to shelter and nurse a wounded man who had fallen in the fight. Householders who were caught 'harbouring a rebel' suffered every kind of cruelty and sometimes death at the hands of the Black and Tans and military. Their houses were destroyed, they were beaten and tortured, yet the civilian population stood by us, and gave us shelter, food and procured medical help for us in spite of all the danger that threatened themselves.

When the men in '144' escaped over the back wall, it was the people in the little cottages in Erne Terrace who kept them through the curfew hours, and gave 'first-aid' to any that needed it. The owner of a dairy shop beside the library saved the life of Tom Kelly, who was seriously wounded, and was lying on the street. He would certainly have bled to death, or have been captured by the enemy, if it had not been for the friendly act of the proprietor of the shop, who carried him indoors, hid him, and gave him what attention was possible, until we were able to fetch him to hospital the next morning. Kelly was later one of those who were captured in the Four Courts in 1922, and afterwards endured thirty-three days hunger strike in prison for the sake of the Republic. That he is alive today is chiefly due to the fact that the dairy owner proved a friend in need.

Two other men, less fortunate than Kelly, were captured in the fight. One of them was Tom Traynor, who was taken prisoner early in the night, and who was executed in Mountjoy jail on 25 April 1921. Traynor was a very typical Volunteer soldier, a Dublin working man, who never shirked a sacrifice and never thought of asking for 'exemption from military duty', although he was a middle-aged man with a large family dependent upon him. He had also taken an active part in the Rising of 1916, and had been involved in many fights with his unit from that time. He went manfully to his death on the scaffold, earning the respect of even his enemies by his bearing on the fatal day.

Another prisoner taken on the same night was Jack Donnelly, who was in prison facing a similar fate when the Truce was announced.

The British casualty list was nearly as heavy as our own, two of their men being killed and five others seriously wounded, a proof that our men though at a great disadvantage, put up a splendid fight. While we were fighting without cover, and with a limited amount of ammunition and small arms, they were attacking from an armoured car, armed with rifles and a machine-gun, and posted in well-protected lorries.

In addition to our military men killed on 14 March, we lost a true friend of the cause in David Kelly, brother of Alderman Tom Kelly, who was accidentally killed while passing along the street. We heard of the death of David Kelly with deep sorrow, for this elderly, quiet man had done great work for the republican movement from the foundation of Sinn Féin.

Early next morning, the men who had escaped into Erne Terrace returned over the back wall, and recovered arms, ammunition and important papers which had to be abandoned the night before. By this prompt action they saved a lot of valuable material as well as preventing the enemy from finding names and other information in the documents left behind.

The following day headquarters was raided by the British, who, finding nothing of importance, wrecked St Andrew's club as revenge.

ATTACK ON RAF UNITS AT RED COW INN

by JIM DONNELLY

'F' COMPANY, 4TH battalion, Dublin brigade, was one of the first companies formed after the inception of the Volunteers. Its first captain was Con Colbert, executed in 1916. It played a prominent part in Easter Week, and a large number of those 1916 men also served in the subsequent struggle from 1918 to 1922. The Dublin brigade area was divided into battalion areas, each under a commandant, assisted by a vice-commandant. These areas were again divided into company areas, each under the command of a captain. The battalion commandant was responsible for the organisation, discipline and training of the units under his command. The area allotted to 'F' company took in the districts south of the Liffey, including the Dublin Union, Old and New Kilmainham, Inchicore, Ballyfermot, Fox and Geese, etc. The company was divided into two half companies, and then subdivided into sections numbering from one to four. No. 1 and No. 2 sections formed the right-half company, under the command of the 1st lieutenant, No. 3 and No. 4, the left-half company under the command of the 2nd lieutenant. Each section was in the charge of a section commander. The sections were divided into squads, numbering one to eight, each under a squad leader.

During the years 1920 and 1921 it might be said that 'F' company was in complete control of the Naas Road from the Third Lock bridge to the Red Cow Inn, and the country on either side of this main artery.

Picked men were out, even by day, sniping the enemy's tenders and caged-in cars, while by night the full company frequently went out on armed patrol for the purpose of attacking troop trains, or any enemy transport that came in their way. Some of the men were armed only with shotguns and weapons of different patterns, the best of our service rifles having been sent to Cork by order of Michael Collins.

A considerable number of the Royal Air Force was stationed in Baldonnell Aerodrome. It was their custom to go into the city in the evenings, where they went to theatres and cinemas, generally speaking to the first house performances. After the show, lorries, accompanied by armed escort cars, were sent to meet them and bring them back to the aerodrome. Our scouts had noted these movements, and it was decided at one of our council meetings to attack one of these escorts and disarm them on their return journey from Dublin. Accompanied by Lieut Frank Banim, I reconnoitred the stretch of road known as the 'long mile' (which paradoxically enough is just a short statute mile) from Conway's Half-Way House to where it meets the Naas Road. We came to the conclusion that the best place to make the attack would be on this Naas Road, near Mr Hanlon's farmhouse, a couple of hundred yards on the Clondalkin side of the Red Cow Inn.

On an evening in May 1921, all available men of the company were ordered to assemble in a low-lying field south of the Grand Canal, between the seventh and eighth locks, and about three hundred yards north of the projected point of attack. Arms, grenades and ammunition, etc., were taken from the different dumps early in the evening, cleaned and conveyed to the point of assembly. While carrying out this work, one young man, Pat Monks, met with an accident; a revolver went off accidentally and wounded him in the thigh. The men were divided into groups, each under the command of a responsible leader. We had the return of the soldiers fairly well timed and allowed for the time it would take our men to move to their different positions. As the Naas Road carried such a stream of traffic, we did not want to take up our positions too soon. If the traffic were interfered with warning might be brought to the enemy. Our party, under the command of a lieutenant and armed with shotguns and hand grenades, was sent off to a point behind a fairly high wall, about two hundred yards on the left side of the road from the Red Cow Inn. This was to be the first party to attack the enemy when they came up.

Another party was sent to Mr Hanlon's farmhouse, where some farm-carts were in the yard which could be pushed out to block the road in a few seconds. This would compel the enemy to stop and the escort would be at our mercy, hemmed in on all sides. A third party armed with short Lee-Enfield rifles was sent to take up a position where there was good cover at the junction of the by-road leading to Clondalkin village and the main road. In the event of the enemy getting through, their work was to open fire with the object of delaying them until the other attacking party had moved up into position. A fourth party took up a position about fifty yards to the right of the road and almost opposite the party who were first to attack. Two men with rifles were placed in the field in front of the Red Cow, where they could enfilade the enemy if necessary. Some unarmed men were in readiness a short distance away to collect the arms if the attack was successful. Another small unarmed party who did not assemble were ready at the Fox and Geese to block the road in the event of the enemy spotting the attackers and turning back city wards.

As we were just in position, and breathlessly waiting for the signal to attack, to my horror and consternation I saw the man in charge of the party who were to have blocked the road, rushing towards me.

'What will I do?' he cried, 'the gate is locked.'

With many words which are not fit for publication here, I ordered him back to smash the lock and demand the key of the farmhouse. Just then the enemy were sighted. They were almost opposite the party who were to attack first before the man I had ordered back to smash the lock had reached his post.

Crash! Boom!! Bang!!! The men behind the wall were doing their stuff. Owing to the failure of the road-blocking party the lorries got through, although under a heavy fire, which was returned by the enemy. To make matters worse the second attacking party, who were to take up a position at the junction of the by-road to Clondalkin and the main road, were not up in time. I would like to explain here that this was not due to any lack of courage on the part of the leader or the men of this third party. It was due to a tactical military error, that is they extended when they moved off and advanced towards their position in this order. Cover was fairly good and they could not be seen from the main road. Therefore it was a serious loss of time to have advanced in open order when they could have reached their position much more quickly by advancing in fours or in file. The result of this was that they got to their positions just as the enemy had passed and were only able to fire a few rounds after them as the cars dashed with full speed along the road. Thus ended the first attack at the Red Cow! We had no casualties on our side, with the exception of Pat Monks, who was accidentally wounded earlier in the evening. We learned afterwards that the enemy had five men wounded. Although we failed in our main objective, namely disarmament of the soldiers, we were quite satisfied with our engagement considering that Richmond barracks (now Keogh Square) was only about two miles away, Tallaght Aerodrome even a shorter distance off, and the Naas Road being the chief route to the Curragh.

THE BURNING OF THE CUSTOM HOUSE

by OSCAR TRAYNOR, TD

THE STORY OF the destruction of the Custom House is one of brave endeavour as well as one of outstanding success. To it has been ascribed, rightly or wrongly, the ending of the war with the forces of occupation. What is certain is that it always will be linked with the ending of that gallant struggle for the restoration of Irish independence, because, in a matter of about one month Mr Lloyd George invited Mr de Valera to a conference. This invitation was followed by the arrangement for a Truce which eventually took place on 11 July 1921, at twelve noon. Thus was brought to an end one of the most successful fights in our long history for the restoration of our independence.

Early in the New Year of 1921, I received a note informing me that there would be a meeting of the army council in the home of the late O'Rahilly in 40 Herbert Park. These meetings were seldom held twice in the one place, and this was the first time I had been summoned to Herbert Park. I was later informed, verbally, that the meeting would be a rather important one and that I should come prepared to discuss the activities of the Dublin brigade and matters pertaining to it. I was also told that the president (Éamon de Valera), who had just arrived back from America, would be present. I arrived at Herbert Park at the appointed hour and found most of my colleagues already there. Those present as far as my memory goes were Cathal Brugha, Austin Stack, Richard Mulcahy, Diarmuid O'Hegarty, Michael Collins,

Gearóid O'Sullivan, Liam Mellows, Seán Russell, J.J. O'Connell, Seán McMahon, Piaras Béaslaí and, I think, Eoin O'Duffy.

There may have been one or two others, but I cannot remember them at the moment. However, we were assembled there for some little time when word was brought to us that the British forces had drawn a cordon across the entrance to the road. It was immediately assumed that this activity was in some way connected with our meeting. The position we were in was being discussed, ways and means to meet it were being planned when to our surprise, the president was ushered into our presence. Everyone naturally wanted to know how he managed to get through the cordon. His reply was simple. He said, 'I was held up, questioned and finally passed through.' Later the word came through that the cordon had been withdrawn. As it was then a very ordinary procedure on the part of the occupying forces to throw out these cordons little further notice was taken.

The meeting proceeded in a very normal way for some time and then the president spoke and he made it clear that something in the nature of a big action in Dublin was necessary in order to bring public opinion abroad to bear on the question of Ireland's case. He felt that such an action in the capital city which was as well-known abroad as London or Paris, would be certain to succeed. He suggested that the capture of the headquarters of the Black and Tans, which was situated in Beggar's Bush barracks, would capture the imagination of those he had in mind, apart from the serious blow it would constitute to the enemy. As an alternative to this he suggested the destruction of the Custom House which was the administrative heart of the British civil service machine in this country. It was finally decided that I, as the officer commanding the Dublin brigade, should examine these propositions and report back to the army council in due course.

I immediately set to work and was given the help of GHQ intelligence. Two weeks were spent on the investigation and examination of the possibilities of capturing Beggar's Bush. The experience of the men engaged on this work was such that they reported against such an operation. My activities were then turned to the alternative suggestion

– the Custom House. I made a personal examination of this building. Armed with a large envelope, inscribed with OHMS on its front, I made my way all over the building. I was greatly impressed by its solidity, its granite walls, and what appeared to me its complete lack of structural material which would burn. However, each office into which I penetrated was surrounded by wooden presses and shelves which held substantial bundles of papers and office files. It could also be presumed that the presses contained papers and other inflammable material. Immediately after my examination I took Commandant Tom Ennis of the 2nd battalion into my confidence and asked him to make a similar examination and let me have his views. He carried out his task by methods similar to my own and his report more or less confirmed my views.

My next step was to secure plans of the building. These were secured for me by the O/C 5th battalion (Liam O'Doherty). A perusal of these indicated the magnitude of the task. There were three floors to be dealt with as well as the basement floor, numerous corridors and hundreds of offices. The staff probably numbered upwards of a hundred with the control of large numbers of telephones. In the course of our investigations it was also discovered that there was a direct line to the Castle for emergency uses. There was also the problem of the general public who were continually entering and leaving the building. There were no military guards on the building, they having been withdrawn some short time before. There was, however, a number of police patrolling both the front and rear of the building. All these and many other points had to be given careful consideration.

I spent nearly three months on the preparation of the plans. They were in my mind day and night. They were altered dozens of times as weaknesses or better points occurred to me. Finally they were submitted to a sub-committee of the army council for their imprimatur or otherwise. This body met at six o'clock one Sunday morning in May in 6 Gardiner's Row, which was the headquarters of the Dublin brigade. Those present were Richard Mulcahy, chief-of-staff, Michael Collins, director of intelligence, J.J. (Ginger) O'Connell, ACS, and a man named Dowling. I got the impression that he was a specialist in engineering. The plans in general were accepted. But one portion which arranged for the throwing up of barricades in the vicinity of the various city barracks was objected to. This operation was designed to operate only if any attempt was made by enemy forces to leave during the twenty-five minutes from 12.55 p.m. to 1.20 p.m. when it was hoped to have the destruction of the building and its evacuation completed. It was designed solely as a delaying action and to give the men operating within the Custom House an opportunity of returning in safety when their task was completed. The barricades were to have been covered by riflemen operating from a distance of two or three hundred yards.

The DI's objection to this part of the scheme was very strong. He regarded the throwing up of barricades all over the city as being suggestive of a general uprising and finally stated, in reply to my arguments, that if it could not be carried out without this precaution it should not be carried out at all. Having withdrawn my arguments in favour of that part of the plan, the date of 25 May was agreed upon for the carrying out of the operation.

My next step was to inform the senior officers of the brigade of the proposed action together with an outline of the plan. They on their part were to start on the selection of their officers for the varying tasks which they would be called upon to fill. In the course of a number of meetings the whole plan was gradually unfolded As the target was in the 2nd battalion area it was decided that the actual destruction of the building would be entrusted to that unit. Commandant Tom Ennis was appointed to take sole control of the party within the building. The 2nd battalion was reinforced by the addition of the Squad, a party of about twelve men who were attached to the DI's department and some men of the ASU.

To the 1st battalion was allotted the task of protecting the outside of the building. In the event of a surprise attack by enemy forces, the battalion was to engage them with grenade, rifle and machine-gun fire. This was a later addition to the plans which I had submitted to the army council's sub-committee. I had hoped to be able to tell the men who had to enter the building that they would be completely protected against surprise by reason of the ring of barricades to which I have already referred, but following the elimination of that part of the plan I decided on this last minute, so to speak, form of at least partial protection. In addition to this task the 1st battalion was also to deal with any fire stations in their area. In other words they were to put all fire-fighting appliances out of action by the removal of vital parts of their machines. The 3rd and 4th battalions dealt in a similar way with the stations in their areas.

To the 5th battalion was given the very important task of cutting off from all communication, telephonic or otherwise, the Custom House with the outside world. This was a highly technical job and the most skilled men of the engineers were called on to carry out the work. Communications could not be cut until the last minute as otherwise suspicions would most likely be aroused. As quite a number of manholes and high telephone poles were involved, the difficulty of their task can well be imagined.

The preparation for the main task of destruction brought about the necessity for a number of lesser actions. For instance, I decided right from the beginning that in no circumstances was petrol to be used. This necessitated the commandeering of a large quantity of paraffin oil and the transferring of the oil from steel casks and tanks to petrol tins. It also necessitated the holding up of an oil concern and their staff for a number of hours and the commandeering of a motor lorry to bring the tinned paraffin to the Custom House precisely on time. When this lorry arrived at the back entrance to the building, which is opposite Lower Gardiner Street, the men detailed for the inside operation entered, at the same time taking with them from off the lorry a tin of paraffin. The building was also entered from the quays and Beresford Place entrance, opposite Liberty Hall. In this way the number going in by any one door was not excessive and did not arouse any suspicion. Their immediate job on entry was to control all telephonic communication as an added safety device, even though these had been cut by our engineers, precisely on the entrance of our men to the building.

Within the building each captain had been allotted a landing or floor and all the officers and men on that landing to deal with. His job was to see that every person employed on that floor was sent down to the main hall where they were kept under the vigilant eyes of the men of the Squad and ASU. With this part of his task completed he was then to see that every office on his landing site was thoroughly saturated with paraffin oil. This could not have been done if petrol was used, as the gas manufactured by the contact of petrol with air would have made a very dangerous explosive mixture. When the job of saturation had been completed the officer was to report to the O/C, Commdt Ennis, on the ground floor and the actual firing was to take place on an order given by him by a single blast of his whistle. Two blasts were to signify the completion of the job and the withdrawal of all men to the ground floor.

Everything went perfectly as per plan expect that just before all floors had given the O/C the 'all ready' or OK signal someone blew two blasts on a whistle and all retired to the main hall. One officer reported, however, that he had not completed his saturation task. The O/C sent him and his men back at once to complete the job. The few minutes lost here, not quite five, was the difference between the successful retirement of all participants and the arrival of a large number of enemy forces in lorries and armoured cars. These forces swept into Beresford Place at exactly 1.25 p.m., just five minutes after the time allotted in the plan for the completion of the operation. They were engaged on entry to Beresford Place by the 1st battalion units with volleys of revolver shots and the throwing of hand grenades. For some unknown reason the machine-gun which our men were to have mounted inside the Custom House Docks at the far end of Beresford Place did not come into action.

Just before the entry of enemy forces, I was talking to Capt. Paddy Daly, just outside the main back entrance. We were discussing the delay in the men leaving as 1.20 p.m. had just passed. The sudden entry of the enemy put an end to our discussion as at this point they were firing wildly from the different lorries as they came through. Capt.

Daly made away towards Abbey Street. I made towards the support of the Loop Line bridge opposite Brooks Thomas' building stores. As I reached the road here I came under fire from a lorry of Black and Tans, but due to the speed and movement of the lorry the fire was erratic. As I reached the pathway, however, the lorry had come to a sudden halt. I was still being fired on and at the same time there were shouts of 'hands up'. At this point I saw a young Volunteer jump out from the cover of the bridge supports and throw a bomb into the middle of the Black and Tan's lorry with disastrous effects to the occupants. I was later told that he was Volunteer Dan Head and that he was killed either then or sometime later during the action. By this time the 'Squad' in the Custom House had gone into action with their Parabellum and Mauser automatics with still further disastrous effects to the Black and Tans who were attempting to storm the main back entrance. Before I managed to get away I saw several enemy bodies lying around the entrance immovable and, as far as one could see and judge, dead. Those who were blown out of the lorry with which I was concerned were unconscious on the ground, if not dead.

I eventually got out through Gardiner Street and Talbot Street and back to Abbey Street where I made touch with Capt. Daly again, just outside the Abbey Theatre. Here we were informed that Tom Ennis who had shot his way out was taken away in a LMS lorry seriously wounded. At this time enemy reinforcements were coming up in lorries together with additional armoured cars. We then knew that the only hope for the men inside was to escape by the Custom House Docks, a slender enough chance considering the strength of the forces now on the scene. Actually, a goodly number did escape by various ways and ruses. Some were killed in their attempt. Altogether we lost five killed and about eighty captured.

Some short time later I received a message to the effect that Tom Ennis had reached his home in Croydon Park House, Fairview, and that he was in a very serious condition. Capt. Daly and myself immediately went to the brigade first-aid post in Gardiner's Row where we collected some first-aid equipment and cycled to Tom's home. His wife, who was nursing a young infant, brought us to Tom's bedside where we found him in a semi-conscious condition. He had an awful-looking bullet wound in his groin. The bullet entered from the buttock and made its exit through the groin. In its passage it was apparently deflected and tumbled on its way through, as the exit wound was a large gaping hole with portions of bone protruding. This looked so bad that I at once ordered Daly to get into immediate touch with Michael Collins' motor driver, Batt Hyland, and ask him to come over at once. While awaiting his arrival I gave first-aid treatment to the wounds, having earlier on in my Volunteer career done a course in that service.

When the car arrived Daly and I had considerable difficulty in getting Tom down the stairs from his flat, every movement causing him excruciating pain. The car then made its way very slowly to the O'Donnell's nursing home in Eccles Street where all our Volunteers were treated. On our way there we twice had to pass through police cordons – once on Ballybough bridge and later on the bridge on Jones' Road. On both occasions the police after peering into the car gave us the 'all clear' and passed us through. I think they sized up the situation and decided on a non-interference policy. On arrival at the home we had to carry Tom to the very top of the building. He was then only barely conscious. He was attended almost immediately and was operated on, I think that night. He spent a considerable period of time in that home. In the course of one of my visits he told me that the doctor assured him that the first-aid attention which he had been given helped considerably in saving his life. I merely mention this to show that the special services in the brigade were of considerable and genuine value, especially when it was not always safe to call in outside help without some knowledge of the individuals called on, or the time to make enquiries as to their friendliness or otherwise.

The operation, apart from these losses, was entirely successful. Everything within the four walls of the building was reduced to ashes. The fire was still burning ten days after the attack. The fire brigade was unable to go into action for a considerable time. This delay, as well as the use of the paraffin oil, played a decisive part in the total destruction of the inside of the building. That evening the Dublin brigade again went into action in a number of places in the city, mainly as a gesture of defiance, as well as to show that our heavy losses that day did not impair our ability to carry on the fight.

The nuns of the Mater Hospital later told me the story of the death of Seán Doyle. As he lay on his death bed, they said his one worry was 'Are the boys beaten' and that night as the sound of nearby explosions shook the air, Seán's face wreathed in smiles, turned to the nun who was attending him and he feebly whispered 'Thank God, Sister, the fight goes on'. That simple statement of a man who had given his all for the cause of Ireland symbolised the determination of the Irish people down through the centuries.

BRITISH FORCES IN SCENE OF CONFUSION

by MICHAEL FITZPATRICK, TD

SHORTLY AFTER THE attack on the Custom House we were given orders by GHQ to intensify the warfare and follow up that victory as closely as possible. I was at that time branch secretary of the barmen's section of the Irish National Union of Vintners, Grocers, and Allied Trades Assistants, and a great number of my comrades in 'K' company of the 1st battalion were members of that branch. As our military duty had to be carried out at dinner hour, after hours, or on our half-holiday, the enemy intelligence soon had suspicions that a number of grocers' assistants were to be found in the ranks of the IRA.

Raids on public houses and union headquarters for suspected men brought the Black and Tans small results, as in the vast majority of cases the owners of the houses, and the men we worked with did not betray us. Even those who were not themselves active Volunteers would stand by the men who were carrying on the fight. As for ourselves, we had learned to be very careful not to keep lists of names which could be caught in a raid, and where it was necessary to preserve a list, we wrote it in code, the key being hidden in a separate place from the list.

The company council planned a series of operations starting the first week in June. On 1 June, a party, under the command of Lieut Billy Bohan ambushed a military lorry near Arran Quay church. The attack was opened by two men with hand grenades that exploded on the lorry which was covered by a wire netting. The attack was followed up by the officer-in-charge and two other men with revolver fire. Their retreat through Smithfield was covered by several other Volunteers stationed at vantage points along the line of retreat to North King Street. Our party suffered no casualties.

On 2 June, a party took up position on Ormond Quay. As no lorry came along, they withdrew after half-an-hour.

On 3 June, I posted a small party at the corner of Dorset Street and Blessington Street. They had just settled in position when a lorry of British troops arrived from the city. Instead of proceeding along Blessington Street as expected, it turned down towards Drumcondra. The men with the grenades decided to attack. As the grenades exploded, a Volunteer stationed at Wellington Street corner opened fire with a revolver to cover the men's retreat. It was reported that several soldiers were wounded in the engagement. Our men retreated via Mountjoy Street and Dominick Street to Parnell Street where the guns were dumped without casualty.

On 4 June I received word that a supply train was due to leave North Wall for the Midlands. I immediately sent a party under Lieut Madigan to Cross Guns bridge with instructions to attack the train with grenades as it entered the tunnel. The officer-in-charge, having posted the men on the bridge, went down Whitworth Road from where he signalled the exact location of the guard on the train. As the van entered the tunnel, our men dropped the bombs; the soldiers immediately opened fire, the terrific noise caused by the exploding grenades and rifle fire echoing from the tunnel caused the republican prisoners in nearby Mountjoy to think that an all-out attempt was being made to rescue them. None of our men were injured. A number of wounded soldiers were taken off the train which stopped at Liffey Junction.

The following week we had planned a series of ambushes on the military and Tans. Proceeding along the quays at about four o'clock on 9 June a party of twenty under the command of the company adjutant, Val Forde took up position along Ormond Quay and intersecting streets. Two men with grenades and the company adjutant with a revolver were stationed on the corner of Swift's Row. Their retreat was covered by revolver men at the corner of Liffey Street and Jervis Street; while Liffey Street, Mary Street and Capel Street were also covered, holding every possible line of retreat, while unarmed scouts maintained a communication link between each outpost. I had just completed an inspection of each post where the men repeated their instructions, and arrived on the south quays where another party was stationed. As I was leaving my bicycle in Fownes Street, one of the men signalled to me that a lorry was coming on the far side. A moment later I heard rifle fire, and saw the British lorry pull up near Swift's Row where our advance party was stationed. Still the grenades did not explode; this was to have been the signal for our attack from the south quays.

Realising that something had gone wrong, and that our party could not escape along Swift's Row if the British were allowed to attack them from the quays, I shouted to our men on the south quays to take up position. They were about twenty yards from me when I issued the order. Fire! By the time I had repeated the order three times, the British had turned from Swift's Row, and were now lined along the Liffey Wall returning our fire. As bullets were hopping off the houses at my back, and knowing that we had served our purpose by giving our comrades a few minutes to retreat past the first cover party, I ordered the retreat. The firing party went via Fleet Street and Butt bridge to Marlboro Street while I cycled towards Parliament Street in an attempt to cross Capel Street bridge and see that all was clear. At the Dolphin Hotel, I was held up by a very vicious-looking Black and Tan. Mustering all the self-control I possessed, I casually asked him what was wrong; without answering, he signalled me with a jerk of his rifle up Dame Court. Later that evening I learned what happened in Swift's Row. The two grenades with which the attack was opened failed to explode. The men retreated as instructed.

When the officer-in-charge of the operations, who was to continue the attack with revolver fire, turned around the corner, he was confronted by the British, who, having spotted the attack with the grenades, were alighting from their lorry. In the exchange of fire which followed, before we came into action from the south quays, he was wounded in the foot, and only escaped arrest by slipping into a nearby cabinet-maker's shop, where, having dumped his gun, he put on an apron and passed as one of the employees.

Meanwhile, the grenade men had made good their retreat across Abbey Street. They had a narrow escape from a load of troops which were being engaged by our cover men from Capel Street. One of them actually ran under the tail of the lorry from which the soldiers were dismounting. Another was held up and searched, while on his finger was the ring and pin attached, which he was bringing back, as proof that he did not throw the grenade with the pin in. Men on the job for the first time were known to make this mistake in the excitement of the moment. Luckily he had the presence of mind, and he held his hands, palm inwards, so that the bomb ring passed for an ordinary finger ring, and went unnoticed.

It was very apparent that the British anticipated this attack some-where along the north quays. At least three lorries laden with troops came down the quays. A detachment of troops came along North King Street and turned down Parnell Street, while another detachment on foot turned up Henry Street from O'Connell Street. The first lorry came down Capel Street and then down into Abbey Street, at the precise moment that the attack started on the quays, and would have cut off the retreat from Swift's Row, were they not engaged by two of our men posted at Mary's Abbey. While our boys fired down Abbey Street they were engaged by the British from a second lorry which had turned into Capel Street. One of these two men was wounded in the shoulder in the Abbey Street firing, but managed to escape because of the confusion caused by the Abbey Street soldiers coming out into crossfire in Capel Street when the British troops fired on each other. Our lads got to Mary Street and Stafford Street where they had to dump the guns and hide in a tenement house, as further retreat was made impossible by a cordon of troops which had taken up position in Parnell Street.

Meanwhile, some 'unknown warrior' of whom we have no record, had opened up an attack on the Black and Tans at the Castle. When a car containing four Auxiliary officers in plain clothes was turning into the Castle gate at Palace Street, this 'unknown warrior' had fired two shots at them from the opposite side of the road. The Auxiliaries' car was followed immediately after by an RIC car, with metal sides, and both these cars, hearing the heavy firing across the river, thought that the whole town was in IRA hands. Coming out from the Castle to Parliament Street, they began firing across Capel Street bridge at their comrades, adding to the confusion which already existed in Capel Street.

Although eight or nine lorry-loads of soldiers and Black and Tans were in action on that day, and were opposed by twenty IRA men, all of our men got away safely, only two being superficially wounded. The British troops unwittingly helped our men to escape, as with the sudden inrush of lorries the men in Abbey, Capel and Mary Streets were in a tight corner, and nothing but the cross-firing of the troops against each other, and Black and Tans against the troops, could have been of much assistance.

The British official report claimed they had captured several of the attackers, a machine-gun, revolvers and the car from which the operation was directed. This was merely propaganda, as we had no car or machine-gun. The success of the operation, which, by the way, was later quoted by GHQ as an example of how street fighting was carried on in Dublin, was due to the loyalty of those lads to each other, and their great discipline in carrying out the jobs allotted to them. Members of 'K' company now scattered to the four corners of the earth – some have passed away, some made good, and some struggle on – wherever you are, I salute you. I was proud to command you and glad to call you friends.

ATTEMPTED RESCUE OF SEÁN MacEOIN FROM MOUNTJOY JAIL

The writer of the account of the attempted rescue of Seán MacEoin from Mountjoy jail on 11 May 1921, Joe Leonard, is a Dublin man. He took part in the Rising of 1916 at the age of twenty, and was deported. In January 1919, he was arrested for drilling, and served a sentence in Mountjoy jail, where he took part in a hunger strike. Later on in 1919, he was one of the first members to join the active service unit in Dublin when it was formed. From that until the Truce of July 1921 he saw a great deal of fighting in Dublin.

The first barracks taken over from the British in 1922 was Beggar's Bush. Members of the Irish army marched in under Paddy O'Daly, (afterwards major-general). Leonard was one of the officers in that party, and subsequently rose to the rank of colonel.

Emmet Dalton had served with the British army in the 1914–1918 war, and was at the battle of the Somme. On his return he became an active member of the Volunteers, as the narrative shows. After the Treaty he rose to the rank of major-general in the National Army.

PHYSICAL FIGHTING AGAINST the British was of a rather different character in the country and in Dublin. In the country, attacks on police barracks were first undertaken by men who assembled at night and after the attack on the barracks, resumed their own ordinary work. Later, small bodies of men in flying columns remained on full-time active service, getting shelter and food from the country people, using assistance from local Volunteers and civilians in their activities, and operating on the 'hit and run' method. Leadership of these columns in different areas required certain qualities. A man had to be fearless, but as well as that he had to be resourceful, alert and responsible. In many cases, he had first to disarm members of the Royal Irish Constabulary or British military to provide his men with arms and ammunition. He had to keep in touch with units in adjoining counties, and with GHQ in Dublin. A point was reached when the RIC were unable to retain their positions in the countryside and the barracks were evacuated. These barracks were promptly burned on orders from Volunteer headquarters in Dublin. But a new problem then presented itself to the local leader because as well as fighting, he had to take his share, sometimes a very important share, in the administration of justice in the area from which the constabulary had been withdrawn.

Seán MacEoin, a young blacksmith from Ballinalee, County Longford, had shown not only great courage, but also ingenuity, military knowledge, and a capacity for taking responsibility. By 1921 he had many exploits to his credit and had become a well-known figure. In March 1921, after a big ambush in which a number of Auxiliary police were killed, MacEoin was wounded and captured. He was tried by court martial and several Auxiliaries gave evidence that after the fighting he had done his best for the British wounded and had, in fact, sent a doctor to see after them. But he was sentenced to death and lodged in Mountjoy jail, Dublin, with a special guard of Auxiliary police to watch over him day and night.

The jail is an old building with a strong outer gate reached by a long passage from the main road and two inner gates which under prison rules have always to be kept closed. The ordinary staff of the jail, all Irishmen, were augmented by Auxiliary police, and regular British military furnished the outer guards. It will readily be understood that the loss of MacEoin was considered a very grievous one and there was passionate anxiety that he should not suffer the supreme penalty, but the problem of effecting his rescue seemed impossible to solve.

Like the flying columns in the country, there had been formed in Dublin, a full-time active service unit to which Colonel Leonard refers in his narrative. In September 1919, General Mulcahy, then chief-of-staff, summoned a number of Volunteers to a meeting at 44 Parnell Square. They included Michael Collins, director of intelligence; Dick McKee,

O/C Dublin; Peadar Clancy, director of munitions; Mick McDonald, brigade quartermaster; Paddy O'Daly; Joe Leonard; Ben Barrett; Seán Doyle; Tom Keogh; Tim Slattery and Vincent Byrne. These men were asked if they would give their whole time to active service and from that time onwards, they operated in Dublin city, getting co-operation not only from members of the Volunteer organisation, but also from many civilians, from some police, prison warders, civil servants and others.

Conditions were different from those in the country, crowded streets instead of lonely places, but intimate knowledge of by-ways and the help of friendly householders often brought men to safety after a 'job'.

After MacEoin's death sentence, Collins called this unit into play to attempt a rescue. The attempt is described in the narrative that follows by Colonel Joseph Leonard.

Michael Hayes

LEONARD'S STORY — OUTSIDE

In May 1921, Collins conceived a plan to rescue Seán MacEoin from Mountjoy jail. The plan was in three parts: (1) To capture and man a British armoured car which would gain entrance to the jail. (2) To gain entrance to Mountjoy and get possession of MacEoin's body. (3) To make sure that it would be possible to come out of the jail again.

British military lorries drew meat rations for various barracks from the Dublin abattoir two or three times a day. The lorries were accompanied by an armoured car, a Rolls, single-turret, whippet. Having in mind the use of the armoured car for the Mountjoy job, Collins instructed Charlie Dalton to take up his quarters in the abattoir superintendent's house and watch through a window the movements of the car. Charlie noticed that on some days, on their first visit, at 6 a.m., the car crew got restless so that eventually the last soldier would get out to stretch his legs and locking the car would ramble about the place. This led to the conclusion that it might be possible to capture the car. Collins took immediate action and in Jim Kirwan's public house, had a consultation with Emmet Dalton, myself and a warder of Mountjoy jail who gave us full information about warders, the positions of military guards, meal times and relief times for police and Auxiliaries. Meantime, through another source, MacEoin was instructed to make some complaint or pretext every day so that at 10 a.m. he would be with the governor in his office. The governor's office is outside of three obstructing gates and the governor was usually alone in his office at 10 a.m. in the morning to interview prisoners. If we could get in at that time and find MacEoin in the office, the rest was easy.

The organisation of the parties was done by Paddy O'Daly, one to capture the car, another to man and drive it, and a third party to force an entrance through the main gate of Mountjoy after the car had driven in. This last party was to reopen the gate and keep it open until the armoured car came out again. I shall take these three parties in order.

One morning Charlie Dalton noticed that on their early visit at 6 a.m. the soldiers were in jaunty mood and he guessed that the last soldier would probably leave the car on their next visit. He made his report, returned to his watch-out post and the job was on.

The car with the same crew returned on its second journey and behaved as Charlie Dalton had guessed it would. The last Tommy got out and went for a stroll. Volunteers, wearing corporation uniform caps who were waiting about the abattoir, at a pre-arranged signal closed in and held up the Tommies shooting some of those who resisted. They secured the keys of the car and a Rolls, single-turret, whippet armoured car, became, for the first time, the property of the Irish Volunteers.

Pat McCrea, a quiet and most reliable man, had never seen the inside of a car like this in his life. But he got in calmly and stepped on the gas. He was accompanied by Tom Keogh, Bill Stapleton and Paddy McCaffrey as machine-gunners and went off down the North Circular Road. Emmet Dalton and myself were waiting for him dressed and armed like British officers. Emmet was wearing his own British uniform and having worn it for a long time before, had all the appearance and manner of a British officer. He knew how to adopt the right tone in serving a Prisoner's Removal Order on the jail authorities. I had served six months in Mountjoy and knew the prison well. Besides, Emmet's second uniform fitted me to perfection.

When he had picked us up, McCrea drove to Mountjoy jail. Emmet Dalton who was sitting outside as the officer usually was, waved an official-looking paper at the look-out warder. The gates opened wide and shut-to with a clang after us. Two more iron gates were opened for us, but McCrea used his long head, driving the car in one long sweep around by the main entrance and back through the two iron gates he had just entered, carelessly jamming both open, and so leaving the main gate only to be negotiated. Dalton and myself jumped smartly out of the car. We posted Tom Keogh, dressed in British dungarees and a Tommy's uniform cap, outside the main entrance door to cover our rear or give the alarm if necessary.

Dalton and I entered the main door at 10.30 a.m., as the warders were coming from their quarters on duty. One of them, Warder Kelly, had known me as a prisoner and was so surprised at seeing me in British uniform that he said, 'Oh cripes, look at Leonard', and then, clapping his hand over his mouth, dashed back upstairs, knocking down all the warders descending. We were refused entrance to MacEoin's wing by the warder in charge, and as it was not possible for us to break down two massive iron gates, and finally MacEoin's cell door, we continued on to the governor's office. The situation in the office at ten o'clock should have been that there was only one warder on duty, but when we went in we received a shock. Instead of finding Governor Munroe alone, there were seven of his staff present, and as we went in the door slammed shut behind us. The governor received us nicely and all went well until he mentioned that he must ring up the Castle for confirmation of the order to remove MacEoin. I sprang for the telephone and smashed it while Dalton, drawing his gun, held the staff at bay, and then began tying the staff up with the hope of securing the master keys, when a fusillade met our ears – it was now or never – we forced the door open – goodbyes were said quickly – we left the building with all haste.

MacEoin was not in the governor's office. We had arrived half-an-hour late for that appointment through no fault of our own.

The plan for holding the main gate open was that Miss Áine Malone was to approach with a parcel and have the wicket opened and that Volunteers in several groups were then to rush the gate. Miss Malone, with her parcel, arrived in good time, the wicket gate was opened and the main gate rushed. But a sentry on the roof, noticing the civilians rushing the gate, fired a shot which wounded one of our men, and raised the general alarm. Tom Keogh, ever on the alert, shot this sentry dead from the courtyard, with a Peter the Painter, and the sentry's rifle fell down to the pavement. As Dalton and myself were rushing to the main door, I spotted the rifle. Auxiliaries were on the roof with their rifles at the ready. A guard of regular soldiers turned out on the ground near the gate, but were naturally confused at the sight of British uniforms. Acting the part of a British officer I ordered them to retire, and on their refusal to obey I took up the rifle, knelt down and threatened to fire. The soldiers, seeing an officer kneeling in the firing position, retired to their quarters. But the Auxiliary police were advancing from the other side so it was time to jump on the back of the whippet and go, taking our rifles with us. We shouted to Pat to let her rip, and Pat McCrea drove down that drive and on to the North Circular Road at a speed that was very satisfactory, seeing we were exposed to rather heavy fire from the prison. Pat McCrea had instructions to drive the whippet to the Finglas bridge area, but on account of the engine overheating badly he decided to abandon the car at Marino and, having stripped it of its guns and ammunition, set it on fire and went back to his brother's shop to continue his daily work.

Dalton and I had no plan of action agreed upon and we transferred into a waiting taxi at the end of the street. We arrived in Howth and dismissed our taxi. It then dawned on me that my sister had good friends among the Sisters of Charity, so we decided to go and see them. We were very nicely received by a sympathetic sister, who listened to our tale of woe, and having produced a lovely cup of tea, and set out the best china, went to see the reverend mother. A messenger was dispatched to Cassidy's public house on the summit, and returned with two suits borrowed for the occasion. Our uniforms were packed away for dispatch and we emerged less showy, perhaps, but feeling more comfortable and more pleased with ourselves and returned to town by tram.

On arrival in Dublin we learnt that the English military had confined all armoured cars to barracks, having got a scare at the loss of their baby whippet.

Joseph Leonard

MacEOIN'S STORY — INSIDE

IN MAY 1921, I received a dispatch from Michael Collins informing me that a new attempt would be made to rescue me from Mountjoy jail. The dispatch instructed me to contact Warder Breslin. Later that evening I received information and instructions from Collins, also in dispatch. This was to the effect that an armoured car, manned by Volunteers would enter Mountjoy jail at any time between ten and twelve o'clock on the following morning and that I must take such steps as were necessary to be in the governor's office and remain there for that time. When I came in from exercise that same evening I made contact with Breslin who informed me that everything was ready for action the next morning. On return to my cell I immediately sent for the deputy governor, Mr Meehan, making a violent attack upon the conduct of (a) the Warders, (b) the Auxiliaries, and (c) the Black and Tans who were in charge of C (1) wing and were our jailers. In accordance with the rules I demanded an immediate interview with the governor and succeeded in arranging the interview for the following morning. Everything was working according to plan, and I arrived in the governor's office escorted by an Auxiliary officer and a warder. I succeeded in remaining in the office with the governor, Charlie Munroe, until about 11.30, when I informed Munroe that I had further complaints on behalf of many of the prisoners and that I would return to my cell and prepare notes for use next morning. This was simply a makeshift as I did not know what had happened.

Going out to exercise after lunch, Breslin contacted me again and informed me that the car had not been taken that day but the attempt would be made on the following day and that the same plan must work. I then sent out a dispatch to Collins informing him that I could be in the governor's office on the following morning, and that I was accompanied by an Auxiliary officer with a revolver, but that when our men would arrive I thought that I could handle him. As arranged on Thursday morning I was once more in the governor's office, and remained there for about the same time, with the same result, and on going out to exercise, I received a repetition of the same message from Breslin. On the third morning the interview was again arranged with the governor for 10 a.m., but something which we had not foreseen now occurred.

The members of the Auxiliaries and Black and Tan guard who were in charge of the wing were being relieved and a new body of Auxiliaries and Tans were taking over the duty. The officer commanding the new party insisted that every prisoner in C (1) wing should be locked in his cell. This was done; then the new party accompanied by the officer commanding the old party came and saw every prisoner. This was for the purpose of identification. Each prisoner was carefully scrutinised and notes taken of him by each member of the guard so that each one would know and recognise each one of the prisoners who was being handed over for the first time into their custody. It was then believed by the authorities that the warders could not be trusted and that prisoners might be enabled to exchange cells so that they would have wrong names and wrong cells.

While this was going on I protested and claimed my interview with the governor, which I had arranged. Mr Meehan, the deputy governor, was present and explained to the commander that I had an interview arranged with the governor. The Auxiliary officer replied that my interview with the governor would be in time enough, that his orders took precedence. While this inspection was taking place the armoured car arrived into Mountjoy and the first indication I had of its presence was the firing of shots. The Auxiliaries manned the inner gate of C (1) wing and in a short time afterwards they returned and opened my cell; they were very excited, and proceeded to search every corner of the cell and my person. While this was proceeding Breslin came into the cell and said to the Auxiliary 'we are all safe' at the same time giving me the 'glad-eye'. From that wink I realised that the car had come in and gone out and that those with it were all safe. I bluffed the Auxiliary a bit by saying 'when you meet the armoured car down town you will have a very hot time if I get much more abuse'. They then informed me that they were aware of my line of communication and that they would be able to find it. I wished them luck in their efforts feeling satisfied that they could not have secured any information upon the line of communication, which was a very simple and very old method. That is another story. When the excitement had died down I was blandly informed that the governor was now ready to receive me, not in his usual office, but in a cell at the end of C (1) wing, and all interviews with the governor thereafter while I was a prisoner in Mountjoy were in this cell.

The capture of the armoured car and the effort at rescue were of a first-class nature, and had they succeeded in capturing it on either of the two first days on which it was planned, I would have been in the governor's room and would have had no trouble in being able to accompany the two Volunteer officers who were dressed up in the uniform of the enemy forces.

Seán MacEoin

CONCLUSION

To GIVE A really satisfactory account of this episode one would require a corroborative narrative from a prison official or from some member of the British military or police force on duty in the prison. An account from the governor, Munroe, or the deputy, Mr Meehan, would have been easy to get, but I do not know whether any steps were ever taken in that direction.

The reason for the failure is clear. The armoured car could only be captured, when, contrary to regulations, the soldiers had left it. Separated from the car they could be mastered. Inside it, they were impregnable. Unfortunately on the morning when an opportunity arose to capture the car, a new guard had come on duty in the prison. As General MacEoin points out, a more stringent and intelligent step had been taken about prisoners. It is clear that the exploit involved risk of death for the crew of the armoured car, and indeed for MacEoin himself, but these things, as Colonel Leonard observes, were all part of the day's work at that time.

Although the prisoner was not rescued, the attempt was not without very valuable results from the point of view of the Sinn Féiners. It was a great shock to public opinion in England to find and that the raiders could escape unscathed in broad daylight in Dublin.

Leonard's story is told with great modesty, but the nature of the exploit itself emerges clearly. There was great daring, resourcefulness and a fierce determination not to be stopped by any kind of danger. Above all, the incident showed well directed organisation, good planning and considerable originality. It came after many other important actions, and afforded added evidence to the British that members of their administration in Ireland, apart altogether from the civilian population, were collaborating with the Volunteers. In fact, British administration in Ireland at that moment, showed symptoms of a complete breakdown. General MacEoin's narrative indicates assistance on the part of members of the prison staff.

Answers by the chief secretary for Ireland in the House of Commons constantly repeated that 'outrages' in Ireland were the work of a small band of 'murderers'. Here in the attempted rescue of MacEoin from Mountjoy was proof positive of the existence of an armed force, widespread in its membership, well led, disciplined and daring.

The exploit therefore made its own substantial contribution to bring about the Truce, and the subsequent negotiations which resulted in the establishment of a sovereign Irish state.

ESCAPE FROM MOUNTJOY

by PATRICK RIGNEY

*Patrick Rigney was captured three days before the Truce, in 1921,
following an unsuccessful raid for military equipment and other goods
on a laundry close to Kilmainham jail. He now tells for the first time the
story of the daring escape he and his comrades made from the jail, where
he had been sentenced to spend fifteen years.*

HAVING PASSED UNSCATHED through the Rising of 1916, when, as a
boy of fifteen I carried dispatches for the Volunteers, it was just my
luck to be captured three days before the Truce with England in 1921.
Following the re-organisation of the Volunteers in 1917 I joined their
ranks, and, up to the time of my capture, I had seen seven months'
service with the active service unit of the Dublin brigade.

With the intensification of the warfare with England, the ASU
was formed of picked men from the 1st, 2nd, 3rd and 4th battalions.
The unit was organised in sections corresponding with the battalions,
and operated as such in their own battalion area and adjoining county
districts. I participated with No. 4 section.

For largescale operations necessitating the employment of stronger
forces the whole unit numbering fifty was employed.

The ASU gave full-time service to the IRA, and, as one of that unit
I participated in about forty attacks of various kinds in and around
Dublin, on Black and Tans, British military, Auxiliaries and members
of the enemy intelligence groups. In an ambush on a party of military
staff officers in Camden Street, I was badly wounded in the leg, but

escaped with the assistance of one of my comrades, so when I was taken prisoner later and sentenced to fifteen years penal servitude, I thought my luck was out permanently.

Having received instructions to remove some military goods from a laundry at Inchicore on 8 July 1921, I went with the late Paddy Kelly and the late Joseph O'Toole of the 4th battalion ASU, and after we had commandeered a Ford van at Dolphin's Barn, we set out for Inchicore. There we were to be met by an advance party, who prior to our arrival occupied the building, should have taken the manager and staff prisoners, and cut the telephone wires.

Having burst through a military patrol, which attempted to stop us at Inchicore bridge, we arrived without further incident at the laundry, where to our dismay we found that there were none of our men to meet us. The laundry was situated only one hundred and fifty yards from Kilmainham jail, where at all times there was half a company of British soldiers on duty. Immediately beyond the jail was the Royal Hospital, which was also strongly guarded. We realised that every second was of vital importance to the success of our mission, and as it was evident that our plans had miscarried in some way, there was no use delaying in the hope of being joined by our comrades. We decided that it would be best to drive down the road past the jail gate in our van, and reconnoitre the position.

As we cleared a bend of the road, which had limited our view to twenty yards, we were appalled to see, bearing right down on us, a party of military numbering about twenty-five, with an officer at their head. They were coming at the double, with rifles at the ready, and as soon as we were sighted, the officer shouted a command to halt. His command was the signal for O'Toole and myself to cock our guns, while we told Kelly who was driving, to accelerate and burst through, as we had done before. Kelly, who thought our decision unwise, pulled up, and undoubtedly saved our lives by his action.

His cooler judgement showed him that we had not one chance in a thousand of getting through that guard, which was later found to have been a picked company of sharp-shooters on duty at Kilmainham jail.

We subsequently learned that they had been warned by the manager of the laundry, who had eluded our comrades when they entered that place, and had succeeded in reaching Kilmainham jail and raising the alarm just before our arrival at the laundry. The raid we were on that day was one of those minor operations carried out at that period. Because rumours were current that negotiations for a truce had commenced, headquarters had issued instructions forbidding the carrying out of major operations until the outcome of the discussions was known. We were to maintain the fighting spirit and morale of the men, always an important consideration when on active service during a period of long or short inactivity. Small engagements such as that one at Inchicore laundry were sanctioned.

On surrendering, we were treated to some barrack-room abuse and to threats from the young and inexperienced officer in charge of the guard. As some of our captors had threatened to shoot us out of hand, it was a distinct relief to hear the officer order our removal to the comparative safety of Kilmainham jail! Once there we were abused and threatened again, and then locked up in the basement cells, where we were kept for three days without light or exercise. During that period the only break in the monotony was the frequent visits of the guards who came in to curse us, from time to time. Often during those three days I thought how strange it was that I should now be an inmate of a cell in Kilmainham, as I had been one of a party who waited outside the jail many nights to rescue Teeling, Donnelly and O'Malley.

On the third day after our arrest we were brought to Arbour Hill detention barracks, where, after some weeks, we were summoned before a court martial. We were charged with being in possession of fire-arms, fully loaded, cocked and ready for immediate use, of commandeering a motor van, and of attempting to seize military goods at the laundry. We refused to recognise the court, and we were returned to Arbour Hill after the trial. Some days later we were informed that each of us had been sentenced to fifteen years penal servitude!

When the officer who had brought me those 'joyful tidings' had left the cell, I began to think over the whole situation. Negotiations were then in progress with England. If an agreement was reached which would satisfy in full the aspirations of Irish republicans, we would be liberated. Otherwise it was certain that the IRA would renew hostilities, and in that event we were certain to be sent to one of the notorious penal settlements in England, where numbers of the IRA prisoners were then experiencing horrible persecution. Having reviewed the situation, I made up my mind to escape, and determined that I would begin making my plans at once with the greatest possible care, and that I would watch every opportunity to put them into action.

We were not left long in Arbour Hill, for as we were 'convicted criminals' in the eyes of the British, even the comparative comfort of a detention prison was then denied us, and we were no longer to be allowed parcels of food, papers, books, tobacco, etc.

In Mountjoy jail, which was our next 'home', we were placed in 'A' wing, where we found that our companions were mostly men who had been captured in circumstances similar to our own, and sentenced to long terms of imprisonment. There was no political treatment in 'A' wing, no visits, parcels, or any other amenities allowed, but it was possible to get smokes occasionally, conveyed through friendly sources, from our comrades in 'D' wing. This wing was receiving political treatment, and after some weeks, our demand for similar treatment in 'A' wing was conceded by the prison authorities. We learnt later that our friends outside had won this amelioration for us by their incessant agitation.

As soon as possible I sent word through a friendly warder, to my dear mother, RIP, asking her to get about half-a-dozen hacksaw blades, bake them into a cake, and attempt to pass it through to me on her next visit to Mountjoy. This she did without a hitch, on her next visit, and I immediately set to work on the first part of my plan, which was to saw away the bars and frame from my cell window. As soon as this first obstacle was removed, and I had made a space large enough to get through, I intended to improvise a rope of prison blankets and sheets, by which I would be able to drop from my cell on the third landing, onto the ground below on the outside of the wing. This, I reckoned, would be the easiest stage of my attempt, for enemies in the shape of warders were everywhere, and I would have to creep along from 'A' wing, through 'B' wing, and so to the end of 'D' wing, where, I had decided from observation, the effort of scaling the boundary wall could best be attempted. At that point, even if I were so fortunate as to avoid meeting other officials, I would certainly have to reckon with an armed Auxiliary. I meant to provide myself with some means of dealing with him. I planned to carry a large piece of the window bar, and on reaching the point at the end of 'D' wing where he was on guard, I would spring on him, and render him unconscious with a few blows of the bar. Fortunately for myself this rather desperate plan did not materialise. But I would like to put on record here the fate of seven of my brave comrades of that time, who made an unsuccessful attempt to get away by the means thus described. They had actually worked their way as far as the end of 'D' wing when they were discovered by the guard, and they had a very bad time as a result; for they were transferred to English prisons, where they remained until the general amnesty.

It was during the time I was busily engaged in the cutting of the window frame that I was approached one day by a non-political prisoner named Fitzgerald, with suggestions of ways of escaping from the prison. I had only known Fitzgerald as a wardsman, whom I saw occasionally working in the wing. His duties were to keep the landings clean, to remove waste matter, to collect dirty linen, and to renew it with clean, and do other like menial work around the prison. He informed me that in pursuit of these duties he had access to most parts of the prison, which had enabled him to acquire an intimate knowledge of regulations, regarding the warders' hours on and off, especially the ones attached to the basements. In addition he could tell me the exact movements of the military and Auxiliary guards, the hours they changed, and all sorts of minute details such as their characters and habits. This information he had compiled for himself, with a view to attempting an escape at the first opportunity.

Not knowing Fitzgerald well I was naturally suspicious of his interest in me on the first day we met, but on our next meeting I listened attentively to the arrangements he had made in the meantime.

We parted, agreeing that there was a sporting chance of a 'get-away' for four or five men.

Fitzgerald had, with the help of friends outside, and of a willing accomplice inside, succeeded in getting in a .45 revolver complete with a couple of rounds of ammunition. He had further arranged for a second revolver to arrive later. With these, and with some Auxiliary 'Glengarries' which he would make for us out of prison blankets, and the wool that binds them, the attempt was to be made.

From that time onwards I was constantly in touch with Fitzgerald, and in due course he informed me that the second revolver had arrived, but he had received no ammunition with it. However, we agreed to act with what we had. For some days following we discussed in detail the relative merits of different plans which he suggested for our escape.

At last our problem was solved for us, and fate decided our plan of action. About the third week of November a party of Auxiliaries from some part of the provinces arrived at Mountjoy, and on the assumption that these Auxiliaries would be complete strangers to the military guards, we decided that the long awaited moment had come. The next matter was the picking of men who were to participate in the risky adventure. After a good deal of consideration four men were selected for the expedition, viz., Fitzgerald, Davis, Troy and myself – although, as you will read later, seven actually escaped in the end.

On a typical evening in the last week of November, having decided to bid adieu to the hospitalities of 'Mountjoy Hotel', we assembled in the cell which I occupied on the third landing of 'A' wing, at four o'clock, five minutes before locking up time. Just before making the attempt I slipped across to the cell of the O/C prisoners, a dear friend of mine. When I told him what we were going to do he was not a bit optimistic of our chances, but, as we parted, he breathed a fervent prayer for our success.

On my return I found that three more of our comrades, O'Brien, Keating and Keegan had arrived, having heard what was on foot. No persuasion would put them off coming with us, although they had not a particle of disguise. We consented to their following us in the effort.

No doubt the additional danger which this introduced can be readily appreciated. In fact it nearly ruined our plans, on reaching the outer main gate.

The four of us who had originally been selected had each been provided with a trench coat and leggings. With these and the 'Glengarries' made by Fitzgerald we made ourselves look the part of Auxiliaries to perfection.

A few preliminaries had to be arranged before we left the cell. Each man had to be rehearsed in the position he was to occupy and the work he was to do, and then, as we had only a few rounds of ammunition, the empty chambers of the revolvers had to be filled with candle grease. The idea of this was to prevent the empty chambers being detected if we had to present the revolvers.

These matters settled, we moved off. On reaching 'B' wing basement we were just in time to capture the warder on duty, and relieve him of his keys. Using these we locked him into a cell, sternly ordering him not to make any attempt to attract attention. We had not reached the end of the basement when our prisoner began to kick the cell door, and make an unmerciful noise, which we were sure would be heard at any minute by the guards. This caused us some very anxious moments, and called forth a heroic effort on the part of Troy. Without any previous experience of forcing of doors, he dexterously unlocked the double locks on some seven doors, which enabled us to take our first steps towards liberty. These doors led by a passage to the reception steps outside 'A' wing, a short distance from the main gates. When we had reached the reception steps, we paused briefly before entering on the final stage of our escape.

The evening seemed specially sent by providence to shield us from watchful eyes, for there was a nice, seasonable fog just falling as Fitzgerald stepped from the cover of the reception steps, leading our party. With his trench coat, leggings and 'Glengarry' he looked the part of the Auxiliary to perfection, but undoubtedly the neatest part of his disguise was a lit cigar stuck in his teeth in the characteristic 'Auxie' fashion. There were three gates at the main entrance which had yet to be passed, and as we approached the inner one we sang out nonchalantly to the British Tommy on guard, 'Gate please'. He jumped to it immediately, and swung the gate open to allow us to pass, and the seven of us filed out with our heads in the air.

A further stroke of luck was still awaiting us. It was usual for an armed Auxiliary to be on duty at the inside of the main gate, and we anticipated an encounter with him to get the keys of the gate. To our great relief he was not there, but instead his box was surrounded by a number of warders going off duty, and included in them was the one that held the keys we wanted so badly on his belt.

Our request here for 'Gate please' was met by a peremptory reply that we would not get out there.

The significance of this retort struck us all simultaneously. It could mean only one thing, and that was that we were detected. The warders must have recognised the three men in civilian dress, and here, within sight of liberty, we saw our hopes fading away. As if moved by one machine, the seven of us jumped simultaneously at the warders, and the next thing of which I was aware was Troy triumphantly shooting the right key, first time, into the lock of the main gate, which responded immediately to his efforts.

As we burst through that gate like seven wild men, the guards opened fire from all directions. Our few rounds were discharged at them in defiance. We had not really a chance against them, as they had a covered position, and plenty of ammunition. Our only hope was to make a dash down the straight drive to the North Circular Road – about one hundred and fifty yards without any shelter, during which we offered a splendid target to the enemy in Mountjoy. The miracle was that none of us was hit. I dragged along after the others, my bad leg preventing me from keeping the pace, and they soon outstripped me. When at last, panting and exhausted I reached the Circular Road, I was alone. My position was really desperate, for I knew that our pursuers would be on top of me any moment. Then I saw a motor-cyclist calmly filling his lamp on the Circular Road seemingly oblivious to the sensational happenings in the neighbourhood. Although the man was a complete stranger, I quickly made up my mind that I would take the risk of asking his help. I was in the position where I had to gamble my chance of liberty, and limping up to that unknown man, I explained my situation briefly and humbly. He listened quietly to my story, never uttered a word, but jumped onto his bicycle, motioned me on to the back, and swept me across the city to within a few yards of my home. And so, thanks to the loyalty and courage of my unknown friend, I was being welcomed by an overjoyed mother, brothers and sisters, whilst the British were hunting all over the city for my comrades and myself. My stay was short. The indescribable feeling of being free urged me to find safety by going to stay with old friends in County Dublin.

Some weeks later, when I thought it safe to venture abroad, I was walking through a lonely part of the city when I came suddenly face to face with one of the Auxiliaries who had been guarding me in Mountjoy. Before I had time to think of escape he had walked up to me, and thrusting out his hand he said, 'Hello Paddy, that was a pretty cool little stunt you fellows pulled off the other day', and having offered his profuse congratulations on our performance, he turned and walked away.

WITH THE SIXTH BATTALION

(SOUTH COUNTY DUBLIN)

by MICHAEL CHADWICK

In the spring of 1917 instructions were received from Commandant Joe O'Connor, O/C 3rd battalion, Dublin brigade, that Andy Mc-Donnell and myself report to Captain Liam Tanham for the purpose of re-organising the Volunteers in South County Dublin. There were units in Dún Laoghaire, Bray, Ticknock, Dundrum and Blackrock. The response was immediate and very soon five companies were formed. Steady training and intensive organisation followed, and in May 1920, the first actions against the British took place.

The RIC barracks at Ballybrack, Stepaside and Kill-o-the-Grange were burned. Two of our officers, Lieutenant Tom Dunne and Adjutant Paddy Meaney, lost their lives at Ballybrack. Armed engagements took place at Sandyford, Bray, Dundrum, Naval Base, Dún Laoghaire; Temple Hill, Blackrock; Merrion and Cabinteely. All these provided useful experience for the men, and their spirit was excellent.

In November 1920, GHQ decided to form the 6th battalion of the Dublin brigade, for South County Dublin. The following were elected to the battalion staff: commandant, Andy McDonnell; vice-commandant, Michael Chadwick; adjutant, Brian MacNeill; quarter-master, Niall MacNeill; transport officer, Tom Cardiff; medical officer, Dr J.J. Loftus; captains, Jack Foley, O/C Deans Grange; Ned O'Brien, O/C Barnaculla; Seán Curley, O/C Dundrum; Larry O'Brien, O/C Bray; and Billy Walsh, O/C Dún Laoghaire.

Arms were difficult to obtain, so trips to Manchester and London were organised. A friend in Whitechapel, London, was found and he arranged to provide them. Plans were prepared for the transport of the arms, and Miss Annie O'Gorman, now married and living in Dublin was placed in charge of the London end of the operation. To the end she carried out her difficult task faithfully and without a hitch.

The area became a hive of activity on both sides, and by 1921 we were a well-organised battalion, playing its part. We had come through a very difficult period in the winter of 1920, and now we had no doubt about the result. Victory was to be ours.

Early in 1921, Andy McDonnell was wounded in an affray near Kilternan. He was taken to a first-aid centre in Peter Little's house at Ticknock, and later to Miss Lily O'Donnell's private nursing home, Eccles Street, Dublin. He later rejoined his battalion. In a raid on Dún Laoghaire railway station members of the local company under Lieutenant George Kelly succeeded in getting away with a large quantity of ammunition consigned to the RIC barracks at Rathdrum, County Wicklow. As the IRA were leaving the station they were fired on by Constable Healy, DMP. He put a bullet through the roof of the car in which the ammunition was being taken away. The fire was returned and he was badly wounded. Returning from escorting a British officer to the mail boat, a party of the Ulster division of the Auxiliaries was ambushed with bombs and rifle fire at the Marine Road, Dún Laoghaire, by Volunteers under Lieutenant Eugene Davis. Several of the enemy were killed. The Royal Marine Hotel, Dún Laoghaire, where a number of the Auxiliaries lived, was the scene of a desperate encounter. A party of Volunteers under Lieutenant James McIntosh went to the hotel to shoot some Auxiliary officers who had arrived there. Inside the main door and up the main stairs a fierce revolver battle took place. Lieutenant McIntosh was badly wounded and later died on the Marine Road. A number of the Auxiliaries were killed.

Steadily the battalion was built for special services. A cyclist company, transport, engineer, signaller and first-aid units were trained.

Officer classes were held weekly. The naval base at Dún Laoghaire was attacked several times with Billy Walsh, George Kelly and Eugene Davis in command. Dundrum company had a sharp encounter and narrow escape when they attacked the local RIC barracks. It was reported after the attack that our men had been fired upon from the rear, and investigations revealed the identity of the man who was responsible for this. The evidence was conclusive and he was executed on the Golf Links Road, Dundrum, the following day. On the day that he was executed several of the officers of the battalion were attending a meeting in the Dublin Corporation Sanitary Department, Chatham Row, when the premises were surrounded by Black and Tans. I was at the time an official in that department, and when the officer in charge of the 'Tans' asked me what all the men were doing there, I told him that they were students attending lectures for their DPH. The officer accepted my explanation and actually escorted our men through the cordon. It was a close shave. The 'Tans' withdrew without finding anything.

After an armoured car had been attacked at Ruby Lodge, Blackrock, the Blackrock company waited all night in the town to prevent burnings such as followed similar attacks in other parts of the county. The 'Tans' did not turn up; they would have got a hot reception if they had.

Cabinteely barracks was sniped time and again. Plans were made for a frontal attack on it, but orders were received from Dublin that the attack was not to take place. A unit of the Cheshire Regiment, then in camp at Powerscourt, was disarmed at Dún Laoghaire. A visit was paid to Enniskerry to secure information regarding the disposition, arms, etc., of the regiment. All the necessary information was obtained from a soldier for a cigarette. One Sunday morning an officers' class had been arranged for Barnaculla, but on our arrival at Sandyford we were informed that the 'Tans' had surrounded the place. This was an opportunity to pay back the shooting of Andy McDonnell, and we immediately proceeded to take advantage of it. Roads leading to the area were blocked and, orders were issued to bring all arms in the battalion to the scene at once. Before we could engage them, however, the 'Tans' withdrew by the road leading to Rathfarnham, and so we missed our chance. One enemy officer, who was O/C of the Magazine Fort in Phoenix Park, was shot resisting capture.

Two spies were executed in the battalion area.

THE FIGHT IN THE BRAY AREA

by JAMES MacSWEENEY

FINDING SUPPORT FOR any Irish-Ireland movement in Bray and district was always very difficult. The population was looked upon as law-abiding and the RIC had very little to do. In such circumstances it was very hard to build up a resistance organisation against British rule. The IRA had few friends and the handful that joined together to fight British domination deserve as much credit as those who did far more in other areas where they had the goodwill of the people. No one of any prominence was connected with either the IRA or the local O'Rahilly Sinn Féin cumann, and anything that would lead to an upset in the normal way in which the townspeople lived was looked upon with great disfavour. The town was, and still is, a haven of rest for retired RIC men and ex-British army and navy officers. During the Black and Tan war some of these gentlemen were suspected of helping the local RIC garrison with information about the IRA. No definite proof could be obtained that they were actual spies or they would have paid with their lives. Members of the local IRA lacked neither courage nor determination and it was not their fault that they did not achieve far greater things than they did. Handicapped by small numbers it was impossible for them to carry out anything in the nature of a major engagement.

Following a meeting in the Rotunda Gardens, Dublin, in November 1913, to organise the Irish Volunteers, where addresses were delivered by leaders, notably P.H. Pearse, the first company of this organisation was formed in Bray. It began with ten members amidst a hostile populace and carried on until July 1914, when as a result of the gun-running at Howth – 26 July – new members, most of them associated with the AOH flocked into it. The company held together until 1 November 1914, when the general split took place. Out of a membership of six or seven hundred only a few remained loyal to the original Volunteer pledge. On the day the guns were landed at Howth a collection for arms at Bray church gates resulted in close on £30. This money was sent by Joseph Kenny, a member of the IRB, to The O'Rahilly, who sent out ten of the Howth rifles to the company.

Following disagreement amongst the local committee of the Volunteers Kenny feared the rifles would be captured by the RIC and he brought nine of them back to Dublin and handed them to Liam Mellows. The tenth he retained for himself. In 1920 he handed it over to Laurence O'Brien the then O/C of the local IRA company. Prior to the gun-running at Kilcool on Saturday, 1 August 1914, Kenny, at the request of Seán MacDiarmada, made a rough sketch of the road from Kilcool to Dublin. In September 1914, Lord Powerscourt addressed the Bray Volunteers and told them he had interviews with Lord Kitchener and John E. Redmond, regarding the recruitment of more Volunteers for the British army. An appeal by him for more recruits was objected to by Joseph Kenny and Lord Powerscourt left the parade ground. Kenny at that time was on the staff of the Congested Districts Board with twenty-one years' service. When he entered his office on the following Monday morning he was informed that he had been reported for interfering with recruiting for the British army.

On Easter Sunday 1916, Arthur Griffith called to Kenny's home in Bray at 11 a.m. with a message from Eoin MacNeill cancelling movement of Volunteers that day. Griffith directed him to hand the message to the secretary of the local Volunteers who at that time was James McCarthy, later employed in the engineering department, at Westland Row station. Kenny was also instructed to show the message to P.J. Farrell, the local IRB centre. A second message of cancellation was received by Kenny at 4 p.m. on the same day from Diarmuid Lynch and was delivered by him to Seán Ó Broin, later a postal inspector (telephones). Shortly after this Kenny was arrested. As a result of the confusion following cancellation of orders the Bray company took no part in the Rising other than cutting telephone communications around the town. However, two of the members took part in the fight. 'Steenie' Mulvey made his way into Dublin on the second day and succeeded in getting through to the post office where he fought until the surrender. The other, Tom Sutton, who later was prominent in the Black and Tan war, was at that time engine driver on the Dublin–Wexford train. When he arrived at Harcourt Street station on the Easter Monday night he was unable to get in touch with the Volunteers owing to the number of British military that were in the vicinity. It had been his practice to carry a miniature rifle on the engine and with this he did some sniping at British soldiers from the canal bridge and between Harcourt Street and Cullenswood bridge near Ranelagh on each night his train arrived.

About the middle of the week a Volunteer from Rathmines area gave him a letter for the O/C of the Volunteers in Enniscorthy. This he delivered to Phelim Murphy for transmission to the O/C. After it was delivered Enniscorthy was taken over by the Volunteers. At the beginning of the week – he thinks it was Tuesday – at 7 p.m. Sutton saw from the railway bridge over Adelaide Road, Harcourt Street, British soldiers with three prisoners handcuffed moving towards the tobacconist shop at 'Kelly's' Corner. He saw the officer in charge point to Kelly's shop and then a soldier throwing a bomb in through the window. After the explosion he fired on the soldier. The soldier staggered towards the shop and fell on the footpath. Sutton fired again and the officer and his men took cover behind their prisoners and forced them to move back behind the corner on the Portobello side of the street. From what was learned afterwards the officer was Capt. J.C. Bowen-Colthurst, Royal Irish Rifles, and his prisoners were F. Sheehy-Skeffington, Thomas Dickson and Patrick MacIntyre. Bowen-Colthurst, later tried for the murder of these men, was found guilty but insane.

Re-organisation of the Volunteers in the Bray and Shankill areas commenced early in 1917. The company was then 'C' of the 3rd battalion, Dublin brigade, and was frequently visited by the battalion O/C, Commandant Joe O'Connor, Dublin. The company O/C was Michael McGarry, Shankill. Weekly parades were held in Mitten's field, Shankill, the drill instructor being 'Steenie' Mulvey, Bray. The members were also trained in the use of the few arms the company possessed – a miniature rifle and a few revolvers of small calibre – as well as in the making of improvised hand-grenades. Weekly parades continued until the end of 1917 while at the same time members did their best to buy additional arms. Coming into 1918 night manoeuvres were held around Puck's Castle, Ballycorus. By this time a few hundred rounds of miniature rifle ammunition had been procured and target practice was carried out in Ballycorus quarry.

In the 1918 general election the company took an active part in helping the local Sinn Féin cumann to secure the return of Seán Etchingham for East Wicklow while the Shankill Volunteers worked in the interest of Gavan Duffy who was a candidate for South Dublin.

A meeting to be addressed by Rev. Michael O'Flanagan at the Town Hall, Bray was proclaimed. When the company attempted to march up the Main Street they were blocked by a strong force of RIC men. Batons were drawn and an ugly situation averted by the intervention of Fr O'Flanagan, who advised the Volunteers not to attempt a breakthrough.

Another parade was held on Lady's Day, 15 August 1918, to the Town Hall, where the 1916 Proclamation was read by the chairman of the Sinn Féin cumann, Paddy Murphy. A well-known Gael from boyhood this local coach-builder was one of the most active Irish-Irelanders in the county. For reading this Proclamation he was arrested and sent to jail. Associated with him in the cumann were: Joseph Lynch, secretary; Paddy Martin, Paddy Waldron, James Hoey, Charlie O'Brien, (Roundwood), Pat Sutton, Stannie McConnery, James Tier and Seamus Rochfort, all of whom at one period or another suffered imprisonment; Joe Sheridan, Bill Earls, Barney Traynor, Nicholas Mulvey, Paddy Hall, James MacSweeney, Tom Bolger, Andy Kavanagh, Frank Leggett, Tom

Martin, Joe Waldron, Mrs Leggett (Nan Nash), Miss Carroll, who worked for a Protestant minister, the Misses Robinson, Misses Griffin (Enniskerry), Rebecca Toole (Kilmacanogue).

Following a general order from HQ the company raided the income tax inspector's house on the Meath Road, Bray, where all his books were seized and taken to Loughlinstown Hospital. This operation was carried out by the O/C, Michael McGarry, Tom Kavanagh, Josie Faulkner, Jimmie McGarry, Dan O'Rourke, all of Shankill; Tom Sutton, 'Steenie' Mulvey and Laurence O'Brien, a 1916 man who had recently come to live in Bray.

The company continued to parade weekly and in the spring of 1920 at a parade held in the Shankill Volunteer Hall members took the oath of allegiance administered by the brigade O/C, Dick McKee, who was accompanied by Commandant O'Connor. At this parade the company O/C resigned in favour of Laurence O'Brien. Michael McGarry was then elected 1st lieutenant; Thomas Mooney, a pawnbroker's assistant in Bray, 2nd lieut; Jim Brien, Bray, adjutant; Jim Toole, Bray, quartermaster; and Mick Brien, Abbeyview, intelligence officer.

On 10 December 1920, a raid was made on the Volunteer Hall, Shankill, by a party of military from Enniskerry under Major Shore. A meeting of the company officers had just concluded. Some members of the company were playing cards when the military arrived. With hands up the occupants were placed against the wall and searched. When the search was over and before they were told to take their hands down a shot was fired from an adjoining room by one of the soldiers and Section Leader Willie Ownes, Loughlinstown, fell dead with a bullet through the head. He had worked in New Ross and was 'on the run' from there where he had been active in the IRA. Another member of the company, Dan O'Rourke, Shankill, was held up outside the premises, a revolver was found on him and he was arrested. Another member of the company from Shankill, James Murphy, was also arrested at the same time.

As the result of a general raid for arms in the area another few revolvers, rifles and shotguns were added to the company's collection.

A list of those licensed to have firearms was hanging in the Bray post office. The names were copied but in the majority of cases when the houses were raided it was found that the arms had been handed over previously to the RIC for safety.

In a raid on the Bray Town Hall for the purpose of disrupting local administration all the council books were seized by Pat Brien and 'Steenie' Mulvey. They were taken to Shankill and handed over to P.J. Farrell who was then assistant clerk, Rathdown Board of Guardians. In order to prevent the British authorities from taking the rates collected by Dublin County Council Rate Collector Murray, Shankill Castle, a raid was made and he handed over a cheque for over £3,000. This was taken by Jim Brien to the secretary of the county council for signature. It was then cashed and the money handed back to the secretary. On this raid were Lieut Pat Brien (McGarry had been arrested); Josie Faulkner, Tom Kavanagh, 'Steenie' Mulvey, Tod Murphy (Shankill); and Jimmie Earls (Bray).

About this time the company was transferred into the new 6th battalion of the Dublin brigade under the command of Commandant Andy McDonnell, the vice-commandant being Mick Chadwick.

The arms taken in the general raid were 'dumped' at Shanganagh in a large box made by Pat Brien. A second 'dump' was then made ready in a double tunnel on the railway line around Bray Head. To it were brought a number of shotguns, shotgun cartridges and revolvers handed over by the Wicklow company at Newcastle. The arms were taken by Volunteers under Pat Brien on a railway bogey from Newcastle to the 'dump'. To allow the bogey to go through, the line was prepared by Signalman Pat Toole, a member of the IRA, who was on duty in Newcastle signal cabin. Two days later military from Kilpeddar questioned Toole about the bogey passing through. He denied knowledge of it and after threatening to shoot him, the soldiers beat him up.

Some nights after, the arms and ammunition were transferred from the double tunnel to an empty cottage at Shanganagh by Tom Sutton, Seamus MacSweeney and Tom Brien. The same men refilled the cartridges with buckshot in preparation for ambushes.

A raid on Bray Urban Council yard at the Fairgreen resulted in the acquisition of cross-cut saws, shovels and picks. These were taken to Shankill and later used for digging trenches and blocking roads in the area. On the raid were: Lieut Pat Brien, Quartermaster Tom Sutton, Section Commander Jack Sterling, Peter ('Lukey') Leggett, Seamus MacSweeney and Gerry Toole (Bray) and Josie Faulkner, Tom Kavanagh, Jimmie McGarry, Jack Sheehan, Tod Murphy, Andy O'Rourke, Bob Walsh and Mick Byrne (Shankill).

The company's first issue of Mills bombs was handed over at Ballsbridge by battalion officers. For this operation the O/C, Larry O'Brien, picked Tom Sutton, Jack Sterling, Seamus MacSweeney, and Jimmie Earls (Bray), and Josie Faulkner and Tod Murphy (Shankill). Armed with revolvers they were told they would be met by some of the battalion officers at the fire-escape that was at that time where Pembroke Road joins Morehampton Road, and that if they were afterwards held up by military or Black and Tans they were to fight it out.

When they arrived at the spot contact was made shortly afterwards as a result of the password, 'Are you from No. 3?' They were then taken to some stables at the rear of Pembroke Road and there handed over four large boxes containing bombs and ammunition. These in turn were carried to Ranelagh railway station and taken on the train to Shankill. On the way to the station a few army lorries with soldiers and Black and Tans passed but nothing happened. On arrival at Shankill the boxes were carried across the fields to Loughlinstown Hospital where they were handed over to Volunteer George Ownes (brother of Willie Ownes) for safe keeping.

The company was now ready for an all-out offensive on the enemy. First spot picked for an ambush was Claffey's Grove, Crinkin, on the main Dublin Road. It was arranged that the Shankill section and the Bray section take about a week at this place. For the first week the former section took up position under Section Leader Josie Faulkner. No lorries passed while they were there. In the second week the Bray section went into positions under Lieut Pat Brien. On the Thursday night about nine o'clock a military lorry going in the direction of Bray came along at a fast speed. At about thirty yards distance 'Steenie' Mulvey and Mick Brien (Abbeyview) who were nearest it opened fire. The lorry zig-zagged and put on speed while the occupants returned the fire. As it passed in front of the main body a bomb thrown by Seamus MacSweeney exploded immediately behind it and lit up the roadway. The Volunteers kept up a steady fire with revolvers and shotguns while bullets from the lorry cut into the trees above their heads. As the lorry passed out of the ambush Tom Sutton jumped over the wall and from a kneeling position on the road fired after it with a service rifle as it raced towards Bray.

In this engagement three of the enemy were wounded. The Volunteers crossed the fields to the moat in Lord Plunkett's demesne where another 'dump' for arms had been made. As well as those mentioned others taking part were Jack Sterling, Tom Brien, 'Lukey' Leggett, Bert Leggett, Jim Toole, Bert Lurring, Billy Lacey and Mick Scariff.

Some time after this a raid was made on the telephone man's hut at Bray railway station. Telephone apparatus, tools and a bicycle were taken. The bicycle was used by members of the company until after the Truce, while the pliers were used for wire-cutting in the area. On the raid were Tom Sutton, Jack Sterling, Seamus MacSweeney and Jim Toole.

In a raid made on Shankill village about thirty men were taken out. With shovels and picks on their backs they were marched to Alley's River Road and to Ballymahon where they were made trench the roads.

Some Enniskerry men, including Mick Dunne, Stephen Barry, Tom Fox, Christy Woodcock and Nick Hempenstall, who had joined the company, reported that a military lorry with four or five soldiers travelled on Sunday mornings about twelve o'clock from Bray to Enniskerry military camp, and it was decided to ambush it on the Enniskerry side of the entrance to the Dargle demesne above the Big Tree. For this operation a long wire hawser belonging to the railway company was taken from around Bray Head. After carrying it for about a mile to the Vevay, Bray, it was agreed that owing to its weight it could not be carried the remaining two miles to the place of ambush. It was decided to take a horse and cab belonging to a carman named Barnwell. The hawser was placed in the cab and taken to its destination. The cab was taken back to its owner who was presented with 10/- for the trouble caused. This operation was carried out by Tom Sutton, Jack Sterling, Seamus MacSweeney, Jack Wheeler and Mick Neary (killed in Dalkey in the civil strife) who drove the cab.

On the following Sunday morning the O/C ordered a parade for the Glen, Ballymahon, where some rifles, revolvers and bombs had been transferred to another 'dump'. After collecting their arms the Volunteers marched to the Enniskerry Road two miles away. In doing so they had to wade knee-deep across the Dargle river. It had been decided to stretch the hawser across the road to block the lorry's progress, but this plan was changed and instead it was decided to rush from a kind of laneway onto the road and attack the lorry as it came along. After waiting for about two hours it was agreed that the lorry must have already gone to Enniskerry and the men marched back to the 'dump'. The following Sunday morning the same position was taken up, but it was ascertained sometime later that the lorry had taken another route along a by-road about one hundred yards below the ambush position and around a bend in the road. On the third Sunday the same position was again taken up but the enemy's luck still held. They had passed sometime previously. With the O/C on this operation were Lieut Pat Brien, Tom Sutton, Jack Sterling, Seamus MacSweeney, Mick Neary, Gerry Toole and Tom Brien (Bray); and Mick Dunne, Stephen Barry and Tom Fox (Enniskerry).

A report was received that a military dispatch rider occasionally travelled in the evening time to Enniskerry via Ballymahon. Several evenings were spent waiting for him but he did not pass. On this operation were Tom Sutton, Jack Sterling, Seamus MacSweeney, Tom Brien and Stephen Barry.

The RIC garrison in Bray at this time numbered about twenty and in addition there was about the same number of Black and Tans. As well as occupying the barracks, the courthouse close by was also occupied.

On a height overlooking the lower portion of the town these buildings were turned into a regular fortress. In a big attack planned to take place on them a number of men from other companies of the battalion were to take part. This operation was to take place on a Saturday night but was called off at the last moment by order of the battalion officers. Outside there was sniping at the barrack and courthouse to keep the occupants in a state of nerves and to get them to waste their ammunition in return fire; little else could be done. Sniping was carried out periodically from the golf links by Josie Faulkner, Jimmie McGarry, Jack Sheehan and Tom Kavanagh from Shankill and from the Dargle Road by Pat Brien, Tom Sutton, Jack Sterling, 'Lukey' Leggett and Tom Brien. Generally after the first few shots were fired Verey lights went up from the barracks and troops came rushing in from Enniskerry and Kilpeddar to 'relieve' the RIC men.

It was amusing to read newspaper reports of the official version after one of these operations which hardly cost the IRA twenty rounds. Reports stated that the barracks and courthouse had been surrounded by a large number of attackers and a most determined effort made to capture them. Most of the IRA, it was stated, were concealed behind tombstones in the grounds of St Paul's Protestant church on the opposite side of the road from where they kept up a heavy machine-gun fire. No member of the IRA ever fired from that position. On other occasions a few revolver shots fired at the courthouse from a side street off the main street were sufficient to keep the RIC firing for hours at nothing.

On Easter Monday 1921, a raid was carried out in the daytime on Shankill post office for the purpose of dismantling the telephone system. The apparatus was taken to Mitten's field where it was hidden. On the raid were Pat Brien, Tom Sutton, Seamus MacSweeney, Jack Sterling and Mick Neary (Bray), and Josie Faulkner, Tom Kavanagh, Jack Sheehan, Andy O'Rourke and Bob Walsh (Shankill).

In a raid on Bray railway parcel office a parcel of Gallagher's tobacco, at the time under boycott ban, was seized by Josie Faulkner and Tod Murphy.

An armed patrol of six RIC men were in the habit of patrolling the streets. Sometimes they went as far as Old Conna Corner and on other occasions to the other extreme of the town, Putland Road corner. For a week Volunteers waited in ambush inside the gates of the now electric bulb factory but the patrol did not show up. The second week was spent waiting for them at Putland Road but again they did not pass that way. On this operation were the O/C Lieut Pat Brien, Tom Sutton, Jack Sterling, Seamus MacSweeney, Tom Brien and Gerry Toole.

It was noticed that on occasions an armoured car and three loads of 'Auxies' came from Dublin to Bray and patrolled up as far as the town hall before going back. The O/C picked ten men to ambush this patrol from behind a wall on the Dublin side of Crinkin church. For this operation each man was armed with two bombs and a revolver. Every night for more than a week they took up their positions but no lorries passed. With the O/C were Lieut Pat Brien, Tom Sutton, Jack Sterling, Seamus MacSweeney, Gerry Toole, Tom Brien, 'Lukey' Leggett, Billy Lacey, Bert Lurring and Mick Neary.

Two Black and Tans were seen on occasions patrolling the old railway line at the North Strand. The O/C and Seamus MacSweeney went to shoot them. It was arranged that 'Lukey' Leggett would bring two Webleys. While waiting the O/C and MacSweeney saw Leggett coming towards them followed at about fifty yards behind by the two Black and Tans. Leggett reported that in crossing the Golf links he had been observed by other RIC men and the O/C decided to call off the operation. The three IRA men got into a field, walked to Shanganagh Junction, 'dumped' the guns and went home by the main road to Bray.

In or about the beginning of April 1921, two British military ambulances arrived on wagons at Bray railway goods yard on their way down the country. To get into this yard to burn them it was necessary to climb a high iron gate. Two tins of petrol were brought for the operation, but fearing they would not be sufficient the man in charge of the railway oil store was held up and a large drum of oil taken. The petrol and oil were poured over the two vehicles and inside a few minutes they were a mass of flames. Present on the operation were Tom Sutton, Seamus MacSweeney, 'Lukey' Leggett and Peter Ledwidge.

On the night of 18 April 1921, at about eleven o'clock, Jack Sterling and —— McCarthy, then a pawnbroker's assistant in Bray, walked along under the wall of the courthouse and threw two bombs in through the door. They then ran across the road, down the Mill Lane, and along by the wall of the Dargle river. As they were making their way along the river they were observed by one of the Black and Tans on his way home. He opened fire across the river. Bullets struck the wall above their heads, but they escaped unhurt. Explosion of the bombs was the signal for fire to be opened on the courthouse and barracks with service rifles from the golf links by the O/C, Lieut Pat Brien and Tom Sutton. The garrison returned the fire with rifles and machine-guns. A hail of lead swept up the main street, breaking shop windows on either side. No fire had been directed at the RIC from that direction. A heavy fire was also maintained in the direction of the golf links and out across Little Bray. Verey lights went up and it was almost two hours before the garrison ceased fire. After the operation the O/C and Lieut Brien handed their rifles over to Tom Sutton, 'Lukey' Leggett and Tom Brien, all of whom lived on the Dargle Road, for safe keeping, and then made their way to Duncairn Avenue where they lived. They were arrested later that night in their homes by a large party of RIC men. Also arrested on that occasion were John Hoey, Pat Hoey, Owen Brien (brother of Pat), Jack Martin, Paddy Martin, 'Steenie' Mulvey and Joe Kenny. Owen Brien and Pat Hoey were released some hours later. The others were taken to Arbour Hill.

The following evening Battalion Adjutant Brian MacNeill (later shot on Benbulben mountain, Sligo, in the civil strife) visited the town. He met Tom Sutton, Jack Sterling, Seamus MacSweeney and Tom Brien in the People's Park, Little Bray. He appointed Tom Sutton, O/C of the company and Jack Sterling, 1st lieut.

In order to strengthen the RIC garrison an army post was established in the town. The Royal Hotel was taken over and upwards of one hundred troops went into occupation.

A conversation overheard by Tom Sutton in the railway sheds led to a raid on a house in Dargan Street, Little Bray, to shoot a man believed to be a British intelligence officer, who was staying with his mother-in-law. Sutton took Jack Sterling into the house and sent 'Lukey' Leggett and Tom Brien to the rear. Sutton was told that the man had left that morning on the mail boat for England. Sutton was arrested the following day by RIC men and taken to Arbour Hill. He was there paraded for identification and identified by one of the women of the house. He was later sent to the Curragh.

The new O/C of the company was Rory McDermott from the Blackrock company. The first evening he arrived he ordered that the head of the RIC, District Inspector Lowndes, be shot. Volunteers took up positions in doorways near the barracks on different nights but they never had the chance of carrying out the order.

The former O/C, Larry O'Brien, was released about a month after his arrest and although 'on the run' again took over the company.

The next sniping operation at the barracks and courthouse had sad consequences for two Shankill men. After firing a couple of rounds from the golf links at nine o'clock one morning, Josie Faulkner and Jack Sheehan made their way back across the fields to Shankill. In doing so they were seen by an ex-member of the RIC. Some hours later they were standing at Shankill bridge with some other men when a lorry load of RIC and Black and Tans from Bray drove up and held up the party. They were all searched. Particular attention was paid to Faulkner and Sheehan and they were placed in the lorry and taken to Bray. Later that day Faulkner's mother went to see him. On the way out she was asked if she would take home her son's overcoat. This was a trap. The coat had been found along the route taken by Faulkner and Sheehan. Faulkner had denied it was his. The mother's recognition was the signal for an onslaught on the two men in the cell. Four local police – the head constable, a sergeant and two constables – beat Faulkner and Sheehan about the heads with batons and kicked them in the legs until they fell to the ground. As they lay there they again received savage kicks in the head and stomach. The two men were later taken to Arbour Hill, court-martialled and sentenced to ten years. Faulkner, an ex-British soldier of the 1914–18 war lost his pension as a result of his conviction. In a search of the fields from the Golf links to Shankill for the rifles used by Faulkner and Sheehan, the RIC found an engine-driver's food basket containing gelignite hidden under one of the railway bridges near Woodbrook. This had been brought from Arklow by Tom Sutton for the Kill-o-the-Grange company and concealed temporarily.

A cheque for £39 payable by a resident of Dorneycourt, Shankill, to the British authorities for road tax on his car was found in a raid on the mails at Dundrum by the local company. This was sent back to the Bray company for the purpose of getting the drawer to make it payable to the republican government. When told what he had to do, he and his three sons adopted a threatening attitude and it was only when a revolver was produced and they were held up that a new cheque was made out. They were warned that if any attempt was made to stop the cheque or to have its bearer arrested when getting it cashed they would be held responsible. The cheque was sent to battalion HQ, then to the corporation offices in Chatham Row, Dublin, where the vice-commandant worked. On this raid were Seamus MacSweeney, Tom Brien and Tod Murphy.

A report was received that two or three Auxiliary officers were stopping at the Powerscourt Arms Hotel, Enniskerry. Stephen Barry and Tom Fox, armed with revolvers, were sent to shoot them. They crept up to a lit window where the 'Auxies' were but could not see in as the blind was almost down to the bottom of the window. They heard the 'Auxies' talking inside and opened fire in that direction. They then had to run about fifty yards for cover and as they did so bullets from the 'Auxies' guns came flying after them.

Shortly before the Truce it was planned to mine a military lorry that passed along the Enniskerry road during curfew. This operation was to be carried out by Battalion Engineer Cummins, the O/C Larry O'Brien, and some of the Enniskerry men. Another party of Volunteers were directed to let down a tree across the road at Valombrossa, near the Dargle bridge, after the lorry had passed in order to delay assistance coming from Bray after the lorry had been blown up. This party was also to attack the relief party when it arrived at the road block. Having cut the tree until it was almost ready to fall they waited for the lorry. When it passed the cutting was finished and the tree fell across the road. The sound of the explosion was awaited but nothing happened. It was later learned that the lorry instead of taking the main Enniskerry road had continued on straight up by Kilbride church on the main road to Wicklow. At the felling of the tree were Peter Ledwidge, Jack Sterling, Seamus MacSweeney, 'Lukey' Leggett, Mick Neary, Tom Brien, Gerry Toole and Pierce Lawlor.

During the greater part of the time the few Volunteers that kept the flag flying in a hostile town were 'on the run'. Favourite sleeping quarters for those on operations on the north side of the town were first-class carriages at the railway siding at the harbour. The O/C and others often slept in 31 Duncairn Avenue, Bray, the house of William Redmond, journalist, who was not suspected by the authorities of being a supporter of the movement. The battalion adjutant, Brian MacNeill, also stopped in this house on occasions.

Members of the company who were arrested in the early stages or who served sentences at different periods were 1st Lieut Michael McGarry, Adjutant Jim Brien, 1st Lieut Pat Brien (brother); Jack Kavanagh, Dan O'Rourke, Pat Sutton, John Hyland, Owen Gallagher, James Tier, 'Lukey' Leggett, 'Steenie' Mulvey, Tom Sutton, Jack Sterling, Jim Toole, Joe Lynch, Paddy Murphy, Paddy Martin, Paddy Waldron, Jack Sheehan, Josie Faulkner, James Murphy, Charlie O'Brien (Roundwood); John Richmond (Ballycorus); Cormac Burke, John Hoey and James Hoey.

NOTE: In compiling the foregoing I had the assistance of Joe Kenny, Pat Brien, Tom Sutton, Josie Faulkner and Dan O'Rourke. They read it over together and agree as to its accuracy. – S. MacS.

IN BRITISH JAILS

by ERNIE O'MALLEY

As soon as the men who fought in Easter Week had surrendered, the Royal Irish Constabulary began to make use of the information which for years they had secreted, concerning an open, armed movement. By that time Richmond barracks, Kilmainham and Arbour Hill held men who had fought, but Richmond barracks was the clearing centre. The detective division of the Dublin Metropolitan Police, prowled around amongst the prisoners, sniffing out leaders. These men were court-martialled when identified and about seventy of them were sentenced to death. That witch-hunt of the 'G' or detective division left many a bitter memory, when fourteen of these men were executed.

Over 3,000 prisoners passed through Richmond barracks, where their presumed rebel thumbs were placed on record. Some captives were released, but to English and Scottish jails went close on 2,000 men. By that round-up the British brought together men who had known each other by name and by rumour. In Richmond, Volunteers from the provinces met the men who had held their capital against British troops. Countrymen who had not fought could now share stories of what could be expanded to an epic by the sympathetic imagination of listeners. As well, they could gather strength and assurance from some of the men they met, and whom they were to meet again in Knutsford, Stafford, Wakefield and Wandsworth.

Resistance to British authority and a demand for prisoner-of-war treatment soon broke the monotony of jail life. In Dartmoor, prisoners sentenced for life and for lesser periods, were a small body who had to serve a rigorous imprisonment, but they too refused to put up with the deadly silence. Soon English penal prisons echoed with Irish shouts and songs.

A camp in Wales, Frongoch, was picked for prisoners who had not been sentenced. In Frongoch, over 1,700 men were interned in huts which had formerly been occupied by German prisoners-of-war. The Irish prisoners' military organisation ran this camp efficiently until the British tried to pick out Irishmen who had been living in England, for compulsory military service. These men, who had belonged to Irish Volunteer companies or had been members of the IRB, had come to Ireland to fight. Most prisoners refused to answer their names, wanted men went on the run in camp, and punishment was inflicted on some hundreds for a long period, but only a few Irishmen were identified and taken away. At times men selected for special punishment disappeared into the great unknown of prisoners who could not be identified. Not until 1921 were as many untried prisoners segregated.

English jails and Frongoch were a means of bringing men together from all over Ireland. Here was a training-ground for ingenuity and improvisation, a school for passive resistance, but the real strength came from the spear-head of unified will with which prisoners pierced and shredded authoritative organisation.

As the strength of Sinn Féin and of the Irish Volunteers grew, men were imprisoned for wearing uniform, for drilling, for seditious speech and for singing songs. In September 1917, prisoners in Mountjoy jail, who had been placed amongst sentenced civil prisoners, demanded prisoner-of-war treatment. They went on hunger strike. Thomas Ashe, a strong, virile man, was dead in a few days. A coroner's jury declared that: 'Hunger-striking was adopted against the inhuman punishment inflicted.' Next week Irish prisoners who were serving a sentence of two years or less were granted free association and other concessions, but when men from Mountjoy, under the leadership of Austin Stack, were removed to Dundalk these privileges were withheld. In each particular jail men had to make their own fight and had to solve their problems by themselves.

In September 1917, in Maryborough jail, Paddy Fleming, who had been sentenced to five years, demanded political treatment. Fleming carried on his own jail war, aided by two other prisoners. He was released in a weakened condition in a month's time, but again arrested in May 1918, when the British made a round-up of men who were supposed to be concerned with a 'German Plot'. Soon he was naked in his cell for twelve hours each day. After a while a brute strength of warders tried to push on him the broad-arrow of grey, but, although handcuffed, he succeeded in destroying a suit daily, until manacles and a body-belt were added. When he broke through this encirclement he was supplied with leather muffs which covered his body from knees to elbows. His uniform at this time consisted of a shirt and muffs, or a shirt and handcuffs fastened behind his back. He repeatedly destroyed muffs, strait-jackets and cell so thoroughly that a specially heated and strengthened cell of two storeys was built for him in which he could spend his naked time. In nine days from his entry to this cell, fitted with special contrivances from a rubber chamber-pot to iron girders as a table support, he had wrecked completely all the new ideas. His sentence of five years had to be reduced to two, so that he could be legally removed to Mountjoy, as no prisoner in that jail could have a longer sentence than two years. On New Year's Day 1919, he was brought to Mountjoy.

In the meantime the 'German Plot' prisoners were scattered in English jails, where grudging concessions were extracted from reluctant governors. In January 1919, Joe McGrath, Barney Mellows, Frank Shouldice and George Geraghty made a rope-ladder in Usk jail and escaped over a wall. In Lincoln jail de Valera took a wax impression of the chaplain's pass-key, which Seán Milroy transferred as a sketch to a humorous Christmas card for friends outside. After many delays a workable key was made inside by de Loughry from a rough facsimile which, with a file, had been baked into a cake. De Valera, Seán Milroy and Seán MacGarry escaped.

In January, also, Paddy Fleming was in charge of the Mountjoy prisoners. There were seven men there who were not receiving political treatment. The remainder of his comrades broke up jail furniture and refused to accept prison rules. They were handcuffed, kept in their cells for a month, then allowed to exercise, handcuffed; at the end of two months handcuffs were removed. Robert Barton, a TD, escaped from Mountjoy jail hospital, where TDs were kept, by filing a bar in his cell window. The file was handed to him by Dick Mulcahy, who had come into the jail posing as a solicitor's clerk. Barton, on a starless night, reached the jail wall at an hour previously arranged. He timed his movements by the prison bell and at the correct moment a rope ladder was waiting for him. Two weeks later Fleming, Piaras Béaslaí and eighteen of the prisoners escaped in daylight, protected by a group of their comrades close to a rope ladder inside. Five prisoners, gripping horn-spoons in their pockets, held up the five warders who supervised the exercise period. A sixth man fiercely read the Proclamation of 1916 and this confirmed the warders' fear that a new Rising had begun and that the jail was being taken over.

In Belfast jail there had been trouble in July 1918. RIC were brought in from outside the jail. These police beat up prisoners with batons, handcuffed them, dragged them downstairs to the basement, where hoses were turned on the men who yet showed fight. There, below, prisoners remained for over a week with their hands handcuffed behind their backs, eating their food in that position. An epidemic of flu struck the prison. A protest meeting in Dublin may have helped to improve conditions in Belfast, for, by September, the prisoners had turned the jail into a convalescent home. One cell functioned as a pub, over the door was the name of the proprietor MULCAHY LYONS, who could supply whiskey, brandy and gin from H.P. Sauce and Yorkshire Relish bottles. Indeed one man who was rather partial to drink had developed his partiality to his stomach's content, for he was not seen to be sober for weeks. During the general election at the end of 1918 the prisoners decided to go over the wall to attend election meetings in Belfast, but the excursion was prevented by an order from GHQ.

A political prisoner, John Doran, was being treated as a criminal in another wing of this jail. At Mass one morning he was surrounded by his comrades and was taken back to the political wing. Austin

Stack, who was in charge of the jail on behalf of the prisoners, had organised a plan of action. Prisoners had already raided store-cells for sledgehammers. They had collected heaps of paving-stones and heavy weights on the second and third landings. With the sledges they broke down the stone stairway which led to the second landing, burst through three passages leading from each landing to another wing, so that their part of the jail was not isolated. As a result of their convalescence, food parcels had accumulated and this food was now used as a reserve. With a ladder and long poles the roof was burst through while slates came down in a heavy shower. The Republican flag waved over the jail while prisoners sat on rafters to see the world below.

Machine-gun units took up positions inside and outside the jail. Prisoners were given twelve hours to surrender Doran, but they refused to hand him over. Flurried negotiations between jail authorities, the lord mayors of Belfast and Dublin, and Dr MacRory, took place. It was agreed that Doran be handed up, to receive political treatment; that political privileges be restored to the men who had held their fortified wing, and that all prisoners be shortly removed to England. Then prisoners, after a five days' occupation, marched out with flags flying and tin cans beating to another wing.

In this wing new warders, who had served with the British army, gradually replaced the old warders who had become friendly or who had been overawed. One morning a prisoner from Cavan had words with a new warder who shouted at him to get out of bed and serve himself with his breakfast. Up to this the sentenced lags had been serving breakfast in the cells. That day the Cavan man asked for a strong dose of jalap. Next morning the warder received the very adequate contents of a chamber-pot when he opened the cell door. The warder fainted from this unexpected salutation. All prisoners were then battened into cells, handcuffed and kept handcuffed for over four months, without exercise. In June 1920, they were brought to Manchester jail where they were treated as politicals.

Piaras Béaslaí had again been captured. He had been sent to Birmingham jail, where with D.P. Walsh he fought for and was granted political conditions. Later they were removed to Manchester, where an escape was planned, which had an amusing connotation. Some of the correspondence was carried on by post through the jail censor. 'Professor Rory' and an 'examination' meant Rory O'Connor, who was in charge of the escape and the 'examination' as mentioned by a supposed school-girl, was the escape itself. They escaped.

The hunger strike had been used as a weapon to demand either prisoner-of-war or political treatment. As a rule, jail authorities, guided by the Ashe precedent, were concerned about the health of prisoners when they had been from five to eight days on hunger strike. Prisoners considered that eight days was a long strike and that they were then in a weak state. In Mountjoy, in April 1920, eighty-eight prisoners went on hunger strike. On the first day of the strike one of the men, O'Reilly, was brought quickly to an outside hospital as he was foaming at the mouth, but his worried jailers were completely unaware that a judicious chewing of soap had produced the alarming symptoms.

British army doctors were called in to supplement the prison medical man. One day an army doctor came in to Andy McDonnell's cell. 'Listen here, MacDonnell,' he said, 'there's no doubt whatsoever but that you have a bad heart. No medical man could deny that nor could he disprove it, but I am convinced that you haven't a bad heart, but how the devil you can also convince me of the contrary I do not know. I won't tell if you tell me, and anyhow I am recommending you for immediate release.'

The officer was a decent human being. He was likeable and friendly. 'I'll tell you if you give me your word of honour never to mention the secret and I'll tell you only when I am on my way out of jail for release.' The officer gave his word of honour. On the night before the release of sixty-six prisoners under the 'Cat and Mouse Act', after a strike of eight days, the medical man came into the cell at night. 'I will not be here tomorrow for your release, but I'd like now to listen to your method for developing a bad heart.'

'All right,' said Andy Mac, 'but first of all test my heart.'

The officer examined the heart. 'Why,' he said in surprise, 'there's nothing whatever wrong with your heart now.'

'Wait for a while,' said Andy. He got out of bed, gave three quick leaps, then returned to bed. 'Now test my heart,' he asked.

The officer examined his heart again. He stood up with a delighted chuckle. 'There's no earthly doubt but you have a bad heart as have the other crowd of devils, and now I'll wish you good luck.' He made a few efforts to restore his face to its settled professional gravity before he walked out of the cell.

In August 1920, Terence MacSwiney, lord mayor of Cork, and brigadier of Cork No. 1 brigade, was arrested. He refused to accept food from the date of his arrest, and demanded unconditional release. MacSwiney died when he was close to seventy-two days on strike. His resistance was a symbol of the nation's resistance, and, as such, daily bulletins were forwarded to Europe and the Americas by a now well-built-up Dáil publicity. As a result of MacSwiney's death the hunger strike was seldom if ever used as a weapon again against the British.

After the shooting of British intelligence and court martial officers in Dublin in November 1920, fighting throughout Ireland became more intense. In many areas there were flying columns on continuous active service and in each battalion officers and men were on the run. An attempt to arrest well-known men meant now a wider police and military net, equivalent to a sweep of troops across country, or a section of a city being thoroughly combed. The British then concentrated on smashing the civil administration of Dáil Éireann. Lord mayors were murdered, men were shot in bed or prisoners were shot 'while attempting to escape'. All this activity meant a large increase in the number of prisoners, extra troops to act as guards and a steady flow of English reinforcements. From 1916 to early in 1920, a prisoner was looked on with admiration. Brass-bands, bonfires and eager listeners awaited his release, but from now on an arrest meant the loss of an officer or official who had important information, or who was essential to the criss-cross puzzle of resistance. Every effort now was made to avoid arrest.

In Dublin and Cork, curfew had closed down the cities between the hours of midnight and five o'clock. In 1921, curfew in Dublin lasted from 9 p.m. to 5 a.m. Curfew gave the British a chance to raid extensively, and to use their intelligence agents and spies under the shield of darkness, for by this the intelligence branch of the Dublin police had been shot off, or had been passing on information to the director of intelligence, Michael Collins. Prisoners arrested in night raids were brought to Dublin Castle or to Richmond barracks where they were interrogated. Interrogation might mean threat, brutality, or various forms of terrorisation; Arbour Hill barracks was used as a place of detention from which prisoners, against whom there was no evidence, could be sent to Ballykinlar camp, or the Rath camp on the Curragh.

The new force of British ex-officers, organised in companies, had been scattered through the country. These Auxiliaries used Beggar's Bush as a base and as well they had a company in Dublin Castle and a company in the RIC depot. Treatment of prisoners varied throughout the country. Captors could comprise RIC, the English recruits to this force, known as Black and Tans, Auxiliaries, or British troops. The invariable treatment by Black and Tans and Auxiliaries was brutal, overbearing and freakish; the regular British troops were severe on prisoners in some areas, depending on the regiment or on their officers; the Camerons in Cork, the Essex in West Cork, the Green Howards in and around East Limerick, all had a very bad name. In the capital, which was close to foreign correspondents, prisoners, save in intelligence rooms, were not badly handled. Auxiliaries sometimes turned their backs as arrested men got rid of papers, or they were kind when other men of their company were brutal. Sometimes 'F' company from the Castle would protect prisoners when they were brought to a military barracks. Once they drew their revolvers in the Royal barracks to ward off men of the Wiltshires who were trying to get at prisoners with their brass-buckled belts.

My own experience may illustrate, perhaps, the average lot of a prisoner. The Auxiliary company which arrested me threatened me with death repeatedly whilst I was with them in Kilkenny. They used their bayonets on me and their nailed boots. I was brought out to be shot one morning. When I was handed over to the military in Kilkenny city, I was kindly treated. On the road to Dublin I was to have been shot by Auxiliaries, but another prisoner, de Loughry of Kilkenny, who had overheard the conversation of some of my guard, told an officer who changed the men in my tender. In Dublin Castle I was well fed by the members of 'F' company in their guardroom. I was badly beaten-up in the intelligence room by a British intelligence officer, Captain Hardy and by Major King, an Auxiliary major, but my Auxiliary guards were sympathetic. In Kilmainham, which was guarded by British troops, we, although untried, were put in solitary confinement at first, but gradually we were able to break down the men of the Welch regiment who acted as warders. They had been told we were notorious murderers – the Tommies always carried revolvers in their hands when they opened our cell doors. They watched us carefully; aggressive in voice, they were ready for our sudden onslaught, but as the days passed they joined in our jokes, listened to our songs and drank our tea, which they had made for us. The deciding factor was, I think, our attitude towards their officers. We all thoroughly disliked the sneak of a captain who was in charge of prisoners. We told him what we thought of him whenever he tried to impose his slippery will. When they heard a young Dublin boy tell a captain to go to hell, or when they listened to our curt and unceremonious language to a lieutenant, whom they themselves thoroughly disliked, their hearts became softened. We could talk to their officers in a way they had often day-dreamed about, or maybe had furtively whispered to each other. I expect their own regimental folklore of our treatment of their officers was joyfully exchanged with other units, and it gained expletives and scurrility as it was passed on. This complete lack of respect by the IRA for their over-lords, and the instantaneous obedience of prisoners to their own elected officers, whose clothing might be in tatters, changed their scale of values.

The British Tommy was a very human individual. He was very poorly paid, harshly disciplined and filled with propagandist fear about our strange race. He was willing to work for money, which was always smuggled in to us, or his natural kindness of heart could meet its stronger reciprocal in his prisoners. At the end of a month the privates could sing our ballads and songs, improvise on them to make fun of us, or teach us their own songs about hated sergeant-majors.

Camps, barracks and jails continued to fill up. Men serving sentences of over two years were sent to England, but in 'A' wing, Mountjoy, before the Truce, there were a number of men, who, on account of Truce negotiations, had been kept in Ireland. Some of the prisoners, advised by Leo Fitzgerald, who had a good knowledge of the prison, decided to escape, dressed as Auxiliaries, for the latter were stationed as a special guard, owing to the number of important men there who had been captured at the destruction of the Custom House. Visits were allowed to 'A' wing prisoners, and, as warders were less stringent and careful, guns were slipped across by visitors during interviews. Two of the guns were useless, a French .42 and a Bulldog .45. Both were fixed with candle-grease to enable them to hold together and to appear loaded when seen from in front against the light.

Leo Fitzgerald made some Auxiliary caps inside by using bed quilts, and the inside lining of a waistcoat for streamers; other caps were tailored outside the prison. Cap-badges were improvised by cutting a crown and harp from the black covers of official prison prayer-books. Trench coats were sent in in parcels to the prisoners.

In November, prisoners came in from exercise as dusk began to come down. Prisoners had a habit of delaying before being locked up, so that eight or nine men would not be missed until the warder returned from locking up the length of the landing. The plan was that the seven men selected would wear trench coats at exercise, keep the Auxiliary caps in their pockets, slip over to 'B' wing from 'A' wing as they came in from exercise, and get to the basement below where they would hold up the warder who was locking up non-political prisoners. His keys would then be used to open a way to the front gate.

On the evening of the escape the seven prisoners were joined by Fitzgerald in the basement. They locked the warder, Dunlevy, into a cell, but before they had reached the end of the basement passage they could hear shouts of 'Help! Help!' The warder had pulled the bell which was in each cell. The convicts there, who were mostly British Tommies, began to roar: 'The Shinners! The Shinners are escaping!' Hurriedly the escapees tried the bunch of keys for the right key to the basement door, whilst they struck a few matches. If the Auxiliaries caught them below in the darkness their guns would be emptied, the prisoners felt, before any of them could get through the door.

The Auxiliaries, hearing the shouts, searched the grounds, as they expected an escape would be made over the wall. In the meantime the men reached the reception rooms beyond the last door of 'B' wing. Further on was a double gate and then three other gates between them and the entrance. They heard the sentries firing their rifles. Four warders, who mistook them for Auxiliaries, ran past as they tried to open the reception-room gate. While one of them tugged at the bunch of keys, the key in the lock stuck tight and it could not be pulled out, but the gate was open.

Fitzgerald and Troy walked across to the sentry at an unlocked gate, which he opened for them as they imitated a Cockney accent. The warders between them and the main gates respectfully refused to open the next gate; 'I'm afraid I don't know you, sir. I'll have to get an Auxiliary to identify you.' Fitzgerald, cigar in mouth, pulled his gun. The warders put up their hands. Behind them Kit Smith stuck his useless weapon into the sentry's back.

At this moment Hipwell, the chief warder, came running towards the group. 'Stop those men,' he shouted, 'they must be identified.' As he shouted Jerry Davis and Paddy Rigney rushed the small office inside the front gate to hold up the guard of two Auxiliaries, but there were no Auxiliaries there. Now six of the enemy was lined up against the wall, and as Troy looked at their upstretched hands he said, 'I think this is what we really want.' Hipwell was holding in one hand the pass-key to the front gate. Troy opened the front gate while Fitzgerald said, 'Go on lads, now, I'll hold them for a while.' Fitzgerald then tried to lock the outer gate, but was not able. The sentry over the main hall was firing at some undefined target, but Fitzgerald stepped inside the gate and lined the warders again shoulder to shoulder against the wall.

Fitzgerald soon afterwards was able to catch up with his companions, and all six got safely away.

This was the last successful escape of prisoners from a British jail before the signing of the Articles of Agreement.

HOW IT WAS DONE –
IRA INTELLIGENCE

by PIARAS BÉASLAÍ

I HAVE HEARD it said more than once that the Fenian movement was 'ruined by spies and informers', whereas in the Anglo-Irish War of 1920 and 1921 there were few informers, and British espionage and intelligence work proved singularly futile.

It is difficult for us, today, to decide how far the statement with regard to 1865–67 is true. I do not believe the Fenian movement was 'ruined by informers'; and though British spies succeeded in penetrating into the secrets of the organisation to a formidable extent, there are other causes to explain the failure of the Fenians.

What is quite certain is that the English administration possessed the same machinery of intelligence in Ireland in 1916 as in 1865, and yet it proved ineffective.

The machinery was – in Dublin – a picked number of 'political' detectives, and, in the country, the RIC. The Volunteers of 1916 had no intelligence service as such. Its importance was not recognised. Yet their leaders prepared an insurrection which took the English entirely by surprise.

The RIC had established a system of espionage which was wonderfully efficient. In every town and village all the movements of persons were watched and reported on. All popular organisations were kept under observation, and all persons who expressed patriotic opinions were the object of surveillance. Even their activities in such matters as teaching Irish, playing Gaelic football or the like were duly reported; and Dublin Castle, as the result of these reports, had the most exact information as to the personnel, strength and methods of all national movements in the country.

In 1916 Dublin Castle had information as to every company of Volunteers in Ireland outside Dublin; their numbers, their officers, the number of rifles they possessed and the feeling among them. Mr Birrell, Irish chief secretary, told the Royal Commission set up to investigate the causes of the 1916 insurrection: 'So far as the country is concerned, we have the reports of the RIC, who send us in, almost daily, reports from almost every district in Ireland, and I have them under the microscope. Their reports undoubtedly do enable anybody, sitting in either Dublin or London, to form a correct general estimate of the feeling of the countryside in different localities.'

In Dublin the work fell upon the 'political section' of the 'G' or detective division of Dublin Metropolitan Police. Their methods were more crude and obvious. They 'shadowed' men known to have what they called 'extreme' views, noted their movements and their associates, and, perhaps, followed this up by also shadowing the movements of their associates. This was done in so open a manner that our being followed around by our 'escort' of 'G' men, was a matter of jest to us.

The result of these activities was seen after the surrender in 1916, when over one hundred and fifty prisoners were picked out by these same detectives for trial by court martial as 'ringleaders'. Some were executed and the rest sentenced to long terms of penal servitude.

The first step towards creating a Volunteer, or (to use the later term) IRA intelligence service came from within this very 'political section' of the 'G' division. Some young men in that body were in secret sympathy with those they were required to spy upon, and made cautious overtures to Sinn Féiners of their acquaintance early in 1918. Through Mr Michael Foley, Éamonn Broy, afterwards chief commissioner of the Garda Síochána came into touch with Michael Collins and arranged a system of sending him information. About the same time another patriotic detective, Joe Kavanagh, and later another, James McNamara (both since dead) got into touch with Thomas Gay, chief librarian of Capel Street corporation library, and through him established a system of communication with Michael Collins. Seán Duffy, a Volunteer, also acted as 'liaison officer' with Kavanagh and himself did intelligence work. This was the beginning of the systematic undermining of the British machinery of espionage in Ireland. Subsequently Michael Collins got in touch with another detective, David Neligan, who later was sworn in as a member of the British secret service!

Apart from the value of the information conveyed to him, Michael Collins was greatly interested in the knowledge he acquired of the methods and system of working of the political detective department, and the idea of establishing a counter-intelligence service, which should take leaves from the work of the enemy, had already begun to dawn on him.

Collins, Harry Boland and others received warning of the 'German Plot' round-up of 17 May 1918, and escaped the net. Immediately after this an intelligence department was set up by GHQ. The late Éamonn Duggan was the first director, and his first intelligence officer was Christopher Carbery. But Michael Collins still continued working in the same direction; though he was at the time adjutant-general and director of organisation – two most exacting positions. Finally, in 1919, Michael Collins became officially director of intelligence and commenced to organise a department on a considerable scale, later resigning from his other positions in order to give it his full attention. He had decided that intelligence was of so much importance in countering enemy activities, that he must concentrate his energies on that branch of the work.

Prior to this, in April 1919, Collins made a daring midnight visit to the headquarters of the 'G' division in Brunswick Street, now Pearse Street. Broy was alone on duty, and had locked the door of the dormitory in which the other detectives were sleeping. A number of secret documents and confidential reports were locked up in a small room on the upper floor, which Broy unlocked with a skeleton key, and Collins spent several of the small hours of the morning studying these papers and making notes. He was particularly amused by a report on himself, which began with the words: 'He comes of a brainy Cork family.'

Two days later the house of one detective was raided by the IRA and a second detective was tied up with ropes in the street and left there. This was intended merely as a demonstration to warn them against being too zealous in their duties, and it had a marked effect on the men concerned and on the detectives generally. But some continued to show special energy and animus in their work against the IRA, and, later, after repeated warnings, more drastic action had to be taken. After some casualties, the once-dreaded 'G' Division had ceased to function effectually. It was undermined and all its information was being 'tapped' by the IRA through those detectives who were working for us; those who had shown special animus against us were known and unable to perform detective duties without risking their lives; and the majority of the force found it prudent never to go beyond the strict letter of their duties.

It was, as I say, early in 1919, that Collins began to create a regular intelligence department. He was fortunate in getting the services of Liam Tobin as chief intelligence officer. Tobin had been previously doing intelligence work for the Dublin brigade. Later the assistant quartermaster-general, the late Tom Cullen, was drafted into intelligence. Next in command came Frank Thornton. The intelligence staff was built up slowly, as suitable men were not easily found. A good intelligence officer is born, not made, but even the man with a great deal of natural instinct for detective work requires to be taught a great deal of the technique of the business.

The knowledge of exactly what information is required, and how to set about obtaining it, the skill in worming information from confiding enemies, the power to perceive the importance of seemingly trivial and irrelevant matters – these were only a portion of the qualifications required.

Office work was almost as important as outside work. The co-ordination of the information obtained, the systematic and carefully planned filing of information, documents, photographs, the accumulation of a mass of information, readily accessible when required, with regard to any person or thing, which was likely to be of value to the IRA in their struggle with their enemies – this indoor work was as essential in its way as the more picturesque work out of doors.

In July 1919, 'The Squad' was formed, a body that played a big part in the subsequent fighting in Dublin. The Squad consisted of a small band of Volunteers attached to the intelligence department, specially selected for dangerous and difficult jobs. The first commanding officer was Michael McDonnell. The second-in-command was Patrick Daly, who afterwards succeeded him as O/C.

The activities of the intelligence department continued to expand. The keys to police, official and military cipher codes were obtained, and gradually a system was established by which English official messages were tapped at various postal centres and decoded. Copies of the necessary codes were sent to intelligence officers in the country to enable them to deal at once with matters urgently concerning their own units.

By the end of 1920, battalion intelligence officers were appointed in every active area in Ireland. These reported to their brigade intelligence officer who, in turn, reported to intelligence headquarters in Dublin, the letters and reports being, of course, conveyed by 'secret post'. Michael Collins was in regular communication with every active brigade intelligence officer in Ireland, and his files show in what an elaborate manner he entered into every detail of their work.

Some of the intelligence officers in the country were selected because they were not known, even to the IRA themselves generally, to be in sympathy with the national cause; and, as their work caused them to seek the society of military officers, and even Black and Tans, they came in for general opprobrium and suspicion from those not in the know. I have encountered some amusing instances of this. That fine Killarney film, *The Dawn*, created a moving and dramatic story out of such a situation.

Postal employees, as I have hinted, came to play a very big part in intelligence work. In London, the late Sam Maguire and his helpers organised an elaborate system of communication with the IRA and of intercepting enemy communications. In Dublin – and even on the mail boats – there was a body of workers operating in collaboration with the intelligence department. In various parts of the country, also, postal employees gave valuable assistance. Besides the interception of letters more direct methods were employed. In February 1920, the mail car containing the day's official correspondence for Dublin Castle was held up in Parnell Square, Dublin, by armed men, and all the letters were seized. All the cross-channel correspondence for fourteen departments, including those of the lord lieutenant, chief secretary, under secretary, military and RIC were captured.

Shortly after this, the very GPO itself (then situated in the Rotunda Rink, after the destruction of the O'Connell Street building in 1916) was invaded by armed men and the Dublin Castle official correspondence was again seized. Of course, the feat was facilitated by inside information from those employed in the GPO.

After this 'raids for mails' became increasingly frequent, and ultimately the holding-up of mail trains and the seizure of official correspondence became a frequent activity in various brigade areas throughout the country. The local brigade intelligence officer inspected the seized correspondence and forwarded to Dublin any documents which he regarded of sufficient importance.

Big bundles of letters of Black and Tans and Auxiliaries to their friends in England were captured from time to time. By this means the home addresses of many of these men were ascertained and the local IRA or IRB men in the district notified.

By the end of 1919 the English authorities had realised the ineffectiveness of the once-dreaded 'G' Division and resorted to other methods. Secret service men and spies were brought over from England. One of their ablest secret service men, Jameson, actually succeeded in imposing on Michael Collins for a time and came within an ace of securing his capture. Ultimately Jameson was shot dead on the Ballymun Road.

By 1920 Dublin was full of British intelligence officers – but these men were heavily handicapped in their work. Unlike the 'G' men, they had no personal knowledge of who was who, they had never seen any of the men who were wanted, they were, for the most part, woefully ignorant of Dublin and their English accents were hardly calculated to allay Irish suspicions. And now began another activity of the intelligence department.

The arrival of certain British intelligence officers in Ireland in March 1920 was followed by the murder of Lord Mayor Tomás MacCurtain of Cork, and later by the murders of other prominent Sinn Féiners in the country and in Dublin. Michael Collins intercepted letters from these British officers, which clearly proved the existence of a 'murder plot', for which they had been 'given a free hand'.

In May 1920, a number of members of Dáil Éireann and other prominent Sinn Féiners received typewritten 'death notices' through the post.

By a wonderful piece of detective work, worthy of a Sherlock Holmes, the director of intelligence, IRA, was able to prove that these notices were typed by the intelligence department of the Dublin district of the English army in Ireland. He ascertained what officers were responsible. He even ascertained the typewriter with which the notices were typed.

Each new discovery opened up new avenues of information. Gradually our intelligence department learned all the personnel of the English intelligence staff, their appearance, hours, habits and haunts. Later a number of English officers living outside barracks as civilians under disguised names were traced, and some of the murders of Irish citizens were definitely traced to these men, a number of whom met their end on 21 November 1920, the day popularly known as 'Bloody Sunday'.

The old RIC had long ceased to be effective as suppliers of information to Dublin Castle. They had been withdrawn from the smaller country barracks and concentrated in the larger centres, and even there a system of social ostracism kept them from getting in contact with the people. Yet even this force had been undermined by the IRA intelligence. A number of RIC men were working in secret for the Irish cause.

Even the very Black and Tans were undermined. The intelligence department had workers in the Auxiliaries. Indeed, by 1921, the department had possessed photographs of practically every Auxiliary and most of the intelligence officers in Dublin, so that they could be recognised even in mufti. Indeed, but for the opening of negotiations for a truce by the British at a certain psychological moment, there would have been a heavy casualty list among these men.

But one outstanding factor, apart from efficiency and system, which helped to explain the success of IRA intelligence work, was the loyalty, courage, enthusiasm, unselfishness and sense of comradeship of the many fellow-workers, high and low, in the cause – workers without whose co-operation success would be impossible. These qualities of loyalty, courage and comradeship characterised all the workers in the IRA and in the national movement in those days of storm and struggle. The impact of foreign violence united the people into a single body. Every man and woman working for the national cause, even in a non-military way, was, in a sense, a soldier in the army of Ireland; and in the same way it could be said that each of them was, in a greater or lesser degree, an intelligence officer anxious to pass on to the soldiers of Ireland any information which they believed to be useful to those fighting for Ireland against the foreign reign of terror.

FIANNA ÉIREANN –
WITH THE DUBLIN BRIGADE

by JOE REYNOLDS

We believe that Na Fianna Éireann have kept the military spirit alive in Ireland during the past four years, and that if the Fianna had not been founded in 1909, the Volunteers of 1913 would never have arisen. – P.H. Pearse, February 1914.

THE FOREGOING IS the testimony of Pádraig Pearse to the work accomplished by Fianna Éireann during the darkest years in the most recent phase of the struggle for Irish independence.

Fianna Éireann, the Irish national boy scouts organisation, was founded by Madame Markievicz, Con Colbert, Éamonn Martin, and others in 1909. Its object, as stated in its constitution, was the re-establishment of the independence of Ireland, and amongst the methods adopted to achieve this primary purpose were: 'The training of the youth of Ireland, mentally and physically, by teaching scouting and military exercises, Irish history and the Irish language.' Thus did the Fianna teach and train Irish boys to work for Irish independence.

The preservation of national independence, strength and unity are the first duties of the people of a nation. In Ireland, successive generations had made sacrifices in the cause of Irish independence, and it was fitting that a new generation of Irish boys should now be trained to take their rightful place in the national struggle for freedom.

The boys who joined the Fianna had to work in sluagh groups, until having passed a preliminary test, they were permitted to make the declaration which admitted them to membership of the organisation. The declaration was as follows: 'I promise to work for the independence of Ireland, never to join England's armed forces, and to obey my superior officers.' Before a recruit was allowed to make the declaration he was required to work in one of the sluaighte for three weeks, following which he presented himself for the preliminary test. Fianna Éireann was the first organisation of recent years to come into the open under the old war-scarred banner, and for a long time it had to contend with public indifference and even derision. Many of the older generation shook their heads and doubted the wisdom of this new movement, whilst there was much talk on every side to the effect that the days of fighting for Ireland were gone forever. We of the Fianna, however, knew that our inspiration was right, and that our organisation was strong in the enthusiasm, faith and high purpose of men like Heuston, Colbert and Mellows. Later, we had the advice and encouragement of Pearse, Connolly and their comrades, and of Roger Casement, too. We were proud and glad that the honour of being the first modern army in the service of Ireland was ours.

The original members of the Dublin Fianna took turns to stand in uniform beneath a large flag, outside their first drill hall, in 34 Camden Street, in order to attract recruits. Those who joined participated in a close bond of comradeship, and later became the nucleus of the Irish Republican Army. The leading figure in the movement was Madame Markievicz, who provided 10/– weekly rent for the hall. Drilling and scout-craft were taught, and in a short time the Fianna became the most efficient and best-trained group amongst those participating in the various public functions and demonstrations, and made the press headlines because of their smart appearance and military bearing. Dr Dunlop was engaged to teach first-aid to the newly formed St Patrick's ambulance brigade. When the course was completed the usual examinations followed, and a large number of boys secured certificates and badges. Many public displays of camping and field drill were given, usually at big open-air demonstrations. Rifle drill and bayonet exercises were demonstrated, too, with dummy rifles, whilst sword drill with single sticks, signalling and first-aid displays all had their place on the programme. In these events the Fianna displayed enthusiasm and knowledge.

The Fianna boys were always welcome at St Enda's College, Rathfarnham, for P.H. Pearse saw clearly the role which they would eventually play in the resurgence of Ireland.

During one of the Fianna camps in the Three Rock Mountains, a young man was drowned in a large quarry hole. Boys of the Fianna made an improvised raft, pushed it into the middle of the quarry and dived from it until they succeeded in recovering the body. The people presented three gold medals to the boys for their bravery and endurance.

Con Colbert compiled a complete course of drill commands in Gaelic, and soon Gaelic became the language in which all commands were given in An Chéad Sluagh. There were sluaighte in Dublin, Limerick, Derry, Cork and Belfast by December 1910, and the first ard-fheis had already been held. The Belfast sluagh wearing their Fianna uniform climbed Cave Hill, and standing at MacArt's Fort, where Wolfe Tone and the United Irishmen had once stood, they promised, as the United Irishmen had promised more than a century before, to work unceasingly for the independence of Ireland.

The second ard-fheis which was held in July 1911, revealed that the organisation had spread to Dundalk, Clonmel, Newry and Waterford. In that year, too, Liam Mellows joined, and by the following year he was secretary to the Dublin district council. Seán Heuston was then in charge of the Limerick sluagh. Prior to 1916 all conventions, which were held annually, took place in the Dublin Mansion House.

The Fianna took a leading part in the demonstrations against the visit to Ireland of the English king, and on numerous occasions the boys came into conflict with the police.

When the executive examined its financial position in 1912, it was shocked into the realisation that our chance of definite achievement in our generation was in jeopardy because of inadequate financial resources. Because of this situation, Liam Mellows proposed early in 1913 that he should give up his prospects in life and take to the road as full-time

Fianna organiser, at the salary of 10/– weekly. He began this work in April 1913, and never relaxed his ceaseless activity for the Republic until his death. When he commenced his task as the first Fianna organiser, he found indifference almost everywhere; yet within a year the roads of Ireland resounded to the tramp of marching feet. Under the guidance of Madame Markievicz plays of Irish character were staged and played their part in the revival of love for Ireland. The Fianna established its own hurling league and athletics, too, held their proper place in the strict military curriculum of the organisation. Headed by their pipe band, the Fianna participated in all national demonstrations, such as the annual parade to Bodenstown, and to the Manchester Martyrs cenotaph in Glasnevin. Seán Heuston came to Dublin in 1913 and took charge of a North City sluagh which paraded in Hardwicke Street. A born leader, he was another of the Liam Mellows kind, and possessed a great capacity for work. He laboured long in the Fianna headquarters, at 12 D'Olier Street, where he was invariably occupied until midnight on details of organisation and training.

The first important clashes between the Fianna and British forces took place during the great Dublin strike of 1913, when the police went completely berserk and batoned the populace indiscriminately. We participated in several affrays with them and because of our loyalty, team work and the support we accorded to each other, we invariably eluded capture and injury. Nevertheless, one of our officers was killed by a blow of a police baton, received whilst he was giving attention to a wounded civilian. One of the biggest clashes took place at Butt bridge, during the height of the strike. We had rolled ship gangways, barricaded the bridge, and then with crates of empty jam jars for missiles, we defied the police to attack us. Eventually, they attempted an encircling movement which we escaped by retreating in good order and mingling with a crowd which providentially emerged from the Queen's Theatre at a psychological moment.

Following the formation of the Volunteers in November 1913, the value of the work undertaken by the Fianna became obvious immediately. The senior boys were then ready and competent to train the Volunteers in the use of arms, to accustom them to discipline, and in short to transform them from raw recruits into effective soldiers. Four Fianna members sat on the Provisional Committee and were elected to the first executive council, of which Liam Mellows was the first effective secretary. Fianna drill halls in Dublin and elsewhere were immediately used by the Volunteers. Fianna officers became Volunteer officers and in many cases they held higher rank in the Volunteers than in the Fianna. The Fianna, too, grew apace with the spread of the Volunteers. A Fianna handbook, which contained articles by Pearse, Colbert, Casement and others, was also adopted by the Volunteers.

The Howth gun-running of 26 July 1914, provided the Fianna with their first event of importance, for on that occasion they marched from Dublin with the Volunteers. They brought their trek-cart with them and were the first to reach Erskine Childers' yacht the *Asgard.* During the return journey to Dublin, some of the ammunition was conveyed in the trek-cart as the Fianna had been entrusted with the task of delivering it safely to its destination, a trust which was not misplaced. A Fianna officer was in charge of the cycle detachment at the Kilcool gun-running, which took place shortly afterwards.

Fianna members on the Volunteer executive were amongst the minority which signed the manifesto opposing the admittance of John Redmond's nominees to the executive, and later were signatories to the manifesto issued after Redmond's speech at Woodenbridge.

The first time we tried out the Howth rifle was in the garden of Surrey House, Leinster Road, the residence of Madame Markievicz, and we were satisfied of its effectiveness.

The Fianna training brought the boys into close association with the City Volunteers, and as they grew up they were transferred fully trained and equipped into Volunteer units. The older or senior boys were already in charge of Volunteer companies, a factor which explains why the Fianna were so strongly represented at every post during the Rising.

From the start of the First World War, the Fianna threw themselves wholeheartedly into anti-British activities. A small printing press which they installed in Surrey House produced anti-recruiting literature which was published in the city. The funeral of O'Donovan Rossa in 1915 was the occasion of a great display of Fianna strength.

Prior to the 1916 Rising, the Dublin Fianna was organised as a battalion of nine independent sluaighte or troops. The battalion was administered by a district council which comprised the battalion staff and commanders of the sluaighte. This council controlled the affairs of the Dublin Fianna until the insurrection. Several of the officers were in direct touch with the military council of the Irish Volunteers, whilst an active service unit comprising officers and picked boys, with the title 'Fianna Commando', was also in existence.

On Easter Monday 1916, Fianna officers were given command of important sections of the operations. A party commanded by a Fianna officer and composed almost entirely of members of the Fianna rushed the Magazine Fort in Phoenix Park, disarmed the guards and destroyed the stock of arms and ammunition which was stored therein. The action was the signal for the Rising. From the fort the party retreated to the Four Courts area and participated in the attack on the Broadstone railway station, in which operation Éamonn Martin, O/C Dublin Fianna, was severely wounded. The party was also involved in the capture of the Linenhall barracks, and in the desperate duel which preceded the surrender in North King Street. In the fighting in that area the British attacking forces were at one time separated from the defenders only by the width of a street. Captain Seán Heuston was in command in the Mendicity Institution on Usher's Island, opposite the Royal barracks. With his small garrison, he held out there for three days during which he directed operations with coolness and ability. He was promoted on the field. Liam Staines, a member of 'F' sluagh, was severely wounded during the fighting at that point. Con Colbert was second-in-command in Marrowbone Lane and assumed charge at the surrender. Madame Markievicz, the Fianna chief, held the College of Surgeons where some Fianna boys fought under her command.

Members of the Fianna were also in the fighting at other posts and in addition carried out the dangerous work of dispatch carrying, scouting and reconnoitring. Two Fianna boys were killed in action, several were wounded, and Seán Heuston and Con Colbert were executed on 8 May 1916.

In an 'Order of the Day', dated 28 April 1916, Commandant-General James Connolly had the following reference to Liam Mellows: '... in Galway, Captain Mellows, fresh from his escape from an Irish prison is in the field with his men'. Mellows' fight, his subsequent escape to America and his activities there on behalf of the Republic would occupy more space than is available for this article. It is sufficient to state that, when he returned to Ireland during a later phase of the Anglo-Irish War, he was appointed director of purchases on the general headquarters staff, Irish Republican Army. He was also elected a member of Dáil Éireann for Galway. Castletown churchyard is the last resting place of this patriot, whose life should be an inspiration to future generations of Irish boys.

Immediately after the Rising the Fianna was reorganised along lines similar to those which had previously existed except that, as some of the members of the district council were then interned in England, they were temporarily replaced by a provisional committee which administered the affairs of the Dublin Fianna until January 1917, when the senior officers were released and returned to duty. These ex-internees found the Fianna well on its feet and determined to continue the fight when they returned to headquarters, then at No. 6 Harcourt Street.

A general re-organisation campaign was initiated for Dublin and the provinces in January 1917. From then until June 1917 the Dublin Fianna was administered by a battalion council which consisted of the battalion staff and sluagh commanders. The general organisation of the battalion, which consisted of nine independent sluaighte, remained unchanged, although the location of some of the sluaighte differed from that which they occupied prior to the Rising. During this time orders prohibiting processions and the wearing of uniforms were issued by the army of occupation. These the Fianna defied. Several incidents occurred as a result, but invariably the police avoided making issue with the Fianna boys, from whom they could always expect strong resistance. The police, too, were often outwitted by the Fianna as on the occasion of a parade by the Dublin battalion at the Fox and Geese, Clondalkin. The parade headed by the company officers in full uniform, gave the slip to the police, who had determined to intercept the battalion on its return to Dublin. The boys marched without interference to the GPO where they were dismissed, and returned home safely, much to the disgust of the Dublin Metropolitan Police. On another occasion a Fianna battalion broke through police cordons at Cromwell's Quarters, Bow bridge.

In June 1917, the Dublin Fianna was reorganised as a brigade of two battalions, the 1st (South City battalion) and the 2nd (North City battalion). A brigade staff was elected which administered the affairs of the brigade, whose area of operations included both the city and county of Dublin. In June 1917, the brigade carried out extensive manoeuvres in the Dublin Mountains. Clashes took place at Terenure and Rathmines in the following month and police cordons were broken when an attempt was made to interfere with the brigade marching in uniform.

Commandant de Valera was unanimously elected chief of the Fianna at the annual convention, which was held at 41 York Street, Dublin, in August 1917. He was proposed by Madame Markievicz, who was elected Chief Scout.

The strength, training and efficiency of the Dublin brigade was evident by its bearing at the funeral of Commandant Tom Ashe in September 1917.

It should be mentioned that during all this time each company carried out its own manoeuvres and marches when not parading with its battalion or brigade. The Fianna carried out several raids for arms in November 1917.

The Dublin brigade commando was formed of senior Fianna boys in 1918, in face of the effort by the British government to impose conscription on the country. The commando was made up of picked members of the brigade, whose duty it was to co-operate with the Irish Volunteers in the event of conscription being enforced. The boys were attached to the Irish Volunteers, but under the control of a Fianna officer.

These developments caused the enemy to increase the pressure of his activities against the Fianna. Drill halls were raided, parades were attacked by police and military, and boys were arrested for wearing

Fianna uniform. Still the desired effect was not obtained by the British, and only resulted in an increase in the membership of the Dublin brigade. About that time too the 'Fianna Post' was established. This provided for the collection and delivery of letters in the Dublin area, employing a similar system to that operating in the post office. Circulars were issued to republican sympathisers advising that correspondence could be left at certain call offices where it would be collected at regular intervals and delivered for the same charges as obtained in the post office.

The transfer of senior boys to the Irish Volunteers also commenced. In March 1918, members of the brigade, returning from an inter-company competition at St Enda's, Rathfarnham, were attacked by RIC at Rathfarnham police barracks. One officer and one NCO were arrested. An attack on the barracks, which was arranged in an endeavour to rescue the boys, was called off by the senior officers in order to avoid unnecessary bloodshed. Two of the headquarters staff, the chief scout and adjutant general, were arrested by the British in May 1918, for alleged participation in a bogus 'German Plot'. Shortly afterwards the British military governor in an address to the Baden Powell scouts referred to the Fianna as 'poisonous insects' who should be stamped out.

The 1918 annual convention, which was held in August, took place at St Enda's, Rathfarnham. During the following month extensive manoeuvres were carried out in the Dublin Mountains, to commemorate the first anniversary of the death of Commandant Tom Ashe. Hooligan elements in the city, assisted by British soldiers, attacked the Fianna headquarters at No. 6 Harcourt Street, on Armistice night, 11 November 1918. The premises were successfully defended by members of 'A' company 1st battalion.

Fianna in full uniform and equipment marched to Glasnevin cemetery in December 1918, on the occasion of the funeral of Dick Coleman who died in Usk prison. A force of Dublin Metropolitan Police under several inspectors, which attempted to break up the Fianna ranks on their return march from the cemetery, were foiled in the attempt by the determination of the boys. Following the setting up of the republican government in January 1919, the activities of the

Fianna grew more intensive and the organisation spread throughout the country. During Fianna manoeuvres in February 1919, a skirmish took place with police and military at Finglas, and one Fianna officer who was arrested was sentenced to six months' imprisonment. Arms were to be carried by Fianna in March 1919, when the brigade was mobilised to take part in a reception to President de Valera, at Mount Street bridge, on the occasion of his return to Ireland after his escape from Lincoln jail. The reception, however, was proclaimed by the British.

Following the return of the chief scout and the Adjutant-General, Barney Mellows, who had escaped from Usk prison, arrangements were made for the annual convention, which took place in the Mansion House, Dublin, and was a huge success. On that occasion the Fianna declaration was altered to read as follows: 'I pledge my allegiance to the Irish Republic, and promise to do all in my power, to protect her from all enemies, whether foreign or domestic, and not to relax my efforts until the Irish Republic is universally recognised. I also promise to obey my superior officers.'

The executive and headquarters staff elected by the 1919 convention undertook full responsibility for the Fianna through the country. The activities of the Dublin brigade increased and the companies carried out intensive training in addition to raids for arms and other material necessary for the propagation of the war with Britain.

Amongst the tasks allotted to the Fianna was the rounding-up by 'A' and 'D' companies of a gang of cycle thieves in the High Street area. The success of this assignment became the subject of a message of congratulations from the Dublin brigade Irish Volunteers.

The annual convention for 1920 took place in August, at 46 Parnell Square. On 17 September 1920, extensive raids for arms were carried out in the Rathfarnham area by several squads from 'A' and 'F' companies. Two days later several armed squads from the same companies recovered arms, explosives and other material lost earlier on the same day at Kilmashogue by engineers who had been surprised by Auxiliaries. During the affray with the Auxiliaries, Seán Doyle, who had been transferred from the Fianna only two days previously, was shot dead.

The Fianna commando offered their services in an attempt to rescue Kevin Barry in October 1920. The boys were ordered to stand by, but the operation was later cancelled. Glenasmole Lodge was raided for arms in November 1920, by 'F' company, 1st battalion.

The brigade took an active part in many of the major operations of the Anglo-Irish War, which was intensified in 1921, and provided a valuable stream of recruits for the Irish Volunteers. Particularly effective was the brigade intelligence department, and the outcome of operations carried out on its information was invariably successful. It would be impossible to give a complete list of the members of Fianna Éireann who fell in the fight for freedom. The casualty list was large.

For some time there had been considerable overlapping on the part of Fianna and Volunteers, and accordingly, about the autumn of 1920 arrangements were made to provide for closer co-operation between the two organisations. A composite council was set up which comprised three general headquarters officers of the Fianna and three general headquarters officers of the Irish Volunteers. The meetings of this council were presided over by a nominee of the minister for defence. It was further decided that the boys should be brought into much closer liaison with the Volunteers and that, in addition to intelligence work, etc., the Fianna should be used as an official training corps for the Volunteer forces. The Dublin brigade Fianna was then reorganised to correspond with the Volunteer organisation, and the existing two battalions were expanded into five. Further activities of the Fianna helped in a large measure to force Britain to call the Truce on 11 July 1921.

'The Fianna Ideal can save the Future' – that last message from Liam Mellows shows how clearly he appreciated the necessity for a continuous and forward policy. The vision of Ireland free has ever been kept and hoped for by the Fianna. One day their work may assist to bring about a sovereign independent Irish Republic, as visualised by Pearse, Connolly, Mellows and their comrades. During all those crowded years that have come and gone since 1909 the proud record of Fianna Éireann has remained inspiring and unsullied.

HOW THE WOMEN HELPED

by R.M. FOX

THOUGH WOMEN HAVE taken a comparatively small part in modern Irish politics they were in the forefront of the national struggle. One has only to recall the way in which the Ladies' Land League sprang into being to keep the flag flying when Davitt and Parnell were imprisoned to see how the women were ready to rise to an emergency.

An immediate forerunner of Cumann na mBan was Inghinidhe na hÉireann founded by Maud Gonne at a meeting held in the Celtic Literary Society rooms in Dublin, as far back as 1900, to work for the national cause. Many of those who afterwards took part in Cumann na mBan owed the initial impulse to the work of the Inghinidhe. Among Inghinidhe pioneers was Mrs Wyse Power who had been in the Ladies' Land League. Maud Gonne also had a record of Land League activities. Helena Molony edited a small monthly journal *Bean na h-Éireann*, which began in November 1908, and ran for about three years. Launched in Dublin this paper numbered among its contributors many women – and men – of literary distinction. James Connolly, who was then in America, commended this journal.

As long ago as 1909, Constance Markievicz gave a lecture to the Students' National Literary Society of Dublin in which she spoke of the need for women fitting themselves to take part in the national movement. 'A Free Ireland with no sex disabilities in her constitution,' said the countess, 'should be the motto of all nationalist women … The old idea that a woman can only serve her nation through her home is gone; so now is the time; on you the responsibility rests.' She concluded with a declaration expressing the spirit which later animated Cumann na mBan: 'Arm yourselves with weapons to fight your nation's cause. Arm your souls with noble and free ideas. And if, in your day, the call should come for your body to arm, do not shirk that either. May the aspiration to life and freedom among the women of Ireland bring forth a Joan of Arc to free our nation.' About this time, too, she interested herself in building up the Fianna to train the boys to be soldiers of Ireland.

When the Irish Volunteers were formed – in November 1913 – there was, at once, a call for a woman's organisation. Cumann na mBan held its first conference at Wynn's Hotel, Dublin, early in 1914. It set out to be an auxiliary to the Volunteer movement. Professor Agnes O'Farrelly, MA, presided at the conference. One object was to assist in arming and equipping a body of Irishmen for the defence of Ireland. A fund was started, known as 'The Defence of Ireland Fund'. But it must not be assumed that Cumann na mBan at its inception, was the militant organisation it afterwards became. For many, in those early days, the idea of a Rising would have appeared fantastic. It was Sir Edward Carson and his 'Ulster Volunteer' movement who were defying the Asquith government and calling for resistance to the Home Rule Act, who fanned the flames of revolt. The Volunteers and Cumann na mBan organised a counter-movement, ready to make a stand against any swashbuckling attempt to cheat Ireland out of a measure of self-government.

Very soon the spirit of growing militancy made itself felt. On 26 June 1914, a detachment of Cumann na mBan marched in the Bodenstown commemoration and listened to Tom Clarke's affirmation of the republican principles of Wolfe Tone. But it was not until the Redmond split in the Volunteers that Cumann na mBan revealed that spirit which marked the whole of its subsequent activities. In August 1914, the First World War began. The Home Rule Act was hung in the air and Redmond supported the war. So the Volunteers broke in two, with the 'National Volunteers' endorsing Redmond and the Irish Volunteers standing for the original independence policy. When the Cumann na mBan annual convention was held in November 1914, one branch – at Ardpatrick – wanted to pledge the organisation to neutrality in the Volunteer conflict. Mary MacSwiney and Madge Daly, among many others, condemned the Redmond faction and the neutrality resolution was defeated. The new executive drew up a manifesto supporting the Irish Volunteers and this was adopted at the central branch by eighty-eight votes to twenty-eight. This Cumann na mBan stand was more remarkable when it is realised that Redmond had by far the largest support of the Volunteers in the country. A good many country branches dropped out. Then, around 1915, the women began to rally again.

With the outbreak of the European war, Cumann na mBan was urged to apply to Geneva for control of Red Cross work in Ireland and they were offered a complete new field hospital. But this was an attempt to link up Cumann na mBan with war activities. They stood firm, declining to apply to Geneva, but reserving the right to use the Red Cross in first-aid or hospital work at home. Each Cumann na mBan member was expected to raise funds to equip one Volunteer besides looking to their own training. They were trained in first-aid, in signalling and in drill. By this time the green uniform and the slouch hats of Cumann na mBan had become a familiar sight in Dublin. Their banner was the design of a rifle with the initials of the organisation entwined about it. And they had a striking badge of similar design. Now they had begun to parade in uniform.

In the hectic period just before 1916, Cumann na mBan found plenty to do. An event which roused great enthusiasm was the funeral of O'Donovan Rossa, whose body was brought from America for burial at home. After the coffin had been lying-in-state at City Hall, a huge procession marched – on 1 August – through Dublin to Glasnevin where Pearse, in Volunteer uniform, his hand resting on his sword hilt, delivered his famous oration. Cumann na mBan took part in this demonstration. Another star occasion was St Patrick's Day 1916, when Volunteers and Cumann na mBan paraded in College Green. This was a most impressive rally. All the activities of the women's organisation were in line with the declaration in their constitution, pledging them 'to work in conjunction with the recently formed Irish Volunteers in any action they would decide … to break the connection with England'.

On the eve of the Rising, Madame Markievicz had been invited to go from Dublin to Tralee to deliver a lecture on the Fenian Rising. This was to take place on 26 March. Detectives waited on her at Surrey House with an order forbidding her to enter Kerry. She was for defying this order, but Connolly vetoed the idea.

'If you go now you will be arrested at some little wayside station in Kerry and we need you just now in Dublin,' he told her, 'for we may be in the middle of things tonight or tomorrow!'

They decided that another woman from Dublin – Marie Perolz – should go to Tralee in her stead. She was to go dressed as Madame Markievicz and was not to reveal her real name. She was about the same build as Madame and the plan was successful. Austin Stack, who commanded the local Volunteers, was informed of her identity and the leader of the Tralee Cumann na mBan was also told. Marie Perolz read the exclusion order, then she read the speech. The Volunteers paraded ready to start a fight if a hair of the countess' head was touched. The meeting was a terrific success. Marie Perolz was in Tralee when the ill-fated *Aud* arrived with Roger Casement and Robert Monteith. But she knew nothing about their landing until she was on her way back to Dublin.

When the Rising began on Easter Monday, Cumann na mBan implemented the clause in their constitution about 'working in conjunction with the Volunteers'. They were mobilised for service in practically every garrison. Thirty-four women served in the GPO. Only one was in at the occupation. This was Winifred Carney, Connolly's secretary, who had been a member of Cumann na mBan since its inception in Belfast, where she had gained the reputation of being a crack shot. She marched into the GPO with a Webley and her typewriter. Together with Elizabeth O'Farrell and Julia Grenan, she remained with the garrison until the surrender.

Apart from these three, the other women members of the garrison were evacuated on Friday morning, after enduring the dangers and difficulties of the week. By that time the upper part of the building was in flames and it was clear that the place could no longer be held. Pearse gave orders for the girls to leave the building and spoke to them before they left. He told them that without the inspiration of their courage the Volunteers could not have made their stand. They deserved, he said, a foremost place in the history of the nation. He shook hands with each of the girls.

At the College of Surgeons – a Citizen Army post – the part in the fighting taken by Madame Markievicz and Margaret Skinnider has been detailed elsewhere. Some of the hardest tasks and the greatest risks were faced by the women dispatch carriers and by those sent out to get food and supplies. Éamonn Ceannt commanded in the South Dublin area, occupying the Marrowbone Lane Distillery, Watkins' Brewery, Roe's Distillery and the South Dublin Union. Margaret L. Kennedy has told how twenty-six girls marched with Ceannt's forces on Easter Monday. Their headquarters was the Marrowbone Lane Distillery, where they remained till the surrender the following Sunday night. Their special job was to attend to first-aid and to the getting, preparing and serving of food.

A bridge was held by the Volunteers and the first casualty was a man who had a bullet wound in his forehead. One of the girls staunched the bleeding and dressed the wound at the first-aid station. The girls were given handmade grenades to drop over the bridge onto the roadway in case of attack. Food and supplies were requisitioned. Parties of girls went out to get stretchers and succeeded in spite of jeers from groups of hostile women. Other sympathetic women, who lived nearby, brought in jugs of tea for the garrison in the mornings. Bread and milk were commandeered. Among the other prizes, a cow and two calves were driven in. One of the calves was killed, but the cow was kept for milking. The girls made butter and soda bread, for they had plenty of milk and buttermilk.

Cathal Brugha sustained many wounds during the repeated attacks on the South Dublin Union. But the garrison kept in cheerful spirits and many were confident of victory. Sleeping accommodation was primitive, beds being made of straw and sacking. Towards the end of the week the garrison felt so elated that the girls got in a supply of cakes and their best frocks, announcing their intention to hold a 'Victory Céilidhe'. As events turned out, this was the night of the surrender.

At the Marrowbone Lane Distillery, a tunnel was constructed by the men, and the girls were told that they could use this avenue of escape if the situation became desperate. But Cumann na mBan did not take this suggestion in a kindly way. 'What do you think we came here for?' asked one of the girls, disdainfully. Later it was found that the tunnel led to a policeman's house near the distillery. When the order to surrender came on Sunday, Con Colbert – a young officer of the Fianna who was in charge – refused to believe it at first. He insisted that Ceannt should come and confirm it. Éamonn Ceannt came in, looking heartbroken – said Margaret L. Kennedy – for he was against the surrender.

The women of the garrison could have evaded arrest. But they marched down four deep, in uniform, along with the men. Miss Mac-Namara, who led the contingent, went to the British officer in charge and explained that they were part of the rebel garrison and were surrendering with the rest. There were twenty-two in this group at the surrender. After being kept at Kilmainham barracks for the night they were taken to Kilmainham jail, where they remained for a week, being released on 8 May. An attempt was made to get them to sign a statement recanting their stand but this failed.

Much of the work done by the women consisted of carrying dispatches during Easter Week. To begin with, some of them were sent out to the country to take the news of the Rising to the Volunteers. Among these was Nora Connolly who went to the north. She had been mobilised with Cumann na mBan at Dungannon but this was a failure owing to the confusion of plans. So she had come to Dublin. Others who took messages were Maeve Cavanagh, Elizabeth O'Farrell, Julia Grenan and Marie Perolz. During the fighting in Easter Week, Pearse asked Julia Grenan to take a letter to the British lines and deliver it to an officer. The letter protested against the firing on a base hospital which Pearse insisted was under the protection of the Red Cross.

'I am going to ask you to do a very dangerous thing,' he told her. 'And you may, if you like, refuse it.'

'I came here to do what was necessary,' Julia Grenan told him.

She asked only that her friend, Elizabeth O'Farrell should be allowed to go with her.

The two set out along the deserted, bullet-swept streets. Soldiers screamed at them to go back but they advanced steadily until they reached a line of soldiers across Dame Street. One soldier held a bayonet to Elizabeth O'Farrell's breast while a young officer came dashing up, a revolver strapped to each wrist. Julia Grenan snatched the letter from her friend and gave it to the officer. The audacity of the proceedings took the soldiers by surprise and the women were able to walk away without cross-examination.

When the GPO was evacuated and the dash made into Moore Street, Winnie Carney went along with Connolly and the rest. They made their way into a shop and barricaded the windows. All were utterly exhausted. A youth guarding the barricade kept falling asleep and slipping down. Winnie Carney lying on the floor, wanted to change places with him but was too worn out to move, whatever happened. Later on, young Volunteers brought her small possessions and treasures to mind for them and wrote their addresses.

'Do you think we will win?' asked one lad. 'I was never in a rebellion before!'

'Neither was I!' Winnie Carney told him solemnly. She repeated this story to Pearse and to Connolly and was pleased to see them both laugh, in spite of the desperate situation.

When Connolly was lying wounded, he called Julia Grenan and said: 'I thought of you and of how many times you had come in and out of it during the week!'

The last episode of the hostilities was Elizabeth O'Farrell taking the message of surrender to General Lowe. An officer in charge at first refused to take any notice. Then he sent her to headquarters where she saw a higher officer. She delivered her message: *The commandant of the Irish Republican Army wishes to treat with the commandant of the British forces in Ireland.*

'Irish Republican Army,' he said, contemptuously. 'The Sinn Féiners you mean!'

'The Irish Republican Army they call themselves and I think it is a good name too,' retorted Elizabeth O'Farrell.

'Take that Red Cross off her and bring her over here to be searched. She is a spy!' he barked.

She was held prisoner in Tom Clarke's little shop for an hour. When General Lowe arrived he behaved courteously. But he demanded unconditional surrender and sent her back with the message. When she brought the answer to this, Pearse came out into Moore Street, and surrendered his sword. Before he was taken away, Pearse extracted a promise that Elizabeth O'Farrell would go free after she had taken the surrender order to the various garrisons. Instead, she was lodged in the Castle hospital, then in Ship Street barracks and finally in Kilmainham jail. She protested repeatedly against this treatment of an envoy and eventually Major Wheeler came to the prison and said her arrest was a mistake and that General Lowe was waiting at the Castle to apologise.

General Lowe offered a car to take her home but she said she would rather walk. So she walked out of the story of Easter Week, independent to the last.

At the end of the Rising, the number of women taken prisoner was seventy-seven. Of these seventy-two were soon released but five were imprisoned. These were Nell Ryan, Brigid Foley, Marie Perolz, Helena Molony and Winnie Carney. This list does not include Constance Markievicz who was court-martialled and sentenced to death, afterwards commuted to imprisonment for life. Madame Markievicz received her sentence gaily.

'Imagine it, Perolz,' she cried, when she met her friend in Kilmainham, 'I was sentenced to be shot, and I'm a lifer now – a *lifer*!'

Other women held at Kilmainham included Mrs Tom Clarke and Mrs Arthur Griffith. Dr Kathleen Lynn was also held.

Linda Kearns – who was a trained nurse – started a Red Cross hospital in North Great George Street, collecting bedding and stores from friends. Six girls helped in this with two youths as stretcher bearers. A number of wounded were attended to, including a British soldier. On Thursday she was ordered to confine her patients to British military or else to close. She closed the hospital, sending her patients to other hospitals and spent the rest of the week helping the rebels in dispatch carrying and first-aid. She was in Moore Street when The O'Rahilly was killed.

Hannah Sheehy-Skeffington came into conflict with the military when her husband, Francis Sheehy-Skeffington, was murdered by Captain Bowen-Colthurst, after being taken prisoner. Sheehy-Skeffington was a pacifist and was actively engaged in preventing looting in the city. Like her husband, Mrs Sheehy-Skeffington was in full sympathy with the aims of the Volunteers and spent much time in Easter Week taking food to various garrisons. After her husband's death she had to endure military raids on her home. Led by Bowen-Colthurst, soldiers fired a volley at her front windows and dashed in with fixed bayonets to be confronted by Mrs Sheehy-Skeffington, her maid, and her young son, aged eight. They had come to secure 'evidence' to justify the shooting of her husband. Bowen-Colthurst brought keys taken from his dead body. Mrs Sheehy-Skeffington faced them with magnificent courage. Later she demanded an inquiry and had the support of a British officer, Sir Francis Vane, who was dismissed from the army for his stand. Eventually she succeeded in getting to America where she told the whole story.

The first account of the Rising from the rebel side to get out of the country after the Rising was written by Patricia Lynch who got across from London during Easter Week, and returned a few days later. This was published in London, circulated widely there, and taken to Paris by W.B. Yeats, where Maud Gonne made it known to the Irish colony.

In the autumn of 1916 Cumann na mBan held a convention in Dublin, presided over by Miss Gavan Duffy, who was in the GPO in Easter Week. Countess Markievicz was elected president although she was in jail. Widows of the executed men were elected as vice-presidents. No note of retreat was sounded by Cumann na mBan in this time of repression. Hundreds of men were interned and the movement came to depend more than ever upon the women. Cumann na mBan funds amounted to £200 and this was used to relieve distress among the prisoners' families. Records were kept of the prisoners and efforts were made to keep in touch with them. On 22 December 1916, some hundreds were released and the others were set free on 17 June 1917. Madame Markievicz was detained until 18 June, when she was released from Aylesbury prison. When the countess arrived in Dublin on 21 June, she had a marvellous reception in the city. In 1917, she presided at the Cumann na mBan convention and branches numbered two hundred. At this convention members were 'pledged to maintain the Irish Republic proclaimed in Easter Week'. A call was made for 'the realisation of the Declaration embodied in the Proclamation of 1916 guaranteeing equal rights and liberties for all'. Among the means chosen was included: 'By educating the people of Ireland in, and urging them to adopt, a social policy as outlined by James Connolly.'

Women were prominent in the anti-conscription movement of 1918 when conscription was a real menace. Cumann na mBan organised an 'All Ireland Women's Day' as part of the campaign against conscription and companies marched to the City Hall to sign the pledge to oppose conscription. This pledge read: 'Denying the right of the British government to impose compulsory service in this country, we pledge ourselves solemnly to one another to resist conscription by the most effective means at our disposal.' Men and women alike took this pledge amid scenes of terrific enthusiasm. The pledge was sealed by a one-day general strike on 23 April.

In 1918 Madame Markievicz was elected as Sinn Féin MP, the first woman to become a member of the House of Commons, although she refused to take her seat. Cumann na mBan was proclaimed as a dangerous organisation – along with other national bodies – and its meetings declared illegal. During the Black and Tan period of terrorism which followed, the women co-operated with the men, carrying arms and ammunition, arranging 'safe houses', taking dispatches and caring for the wounded. In 1919 the Dublin offices of Cumann na mBan were twice raided and finally closed up. This was a period of terror throughout Dublin and the country, when hordes of armed ruffians tried to break the national spirit. A rigorous curfew was imposed. But the women carried out publicity and propaganda work, issuing leaflets and painting slogans on the walls. So effective was this work that the whitewash brush was described as 'an instrument of the conscience of Ireland'. During this Black and Tan period Linda Kearns was arrested for carrying arms and ammunition. She received a sentence of ten years by court martial. Some of this sentence she served under bad conditions in Walton jail. Afterwards she was transferred to Mountjoy where she succeeded in escaping with three others, including Ethne Coyle, who became president of Cumann na Ban, and who had a great personal record of militant action. Although it is impossible to dwell on individual exploits, the highest level of devotion and heroic sacrifice was reached during those years of intense struggle.

At its peak period before the Truce, Cumann na mBan had over 1,000 branches. At its convention in Dublin held in February, 1922, its opposition to the Treaty was registered by a vote of 419 to 63. It was the first organisation to declare against the Treaty and all the women deputies in the Dáil voted against. With the coming of the Treaty this record of women's activities comes to an end. There was, it is true, a further stormy period of struggle inside and outside jail. Events and personalities of this latter period have been recorded in Margaret Buckley's *The Jangle of the Keys*.

The test of a real national movement is how far it reaches down into the people. And it is clear from this record that thousands of girls and women – ranging from the very young to the very old – were caught up by the spirit of national regeneration, expressed in the 1916 Rising and the subsequent events. Most of these girls and women would have been content, in normal circumstances, to lead quiet, home-loving lives. But they came out into the streets of Dublin, into the rebel garrisons and into the jails; they carried out all the arduous and dangerous work of the national struggle. The demand made by a handful of men and women in Dublin in 1916 resounded through the country and so stirred the hearts of the people everywhere that their victory became certain.

MICHAEL COLLINS

by SEÁN McGARRY

To WRITE ABOUT Michael Collins a generation after his death and
for a generation so lamentably ignorant of his achievements, without
running into the superlative is next to impossible for anyone who
knew him and worked with him. It should be remembered by those
who may be inclined to regard even a brief outline of his public career
as savouring of adulation that, in the short time of three-and-a-half
years – from the beginning of 1918 until the Truce of 1921 – he had
through his own efforts emerged from the unknown into the position
of leader of the only successful revolutionary campaign in the history
of this country.

He had, of course, gathered round him a number of brave and
gallant souls whom he fired with his own enthusiasm; if I omit the
mention of their names it is only because space forbids it. But, let there
be no doubting the fact that during the last couple of years of the
struggle Collins was the inspiration and guiding spirit of the whole
movement.

Born in 1890 in the Rosscarbery district of West Cork, Michael
Collins entered the British civil service in 1905, but, finding the
routine unsuited to his temperament, he changed to a stockbroker's
office. There he acquired knowledge of financial matters which he put
to good use later. At the outbreak of war in 1914 he was compelled to
find another position which he found in a bank, where he remained
until the end of 1915. His activities outside working hours in London
do not concern us here, save to say that he became treasurer of the

Irish Republican Brotherhood for the area of London and the south of England. It was through the IRB that he met Seán MacDermott when Seán visited London on behalf of the supreme council. A fine friendship developed between the two, and Collins, having learned from MacDermott that a rising was contemplated, determined to go to Dublin to take part in the preparations. I remember his arrival at the office of *Irish Freedom* where he came to report to MacDermott. Tall, athletic and rather boyish, his face wreathed in smiles, he gave the impression of being carefree, full of life, energy and enthusiasm, and ready to undertake anything on behalf of his country.

Collins soon obtained a position with a firm of auditors, but left at the request of Joe Plunkett, who asked him to undertake some work of a personal nature which occupied the months between then and the Rising. During these months his spare time was spent in various Volunteer activities, notably the training camp started at Kimmage for men from Britain who were being prepared for 'The Day'. During the Rising he was in and around the GPO and seemed to enjoy every moment of it. He radiated cheerfulness and good humour and acted like a tonic to the spirit of the tired and sometimes downcast garrison. After the surrender he grew silent and when the news of the first executions came he had little to say. Collins wore a set and determined look as he left Richmond barracks for Frongoch internment camp. He was not long there before he set to work amongst his fellow internees, a mixed lot, some of whom had never contemplated the use of physical or any other kind of force. Others, like himself, regarded the Rising merely as one battle in a war which must be continued until victory was achieved. To these latter he devoted his attention and started to reorganise the IRB with the help of some members, a project for which he has been criticised in many quarters. But his reasons were clear and logical. Collins held strongly that the IRB was necessary to the successful maintenance of an armed force and to ensure its continuity, because as a secret organisation with a selected membership, it could not be suppressed without the greatest difficulty. On the other hand, the Irish Volunteers was of necessity an open organisation whose officers could be picked off at will by the enemy, and further to use a phrase of his own: 'The IRB would always contain the leaven in the movement.'

Released with the others in December 1916, Collins went home on a short holiday, and returned to Dublin early in 1917. It was then that his real work for Ireland started. Though not unmindful of the importance of a strong political organisation, he was more immediately concerned with the development of the Irish Volunteers, which work he began by getting in touch with ex-internees and others who had escaped internment. His appointment to the secretaryship of the National Aid Association in February 1917, gave him his great opportunity, as his work in this association enlarged his sphere of influence by bringing him into contact with people from all parts of the country. He made hosts of friends everywhere.

The early months of 1917 were memorable; there were two by-elections fought and won by Sinn Féin and excitement was kept at white heat until the general release of the sentenced prisoners, followed by the Clare election in which de Valera was victorious. Recruits were steadily coming into the Volunteers and the organisation of Sinn Féin was rapidly brought into good shape. So far as the general public was concerned, Collins might not have existed at that time, so little was known of him outside his sphere of activities; but his influence amongst the young men was growing. He was elected to the executive of Sinn Féin and, in the same week, to the executive of the Irish Volunteers of which he became director of organisation. With a small committee he tackled the writing of a new constitution and this was followed shortly afterwards by a scheme of organisation drafted entirely by himself. The work progressed steadily despite occasional arrests for drilling and seditious speeches, until the arrests in 1918 when Lloyd George invented the infamous 'German Plot'. The imprisonment of about forty men who mattered in the movement, allied to the fact that many others had to go on the run, might have created a serious problem. It did, I suppose, have repercussions through the country but it also provided Collins with the opportunity to show his genius for organisation and his capacity for hard work. He immediately set about establishing a system of communications, which, by the way, functioned throughout the fight. In a short time it was found that the direction of the whole movement had fallen on his shoulders, a more or less inevitable development. No matter who was arrested or who went on the run Collins was always available and could be found as required. The demands upon his time reached enormous proportions as a result of the growth of the Volunteer organisation, accentuated by the threat of conscription. Simultaneously with this work he found time to perfect a system of counter-espionage, as he had long previously realised that if we were to beat the British, we should first beat their excellent espionage. With that end in view he had already made contact with some friendly members of the 'G' (detective) division of the Dublin Metropolitan Police. The overwhelming success of Collins' endeavours in this field, now a matter of history, is dealt with elsewhere in this volume.

With the aid of the Liverpool IRB Collins organised a number of seamen, plying between that port and Dublin, to carry arms and munitions. He eventually arranged for personnel to be carried, too, so that travel between Great Britain and Ireland could be undertaken by IRA elements without grave risk. In addition to his duties as director of organisation and adjutant-general of the Volunteers, Collins also had to undertake the work of the secretary who was one of those arrested as a result of the 'German Plot'. Thus, it is no exaggeration to state that he was then the mainspring and guiding force of the whole Volunteer movement.

The general election of 1918 brought with it an additional mountain of work. Workers there were aplenty, but there was lack of direction, until Collins co-ordinated the efforts of the different available elements, even though the routine demands on his time had already increased so that his energy and capacity for work had become the wonder of his associates. The election, which resulted in the complete victory of Sinn Féin, was followed by the establishment of Dáil Éireann. Collins missed the first meeting of the Dáil as he was in England with Harry Boland to attend to the escape of de Valera, Milroy and McGarry, from Lincoln jail. Having seen them safely off the premises he returned immediately to Dublin and to work.

As though his time was not fully occupied by all these matters, Collins managed to write a monthly article on organisation for *An t-Óglach*, the official organ of the Volunteers, the direction and publication of which he personally supervised.

The general release of the 'German Plot' prisoners took place in March 1919 and the tempo of events increased. There had been some skirmishing in the country and war was coming gradually but surely. Collins was inclined to be cautious then. He induced headquarters to issue an order to the effect that its permission should be obtained before major operations could be undertaken. The object of the order was not the prevention of such engagements; rather it was an attempt to ensure that all necessary precautions were taken, that arms, personnel and dispositions were such as would entail the minimum loss of life. It was carried out for some time but its observance became impossible as the struggle developed.

One is apt to forget that from 1919 Collins was minister for finance and that in pursuance of a Dáil Éireann decree he had to take charge of the flotation of a loan of £250,000. Under ordinary circumstances that task would have been a whole-time occupation for a director with considerable staff at his disposal; yet despite his already very full programme, Collins took the job in his stride with the help of a couple of clerks and a few organisers. Then there were the ever-increasing military operations, the burning of tax offices, Sinn Féin courts for which protection had to be provided, major operations like the burning of the Custom House, the provision of arms and munitions for the fighting men and the hundred-and-one other activities all of which to some extent claimed his attention. As the struggle developed his name became the symbol of resistance to British rule. Spies and Castle touts were set on his track and on those of his colleagues, but because of his splendid counter-espionage he was able to cope adequately with all such hazards. In dealing with them, however, he was scrupulous to the point of danger. In fact his attitude in this regard was often a source of worry and even of annoyance to the lads whose task it was to bring in evidence of the guilt of spies. Nothing is more certain than that no spy was executed until the certainty of his guilt had been established.

It is difficult nowadays to recapture the atmosphere of those times in which a veritable reign of terror prevailed. The Auxiliaries and Black and Tans formed the spearhead of a campaign of frightfulness which was carried on by the British with all the force at their command. Ambushes and fights between IRA elements and the enemy were of daily occurrence, whilst the murder of civilians and IRA prisoners, burning and looting by the British, street searches and night raids became more and more frequent. All the while frantic but unavailing efforts were made to capture Collins. Eventually peace feelers began to emanate from different enemy sources. These were not allowed to interfere with the conduct of the war, but ultimately when Collins' correspondence shows that he was preparing to intensify operations, de Valera received from Lloyd George a letter suggesting the former's attendance at a conference in London and expressing a fervent desire to end what he called: 'The ruinous conflict which has for centuries divided Ireland and embittered the relations of the peoples of these two islands.' That letter was dated 24 June 1921, and it led up to the negotiations which resulted in the Truce on 11 July. It must have been a source of pride to Collins in his thirty-first year that the British government by agreeing to a Truce had recognised the IRA as an army with which negotiations could be discussed. Only a short while previously we were merely a 'murder gang' in the opinion of Lloyd George.

In appraising Collins the man one can only write of him as one found him. He has been the subject of much detraction by writers who did not know him and who might usefully be reminded of Mitchel's reference to Davis. Mitchel wrote: 'It is difficult for those who did not know Davis to understand and appreciate the influence which that most puissant and imperial character exerted upon the young Irishmen of his day.' If this were true of Davis whose writings in verse and prose had warmed the hearts of his generation as they were passed from hand to hand to be read round the firesides through the country, how much more true of Collins who, to the great majority of the people, was but a name – a name, however, which had come to mean even more than that of Davis.

Collins was neither weak, mild nor saintly. He was never the schizophrene that some writers have dubbed him, nor was he a mystery man endowed with occult powers which enabled him to avoid raiding parties. He could no more sense a raid than I could. What was extra-ordinary about him was his colossal capacity for work, his boundless energy and fixed purpose bent upon paralysing British power in Ireland. He had the gift of friendship and the gift of enthusiasm which inspired all his colleagues to work for him and with him. He did not spare anyone as he did not spare himself. He has been wrongly accused of violent tempers. True he had no patience with laziness nor could he tolerate inefficiency; but his so-called fits of temper were merely sudden explosions which disturbed but momentarily his invariable good humour. He hated the loss of a man and never acquired the soldier's outlook that a casualty was merely a casualty. The news that somebody was killed would depress him greatly, irrespective as to whether it related to a dear friend or to a Volunteer whom he had never seen. He made it his duty where possible to visit the friends and relatives of those killed or arrested, and many a mother and many a wife can testify to his gentleness.

He had an unwonted respect for older people and his deference in dealing with them was notable. His almost childish sense of loyalty to colleagues was particularly in evidence during the last month of the war, when differences arose between himself and some members of the Dáil cabinet, occasioned it would seem by jealousy of the part he had played and of the position he had attained. He never spoke of them himself and so far as could be seen he never let them influence the carrying out of any of his numerous duties. The picture I like to retain is that of a hunted man who resolutely refused to be hunted; whose job, as he often described it, was to get on with the work, who met every difficulty with a smile and who remained through it all, as he said of himself, 'just a representative of plain Irish stock'. Such was Michael Collins, and no man can measure the loss sustained by Ireland when he met his death beside his own homestead.

ÉAMON DE VALERA

by M.J. McMANUS

ON A JUNE morning in 1917, there was intense excitement in Dublin city. All night long crowds had waited upon the quays, singing 'rebel' songs, straining their eyes as the dawn came for the sight of an incoming ship. The last of the prisoners of the Easter Week Rising were coming home.

Somebody eventually brought word that they were being landed at Kingstown (not yet Dún Laoghaire), whereupon the people got into military formation and marched to the Westland Row terminus. As soon as the boat-train steamed in, there was a tremendous outburst of cheering and the crowd began to sing 'The Soldiers' Song'. Then the prisoners were packed into brakes and escorted, with bands and banners, though the densely packed streets, where a little more than a year before they had gone out to challenge the might of an empire. One tall, spare figure, with sombre brown eyes and ascetic-looking features, seemed to attract universal attention. 'There he is!' people exclaimed, 'there's de Valera!' Dublin was welcoming home the last surviving commandant of the Rising. The fame of Boland's Mills had gone abroad.

To the vast majority of them, it was their first sight of de Valera. A little more than a year before, outside Volunteer circles and the class-rooms of a few colleges, he had been unknown. Born in New York in October 1882, of a Spanish father and an Irish mother, he was brought to Ireland by an uncle when he was two years old and grew up with his mother's relations at Bruree. Bruree and the Maigue river – a stream that once nourished a nest of Gaelic poets on its banks – stand where there was an ancient pass-way from the hills of Clare into the rich lands of Limerick and the Golden Vale that runs past Slieve Phelim to the Rock of Cashel. The ruined castles that stud the valley speak eloquently of ancient wars and the City of the Broken Treaty is not far away.

Around the fireside in Patrick Coll's cottage young Éamon began to learn something of his country's history. The old tales would be told and re-told of a winter's night when the neighbours dropped in, and the old ballads would be sung. There would be talk, too, of the Land War that was setting the country on fire and names like Parnell and Davitt would crop up again and again. Sometimes the conversation would be in a language he did not understand, for around Bruree the old people still spoke Gaelic.

At thirteen he went to the school of the Christian Brothers at Charleville – now Rath Luirc – a distance of some six miles, making the journey by train in the morning, returning on foot if the weather was fine. The Christian Brothers found him an easy pupil – serious-minded, industrious and talented. He liked his books and his lessons. At home of a summer's evening he would sometimes be found, like Abraham Lincoln, lying with a book on the top of a haystack or working out sums by the light of the kitchen fire when he should have been in bed. There was a *Life of Sarsfield* lying about and a copy of Jane Porter's *Scottish Chiefs* – a great favourite in the countryside in nineteenth-century Ireland – and it was books like these that first fired the boy's imagination and set him dreaming romantic dreams as he lay reading on the grassy banks of the Maigue. From the Christian Brothers he got tales of Spanish ships in Galway Bay, of Spanish soldiers at Kinsale, and of a lonely grave in Valladolid, and it gave him a pride in his Spanish ancestry.

At fifteen, a scholarship took him from Bruree to Blackrock College, near Dublin. He had grown up tall and thin, but strongly built and athletic. He proved himself as good at games as he was at books and distinguished himself both on the running track and on the football field. The year of his arrival at Blackrock was 1898 – the centenary year of the great rising. In Dublin there were meetings and banquets and processions. The parliamentarians were vocal with sunburst oratory, but it was the young men and women of the recently founded Gaelic League and the Irish Republican Brotherhood who were making the celebrations an occasion for national resurgence. Even within the cloistered walls of the college of the Holy Ghost Fathers some rumour of these happenings must have found their way. But Éamon de Valera, preoccupied with his studies and his games, took little heed of them. At Christmas and mid-summer he would return to Bruree, where he would lend a hand in the work of the farm. 'There is not an operation on the farm,' he said in later years, 'that I as a youngster had not to perform, from the spancelling of a goat to the milking of a cow. I followed the tumbler rake. I took my place on top of the rick. I took milk to the creamery. I harnessed the donkey, the jennet and the horse.'

After reading a brilliant intermediate and university course he was appointed a junior master at Blackrock, the first step on what seemed to be the destined road to a scholastic career. Before he was twenty he was entrusted with the higher classes and a little later he left Blackrock to take a professorship at Rockwell. The year was 1904 and he was twenty-two.

The young man had made good. With a degree to his name he came back to Dublin, where there were plenty of openings awaiting him. His industry was amazing. In addition to reading a post-graduate course in higher mathematics and taking a diploma in education, he taught at different periods in University College, in Belvedere, in Clonliffe, and in the Carysfort Training College for teachers. His career appeared to be settled. All the gathered records agree that he was a born teacher, painstaking, patient, lucid, master of his subject and, despite a gravity and high-mindedness beyond his years, popular both in the classroom and on the playing-field.

In 1908 an event happened that was destined to have a profound effect not only on his cultural and educational development, but on his domestic life and later career. He joined the Gaelic League. De Valera had learnt his first Irish phrases from his grandmother and there was an old Gaelic shanachie at Bruree with whom he conversed, in order to improve his knowledge of the language, when he visited his home. Now, infected by the spreading enthusiasm for native culture, he enrolled himself as a student at the Leinster College of Irish. There he met a young teacher who was equally enthusiastic for the language revival. She was pretty and talented; an amateur actress who had appeared in some of the first Gaelic plays ever produced. Her name was Sinéad Ní Fhlannagáin. Friendship ripened between them, and in January 1910, they were married.

The fateful years of the second Home Rule struggle came, bringing excitement that penetrated even into the Gaelic classrooms. Carson was arming the Orangemen; Winston Churchill was mobbed in Belfast; the shadow of civil war – with Ireland as its focal point – was over the two islands. In Dublin, in the year 1913, at the call of James Larkin and James Connolly, the Dublin workers swarmed out of the slums to engage in unequal combat with Mr William Martin Murphy's all-powerful Federation of Employers. There were riots and batonings and in Liberty Hall Countess Markievicz was running a soup-kitchen. In August of that year Larkin called upon the workers to arm. 'What is legal for the Orangemen is legal for us,' he declared. Then and there the Citizen Army was born.

De Valera's sympathies, like those of the average citizen, were with the workers. At home in Bruree, uncle Patrick Coll was doing in a small way what Larkin was doing in Dublin, organising a branch of the Trade and Labour Society, a body formed to further the interests of landless men and agricultural labourers. But in Dublin, for the moment, there was no contact between the collar-and-tie class to which de Valera belonged and the men who followed Larkin and Connolly. The soldiers of the Citizen Army were nearly all manual workers. Before the end of 1913, however, another army sprang into existence. A new body of Volunteers, with men like Eoin MacNeill and Pádraig Pearse at its head, was formed. The parliamentarians frowned on it at first, but soon, realising that it was too powerful to be ignored, sought to obtain control of it. De Valera was one of the first to join. Here, at last, was something more tangible, more purposeful than the wordy conflicts of political warfare. The young men were leading the way, earnest young men of the Gaelic classes and resolute young men from the hurling fields, young men who had read Arthur Griffith's *Sinn Féin* week by week, who had heard the separatist doctrine expounded in Tom Clarke's little shop in Parnell Street, who had cheered Yeats' *Cathleen Ni Houlihan* at the Abbey Theatre.

De Valera did not make his decision lightly. As a married man he had to consider his responsibilities. It was only after deep thought that he decided to take active part in a movement which was almost certain to end in war and bloodshed.

As a Volunteer, he soon made his mark, and within a few months had attained the rank of captain. He was now in his thirty-first year, 'exceptionally tall' – to quote one who was in his company at the time – 'considerably over six feet in height, a very serious-looking man with a long nose and spectacles and a foreign complexion, wearing Irish homespuns'. A singularly impressive figure he must have been, with his commanding stature, his strong voice, his foreign look and his homely garb. The men he drilled on the Dublin hills soon came to respect him. He brought the same zeal and the same high order of intelligence to field tactics that he had formerly devoted to problems of mathematics and he studied the art of street fighting as assiduously as Robert Emmet had done more than a century before.

In 1914 the cauldron which had been bubbling since Carson had started to raise an army in the North began to boil over. In March there was mutiny at the British army headquarters at the Curragh. In April the Carsonites, with the connivance of the British authorities, landed 35,000 German rifles at Larne. In July the National Volunteers marched to Howth to aid in the landing of a similar cargo of rifles brought across the North Sea by Erskine Childers and his wife. This time there was no connivance. Dublin Castle called out its soldiery to prevent the nationalist gun-running and there was shooting in the streets of Dublin. It was de Valera's first approach to real fighting.

A few days later the First World War broke out and John Redmond virtually offered the Volunteers to Britain. A split followed at once. 'Ireland,' said Roger Casement, 'has no blood to give any land or any cause but that of Ireland.' The majority of the Volunteers were swayed by Redmond and thousands of them joined the British army. Some 10,000 or 12,000 remained with MacNeill and the other leaders who believed that if Irishmen were to fight for liberty it should be on Irish soil. De Valera was one of the minority.

Steadily, his influence grew in the Volunteer ranks, and in 1915 he was appointed adjutant of the Dublin brigade, of which Thomas MacDonagh was commandant. All through that year the IRB went resolutely ahead perfecting their plans. From the moment the European war had broken out they were determined that a Rising would take place. The only question was when? Connolly with his Citizen Army was all for immediate action, but the IRB – represented by Clarke, Pearse, MacDonagh, MacDermott and others – were not quite ready. There was constant communication with men like John Devoy in America and ceaseless activity behind the scenes.

Easter Sunday 1916, was finally selected as the day for the great adventure, and Pearse gave orders for a route march and field operations on that day. A rumour of what was happening reached MacNeill – who had not been informed and who disapproved – and he issued an order cancelling the manoeuvres. At the same time, he sent a dispatch to de Valera – now a commandant – ordering that there should be 'no movement whatsoever' of Volunteers under his command. De Valera was sorely troubled. For MacNeill he had not only the highest personal regard, but all the respect due to Ireland's greatest living scholar. Not only that, but he was not altogether convinced that the moment to strike had arrived. Yet he knew that a rising was now inevitable. On Easter Sunday morning the revolutionary council had met and final plans were made. The Rising was fixed for noon on the following day. For de Valera that was sufficient. However slender the chances of success, he would play his part.

On Holy Thursday night he had slept at home without taking off his uniform and with his revolver lying at his bedside. He did not sleep there again. Good Friday and Saturday were filled with feverish activities, giving orders, sending and receiving messages. On Easter Sunday night he returned home for a few hours and left late, after having gone upstairs for a few moments to have a look at his sleeping children. To his wife he gave no inkling of what was about to happen.

Early on Easter Monday morning the men of the Volunteers and of the Citizen Army were astir. At Liberty Hall the last salutes were taken and Commandant de Valera's little column – something less than a hundred men – wheeled southwards through the city. The task assigned to him was one of great difficulty and was evidence in itself of the complete confidence reposed in his ability by the men at the top. Reinforcements would inevitably be dispatched from Britain as soon as news of the Rising reached the authorities and it was the business of de Valera and his 3rd battalion to hold them up when they marched on the city from Kingstown.

Leaving a handful of men guarding the Westland Row terminus, which was seized without difficulty, he halted at Mount Street bridge, which crosses the canal where it bisects the coastal road. Here, with enforced economy, he placed other handfuls – not much more than a dozen altogether – in houses overlooking the bridge. The remainder, some seventy or eighty, he marched to the building he had selected as his headquarters – Boland's Flour Mills, a tall, many-windowed edifice. There, and on a nearby distillery (this was a blind, for during the week it remained unoccupied) he hoisted the tri-colour. All through Easter Monday the work of barricading the place went on. Curious crowds who had gathered were dispersed – for there was grim work ahead – and sentries posted.

Tuesday brought little change in the situation. The men at Westland Row were recalled and joined their comrades in the Mill. But it was mostly a day of waiting. On Wednesday the insurrection blazed up fiercely in other parts of the city. Troops had advanced from the Curragh and the gun-boat *Helga* was shelling Liberty Hall. The upper storey of the GPO – the Volunteer headquarters – was battered by other shells and many buildings in O'Connell Street were set on fire.

Troops had now been landed at Kingstown and were marching along the route held by de Valera's men. Many of them would seem to have been raw recruits without any war experience. They walked straight into a trap. As they approached Mount Street bridge they were met by a withering, concentrated fire from the houses where de Valera had placed his men. Half a dozen times they retired and advanced, always with the same result. The commandant's aide-de-camp, Captain Malone, was in command at this spot and he made the most of his strategic position. It was not until Clanwilliam House, which he held, attacked by a gatling gun and hand-grenades, had crashed in flames, burying him and some of his comrades under the debris, that the bridge was stormed. In his report to the British government afterwards, General Sir John Maxwell described how 'after careful arrangements the whole column, accompanied by bombing parties, attacked the schools and houses where the chief opposition lay, and the battalions charging in successive waves carried all before them'. But Sir John did not reveal – perhaps he was not aware – that the opposition came from no more than fourteen men. The British losses were two hundred and thirty-four killed and wounded, or about half the total number of their casualties in the Rising. The Volunteers lost six. The battle had lasted for five hours.

Out at Ringsend the fighting grew more intense as the week wore on. British snipers took up positions in the tall Mount Street houses and the Mill was continually under fire. A field gun was mounted in Percy Place and a shell crashed through an outer wall of the Bakery. To divert the enemy's fire, de Valera dispatched an officer to send out semaphore messages from the roof of the empty distillery nearby. The messages meant nothing, but they had the desired effect. The British, believing that the distillery was the area headquarters of the Volunteers, began to pound it with artillery. Some of the shells fell into the river near the *Helga*, which had steamed down to take part in the bombardment. The *Helga*'s captain mistook the shells for republican artillery fire and trained his guns on the distillery, which was thus shelled from land and sea. But the Mill remained intact and the barricades unbreached. Along with the Four Courts, held by Commandant Daly, Boland's Mill remained to the end the most strongly defended post in the city.

The fires of Thursday night told de Valera that all was not well with his comrades in the central positions. Communications with the Post Office had been severed and the orange-red midnight sky above the heart of Dublin told its own tale. No thought of surrender, however, had as yet occurred to his mind and he went about giving orders quietly and methodically. His grey-green uniform was white with flour-dust; his unshaven face was haggard, his eyes were weary from lack of sleep; but he still contrived to maintain his cheerfulness and encourage his men. All through Friday and Saturday, when the burning Post Office was evacuated and Pearse had surrendered his sword, when every other position had fallen, the Mill was still offering defiance and the men of the 3rd battalion were still fighting fiercely on roofs, at barricades and at street corners. But, as the week drew to a close, the end came in sight and for the first time de Valera betrayed any emotion. 'Ah,' he said to a bakery employee who had been allowed in to tend the horses, 'if the people had only come out with knives and forks!'

It was not until Sunday that the order to lay down arms reached him. He marshalled his men, thanked them for what they had done and endured, saw to it that the doors of the Mill were made safe against possible looting, and then marched them to the nearest British military post. To the officers with whom he parleyed he made only one request – that his men should not be molested when surrendering.

With the surrender, de Valera's career as a soldier was – with the exception of a short period in the tragic year of 1922 – at an end. Eleven days after the surrender he was put on trial and sentenced to death, but, possibly on account of his American birth, the sentence was commuted to penal servitude for life.

In Dartmoor his chronicle of jails began. Brooding in his cell he was determined that he would pit his resolution against that of his jailors; that no solitude would break his spirit or make him morose or bitter. There might be long years of penal servitude ahead, but some day release would come and he would be faced again with the task of supporting his wife and children. Carysfort or Blackrock might take him back when the jail gates opened.

It was a dreary existence at Dartmoor, with hardly a break in the deadly demoralising monotony. Once only in the early months was there a touch of drama. Eoin MacNeill, who had done his best to stop the Rising, had come to serve a sentence along with those who had fought in it. One morning when the Irish prisoners were lined up for inspection, MacNeill's spare figure was seen descending the iron stairs to take his place in their ranks. Immediately, disregarding all prison rules, de Valera stepped out and faced the prisoners. 'Irish Volunteers!' his voice rang out: 'Attention! Eyes left!' The command – a salute for MacNeill – was obeyed with military precision. 'Then,' wrote one who was present, 'de Valera stepped back into the ranks, leaving us a bit dazed by his chivalry and courage.' The senior officer of the Volunteers – the last surviving commandant of Easter Week – was honouring his former chief-of-staff.

Before the end of the year all the long-term prisoners of Easter Week were removed to Lewes jail, where, under de Valera's leadership, they staged a revolt. Rebelling against their 'convict' status, they demanded the right of prisoners of war and, when they were refused, proceeded to make things as unpleasant as possible for the prison authorities. The authorities retaliated by dividing them up into small handfuls and scattering them through other English prisons.

Release, which had been decided upon by Lloyd George to appease American opinion, came in June 1917. As he walked out of Pentonville, where he had spent the last weeks of his imprisonment, de Valera was handed a telegram. It informed him that he had been selected to contest a forthcoming by-election in East Clare. It was the turning point in his career. Up to then he had thought of release in terms of taking up the old interrupted existence in terms of home and family, of teaching posts to be looked for. Now there loomed up before him a new road, a road where there would be few signposts and many pitfalls, a road that might lead anywhere. The prospect was as disturbing as it was exciting.

But he did not hesitate long. He had heard, in jail, of the extraordinary change that had come over the political situation; of the quickening of the nation's pulse; of the republican triumphs in Roscommon and Longford. Easter Week was not an end, but a beginning and Clare had called on him to raise the standard. Well, to Clare he would go.

A week later there were scenes of rejoicing in the Banner County such as had not been witnessed since O'Connell's historic victory ninety years before. De Valera, having beaten the strongest candidate that the Parliamentary Party could put forward, was member for Clare. The bonfires blazed from Burren to Bodyke.

The Clare election was the beginning of his political career. The roar of cheering that greeted him as, wearing his Volunteer uniform, he mounted a platform in the market square at Ennis, was not a welcome to an orator from whom golden eloquence was expected, it was a tribute to a soldier who had fought a gallant fight in Easter Week. Yet, unknown as he was, inexperienced as he was, devoid as he was of the natural gift of oratory, he nevertheless impressed when he spoke. He was lucid and vigorous; he hammered home his points with force and sincerity. There were no personalities, no conventional flourishes; instead, there was a grave dignity which has ever since remained the most striking characteristic of his public speeches.

What remains does not, strictly speaking, belong to *Dublin's Fighting Story*. It belongs to the general history of the last phase of Ireland's struggle for independence. From 1917 to 1921 Éamon de Valera was not merely president of Sinn Féin, president of the Volunteers, and, later, first minister in Dáil Éireann and president of the Irish Republic; he was the accepted leader of the nation, with a power and prestige as great, or perhaps greater, than that of O'Connell or Parnell. The position he had attained was an extraordinary tribute to a man whose name was virtually unknown in Ireland before 1916, who had had no political training, and who was endowed with none of the more obvious political gifts. Yet nobody seemed to doubt the wisdom of the nation's choice. Even in Britain, people soon began to awaken to the fact that a new Irish leader of outstanding character, and pledged to use different methods to attain the ancient goal, had suddenly come forward. 'Mr de Valera,' said Lloyd George, within a week of the East Clare election, 'is obviously a man of great ability and great influence.' And when, a year later, after he had successfully led the anti-conscription campaign and then made his dramatic escape from Lincoln jail, he toured the United States in Ireland's cause, he became known and respected across the Atlantic. As Arthur Griffith said in the Dáil: 'The work accomplished by the president in America has been extraordinary; he has welded the Irish race into a united force and has raised the Irish question there into the position of an international issue.'

When de Valera returned from America at Christmas 1920, the War of Independence had reached its peak point, and a resolute effort was being made to give the Republic the requisite machinery of government. It was the president's duty, in his hiding-place in Dublin, to keep his finger on every key and to direct the activities of both the departmental and fighting machines. Day after day, he worked far into the night, reading reports, giving instructions, receiving messages, conferring, advising, planning.

The fighting men were his special concern and one of his first acts after returning from America was to clarify the position of the IRA. British ministers and propagandists still endeavoured to represent the army of the Republic as composed of undisciplined bands of blood-thirsty irresponsibles (Lloyd George's 'murder gangs'). In a public state-ment he issued de Valera put the matter beyond ambiguity:

> 'One of our first governmental acts,' he said, 'was to take over the control of the voluntary armed forces of the nation. From the Irish Volunteers we fashioned the Irish Republican Army to be the military arm of the government. This army is, therefore, a regular state force, under the civil control of the elected representatives, and under organisation and discipline imposed by their representatives, and under officers who hold their commissions under warrant from those representatives. The government is, therefore, responsible for the actions of this army.'

On the question of the morality of the methods and tactics used by the army, he was equally explicit. In the British parliament and in British newspapers, ambushing was constantly being referred to as a cowardly and indefensible method of warfare. It was a charge that de Valera felt should be answered. To an American interviewer he said:

> If the British may use their tanks and steel-armoured cars, why should we hesitate to use the cover of stone walls and ditches? Why should the element of surprise be denied to us? If German forces had landed in England during the recent war, would it have been held wrong for Englishmen to surprise them?

Ireland, it is obvious, had, in those days of stress and danger, a leader whose pronouncements were marked by courage, dignity and sincerity.

ARTHUR GRIFFITH

by LIAM Ó BRIAIN

TWO ALTERNATING CURRENTS, so to speak, have supplied the motive power for the march of the Irish people since the Act of Union and perhaps for centuries before that ill-omened piece of legislation – the revolutionary current and the evolutionary. Passing over the earlier periods, we find the course of Irish political activity in the nineteenth century and almost to our day changing from the tradition of Tone to that of O'Connell and back again. We think of the '48 men, of the Fenians, of the Invincibles, of the Irish Volunteers, of the IRA when we mention the Tone tradition. We think of constitutionalism, of Isaac Butt, of parliamentary parties, of the movement which held the stage when some of us were young, the O'Connell tradition.

Two names occupy a middle position, more or less between the two currents, those of Parnell and Arthur Griffith, but Griffith stands more to the left than Parnell. When Parnell called on the people to hold fast to their homesteads, when he gave the word to use the weapon of boycott, he was being essentially revolutionary rather than evolutionary – he was applying the fundamental principle of the revolutionary tradition, namely that action at home, carried to the point of defiance of British law and constitutionalism, was the only way by which really decisive progress could be made towards the goal of national independence. The use of force had always to halt before British military superiority. But the spirit aroused by a military insurrectionary movement could drive on a semi-military, semi-constitutional, semi-legal movement which would come immediately afterwards.

The Famine nipped in the bud such a vigorous movement led by the Young Irelanders, which might have made of the 1850s a very stirring period in our onward march instead of being one of torpor. The chance recurred when, at the very end of the 1870s, Michael Davitt in Ireland, supported by John Devoy in America, placed the flickering torch of Fenianism into the strong hands of the youthful Parnell. For that was the significance of the 'New Departure' initiated by these two men who saw that the splendid spirit of devotion and sacrifice created or recreated by Fenianism was wasting away and would die unless some practical outlet for it was provided. Davitt saw also that it was necessary to break first the grip of feudalism, as he called it, before men economically freer, could be led directly against the bastions of foreign domination. So the revolutionary passed into the semi-evolutionary, into the passive resistance of the Land League.

Pure old Fenians cursed Davitt for 'betraying' the cause of physical force, but did he not rather save it for another day and has he, even now, the high rank he deserves among Ireland's men? Had the boycott weapon been applied by Parnell during his Home Rule campaign to government institutions, after its employment in agrarian conflict, might not, nay, in the light of subsequent experience, would not that campaign, after a short and sharp clash of forces, have been successful? But his movement went down in disunion and despair, as had happened to the movements of the 1840s and 1860s. By the middle of the 1890s, the Fenians, growing old, and the few young men who were attracted towards them, seemed to be a completely spent force. The people in general were content with a mild, mannerly 'demand' for Home Rule made by Parnell's former followers who were also beginning to grow old. It was then that a new man, an unknown man gave the dying spirit of Fenianism a hope and a programme just as Davitt had done nearly twenty years previously. That man was Arthur Griffith.

Griffith was a product of the Dublin working class. Born in 1872, he was apprenticed to the printing trade. One of his boyhood tasks, he used to relate, was to carry periodically printers' galleys to the Freemason headquarters in Molesworth Street. Being always kindly received there, he developed early a certain esteem for the unionist element in Irish life, which was reinforced by his close studies of the lives of the Protestant patriots from Grattan to Davis. For we must picture to ourselves the youthful Griffith spending nearly all his spare time and nearly all his spare pennies and sixpences among the second-hand book shops and book stalls of the Dublin quays. The study of Irish history, the history of the eighteenth and nineteenth centuries in particular, and more particularly still, the history of Grattan's parliament and of the Young Ireland movement, became his all-absorbing occupation, one might say his passion.

Contemporary politics began to interest him just when the great movements of the 1880s were coming to their disastrous close. Though only eighteen years of age, Griffith witnessed the Parnell split somewhat from the inside, as he was a member of one of the Parnell election committees in Dublin. He used relate some curious anecdotes of that tragic period. Two lessons he learned then which he never forgot, one was that in dealing with English politicians, Irishmen must never allow passion or emotion to run away with them, must keep their heads icy cool; the other was that Irishmen must have their own standards of conduct and honour and allow neither the sneers nor the strictures of their opponents to influence them.

For a while after the split, in the extreme depression which followed, Griffith was a member of the National Club which met in Rutland (subsequently Parnell) Square. He belonged to the extremist group there, which studied Irish history and brooded over the recent disaster. But after a few years, in the middle 1890s, Griffith suddenly emigrated to South Africa. He was poor, there seemed no prospect for him either as an individual or as a nationalist. The Fenian movement to which in all probability he already belonged (if not then, certainly on his return from South Africa) was in a hopeless condition and the constitutional movement not much better. But there were probably other reasons; a desire to see the world, to see the British Empire in action (a subject that interested him greatly; the writer once heard him say that he would like to retire and write the real history of the Empire!), and some of his old friends of that period suspected a disappointment in love as a primary cause of his emigration.

Be that as it may, Griffith spent a year or two in different places in South Africa working at his trade. At Middelburg in the Transvaal he published, according to himself, a paper for a short while. This would be the first of his many editorships. The paper was anti-English, the Boers were delighted but didn't buy it as the paper was in English. He was also popular among the natives in one job where he was a 'baas' over them and they nicknamed him 'Cuguan'. This word means 'dove' and the writer heard him tell with a broad smile once how an old native explained that he had a waddling or rolling walk like that of a dove! He used to sign articles in *Sinn Féin*, in later years as 'Cuguan'. It has been stated that he learnt to speak Kaffir, but this is probably an exaggeration. He had a constitutional incapacity for learning languages. He struggled with Irish for years in the intervals of the long, hard, poverty-stricken campaign which occupied the best years of his life, but it was only on his return from his imprisonment in Gloucester in 1918 that he informed SeanPhádraic Ó Conaire with great satisfaction that while in prison, he had succeeded in reading one of Padraic's books without the aid of a dictionary.

Griffith witnessed the parliamentary diplomatic sparrings between British and Boer which led to the South African war. He related once that astonishment was caused at the period, by the competent knowledge of international law displayed in the replies sent from the former Republic's government to the British Foreign Office. This knowledge, according to Griffith, came from a drunken Irishman out there, whom he named and who had been a professor or graduate of international law in Trinity College. Whenever a missive arrived from Joe Chamberlain the call went out for O'F_____ and Griffith or some other Irishman would search the bars for him, cool his head with cold water and send him along to help compose the reply of 'Oom Paul' Kruger's government to Her Britannic Majesty's minister!

He returned home, via East Africa, Naples and Lisbon, towards the end of 1897, well before the Boer War started. He was thus in Ireland for the resurgence of patriotic sentiment caused by the '98 anniversary celebrations; for the great wave of anti-British feeling all over Europe which accompanied the unprovoked attack on the two little Boer states; and for the beginning of the great Irish-Ireland movement which, starting about 1899, carried us onto 1916 and beyond and to which he was to give its political expression.

The sundered wings of the Parliamentary Party had been re-united under the leadership of John Redmond and were to represent in the House of Commons the constitutional demand for Home Rule within the Empire for the next eighteen years. In a very few years the Land Act of George Wyndham, an event of real importance, was to give a belated crowning to the fight of the Land League and remove the fear of landlordism. Of much greater significance was the spiritual awakening of the nation with the turn of the century. The Gaelic League, the dramatic movement, the poetic movement, the industrial revival, the general resurgence of national spirit, the intense desire to make Ireland 'self-respecting, self-relying, self-advancing', the reaction from the prolonged self-depreciation and aping of the ways of foreigners and gentry, so-called – all this, to a generation disillusioned with parliamentary action by the Parnell split, to an eager, on-coming, new generation to whom that split meant nothing, needed for its completion a new political philosophy and a more intellectual and constructive form of political activity. Griffith supplied it.

For a very few years after his return from South Africa, his closest political friend was Willie Rooney, 'Fear na Muintire', one of the most earnest workers of what I might call the pre-historic Irish-Ireland movement, one of its earliest martyrs from over-work. From him Griffith learned of and accepted the essential importance of the national language in the work that lay ahead. He had seemingly paid no attention to the tiny Gaelic League of his pre-South African days. But one has only to peruse the columns of Sinn Féin in the subsequent years to see how constantly and how firmly Griffith kept the language ideal in the very forefront of his programme. He now founded his first paper in Ireland, *The United Irishman*. Anti-imperial and violently pro-Boer, specialising in 'anti-recruiting' for the British army, it was classed as seditious and had the honour of frequent attentions from the Castle authorities. Who supported it? There were many old Fenians still active and a growing body of extremists among the new Irish-Irelanders. Maud Gonne, then in the prime of her radiant beauty, gave financial support. One way or another Griffith maintained himself and his political programme, fruit of his youthful readings, matured in his mind. In opposition to the dominant political party he began to preach the policy of abstention from Westminster. The Renunciation Act of 1783 by which the British parliament had renounced 'forever' the right to control an Irish parliament, was to be the basis of his political movement which he claimed was the real constitutional one, looking at things from an Irish standpoint. By that Act, the Union of 1800 was invalid, the authority of all British legislation, the right of Dublin Castle to govern Ireland could and should be challenged.

This was the policy of the Sinn Féin organisation which he founded in 1905 and of his famous weekly *Sinn Féin* which he edited, with a daily *Sinn Féin* for a period in 1907, until the war of 1914, when it was succeeded by *Nationality* and then by several smaller papers, as each in turn was suppressed. Or rather it was only the basis of his policy. Irish representatives denying the right of Westminster, should refuse to go there and instead form a national assembly in Dublin; govern Ireland with the help of the local bodies, pursue a constructive policy of national development in every sphere, language, games, industry, education, the arts. This policy had been pursued by the Hungarians under Deak when the Austrians had wanted them to attend the Vienna parliament and Griffith insisted that that was our model.

The idea of abstention from Westminster was not absolutely original. O'Connell had had the idea of bringing his party home in 1843 and setting up a national assembly. Griffith, who was not at all a worshipper of O'Connell, said that it was the only really statesmanlike idea that O'Connell ever had and that it caused more alarm in Dublin

Castle than anything he ever did. But most unfortunately O'Connell abandoned his purpose. In 1858 one Charles Beggs published a pamphlet *The Road to Irish Liberty* advocating withdrawal from Westminster.* The Hungarian policy was occasionally referred to in the Parnell period and Parnell would probably have come to the abstention policy if Westminster had continued to reject Home Rule. But it was Griffith who with his masterly journalistic style hit the imagination of the new intelligentsia with his policy when he published his revolutionary pamphlets *The Resurrection of Hungary* in 1904 and *The Sinn Féin Policy* in 1905. He first made it a serious political policy. Year in and year out, week in and week out, Griffith hammered home this policy and lent the support of his pen, the most incisive probably in the history of Irish journalism, to every worthy nation-building effort as well.

The history of these years, the most hopeful, the most inspiring that the Irish race had until then experienced, is familiar. Various groups all marched towards the Irish-Ireland goal, and finally, after the Home Rule Bill of 1912 had produced Carsonism, and Carsonism had given Irishmen the chance of bearing arms openly, the IRB launched the insurrection of 1916. A voluntary armed revolt had never been part of Griffith's programme, for obvious reasons, though it was clear to him that his policy of setting up a national assembly and attempting to take the government of the country out of the hands of the Castle and the police was a much more violent one than it appeared on the surface. He would not have shrunk from resisting attack. He had been a member of the IRB until 1910 when he formally asked to be released from membership on account of his presidency of the independent Sinn Féin organisation.† Truth to tell, events had run ahead of the Sinn Féin policy since Edward Carson had begun to set the pace. The leaders of the Rising expressly asked him to stay out of the fighting and keep his pen and his brain for

---

*   I am indebted to Mr P.S. O'Hegarty for this reference.
†   P.S. O'Hegarty in *Sunday Independent*, 24/8/1947.

Ireland; but he, during Easter Week, was trying, in consultation with John MacNeill, to call on the country to rise in support of Dublin.[‡]

The result of the Rising was, ironically enough, to convert the people to the Sinn Féin policy. Withdrawal from Westminster, and the setting up of a national assembly claiming to be the government of Ireland became suddenly the obvious things to do. Among the rush of events of the five great years that followed there stands out: Griffith's modest withdrawal from the presidency of his own organisation in favour of the more glamorous personality of Éamon de Valera; and the steady rapprochement of the young leaders of the fighting men, led by Michael Collins, and of Griffith, according as the former realised that the absolute Republic was not to be gained by military means alone against the might of Britain and that they would be lucky to attain the practical goal which Griffith had always set to his striving, namely, the restoration of the position of Grattan's independent parliament with a responsible Irish executive in addition. For this Griffith worked steadily at that Peace Conference of 1921, from which all discussion of an independent Republic had been barred in advance. Faithful to his life-long principles Griffith resisted to the last the determined British effort to impose a Privy Council ban on Irish legislation and a limitation to our fiscal autonomy.

All the old separatists of Griffith's youth had been practical men looking for the essentials of liberty rather than doctrinaire Republicans. Griffith brought home what he believed to be the essentials of liberty and a firm basis for the future advance of the Irish nation, both economic and constitutional. All subsequent progress has justified this belief. He brought home more. Most significant among the events of that memorable year of 1921 is that the British set going a parliament in Belfast before they offered a truce to Dáil Éireann. Griffith brought back in the partition clause of the Treaty, something which he believed was capable of undoing that hard fact of partition. Who can be sure that this belief would not have been justified if heads had kept cool,

---

‡   Communicated to the writer by Arthur Griffith a year or two before his death.

if difference of opinion had not been allowed to degenerate into civil strife and if he and Collins had lived?

The last and hardest decision of Griffith's life was the order which as president of the Republic's cabinet he gave, in conjunction with his colleagues, to recover possession of the Four Courts by military action. The issue for him was clear: either order or anarchy. He stood for order and democratic rule. He would have been the last man in the world to shirk his full share of personal responsibility for that action.

He died that fatal year, mourned by the nation. In private life those of us who knew him, loved him for his straightness, his honesty, his iron will when principle was involved; for his complete and absolute modesty, for his humour, his sociability, his devotion to his family, his keen and typically Dublin relish for simple pleasures like a walk in the Phoenix Park or a swim at the 'Forty-Foot'. In Irish history, he was the last of the great political leaders of the union period. Time will show that he was the most national of them all, the profoundest thinker of them all, and one of the greatest men that Ireland ever produced.

Index

A

Abbey Street 43, 44, 133, 134, 137, 141,
    142, 143, 144, 319, 325, 326
Abbey Theatre 36, 183, 184, 319, 417
Aberdeen, Lord 39, 45
Adelaide Hospital 82
Adelaide Road 352
Æ (George Russell) 35, 49, 166, 183
Albert, Father 101, 211
All-For-Ireland League 227, 228
Allan, Fred 179
Aloysius, Father 186
Amiens Street 180, 275
Ancient Order of Hibernians (AOH) 32,
    176, 229, 351
Annesley bridge 169
Antient Concert Rooms 188
Aran islands 182
Arbour Hill 339, 340, 361, 362, 363, 365,
    372
Archer, Liam 102
Ardee Street 72, 80
Arran Quay 322
Ashbourne 64, 117, 119, 120, 257
Ashe, Thomas 100, 119, 120, 122, 123,
    124, 126, 127, 129, 130, 257, 366,
    370, 391, 392
Ashtown 247, 248, 249, 252
Askwith, George 48
Asquith, H. 30, 55, 116, 396
Athea 208
Athlone 72, 114, 119
Aud 17, 33, 398
Augustine, Father 101, 151
Auxiliaries 269, 270, 275, 284, 289, 290,
    291, 293, 305, 326, 328, 332, 333,
    334, 335, 337, 341, 342, 343, 344,
    345, 347, 360, 363, 372, 373, 374,
    375, 381, 383, 393, 411
Aylesbury 218, 404

B

Bachelor's Walk 29, 43
Baggot Street 91, 93, 94, 288
Baldonnel Aerodrome 304, 310

Balfe, Richard 101
Ballinalee 328
Ballsbridge 86, 88, 89, 91, 96, 97, 207,
    216, 356
Ballybough bridge 320
Ballybrack 346
Ballycorus 353, 364
Ballyfermot 309
Ballykinlar 372
Ballykissane 33
Ballymahon 357, 358
Ballymun Road 64, 381
Banim, Frank 310
Banna Strand 33
Barmack's factory 72
Barnaculla 346, 348
Barrett, Ben 329
Barron Street 84, 85
Barry, Kevin 253, 255, 278, 279, 280, 281,
    282, 394
Barry, Stephen 357, 358, 363
Barton, Robert 235, 368
Batterstown 120
Béaslaí, Piaras 23, 98, 233, 314, 368, 369,
    376
Beaumont Convalescent Home 270
Beggar's Bush barracks 84, 86, 87, 270,
    289, 314, 327, 372
Belfast 37, 40, 71, 72, 114, 164, 166, 176,
    177, 182, 197, 208, 228, 233, 368,
    369, 386, 398, 416, 433
Beresford Place 41, 42, 43, 45, 136, 317,
    318
Beresford Street 104
Beverley, J. 33
Birkenhead, Lord (F.F. Smith) 24
Birrell, Chief Sec. 377
Bishop Street 77, 78, 79, 81, 140
Black and Tans 9, 18, 59, 76, 247, 268,
    270, 297, 301, 306, 314, 319, 322,
    323, 324, 326, 333, 334, 337, 348,
    349, 350, 352, 356, 358, 360, 361,
    362, 372, 380, 381, 382, 404, 405,
    411
Blackhall Street 100
Blackrock 84, 346, 348, 362, 414, 415, 422

Blake, Colonel 198
Blanchardstown 250
Blessington Street 323
Bohan, Billy 322
Boland's Bakery/Mill 63, 82, 83, 84, 85,
        90, 96, 140, 150, 151, 152, 215,
        413, 419, 421
Boland, Harry 229, 232, 234, 378, 409
Bolger, Tom 353
Bolton Street 104
Borranstown 119, 120, 127
Botanic Avenue 259, 266, 268
Botanic Road 64
Bow bridge 391
Bowen-Colthurst, Capt. 80, 81, 352, 403
Brady, Christopher 113
Bray 346, 350, 351, 352, 353, 354, 355,
        356, 357, 358, 359, 360, 361, 362,
        363, 364
Breen, Dan 246, 247, 248, 249, 250, 251,
        257, 258, 259, 260, 261, 262, 263,
        264, 265, 266, 267, 268, 269, 270,
        271, 273, 274
Brennan, Maurice 268, 269
Brennan, Robert 231
Brereton, R.K. 207
Breslin, Peadar 241, 243
Breslin, Warder 333, 334, 335
Brett, Corporal 222
Bride Street 151, 152
Brien, Jim 354, 355, 364
Brien, Mick 354, 357
Brien, Owen 361
Brien, Pat 355, 356, 358, 359, 360, 361,
        364
Brien, Tom 355, 357, 358, 359, 360, 361,
        362, 363, 364
Broadstone 100, 102, 389
Broy, Éamonn 377, 378
Brugha, Cathal 64, 74, 75, 159, 160, 161,
        189, 209, 229, 232, 234, 235, 286,
        287, 313, 399
Brunswick, Seán 274, 275, 276, 277
Brunswick Place 151
Brunswick Street 101, 104, 305, 378
Bruree 413, 414, 415, 416
Bryan, Thomas 296
Burgh Quay 136
Burke, Cormac 364
Burke, J.J. 203
Burke, W.F. 71
Butt Bridge 133, 150, 324, 387

Byrne, John 43
Byrne, Mick 356
Byrne, Tom 197
Byrne, Vincent 247, 249, 329

C

Cabinteely 346, 348
Cabra Road 102
Caffrey, Chris 111
Camden Street 78, 79, 81, 337, 385
Capel Street 104, 149, 324, 325, 326,
        378
Carass, Section Commander 305
Carbery, Christopher 378
Cardiff, Tom 346
Carlow 57, 200
Carney, Winifred 144, 146, 150, 154, 155,
        398, 401, 402
Carolan, Professor 257, 260, 261, 266
Carrisbrooke House 91
Carroll, Patrick 276
Carson, Edward 23, 24, 29, 42, 52, 54,
        396, 416, 417, 432
Casement, Roger 17, 27, 28, 32, 33, 156,
        192, 193, 194, 385, 388, 398,
        418
Castle Street 114
Castletown (Wexford) 390
Cathedral Place 137
Cathedral Street 141
Cavanagh, Maeve 116, 400
Ceannt (Kent), Éamonn 16, 24, 25, 27,
        61, 62, 67, 69, 70, 71, 72, 73, 74,
        75, 76, 77, 132, 140, 152, 160,
        168, 181, 186, 187, 188, 189, 209,
        214, 399, 400
Chadwick, Michael 346, 355
Chamberlain, Joe 429
Chancery Street 149
Chapelizod 208, 301
Charlemont House 88
Charles Street 101, 149, 269
Charleville 414
Charlotte Street 80
Chatham Row 348, 363
Childers, Erskine 28, 388, 417
Christchurch Place 238
Christian, Francis 274, 275, 276, 277
Christian, William 89
Church Street 99, 100, 101, 102, 103, 104,
        105, 106, 134, 149, 155, 280

Citizens' Defence League 48

City Hall 59, 63, 113, 114, 115, 117, 228, 234, 397, 404

Clancy, Peadar 103, 246, 253, 254, 270, 271, 273, 274, 286, 287, 288, 290, 291, 293, 329

Clan na Gael 31, 172, 173, 174, 193, 194

Clanwilliam House 86, 87, 89, 90, 91, 92, 93, 94, 95, 96, 98, 238, 420

Clanwilliam Terrace 85

Clarence Hotel 270

Clarence Street 86

Clare Street 150, 151

Clarke, James 171

Clarke, Joe 89, 90, 98

Clarke, Liam 133

Clarke, Sergeant 171

Clarke, Thomas 15, 16, 24, 30, 47, 54, 131, 132, 145, 146, 147, 149, 154, 155, 157, 167, 168, 171, 172, 173, 174, 175, 176, 177, 178, 179, 180, 181, 205, 207, 208, 396, 402, 417, 418

Clery's 134, 137

Clondalkin 301, 303, 304, 310, 311, 312, 390

Clonmel 386

Cloughjordan 181

Clune, Conor 287, 291, 293

Coghlan, F.X. 102

Colbert, Con 26, 27, 71, 72, 80, 208, 209, 210, 309, 384, 385, 386, 388, 389, 390, 400

Coleman, Dick 392

Coliseum Theatre 142, 143

Coll, Patrick 414, 416

College Green 32, 37, 63, 397

College of Surgeons 63, 79, 81, 109, 110, 111, 112, 140, 150, 184, 203, 204, 215, 389, 399

College Street 133, 150

Colley, Harry 292

Collins, Con 233

Collins, Michael 18, 20, 32, 178, 221, 222, 229, 232, 234, 235, 246, 258, 268, 270, 272, 274, 285, 286, 287, 288, 290, 293, 310, 313, 315, 320, 328, 329, 330, 333, 334, 372, 377, 378, 379, 380, 381, 382, 406, 407, 408, 409, 410, 411, 412, 433, 434

Collinstown Aerodrome 241, 242, 243, 244

Colum, Pádraic 183, 191

Columbus, Fr 149, 153, 155

Conlon, Martin 102

Connolly, George 113

Connolly, James 16, 30, 31, 32, 35, 39, 40, 42, 45, 46, 47, 49, 51, 53, 55, 56, 57, 58, 59, 110, 111, 112, 113, 116, 117, 118, 130, 131, 132, 138, 140, 142, 144, 145, 146, 147, 148, 149, 154, 157, 160, 161, 162, 163, 164, 165, 166, 167, 168, 169, 170, 181, 188, 194, 202, 203, 206, 208, 211, 224, 385, 390, 394, 395, 398, 401, 404, 416, 418

Connolly, Joe 109

Connolly, Nora 164, 170, 400

Connolly, Seán 59, 113, 114

Cooper, Becky 288

Cork 21, 37, 38, 40, 140, 156, 186, 310, 371, 372, 378, 382, 386, 406

Cork Street 72

Corporation Street 44

Corringham, Joseph 276

Cosgrave, Liam 235

Cotter, Brigid 216

Coyle, Ethne 405

Crinkin 356, 360

Crofts, Gerard 134, 216, 222

Croke Park 178, 222, 292, 293

Cross Guns bridge 323

Crowe Street 285

Croydon Park 43, 45, 49, 53, 54, 55, 57, 167, 319

Crozier, General 290

Cuffe Street 78

Cullen, Tom 274, 285, 287, 293, 379

Cullenswood 183, 352

Cumann na mBan 19, 71, 77, 79, 102, 105, 133, 134, 146, 147, 152, 155, 184, 201, 202, 224, 232, 395, 396, 397, 398, 400, 403, 404, 405

Cumann na nGaedheal 177

Curley, Seán 346

Curragh 27, 63, 72, 114, 116, 312, 362, 372, 417, 419

Cursham, Capt. 95

Curtin, John 173

Cusack, Michael 197

Custom House 130, 136, 137, 141, 241, 313, 314, 315, 316, 317, 318, 319, 322, 374, 410

D

Dáil Éireann 18, 100, 102, 233, 234, 235,
	279, 284, 286, 290, 371, 382, 390,
	405, 409, 410, 412, 423, 424, 433
Dalkey 216, 358
Dalton, Charlie 329, 330
Dalton, Emmet 327, 330, 331, 332
Daly, Edward 206
Daly, Edward (Ned) 31, 61, 101, 105, 106,
	107, 139, 146, 149, 174, 204, 205,
	207, 215, 421
Daly, Frank 102
Daly, John 172, 173, 174, 205, 208
Daly, Kathleen 174, 205
Daly, Laura 207
Daly, Madge 207, 397
Daly, P.T. 42
Daly, Paddy 247, 248, 250, 251, 271, 318,
	319, 320
Daly, Patrick 380
Daly, Tom 113
Dame Court 324
Dame Street 63, 133, 151, 154, 295, 401
Darcy, Charlie 115
Dargan Street 362
Dargle 357, 358, 359, 361, 364
Davis, Brigid 224
Davis, Eugene 347, 348
Davis, Jerry 342, 375
Davis, Thomas 411, 412, 428
Davitt, Michael 172, 395, 414, 427
de Loughry, Peter 367, 372
de Valera, Éamon 18, 81, 84, 96, 140, 151,
	152, 160, 215, 216, 217, 227, 229,
	233, 234, 235, 313, 367, 391, 393,
	408, 409, 411, 413, 415, 416, 417,
	418, 419, 420, 421, 422, 423, 424,
	425, 433
Denzille Street 86
Derrig, Thomas 20
Derry 172, 230, 386
Devlin, Joe 229, 230, 233
Devoy, John 31, 32, 174, 175, 192, 193,
	195, 418, 427
Dickson, Thomas 80, 352
Dietrichsen, Capt. 97
Dillon, John 228, 230, 231, 233
Dockrell, Maurice 233
Dolan, Charles 177
Dolan, Joe 254, 255
Dolphin's Barn 61, 71, 72, 252, 338

Dominick Street 286, 323
Donelan, Brendan 66
Donnelly, Jack 307
Donnelly, Simon 84, 96, 290, 295
Donnybrook 96
Doran, John 368, 369
Dorset Street 269, 323
Doyle, Andy 292
Doyle, Arthur Conan 192
Doyle, P.J. 89
Doyle, Pat 241, 242, 296
Doyle, Patrick 91, 92, 95
Doyle, Seán 241, 242, 321, 329, 393
Drangan 277
Drumcondra 195, 257, 258, 259, 260, 262,
	263, 268, 323
Dublin Castle 18, 36, 41, 45, 49, 55, 63,
	65, 76, 78, 79, 112, 113, 114, 115,
	133, 140, 144, 151, 152, 153, 154,
	170, 180, 229, 232, 246, 259, 260,
	264, 267, 279, 283, 284, 285, 288,
	290, 291, 292, 294, 295, 315, 326,
	331, 372, 373, 377, 381, 382, 402,
	410, 417, 431, 432
Dublin Metropolitan Police (DMP)
	28, 41, 145, 155, 181, 236, 238,
	283, 286, 347, 365, 377, 391,
	392, 409
Dublin Steam Packet Co. 40
Dublin strike [1913] 35, 37, 38, 39, 40,
	41, 42, 45, 47, 48, 49, 50, 51, 52,
	54, 55, 123, 125, 160, 166, 167,
	228, 232, 307, 327, 370, 371, 387,
	404, 418
Dublin Trades Union Council 39, 41,
	47, 54
Dublin Tramway Co. 40
Duffy, Seán 378
Duggan, Éamonn 102, 378
Duke of Wellington's Regiment 280
Dunboyne 269
Dundalk 37, 140, 306, 366, 386
Dundrum 346, 348, 363
Dungannon 171, 172, 177, 400
Dún Laoghaire 83, 84, 86, 88, 91, 96, 346,
	347, 348, 413
Dunlevy, Warder 374
Dunlop, Dr 385
Dunne, Andy 203, 210, 215, 222
Dunne, Mick 357, 358
Dunne, Tom 346

E

Earls, Bill 353
Earls, Jimmie 355, 356
Earlsfort Terrace 83, 84
Earl Street 43, 134, 137, 142
Eccles Street 269, 320, 347
Echlin Street 72
Eden Quay 43, 134, 142
Employer's Federation 46
Ennis, Tom 288, 289, 315, 316, 318, 319, 320
Enniscorthy 137, 352
Enniskerry 348, 354, 357, 358, 359, 363, 364
Ervingstown Lane 62
Etchingham, Seán 353

F

Fahy, Frank 100, 161, 176, 208, 215
Fairview 137, 319
Fane, Lieut-Col 97
Farrell, Kit 226, 237, 238
Farrell, P.J. 351, 355
Faulkner, Josie 354, 355, 356, 359, 362, 363, 364
ffrench-Mullen, Douglas 218, 222
ffrench-Mullen, Madeleine 108, 109, 155
Fianna Éireann 26, 60, 61, 71, 77, 100, 144, 164, 203, 208, 210, 306, 384, 385, 386, 387, 388, 389, 390, 391, 392, 393, 394, 396, 400
Fianna Fáil 20
Figgis, Darrell 28
Fingal 101, 117, 118, 236
Finglas 117, 118, 263, 266, 269, 271, 332, 393
Fitzgerald, Dick 222
Fitzgerald, George 242, 288, 291
Fitzgerald, Leo 306, 341, 342, 374, 375
Fitzgibbon, Seán 25, 27, 189
Fitzpatrick, Section Commander 254
Fitzwilliam Square 82
Fitzwilliam Street 82
Fleet Street 324
Fleming, Dot 259, 263, 265, 266
Fleming, James 257, 264, 265, 267
Fleming, K. 258, 259, 263, 264, 265, 266, 268
Fleming, Michael 257, 259, 267
Fleming, Paddy 367, 368
Flood, Frank 296

Flood, Seán 256
Foley, Brigid 402
Foley, Jack 346
Foley, Michael 377
Forbes Lane 72
Forde, Seán 275
Forde, Val 323
Four Courts 64, 100, 101, 102, 105, 106, 134, 146, 149, 150, 154, 155, 207, 211, 215, 307, 389, 421, 434
Fownes Street 324
Fox, Tom 357, 358, 363
Fox and Geese 309, 311, 390
French, Lord 246, 247, 248, 249, 250, 251, 252, 279
Frongoch 213, 219, 221, 222, 223, 366, 407
Fumbally Lane 78
Furlong, Matt 269

G

'G' Division/men 283, 284, 285, 291, 377, 378, 379, 381
Gaelic Athletic Association (GAA) 15, 197, 200, 292
Gaelic League 15, 24, 26, 36, 158, 159, 160, 176, 182, 186, 187, 200, 201, 415, 430
Gaffney, St John 194
Gallagher, Owen 364
Gallagher, Thomas 173, 174
Galway 40, 140, 186, 390, 414
Galwey, Johanna 186
Gardiner's Row 315, 319
Gardiner Street 44, 287, 317, 319
Garristown 119
Gavan Duffy, George 233, 353
Gay, Thomas 378
General Post Office (GPO) 17, 63, 64, 79, 83, 102, 104, 106, 111, 112, 113, 117, 118, 130, 131, 133, 134, 135, 137, 140, 141, 142, 143, 144, 145, 146, 148, 149, 154, 169, 175, 181, 211, 214, 221, 224, 352, 381, 391, 398, 401, 403, 407, 419
Geraghty, George 367
Germany/German 17, 28, 30, 31, 32, 33, 139, 140, 180, 191, 192, 193, 194, 195, 219, 229, 232, 235, 261, 366, 367, 378, 392, 408, 409, 410, 417, 425

Gifford, Grace 196
Gifford, Muriel 185
Gifford, Nellie 184, 215
Ginnell, Laurence 220, 235
Glasgow 32, 37, 176, 205
Glasnevin 64, 96, 200, 224, 387, 392, 397
Glenasmole Lodge 394
Globe Hotel 275
Gógan, Liam 27
Golden Lane 151
Gonne, Maud 165, 395, 403, 431
Gore, John 27
Gorman, Eric 184
Gough, Jim 215
Grace, James 87, 89
Grafton Street 63, 150, 239
Grand Canal 62, 63, 108, 310
Grand Canal Street 83, 84, 85, 151
Grantham Street 79, 80
Grattan bridge 246
Grattan Street 86, 215
Great George Street 402
Great Southern and Western Railway
        209, 301
Greenwood, Hamar 18
Grenan, Julia 111, 146, 150, 154, 155,
        175, 181, 398, 400, 401
Gresham Hotel 150, 154, 290
Griffith, Arthur 14, 20, 177, 201, 225,
        229, 233, 234, 235, 351, 417, 424,
        426, 427, 428, 429, 430, 431, 432,
        433, 434
Guilfoyle, Seán 236
Guinness Brewery 64, 77, 85, 140
Gwynn, R.M. 53

H

Hackett, Rosie 224
Haddington Road 85, 86, 87, 88, 92, 94,
        96, 97, 98
Haig, Major 29
Hall, Paddy 353
Halley, Detective-Sergeant 250
Hanratty, John 113
Harcourt Street 81, 108, 233, 352, 390
Hardie, Keir 45, 47
Hardwicke Street 184, 212, 387
Hardy, Capt. 291, 292, 295, 373
Harrel, William 28, 29
Hayes, Richard 119, 126, 128
Head, Dan 319

Healy, Constable 347
Healy, T.M. 48
Hempenstall, Nick 357
Henderson, Leo 273, 274, 275
Henrietta Street 254, 255
Henry Place 143, 145, 146, 149, 154
Henry Street 43, 142, 143, 145, 146, 273,
        325
Herbert Park 91, 313
Heuston, Seán 101, 103, 208, 209, 210,
        211, 385, 386, 387, 389, 390
Heytesbury Street 271
High Street 237, 393
Hipwell, Chief Warder 375
Hobson, John Bulmer 16, 24, 25, 27, 28,
        31, 33, 177, 180, 209
Hoey, James 353, 364
Hoey, John 361, 364
Hoey, Pat 361
Hogan, Seán 246, 247, 250, 257
Holland, Bob 271
Holles Street 150, 151
Holohan, Paddy 106
Home Farm Gardens 266
Home Farm Road 260
Home Rule 13, 15, 17, 23, 24, 25, 26, 29,
        42, 161, 229, 396, 416, 427, 430,
        432
Hopkins and Hopkins 134, 137
Houlihan, Garry 210
Houlihan, Paddy 210
Houston, David 183, 191
Houston, Professor 53
Howth 28, 54, 71, 88, 180, 189, 206, 332,
        351, 388, 417
Humphries, Sheila 228
Hurley, Seán 106
Hyde, Douglas 159, 182, 192
Hyde, Seán 289, 294
Hyland, Batt 320
Hyland, John 364
Hyland, Mary 110

I

Inchicore 63, 271, 301, 302, 304, 309,
        338, 339
Inghinidhe na hÉireann 395
Irish Citizens Army (ICA) 14, 16, 31, 51,
        52, 53, 54, 55, 56, 57, 58, 59, 63,
        77, 79, 107, 108, 110, 112, 113,
        114, 115, 116, 130, 132, 164, 167,

168, 169, 170, 203, 215, 221, 224,
225, 399, 416, 418, 419
Irish Labour Party 38, 219, 227, 228
Irish Parliamentary Party (IPP) 13, 14,
24, 25, 26, 28, 29, 30, 32, 36, 37,
193, 220, 225, 227, 228, 229, 230,
231, 233, 234, 423, 430
Irish Republican Brotherhood 13, 14, 15,
16, 23, 24, 25, 26, 27, 30, 31, 33,
132, 161, 171, 172, 177, 178, 179,
180, 204, 351, 366, 381, 407, 408,
409, 415, 418, 432
Irishtown 238
Irish Transport and General Workers'
Union (ITGWU) 38, 39, 40, 41,
42, 43, 45, 46, 48, 51, 53, 54, 109,
166, 167, 202
Islandbridge 60, 61, 62

J

Jackson, Frank 224
Jacob's factory 63, 72, 77, 78, 79, 80, 81,
82, 133, 151, 152, 182, 184, 185,
198, 199, 201, 257
James' Street 62, 63, 64, 65, 68, 69, 70, 71,
74, 140, 215, 238, 301
Jameson, John 381
Jameson Distillery 62, 69, 71, 101
Jameson raid 199
Jeffares, Capt. 97
Jervis Street 141, 144, 324
Jervis Street Hospital 43, 142, 143, 145,
270
Johnson, Judge 86
Jones' Road 292, 320
Judge, M.J. 27, 193

K

Kane, Tom 113
Kapp and Peterson's 134
Kavanagh, Andy 353
Kavanagh, Jack 364
Kavanagh, Joe 377, 378
Kavanagh, Tom 354, 355, 356, 359
Kearns, Linda 402, 405
Keating, Con 194
Keating, J.J. 134
Keating, Matthew 199
Keely, Sarah 201, 202
Kelly, Billy 171, 172

Kelly, Brian 242
Kelly, David 308
Kelly, George 347, 348
Kelly, J.J. 80
Kelly, M. 108
Kelly, Paddy 338
Kelly, Tom 194, 268, 269, 307, 308
Kempson, Lily 110
Kenmare 134
Kennedy, Margaret L. 399, 400
Kenny, Joseph 351, 352, 361, 364
Kent, Thomas 156
Keogh, Myles 95, 98, 281
Keogh, Nurse 67, 68, 71
Keogh, Tom 247, 248, 249, 250, 271, 289,
329, 330, 331, 332
Kerry 7, 8, 10, 11, 32, 33, 135, 137, 140,
145, 195, 222, 398
Kerryman, The 7, 9, 10, 21
Kettle, Laurance 25
Kettle, Thomas 25, 26, 27, 42, 48
Kevin Street 78
Kiernan, Seán 274
Kilbride 364
Kilcool 28, 189, 206, 351, 388
Kilcoyne, Tom 247
Kilkenny 182, 199, 372
Kill-o-the-Grange 346, 363
Kilmacanogue 354
Kilmainham 64, 65, 153, 155, 186, 196,
207, 214, 215, 290, 295, 296, 297,
300, 303, 304, 309, 337, 338, 339,
365, 373, 400, 402
Kilmashogue 393
Kilpeddar 355, 359
Kilternan 347
Kiltyclogher 176
Kimmage 32, 130, 189, 193, 195, 407
King's Inns 253, 254, 256, 288
King's Own Scottish Borderers 28
King, Major 373
Kingsbridge station 57, 63, 114, 210, 301
Kingstown (Dún Laoighaire) 96, 413,
419, 420
King Street 61, 98, 101, 103, 104, 105,
106, 110, 206, 323, 325, 389
Kinsale 414
Kirk, Paddy 255
Kirwan, Jim 272, 273, 330
Knocklong 257, 277
Knutsford 365

L

Lacey, Billy 357, 360
Lacey, Dinny 257, 261, 264, 267
Laffan, Nicholas 102, 104, 106
Lancashire Fusiliers 280
Lancers 79, 90, 101, 106, 133, 134
Land League 46, 395, 427, 430
Lansdowne Road 85, 86
Larkfield 193, 194, 195
Larkin, Jim 37, 38, 39, 40, 42, 43, 44, 45, 47,
        49, 52, 53, 54, 55, 59, 166, 167, 416
Lawless, Frank 119
Lawless, Joe 266, 268, 269
Lawless, Mary 266, 269
Lawlor, Pierce 364
Lawlor, Thomas 42
Leddy, Phil 242
Ledwidge, Peter 361, 364
Leeson Street 82, 108, 288
Leggett, Bert 357
Leggett, Frank 353
Leggett, Peter 'Lukey' 356, 357, 359, 360,
        361, 362, 364
Leinster Road 388
Lenehan, James 27
Leonard, Joe 247, 271, 327, 329, 336
Leslie, John 163
Leslie-Neville, Col 92
Liberty Hall 34, 43, 47, 52, 53, 55, 56, 57,
        58, 115, 130, 136, 141, 164, 166,
        167, 181, 203, 224, 317, 416, 419
Liffey 63, 85, 100, 101, 143, 144, 165,
        289, 290, 309, 323, 324
Limerick 7, 8, 9, 10, 32, 130, 174, 199,
        204, 205, 208, 210, 372, 386, 414
Lincoln jail 234, 235, 367, 393, 410, 424
Lincoln Place 86
Linenhall barracks 99, 103, 104, 139,
        206, 389
Lisburn Street 99, 103
Little, Peter 347
Littlechild, DI 170, 173
Little Mary Street 149
Liverpool 32, 37, 229, 233, 409
Lloyd George, David 18, 225, 227, 229,
        313, 408, 411, 422, 424
Loftus, J.J. 346
Logue, Cardinal 230, 231
London 32, 35, 49, 106, 156, 170, 197,
        221, 314, 347, 377, 380, 403, 406,
        407, 411

Lonergan, Michael 26, 27
Long, Nurse 265, 266, 268
Longford 7, 225, 328, 423
Lord Edward Street 63
Lotts Road 83, 84
Loughlinstown 354, 356
Lowe, Brig. Gen. 116, 148, 149, 151, 152,
        153, 401, 402
Lowndes, DI 362
Lurring, Bert 357, 360
Lynch, Diarmuid 131, 146, 181, 351
Lynch, Fionán 102, 106
Lynch, Joseph 353, 364
Lynch, Michael 218, 222
Lynch, Paddy 227
Lynch, Patricia 403
Lynn, Kathleen 54, 114, 115, 402

M

MacBride, John 72, 78, 80, 81, 174, 197,
        198, 199, 201
MacCaffrey Estate 64
MacCartan, Patrick 178, 179
MacCarthy, Eugene 196
MacCrae, Pat 244
MacCullough, Denis 177
MacCurtain, Tomás 246, 382
MacDiarmada (MacDermott) Seán 16,
        24, 25, 27, 30, 33, 116, 131, 132,
        135, 136, 145, 147, 154, 155, 160,
        168, 175, 176, 177, 178, 179, 180,
        181, 188, 205, 351, 407, 418
MacDonagh, John 182, 184, 198
MacDonagh, Joseph 182
MacDonagh, Richard 197
MacDonagh, Terence 182
MacDonagh, Thomas 15, 27, 33, 77, 81,
        83, 132, 140, 151, 152, 155, 160,
        161, 168, 175, 178, 180, 181, 182,
        183, 184, 185, 186, 189, 191, 192,
        196, 198, 201, 207, 418
MacDonnell, Andy 370
MacDowell, Cathal 222
MacDowell, William 66
MacEoin, Seán 327, 328, 329, 330, 331,
        332, 333, 335, 336
MacGarry, Seán 367
MacGlynn, Seán 214
MacGrath, J. 89
MacIntyre, Patrick 80, 352
Macken, Peadar 27, 96, 160, 188

MacLoughlin, Seán 144
MacMahon, Seán 239, 240
MacMullen, Louis 171
MacNeill, Brian 346, 361, 364
MacNeill, Eoin 15, 16, 17, 24, 25, 27, 32,
    33, 34, 138, 180, 187, 193, 196,
    206, 230, 231, 233, 235, 351, 416,
    418, 422, 433
MacNeill, Niall 346
MacRory, Bishop 196, 369
MacSweeney, James 350, 353
MacSweeney, Seamus 355, 356, 357, 358,
    359, 360, 361, 363, 364
MacSwiney, Mary 397
MacSwiney, Terence 371
Madigan, Lieut 323
Magee, Mick 242
Maguire, Sam 380
Mahon, Gen. Bryan 224
Mallin, Michael 55, 57, 58, 59, 79, 108,
    109, 110, 111, 112, 140, 150, 165,
    167, 202, 203, 204
Malone, Áine 332
Malone, Captain 420
Malone, Michael 86, 87, 89, 91, 93, 95
Mannix, Archbishop 227
Mansion House 25, 30, 31, 55, 228, 233,
    234, 386, 393
Marine Road 347
Marino 332
Markievicz, Constance 13, 47, 53, 58, 59,
    109, 110, 111, 112, 148, 150, 155,
    160, 164, 166, 167, 168, 169, 175,
    204, 208, 210, 226, 232, 235, 384,
    385, 387, 388, 389, 391, 395, 398,
    399, 402, 403, 404, 416
Marks, Doctor 95
Marlboro Street 44, 137, 141, 324
Marrowbone Lane 62, 71, 72, 140, 152,
    209, 389, 399, 400
Martin, Éamonn 27, 210, 384, 389
Martin, Jack 361
Martin, Paddy 353, 361, 364
Martin, Tom 353
Martyn, Edward 184
Mary's Abbey 325
Mary's Lane 101, 106
Maryborough jail (Portlaoise) 367
Mary Street 149, 324, 325, 326
Masterpiece cinema 274, 275
Mater Hospital 268, 269, 270, 274, 275,
    321

Maxwell, Gen. 65, 79, 96, 97, 199, 207,
    220, 224, 420
May Lane 101
McCaffrey, Paddy 330
McConnery, Stannie 353
McCormack, Mick 269
McCormack, R. 57, 108, 110, 112
McCrae, Pat 269
McCrea, Pat 330, 331, 332
McCullough, Denis 15
McDermott, Rory 362
McDonald, Mick 329
McDonnell, Andy 346, 347, 348, 355, 370
McDonnell, Michael 380
McDonnell, Mick 247
McGarry, Jimmie 354, 356, 359
McGarry, Michael 353, 354, 355, 364
McGarry, Seán 20, 177, 406, 409
McGrath, Joe 367
McGuinness, Joseph 100, 106, 225
McIntosh, James 347
McKee, Dick 229, 253, 266, 268, 269,
    270, 271, 273, 274, 275, 286, 288,
    290, 291, 293, 328, 354
McLean, Mr 267
McMahon, Seán 314
McNamara, James 377
Meaney, Paddy 346
Meath Road 354
Meehan, Deputy Gov. 333, 334, 335
Mellows, Barney 367, 393
Mellows, Liam 26, 27, 140, 160, 175, 178,
    208, 209, 210, 233, 314, 351, 385,
    386, 387, 388, 390, 394
Mendicity Institution 64, 100, 101, 117,
    144, 210, 211, 389
Merrigan, Tom 242, 243
Merrion Square 81, 82, 86, 96, 98, 140,
    151, 247
Metcalfe, Fr 82
Metropole hotel 133
Meyer, Kuno 159, 192
Michael's Hill 237
Milligan, Alice 228
Milltown 95
Milroy, Seán 367, 409
Mitchel, John 163, 411
Molesworth Street 427
Molony, Helena 114, 153, 224, 395, 402
Monalena 208
Monks, Pat 310, 312
Monteith, Robert 32, 33, 194, 398

Mooney, Thomas 354
Moore, Hugh 197
Moore, Maurice 27
Moore Lane 143, 145, 146, 149, 154
Moore Street 141, 143, 145, 146, 147,
        148, 149, 150, 154, 155, 273, 401,
        402, 403
Moran, Paddy 296, 299
Morehampton Road 356
Morehampton Terrace 216
Morkan, Éamonn 102, 105
Mount Brown 62, 64, 65, 68, 71
Mountjoy jail 155, 204, 241, 267, 278,
        279, 281, 307, 323, 327, 328, 329,
        330, 331, 333, 334, 335, 336, 340,
        342, 344, 345, 366, 367, 368, 370,
        374, 405
Mount Street 82, 84, 86, 87, 91, 92, 95,
        97, 115, 215, 288, 289, 290, 393,
        419, 420
Mulcahy, Richard 119, 122, 123, 126,
        127, 129, 235, 257, 258, 313, 315,
        328, 368
Mulkearns, Jimmie 223
Mulvey, Nicholas 353
Mulvey, 'Steenie' 352, 353, 354, 355, 357,
        361, 364
Munroe, Gov. C. 331, 333
Munster Street 217
Murphy, James 354, 364
Murphy, Paddy 353, 364
Murphy, Phelim 352
Murphy, Richard 95
Murphy, Tod 355, 356, 359, 363
Murphy, William Martin 40, 42, 45, 416
Murray, Christy 237, 238
Murray, Éamonn 210
Murray, Seamus (Jimmy) 226, 236

N

Naas Road 309, 310, 312
Nally, P.W. 197
Nash, Nan 354
Nassau Street 239
Neary, Mick 358, 359, 360, 364
Neligan, David 378
Nelson's Pillar 43, 44, 131, 133, 134, 149,
        154, 258, 273, 275
Newcastle 355
Newry 37, 201, 386
Nicholas Street 115

Nic Shiubhlaigh, Máire 184
Ní Fhlannagáin, Sinéad (de Valera) 416
Nolan, James 43
Norgrove, Annie 113
Norgrove, Emily 113
Norgrove, George 113
North Circular Road 102, 215, 290, 330,
        332, 344
North Dublin Union 100, 101, 253, 256,
        280, 281
North Frederick Street 134
North Richmond Street 186, 208
North Strand 226, 360
Northumberland Avenue 97
Northumberland Road 86, 87, 91
North Wall 304, 323
Nunan, Ernest 221
Nunan, Seán 221, 234

O

O'Brennan, Áine 187
O'Brennan, Kathleen 187
O'Brennan, Lily 187
O'Brien, Charlie 353, 364
O'Brien, Con 98
O'Brien, Eamonn 257, 258, 259, 266
O'Brien, Laurence 346, 351, 354, 356,
        362, 363
O'Brien, Ned 346
O'Brien, Peadar 223
O'Brien, Vincent 206
O'Brien, William 42, 219, 220, 227, 228
Ó Broin, Seán 351
O'Callaghan, Denis 102, 103
O'Carroll, Kevin 189
O'Carroll, Richard 79, 81
O'Casey, Seán 53
Ó Ceallaigh, Seán T. (see also O'Kelly,
        Seán T.) 160, 233
Ó Cearbhaill, Liam 102
Ó Conaire, SeanPhádraic 429
O'Connell, J.J. 314, 315
O'Connell, Mortimer 102
O'Connell bridge 43, 63
O'Connell Street [Sackville] 42, 43, 45,
        52, 59, 64, 79, 90, 104, 105, 107,
        111, 117, 134, 136, 137, 141, 142,
        143, 149, 150, 153, 154, 155, 161,
        194, 224, 258, 275, 292, 325, 381,
        420
O'Connor, John S. 102

O'Connor, Joseph 83, 84, 215, 216, 217, 218, 237, 346, 353, 354
O'Connor, Patrick 137
O'Connor, Rory 194, 229, 370
O'Connor, Seamus 27
O'Connor, Tommy 32, 106
O'Connor, Úna 184
O'Daly, Paddy 327, 329, 330
O'Doherty, Liam 315
O'Donnell, Lily 347
O'Donoghue, Thomas 221
O'Donovan Rossa, Jeremiah 161, 175, 184, 234, 389, 397
O'Duffy, Eoin 314
O'Dwyer, Bishop 199
O'Farrell, Elizabeth 111, 146, 147, 148, 149, 150, 152, 153, 154, 185, 398, 400, 401, 402
O'Farrelly, Agnes 228, 396
O'Flanagan, Michael 232, 234, 353
O'Flanagan, Patrick 105
O'Gorman, Annie 347
O'Grady, John 82
O'Hanlon, Bernard 306
O'Hanrahan, Eily 202
O'Hanrahan, Henry 201
O'Hanrahan, Michael 200, 201, 202
O'Hanrahan, Richard 200
O'Hare, Dan 197
O'Hegarty, Diarmuid 102, 313
O'Higgins, Brian 155, 160, 188
O'Keefe, Seán 305, 306
O'Kelly, Seán T. (see also Ó Ceallaigh, Seán T.) 220
Ó Laoghaire, Diarmuid 131
Ó Lochlainn, Colm 27, 195
O'Leary, John 165
O'Leary, Philip 113
O'Malley, Christy 241, 242
O'Malley, Ernie 283, 290, 295, 296, 299, 339, 365
O'Mara, Catherine 204
O'Mara, James 233
O'Meara, Peadar 226, 305
O'Neill, James 59
O'Neill, John 108
O'Neill, Martin 306
O'Rahilly, The 25, 27, 130, 134, 142, 145, 147, 148, 160, 161, 188, 313, 350, 351, 403
O'Reilly, Joe 258, 272, 274
O'Reilly, M.W. 219, 220

O'Reilly, Mollie 58
O'Reilly, Peter 27
O'Reilly, Richard 66
Ó Riain, Padraic 27
O'Rourke, Andy 356, 359
O'Rourke, Dan 354, 364
O'Shea, James 56, 110
O'Sullivan, Gearóid 272, 293, 314
O'Sullivan, James 102
O'Sullivan, Seamus 183
O'Toole, Joseph 338
Oates, Col 72
Old Conna Corner 360
Oola 262, 277
Ormond Quay 323
Owens, John 65
Ownes, George 356
Ownes, Willie 354, 356

P

Page, Robert 27
Palace Street 326
Parliament Street 324, 326
Parnell, Charles Stewart 13, 43, 173, 174, 197, 395, 414, 423, 426, 427, 428, 430, 432
Parnell Square 30, 254, 328, 381, 393, 428
Parnell Statue 141, 147, 149, 150
Parnell Street 43, 141, 143, 146, 147, 149, 175, 177, 208, 272, 273, 323, 325, 417
Partridge, William P. 42, 111, 204
Pearse, James 160
Pearse, Margaret 160
Pearse, P.H. 15, 16, 17, 27, 33, 47, 107, 112, 116, 130, 131, 132, 137, 140, 144, 145, 146, 147, 148, 149, 151, 152, 154, 155, 157, 158, 159, 160, 161, 168, 169, 175, 178, 179, 180, 181, 182, 183, 184, 185, 186, 188, 192, 204, 207, 208, 210, 213, 214, 350, 384, 385, 386, 388, 394, 397, 399, 400, 401, 402, 416, 418, 421
Pearse, Willie 147, 154, 158, 160, 184, 211
Pearse Street 240, 305, 378
Pembroke Road 356
Penrose, Joseph 266
Pentonville 422
Percy Lane 89, 93
Percy Place 90, 420

Perolz, Marie 398, 400, 402
Peter's Row 78
Peter Street 151
Phibsboro 251, 268
Phoenix Park 60, 62, 72, 247, 250, 251,
        349, 389, 434
Plunkett, George 130, 190, 216, 223, 234,
        235, 357
Plunkett, Joseph Mary 27, 130, 131, 132,
        145, 147, 154, 155, 161, 167, 168,
        175, 178, 181, 183, 184, 190, 191,
        193, 194, 195, 196, 197, 216, 407
Plunkett, Philomena 195
Poole, C. 57
Port Leinster House 302
Portobello 78, 79, 80, 88, 114, 133, 306,
        352
Power's Court 92
Powerscourt 348
Prendergast, Seán 255
Price, Gilbert 276
Prince's Street 43, 44, 133, 143
Protestant infirmary 67
Putland Road 360

Q

Quinn, James 66

R

Ramsay, Lieut 70
Ranelagh 352, 356
Rathdown 355
Rathfarnham 133, 180, 183, 349, 386,
        392, 393
Rathgar 233
Rathmines 80, 210, 233, 352, 391
Reading jail 220, 223
Red Cow Inn 309, 310, 311, 312
Redmond's Hill 79, 140
Redmond, John 13, 14, 15, 23, 24, 27, 28,
        29, 30, 168, 180, 209, 228, 229,
        351, 388, 396, 397, 418, 430
Redmond, William 364
Republican Outfitters 271, 272, 273, 274,
        275
Reynolds, George 86, 87, 95
Reynolds, Lily 163
Rialto 62, 64, 65, 66, 69, 70, 72, 73, 77,
        300
Richmond, John 364

Richmond barracks 62, 64, 65, 77, 112,
        114, 133, 153, 155, 181, 214, 215,
        216, 223, 300, 302, 303, 304, 312,
        365, 372, 407
Rigney, Patrick 337, 375
Ring, Tim 134
Ringsend 151, 215, 420
Robert Street 71
Robinson, Seamus 134, 220, 246, 247,
        248, 249, 250, 251, 252, 257, 267,
        271
Rochfort, Seamus 353
Rockwell 182, 415
Rooney, Willie 430
Roscommon 7, 181, 223, 423
Rosegreen 262
Rose Road 152
Rosscarbery 406
Rotunda Gardens 350
Rotunda hospital 43, 133, 150, 154, 175,
        207, 381
Rotunda Rink 25, 26, 167, 189, 381
Roundwood 353, 364
Royal barracks 61, 114, 133, 372, 389
Royal Canal 226
Royal Dublin Fusiliers 79, 131
Royal Dublin Society 86
Royal Hibernian Academy 134
Royal hospital 62, 64, 66, 70, 72, 96, 215,
        338
Royal Hotel 361
Royal Irish Constabulary (RIC) 14, 18,
        33, 41, 72, 117, 120, 128, 186,
        251, 283, 284, 293, 326, 328, 346,
        347, 348, 350, 351, 353, 355, 358,
        359, 360, 361, 362, 363, 365, 368,
        372, 376, 377, 381, 382, 392
Royal Irish Regiment (RIR) 65, 70
Royal Irish Rifles 79, 352
Royall, Capt 149, 150
Royal Marine Hotel 347
Russell, Seán 137, 292, 314
Ryan, Barney 242
Ryan, Bernard 296
Ryan, Fred 110
Ryan, Nell 402
Ryan, P.J. 242
Ryan, Phil 263

S

Sackville Lane 143, 147, 148

Sackville Place 134
Salkeld, Blanaid 184
Sandwith Street 306
Sandyford 346, 348
Sandymount Castle 193
Sarsfield Road 301, 303
Savage, Martin 247, 248, 249, 250, 251
Scanlon, Jim 257
Scariff, Mick 357
Sebastian, Father 197
Seerey, James 113
Shanahan, Jane 224
Shanahan, Phil 272, 273
Shanganagh 355, 360
Shankill 352, 353, 354, 355, 356, 357,
    359, 362, 363
Shaw, George Bernard 49
Sheehan, Jack 356, 359, 362, 363, 364
Sheehy-Skeffington, Francis 53, 80, 111,
    166, 195, 209, 352, 403
Sheehy-Skeffington, Hannah 166, 403
Shelbourne Hotel 48, 82, 86, 109
Sheridan, Joe 353
Sherlock, Lorcan 25
Sherwood Foresters 72, 89, 91, 96, 97, 98,
    206, 207
Ship Street 79, 151, 153, 402
Shore, Major 354
Shortis, Patrick 145
Shouldice, Frank 102, 367
Shouldice, John 102, 104
Silk Weaver's Union 202
Sinn Féin 15, 17, 18, 20, 23, 26, 68, 79,
    81, 147, 177, 182, 187, 198, 201,
    207, 219, 220, 221, 225, 227, 228,
    229, 230, 231, 232, 233, 234, 308,
    336, 350, 353, 366, 377, 382, 404,
    408, 409, 410, 417, 423, 429, 430,
    431, 432, 433
Sir Patrick Dun's hospital 93, 151
Skinnider, Margaret 110, 399
Slattery, Tim 329
Sligo 13, 40, 361
Smith, County Insp. 129
Smith, Kit 375
Smithfield 323
Smyth, Major 260, 262, 265
Soloheadbeg 277
South Circular Road 108, 227, 280
South Dublin Union 62, 63, 64, 65, 69,
    70, 71, 72, 75, 76, 140, 214, 218,
    234, 399

Squad, the 268, 269, 271, 274, 285, 287,
    288, 293, 318, 319, 380
St Augustine Street 237
Stack, Austin 228, 313, 366, 368, 398
Stafford jail 365
Stafford Street 325
St Enda's 158, 161, 183, 191, 209, 210,
    212, 386, 392
Stepaside 346
Stephens, James 108, 183, 191
Sterling, Jack 356, 357, 358, 359, 360,
    361, 362, 364
Stillorgan 96
St Mary's Place 242
St Mary's Road 91
Stopford-Green, Mrs 228
St Patrick's Park 78, 83, 150, 151
St Stephen's Green 55, 59, 63, 77, 79, 82,
    90, 107, 108, 109, 110, 112, 113,
    117, 140, 149, 150, 151, 198
Surrey House 388, 398
Sutton, Pat 353, 364
Sutton, Tom 352, 354, 355, 356, 357, 358,
    359, 360, 361, 362, 363, 364
Swift's Row 324
Swords 211
Synod House 115

T

Talbot Street 134, 271, 272, 274, 275, 319
Tallaght 304, 312
Tanham, Liam 346
Tara Street 136, 150
Teeling, Frank 290, 296, 297, 299, 339
Templemore 72
Terenure 391
Theatre Royal 137, 141
Thomas' Lane 137, 141
Thomas Street 63
Thornton, Frank 130, 251, 274, 285, 286,
    293, 379
Ticknock 87, 346, 347
Tier, James 353, 364
Tierney, Éamonn 106
Tipperary 10, 181, 186, 257, 260, 277,
    292
Tivoli Theatre 136
Tobin, Liam 285, 287, 379
Tolka bridge 260
Toole, Gerry 356, 358, 360, 364
Toole, Jim 354, 357, 364

Toole, Pat 355
Toole, Rebecca 354
Trade Union Congress 37, 39
Tralee 9, 33, 40, 398
Traynor, Barney 353
Traynor, John 69
Traynor, Oscar 137, 313
Treacy, Seán 246, 247, 251, 252, 257, 258,
   259, 260, 261, 262, 263, 265, 266,
   267, 269, 270, 271, 272, 273, 274,
   275, 276, 277
Treacy, Séan 251, 259, 260
Trinity College 53, 63, 82, 86, 96, 97, 136,
   150, 151, 152, 203, 246, 429
Tyrconnell Road 301

U

Ulster Volunteer Force (UVF) 15, 24, 26,
   27, 42
United Irish League 230
United Services Club 82, 109
United States 27, 31, 32, 39, 55, 132, 135,
   140, 165, 166, 167, 170, 172, 173,
   174, 175, 178, 191, 192, 193, 194,
   195, 197, 198, 205, 216, 217, 225,
   258, 313, 390, 395, 397, 403, 413,
   418, 424, 427
Upper Dominick Street 286
Usher's Quay 101
Usk prison 367, 392, 393

V

Valentia 134
Valombrossa 363
Vane, Francis 72, 209, 403
Vaughan's Hotel 287
Vize, Joe 268, 269, 273, 275

W

Wafer, Thomas 137
Wakefield prison 217, 365
Waldron, Joe 354
Waldron, Paddy 353, 364
Wall, Fr 96
Walsh, Archbishop 50, 136, 227, 279
Walsh, Billy 346, 348
Walsh, Bob 356, 359
Walsh, D.P. 272, 273, 369

Walsh, George 27
Walsh, J.J. 134, 233
Walsh, Jim 238
Walsh, Leo 238
Walsh, Pierce 238
Walsh, Tom 238
Walton jail 405
Wandsworth prison 218, 365
Warmington, Major 70
Warrington Place 86, 94
Waterford 40, 386
Watkins' Brewery 62, 71, 72, 80, 209, 399
Wellington Street 323
Wentworth Place 150
Westland Row 63, 84, 85, 86, 140, 150,
   159, 225, 226, 351, 413, 419
Westminster 13, 220, 230, 233, 431, 432,
   433
Westmoreland Street 134, 136
Westport 197
Wexford 40, 140, 200, 352
Wheeler, Capt. 149, 150, 151, 152, 153
Wheeler, Jack 358
Whelan, Thomas 296
Whelehan, Seán 237
White, George 52
White, Jack R. 49, 52, 53, 167, 170
White, Peadar 27
Whitefriars' Street 151
Whitehead, Alfred 173, 174
Whitworth Road 323
Wicklow 28, 43, 140, 163, 347, 353, 355,
   364
Williamstown 88
Wilson, Henry Hammond (Tom Clarke)
   170, 172
Wilson, Lee 207
Wimborne, Lord 135
Winters, Colonel 292
Wolfe Tone, T. 54, 159, 163, 386, 396
Woodbrook 363
Woodcock, Christy 357
Woodenbridge 30, 388
Wynn's Hotel 25, 189, 193, 396

Y

Yeats, W.B. 165, 403, 417
York Street 82, 150, 391